Linguistic controversies

Essays in linguistic theory and practice in honour of F.R. Palmer

Edited by David Crystal

Edward Arnold

First published 1982 by
Edward Arnold (Publishers) Ltd
41 Bedford Square, London WC1B 3DQ

Set in 10/11 Times by Huron Valley Graphics, Ann Arbor USA

British Library Cataloguing in Publication Data

Linguistic controversies: essays in linguistic
   theory and practice in honour of F.R. Palmer.
   1.   Linguistics—Addresses, essays, lectures
   2.   Palmer, F.R.
   I.   Crystal, David   II.   Palmer, F.R.
   410   P125

   ISBN 0-7131-6349-6

Printed in Great Britain by Richard Clay
(The Chaucer Press) Ltd, Bungay, Suffolk.

Contents

iv *Contents*

Part V Applications: language teaching and language pathology

Foreword

The motivation for this volume has come from the desire of the departmental colleagues of F.R. Palmer to provide him with a fitting tribute for his 60th birthday. But as soon as this aim was first formulated, a problem became apparent: a collection of papers in the 'festschrift' tradition would be little tribute to someone who has long been unhappy about the way many such volumes are routinely constructed—often with little or no thematic coherence, and lacking an orientation that would relate the finished volume to current issues in teaching or research. Any Palmer collection, we felt, should be based on principles of which we know he would approve—three, in particular:

the volume should aim to find unity within diversity, by focusing on core theoretical issues that would seem to permeate the discipline of linguistics, in its several branches and applications;

the volume should have research relevance, in that its theme should recur in any evaluation of the discipline's progress;

the volume should have pedagogical relevance, in that it should relate to the kind of problem regularly encountered in undergraduate or postgraduate courses in linguistics.

How, then, to satisfy such stringent criteria? Our first discussion to find a unifying issue for the volume covered a wide range of topics and brought to light some interesting areas of disagreement amongst us. Such comments were made as 'But is that a *real* issue, or just an artefact of your approach?', 'But is that doing linguistics, rather than philosophy/psychology/sociology . . . ?', 'But is that a helpful way of looking at the problem?' Upon reflection, we felt that questions such as these might perhaps be viewed as evidence of a more deep-rooted difficulty, which affects students as well as researchers. Certainly, one of the major problems facing students of linguistics, once they have taken an introductory course in the subject, is how to come to grips with the diversity of theoretical and methodological positions adopted by linguists, in their investigations of language. The realization that there are several ways of looking at a problem, and several alternative solutions, is something one learns early on. What is much more difficult is to learn how to draw back a step further, and to evaluate the positions and solutions themselves, and it is here that confusion readily arises—and not only for the student. Critical comments regularly voiced by linguists reflect the problem: while accepting that what a certain author says may be of interest, such questions as the above are often heard in common rooms and conferences. They are, however, not so commonly raised in print, and it is accordingly difficult to provide students with reading which will sharpen their intuition about such matters. We know of no volume which addresses this problem directly, in relation to the many subject areas within linguistics; and the topic has received little attention, even in article form, since the days when God's truth and hocus-pocus views of the subject were being discussed. It is this neglect which the present volume is concerned to help remedy.

At the very least, we hope to focus attention on a range of neglected questions. What makes a topic controversial in linguistics, and how can such controversies be constructively approached? What counts as a Big Issue in linguistics? Can a set of criteria be established for evaluating linguistic positions? Do these criteria change as we move from one area of linguistics to another? How far are there differences between what linguists do and what they think they do? How far is it possible to develop an intellectual justification for the way linguists work—a kind of grammar of their own performance? Linguists expect their students to develop this kind of meta-metalinguistic awareness; their comments on students' work repeatedly indicate it. But if these comments were analysed, they would bring to light many differences of opinion and belief concerning the nature of the subject, and there is rarely an opportunity to have these differences openly discussed. If 'linguistics is what linguists do', then this volume is attempting to look behind this old saw, and to ask 'Why do they do what they do?', and perhaps, 'Is everything that they do worth doing?'

In order to give this theme adequate coverage, it was essential to parcel out the field of linguistics in such a way that all of its main branches would be represented. Only thus would an interesting characterization of the notion of linguistic controversy emerge. A fairly natural means of ensuring a balanced coverage is to have the teaching members of a large and varied department contribute a chapter—and this is what we have done. To be precise, we have restricted participation in the volume to present and past full-time colleagues at the University of Reading, where Palmer is Head of the Department of Linguistic Science; his previous headship of department at the University College of North Wales, Bangor, is represented by one further contribution. Each contributor was asked to take his main research field, and to select from it a topic which he felt represented a currently controversial issue. He was to provide an account of the controversy, an evaluation of it, and, perhaps, some guidelines as to how it might be resolved.

The eighteen contributions have been grouped into five main sections, which reflect some of the conventionally-held divisions within the subject.

Part I raises questions concerning some of the fundamental notions to be encountered in linguistic theory and history. Matthew's critical review of the notion of formalization is timely, in view of the controversies surrounding its use and interpretation in the last 20 years. His survey shows the wide variety of different ways in which linguists have used the term, ranging from the simple use of abbreviatory notations, to the formalization of mathematical systems. His chapter raises several questions about matters which many linguists might at first glance feel to be non-controversial—such as whether there is any validity in the idea that a 'formalized' account is necessarily clearer than one which is not 'formal', and whether there are still grounds for believing in formalization as a basis for the evaluation of grammars. Crystal's chapter raises the question of the autonomy of linguistic theory. Several linguists have argued the importance of constraining linguistic theory with reference to the findings of other disciplines, such as psychology and neurology. The 'aphasia paradigm', in particular, has been cited as providing evidence which would count for or against particular theories. The chapter examines this evidence, and the controversy which it aroused in neurolinguistics, and finds it wanting in several respects. The controversy, in its relationship to linguistic theory, is held to be irrelevant and ambiguous—a 'pseudo-controversy'. Lepschy's chapter reviews the field of linguistic historiography, which has attracted increased interest in recent years, especially since Chomsky's regular references to the historical background of his theories. Lepschy points out several problems in the field: the need, which is widely felt but rarely met, to look at the history of linguistics as part of general cultural history; the influence which different theoretical assumptions about language and linguistics have on the perspective (the definition of the object) of linguistic historiography; and the lack of a comprehensive, large-scale reference work on the history of linguistics. He illustrates these problems with a discussion of two historical episodes from the work of Saussure and Freud, where the lack of historiographical data has a direct bearing on our understanding of their theories, and thereby on the evaluation and application of these theories in contemporary linguistic controversy.

Part II provides three chapters on controversial issues in phonetic research. Hardcastle's chapter examines the little-understood domain of coarticulatory processes. He begins by reviewing the way in which articulatory movements overlap in real time, resulting in a lack of invariance between particular phonemes and a given set of articulatory manoeuvres. He argues that previous attempts to account for these processes have been unsuccessful, in that they have attributed coarticulation solely to low-level mechano-inertial characteristics of the speech-producing mechanism (such as the relative velocities of muscle contractions). Hardcastle, by contrast, sees some coarticulatory processes as the direct result of high-level processing during the neural programming stage in the generation of a speech utterance; and he presents experimental evidence in support of this view. Both Butcher's and Roach's chapters raise basic questions concerning the traditional practice of phonetic research. Their concern is to see a science of phonetics based on objectively measurable and independently motivated parameters, rather than on shared experience and imitative skills. Butcher reviews recent (and not so recent) evidence which points to the scientific inadequacy of the cardinal vowel model—such as the difficulties inherent in defining the reference sounds unambiguously, or in relating articulatory movement to auditory perception. Roach takes another traditional theory—the binary classification of languages into stress-timed and syllable-timed rhythmical types—and questions its reliability in objective terms. He argues that there is no support for the assignment of a language to one or other of these categories on the basis of the measurement of time intervals in speech. Taken together, the three phonetics chapters provide an illustration of the way in which the phonetician always needs to look critically at his traditional paradigms of enquiry, especially in the light of new methodological techniques, which can provide fresh dimensions of knowledge. New instrumentation does not merely add new facts; it forces—or should force—a re-examination of old findings.

In Part III, the first three contributors provide chapters representing other traditional foci of linguistic inquiry—phonology, grammar and semantics. Brasington's paper investigates the problem of naturalness and the controversial notion of strength, as propounded by some phonologists as an explanation of phonological change, distributional pattern, and the form of phonological systems. He discusses its relationship to the Chomskyan version of markedness, and then points to certain current deficiencies—in particular, the need to take more explicitly into account the properties of positions in structure. He suggests a methodology for characterizing structural positions, based on the statistical analysis of texts and vocabularies. Warburton's chapter is concerned with an aspect of the controversy over linguistic universals. She takes as her example the range of subject-to-object and object-to-subject raised structures in Modern Greek, and discusses these in relation to the claimed universality of the Tensed S condition (or Nominative Island Constraint) in generative grammar. She finds that both structures violate the constraints, but while the former type can be accounted for (through Chomsky's proviso that languages which allow subjectless sentences are exempted from the constraint), the latter type has to be described by special rules with different properties (rules of predication). This challenges the universality of the condition, and its accompanying proviso; and while a unitary treatment is possible, it requires a major amendment to the present formulation of the theory. Biggs begins his chapter with a review of the special kinds of controversial issue facing anyone wishing to research in semantics, as a preamble to a discussion of whether a general theory of word semantics is possible, given the figurativeness, vagueness and indeterminacy of so much of meaning. He argues that, despite some recent criticisms which have been made of word semantics, and despite the demonstrable weaknesses in the approaches of field theory and componential analysis, the machinery for a plausible theory is available in the meaning-postulate approach to the subject. Sussex's contribution to this section provides an example of a descriptive controversy in Russian, in relation to which all three of the above levels are relevant. He reviews previous solutions to the syntactic area selected, which is given detailed illustration. The analysis he prefers is in terms of the semantic scope of the constituents, which he relates to the functional sentence perspective structure of the sentence.

Part IV brings together papers on psycholinguistics and language acquisition, on the one hand, and sociolinguistics and dialectology, on the other. Fletcher's chapter questions the relationship often claimed between adult grammars and child language acquisition, as propounded by rule-based accounts of learning. He uses studies of the acquisition of question-forms and of the verb phrase to illustrate the limitations of the classical generative position, and suggests some prerequisites for an alternative approach. Garman's chapter deals with a recent psycholinguistic argument, according to which Broca's aphasia is to be interpreted as resulting from a purely phonological disorder—this being opposed to the commonly held view of the syndrome as a function of multiple disorders involving morphology and syntax ('agrammatism') as well as phonology. He argues that more refined linguistic analysis is required before we can seriously debate such issues, and that in any case the 'phonological deficit hypothesis' is suspect, in psycholinguistic terms.

The remaining three papers in this section provide various perspectives on the phenomenon of language variety and social change. Trudgill reviews the notion of polylectal grammar, raising the question of how far it is legitimate to include more than one variety of language in a rule-based grammar. He uses the results of a series of tests of grammaticality and of comprehension to argue that the limits on native speaker passive competence are sometimes so severe that polylectal grammars may not provide a fruitful model of investigation. Like Fletcher, his results raise serious questions as to whether a rule-based system is the best way of explicating competence. Petyt's chapter contrasts traditional and modern approaches to English dialectology, the former concentrating on what is regarded as 'pure' dialect and tracing the development of Old and Middle English sounds and forms, the latter examining variation among the different social groups in a large representative sample, concerned not with history but with present-day systems. He reviews several criticisms of traditional dialectology, and then illustrates some of the difficulties he sees in the modern approach (such as the over-precise notion of 'speech community'), using data drawn from studies of West Yorkshire dialects. He concludes that relevant insights can be obtained from both approaches. Thomas's chapter looks at the phenomenon of language contact in communities which are in a state of transitional bilingualism—particularly at the nature of the competence of speakers of languages that are said to be dying. The speakers' reduced competence may be reflected both in the 'completeness' of their grammatical structures and in the range of stylistic options available to them. He discusses the type of linguistic changes encountered in the present-day Celtic languages, arguing that the structural changes involved are less revealing than a sociolinguistic account of the reduced stylistic choices that are available.

Part V of the book provides examples of controversial issues taken from some of the main areas of applied linguistics. Wilkins and Hughes address several issues from the fields of foreign language teaching and learning. Wilkins identifies four dichotomous research positions often adopted, and argues that to see these positions as being mutually exclusive is to lead to procedures and interpretations of doubtful validity. His illustrations derive from the widely used distinctions of interference and generalized learning processes, behaviourism and mentalism, structure and function, and language and communication, as encountered in the language-teaching field. Hughes's chapter looks especially at a controversy in foreign-language testing, concerning the nature of language proficiency—whether it is capable of being broken down into a number of separately testable components. He argues that recent criticism of the traditional, 'divisibility' view of proficiency is itself questionable, and that an alternative direction for research into testing is required. Whurr addresses a central issue in the relationship of linguistics to the study of language pathology. She reviews Jakobson's attempt to provide a linguistic typology of aphasic impairment, and argues that the limitations of this view motivate a fresh direction for aphasia studies, in which more detailed descriptions of language break-down are made at different linguistic levels. But we are still left with the question of how to integrate these detailed descriptions with the psychological and neurological accounts of the phenomenon.

In spite of this topical diversity, it is possible to see certain attitudes and emphases emerge, independently of the subject-matter with which the authors deal. Most of the chapters are critical, in varying degrees, of prevailing orthodoxies in linguistic and phonetic research. There are several general themes, such as the ambiguities in linguists' use of formalization (Matthews), the unfruitfulness of certain notions in the evaluation of linguistic theories (Crystal), the inadequacies of linguistic historiography (Lepschy), the limitations of rule-based accounts of child language acquisition (Fletcher), the analysis of several basic antinomies in language teaching (Wilkins), the critique of the contributions of traditional and modern dialectology (Petyt), and the weaknesses of polylectal grammars (Trudgill). More specific issues are illustrated by the inadequacies of the cardinal vowel system (Butcher), the implausibility of syllable- v. stress-timing as a basis for language classification (Roach), the significance of coarticulation in revising models of speech production (Hardcastle), the modifications needed to implement the notion of phonological strength (Brasington), the inadequacies in the formulation of a claimed linguistic universal (Warburton), the descriptive controversies presented by an area of Russian syntax (Sussex), and the theoretical controversies involved in handling word semantics (Biggs). Somewhat related to these attitudes are those authors who question an *unorthodoxy* in linguistic research—the problems inherent in a phonological view of Broca's aphasia (Garman), the difficulties involved in attempting to provide a unitary view of language proficiency (Hughes), the inclarities of the role of linguistics in aphasiology (Whurr), and the neglected topic of language death (Thomas).

No small collection can cover the whole field of linguistic controversy, but it is certainly possible to project several themes raised by these authors well beyond the confines of this volume. A recurrent theme is the way in which it is felt that the process of theory construction and model-building has left empirical research too far behind: the need for better data-bases is a major conclusion of over half the chapters in the book (Crystal, Butcher, Roach, Hardcastle, Brasington, Fletcher, Garman, Trudgill, Petyt, Thomas, Hughes). Another strong theme is the importance of an accurate historical perspective for the interpretation and evaluation of current positions (Matthews, Butcher, Biggs, Wilkins, and above all, Lepschy). Several chapters argue the need for more sophisticated linguistic models to handle the data we have already—especially models in which the interaction between linguistic levels is better taken into account (Hardcastle, Fletcher, Warburton, Garman, Hughes, Sussex, Whurr). There is an anxiety not to idealize prematurely from the complexities of observed performance (Crystal, Fletcher, Garman, Trudgill, Petyt), and a corresponding concern to establish the nature of these complexities as accurately as possible (a particular concern of the phoneticians, in Part II, but implicit in the suggested survey work of several others).

In writing this book, we have tried to avoid producing a set of papers which merely illustrate the routine application of standard theoretical positions and conventional analytic techniques. Our concern has been more fundamental: to investigate the ways in which linguistic knowledge has grown, and to see whether changes in direction are needed. At best, we hope that our volume will constitute a small contribution to the developing field of linguistic epistemology; at the very least, we hope that we have been able to produce enough of a critical perspective on individual issues to enable our understanding of these issues to progress. Our criticism is an inevitable consequence of our chosen theme; but we have always tried to make it a constructive criticism, and one which expresses something of the excitement which comes from dealing with matters at the heart of an academic discipline. It is at once an exciting and a humbling exercise. We are all of us aware that, if we have been able to see a little further into the nature of linguistic controversy, it is largely because we have been stimulated so much by the insights of our colleagues in the wider linguistic community.

Frank Palmer, in our view, has done more than most in focusing the attention of his colleagues and students on the issues raised by this volume. Indeed, it is from his generous criticism, and his persistent reminders to us as to what we are about when we say we are 'doing linguistics', that the idea for this book derives. Each of us in his department knows how much he has gained, individually, from having his work subjected to Palmer's close, cogent, intellectual scrutiny; and we appreciate the interest he has always shown in our varied research proposals and theoretical stances. There has never been a 'party line' at Reading—unless, that is, it is to question the limitations inherent in all party lines! Palmer's policy of paying serious attention to all schools of linguistic thought, and to allow his junior colleagues the freedom to follow their own theoretical inclinations, is well reflected in the diversity of attitudes represented in the present volume.

But we in the department are far outnumbered by the many other linguists who have personally benefited from Palmer's guidance, whether as Chairman of the Linguistics Association of Great Britain (1965–8), editor of the *Journal of Linguistics* (1969–79), or in his many other roles as editorial adviser, committee member, external examiner and lecturer in many parts of the world. Perhaps most readers of the present book will know him only for his main publications, which we list below, and which illustrate precisely that balance between theoretical statement and empirical illustration, between expository clarity and subtle criticism, which we would do well to emulate. What this list does not provide, of course, is an indication of his considerable administrative and political skills: in the past 15 years, he has developed at Reading a strong theoretical core of linguistic studies, at the same time supporting the growth of multidisciplinary courses and applied projects, so that his department must now be one of the most diversified within the linguistics world. His personal concern for the well-being of his colleagues and students, throughout these years, has been salutary; as has his enthusiastic commitment to teaching and to research. *Linguistic controversies* repays only a fraction of the debt we owe him.

F.R. Palmer: a select bibliography

The 'broken plurals' of Tigrinya. *BSOAS* **17.3**, 548–66 (1955).

'Openness' in Tigre: a problem in prosodic statement. *BSOAS* **18.3**, 561–77 (1956).

The verb in Bilin. *BSOAS* **19.1**, 131–59 (1957)

Gemination in Tigrinya. *Studies in linguistic analysis* (Special volume of the Philological Society), 139–48 (1957).

The noun in Bilin. *BSOAS* **21.2**, 376–91 (1958).

Linguistic hierarchy. *Lingua* **7.3**, 225–41 (1958).

Comparative statement and Ethiopian Semitic. *TPS*, 119–43 (1958).

The verb classes of Agua (Awiya). *Mitteilungen des Instituts für Orientforschung* **7.2**, 270–97 (1959).

An outline of Bilin phonology. *Atti del Convegno Internazionale di Studi Etiopici,* Rome (1959).

The 'derived forms' of the Tigrinya verb. *African Language Studies* **1**, 109–16 (1960).

Relative clauses in Tigre. *Word* **17.1**, 23–33 (1961).

Review of M.A.K. Halliday, *The language of the Chinese 'Secret history of the Mongols'. ArchLing* **13.1**, 94–6 (1961).

Relative clauses in Tigrinya. *JSS* **7.1**, 36–43 (1962).

The morphology of the Tigre noun. (O U P, 1962).

Grammatical categories and their phonetic exponents. *Proc. IXth Int. Cong. Lings.,* 338–45 (1962).

'Sequence' and 'order'. *Georgetown Monograph Series on Language and Linguistics* **17**, 123–30 (1964).

Review of W. Leslau, *Etymological dictionary of Harari. Word* **20.3**, 453–6 (1964).

A linguistic study of the English verb. (Longman, 1965).

The oral approach to language teaching. *The European Teacher* **1.3**, 6–10 (1965).

Bilin 'to be' and 'to have'. *African Language Studies* **6**, 101–11 (1965).

Review of P.S. Ray, *Language standardization. JL* **1.1**, 83–7 (1965).

Review of P. Postal, *Constituent structures. FL* **1**, 346–53 (1965).

Review of B.W. Andrezejewski, *The declension of Somali nouns. Lg* **41.4**, 676–80 (1965).

Review of W. Leslau, *Ethiopian argots. Lg* **42.3**, 700–3 (1966).

Review of J.R. Firth, *The tongues of men and Speech. FL* **4**, 84–6 (1966).

Bilin word classes. *Lingua* **17.1/2**, 200–9 (1967).

Affinity and genetic relationship in two Cushitic languages. In *To honor Roman Jakobson,* 1489–96 (1967).

Review of W.A. Hirtle, *The simple and progressive forms. StudNeophil* **39.2**, 363–5 (1967).

Review of M. Joos, *Semantics of the English verb. Lingua* **18**, 179–95 (1967).

(ed.) *Selected papers of J.R. Firth, 1951–8.* (Longman, 1968).

Will, can, may and must. *Filologia Moderna* **31.2**, 203–12 (1968).

Review of S.M. Lamb, *Outline of stratificational grammar. JL* **4**, 287–95 (1968).

Review of J. Svartvik, *On voice in the English verb, Lingua* **20.2**, 187–94 (1968).

Review of C.F. Hockett, *The state of the art. Lg* **45.3**, 616–21 (1969).

(ed.) *Prosodic analysis.* (OUP., 1970).

Cushitic. *Current trends in linguistics,* Vol. 6, 571–85. (Mouton, 1970).

Review of F.P. Dineen, *An introduction to general linguistics. FL* **6**, 150–1 (1970).

Review of R. Hetzron, *The verbal system of Southern Agaw. Lg* **46.1**, 205–8 (1970).

Grammar. (Penguin, 1971).

Review of B. Sundby, *Front-shifted -ing and -ed in present-day English.* *StudNeophil* **44.1**, 204–6 (1972).

Review of S. Yotsokura, *The articles in English. Linguistics,* 87–94 (1972).

Noun-phrase and sentence: a problem in semantics/syntax. *TPS,* 20–43 (1973).

Review of D. Bolinger, *The phrasal verb in English. LangStyle* **6.3**, 230–4 (1973).

Review of D. Steinberg and L. Jakobovits (eds.), *Semantics. JL* **9**, 361–4 (1973).

Review of M. Grady, *Syntax and semantics of the English verb phrase. Linguistics* **99**, 110–15 (1973).

Review of M. Ljung, *English denominal adjectives. Linguistics* **105**, 121–8 (1974).

The English verb. (Longman, 1974).

Some remarks on the grammar and phonology of the 'compound verbs' in Cushitic and Ethiopian Semitic. *IV Congresso Internazionale di Studi Etiopici, Accademia Nazionale dei Lincei,* 71–7 (1974).

The English modals. In *Linguistik: Beschreibung der Gegenswartssprachen* (Kongressbericht der 6. Jahrestagung der Gesellschaft für Angewandte Linguistik GAL e. V, Band IV.), 85–91 (1975).

Language and languages. In W.F. Bolton (ed.), *The English language* (Sphere History of Literature in the English language, Vol. 10), 12–37. (Sphere Books, 1975).

Review of F. Liefrink, *Semantico-syntax. IRAL* **13**, 355–8 (1975).

Review of W.J. Meys, *Compound adjectives in English and the ideal speaker-hearer. Linguistics* **176**, 99–103 (1976).

Modals and actuality. *JL* **13.1**, 1–23 (1976).

Semantics. (C U P, 1976; 2nd edn. 1981).

Review of A. Zaborski, *The verb in Cushitic. BSOAS* **40**, 197–202 (1977).

Review of R. Hetzron (ed.), *Afroasiatic linguistics. Lg* **53.1**, 237–9 (1977).

Possessive pronouns in Dongola. *BSOAS* **41.2**, 352–4 (1978).

Past tense transportation: a reply. *JL* **14**, 77–81 (1978).

Why auxiliaries are not main verbs. *Lingua* **47**, 1–25 (1979).

Non-assertion and modality. In D.J. Allerton *et al.*(eds), *Function and context in linguistic analysis* (C U P), 185–95 (1979).

Modality and the English modals. (Longman, 1979).

Can, will and actuality. In S. Greenbaum *et al.* (eds.), *Studies in English linguistics* (Longman), 91–9 (1980).

Part I
General issues

1

Formalization

P. H. Matthews

What do linguists mean by formalization, and why is it important? Throughout the 1960s I would have given simple answers to these questions, which would have been accepted by most scholars writing (as I then was) in the generative style. But at the beginning of the 1980s such answers are no longer convincing. This is partly because the term has not been used consistently: at best it has both strict and loose senses. But it is also because the programme of formalization has less and less connection with the research that linguists are actually pursuing. It is therefore time to take a fresh look at the issue. I am especially glad to do so in this volume, which is dedicated to a scholar who has himself thought deeply about them, and has often helped to set my own thoughts straight.

Our first problem involves the relation of *formalize* and its derivatives to the base term *formal*. The sense of the latter, in collocations such as *formal model* or *formal theory*, often matches that of *formalized*: a formal theory is one for which a formalism has been proposed. But *formal* is an ordinary word, as in *a formal requirement* or *a formal invitation*, and is also used more widely by linguists, in talking, for instance, of formal versus notional criteria or of formal versus substantive universals. It is therefore customary to distinguish at least three strands of technical or semi-technical usage, only one of which might at first seem relevant.

The first derives from Hjelmslev's theory of form and substance (expounded by, for example, Corneille 1976, 180ff.). On one level we are dealing with substantive features: for example, voiced and voiceless as categories of phonic substance, or animate and inanimate as categories of content. On the formal level we are dealing with abstract relationships, independently of substance. Thus phoneme *a* will be opposed to phoneme *b*, and can precede or follow phonemes *c* and *d* within the syllable; likewise word *a* will be opposed to word *b*, and so on. It is in this sense that we may talk of formal universals (Chomsky 1965, 29). For example, constituency

1

structure is based on a relation in which units *a* and *b* together form a larger unit *c*. It does not matter how *a, b* and *c* are realized: it is a purely abstract relation, and constituency structure is thus a formal universal, assuming that all languages exhibit it.

The second usage derives from a distinction between form and meaning: obvious sources are in Bloomfield's definition of a linguistic form (1935, 138) or Jespersen's opposition of form and notion (1924, 55ff.). A formal criterion or definition will refer to form alone: for instance, the definition of a noun, or of a major class of nouns, as a word that can directly follow an article. A notional criterion would instead refer to categories of meaning, as in the traditional definition of a noun as denoting an individual or thing. The collocation *formal grammar* may then be used of a grammar or an approach to writing grammars which eschews notional criteria and relies on formal tests alone (so, for example, Robins 1964, 182ff.).

The third usage derives from mathematical logic, but is explained by most textbooks as referring to no more than a certain standard of exactness. An informal statement (of a rule, a theory, and so on) is in some way less explicit than a formal statement, just as, in an ordinary sense, an informal requirement either avoids or fails to achieve the precision expected of formal requirements. Standards of exactness vary, in practice especially. The general sense, however, is that an informal account will leave things to the reader's imagination and background knowledge. For example, if I say that the passive in English is formed by *be* with the past participle, it must be understood that by *be* I mean whatever form of 'to be' is determined by the subject and the remainder of the verb phrase, that the participle follows, is a separate word, and so on, and the reader is perhaps at a loss to know whether I would identify this structure with that of *be* plus an adjective or noun phrase. A formal account (it is said) would spell out this and everything else mechanically.

The first two senses might be further subdivided, as in the influential account by Lyons (1968, 136f.). But they are distinct from the third, and it is to that in particular that our notion of 'formalization' is commonly related. According to Lyons, *formal* is here 'equivalent to "formalized" or "explicit", in contrast with "informal" or "intuitive" '; in a slightly later work *generative* is also 'held to imply "formalized" or "explicit" ' (1970, 24), and it is this 'more or less mathematical' sense of *generate* that is said, again in his textbook, to 'presuppose the *formalization* of grammatical theory' (1968, 157). Lyons has been followed by many writers, among them myself (Matthews 1972, 9f.), and a student might easily conclude that *formalized, generative* and *explicit* are equivalent.

But usage is not in fact so simple, for reasons that have to do both with the development of ideas within linguistics and with the logical tradition from which it has borrowed. We have seen that a formal grammar can be one that ignores meaning. Alternatively, it ignores semantic 'substance': in that respect a Bloomfieldian and Hjelmslevian approach are not, in practice, very different. But to abstract from meaning is also the essential step in logical formalization (see, for instance, Edwards 1967, vol. 5, 191f.). This is clear in ordinary dictionaries. In *Webster's Third International* to *formalize* is 'to state precise rules for the combination and transformation of . . . usu. by replacing the original words by symbols that can be discussed without reference to their meaning' (§3.b). In the New Supplement to the *Oxford English Dictionary, formalism* is defined as 'the conception of pure mathematics as the manipulation according to certain formal rules of symbols that are intrinsically meaningless' (§3.a). I have seen no account outside linguistics which points to the explicit character of formalisms without making clear the abstract level at which it is to be achieved.

The reasons for formal grammar in the sense of Robins's textbook (1964) are not the same as those which justify a logical formalization in, for instance, Carnap's (1958). But the currents had already met in Chomsky's earliest proposals. On the one hand there is a connection, both historical and rational, between a formal or distributional analysis of language, as expounded at the beginning of Harris's *Methods* (1951, 5f.) or in his article on 'Distributional structure' (1954), and the concept of a grammar as a set of rules which state which combinations of words or morphemes are possible. We may compare the section at the end of Harris's own book in which he talks of 'statements which enable anyone to synthesize or predict utterances in the language' (1951, 372f.). At the same time a Chomskyan grammar provided a calculus for grammaticality in a so-called 'natural language', just as a 'syntactical system' in Carnap's sense provided a calculus for a symbolic language (Carnap 1958, 78ff.). The notion of grammaticality was naturally seen as independent of meaning (Chomsky 1957, 15).

Chomsky's later model incorporated Katz's semantic component (Chomsky 1965; Katz and Fodor 1963). But this was said to 'interpret' the syntactic descriptions of sentences, in the same sense (one supposed) that a semantic system in the tradition of Carnap and others assigned an interpretation, with respect to certain designata, of the formal expressions in a given calculus. The syntax of *Aspects* remained, in itself, 'uninterpreted'. There was also more than a passing resemblance to Hjelmslev's model. Just as the formal expression and content imposed an analysis of their respective purports (Hjelmslev 1953, §13), so Chomsky's syntactic descriptions were related if not to the substance of sound and meaning then to mental representations of them, which were said to be 'determined' (Chomsky 1965, 16) by the surface structure or deep structure.

It is in this light that we must read secondary discussions such as, for example, that of the Larousse *Dictionnaire de linguistique* (Dubois *et al.* 1973, 220). Its entry begins by talking of 'la généralisation des règles linguistiques explicites, exprimée par des règles formelles ou *formalisation*'—which might appear to say no more than Lyons's textbook. But, in the next sentence, 'Une description formelle décrit des relations entre les unités d'une langue donnée sans faire état de leur interprétation . . . ', where the word *interprétation,* as is made clear in the following paragraph, covers 'aussi bien la description du phonétisme d'une phrase que la description de son contenu sémantique'. 'Une grammaire formelle' will thus supply no more than 'une hypothèse sur l'ensemble des conditions que doit remplir une phrase pour recevoir, pars ailleurs, une interprétation phonétique et sémantique', and this 'ensemble formalisé'—and presumably this alone—'est appelé *description structurelle*'. This causes problems if one is to talk of the formalization of semantics. In a final paragraph the authors refer to the attempt by certain linguists (that is, by proponents of generative semantics) to reintroduce 'tout ou partie de la composante sémantique à l'intérieur de la syntaxe'. That does not mean, they say, that formalization is abandoned; 'mais la formalisation des données sémantiques nécessaires à la construction d'un modèle de compétence (dans le cadre d'une grammaire formelle) complique beaucoup le projet initial'. Indeed it is not clear how the project could survive, if stated in their terms.

It is also worth asking what exactly is meant by *formal syntax* as, for example, the title of a recent collection (Culicover *et al.* 1977). The thesis which unites the contributors is that of the autonomy of syntax—or the 'autonomous systems view' of language generally. That means, in particular, the autonomy of syntax in relation to semantics. But the issue is bound up, in the editors' minds, with that of formal statement. It is not coincidental (they remark) that an opponent who insists that the study of grammar should take account of meaning and use should also call for a return to informal description (5, citing and commenting on Lakoff 1974). For comparison they return to an important passage in *Syntactic structures,* in which Chomsky dismisses the notion that 'one can construct a grammar WITH appeal to meaning' (1957, 93); 20 years later, nevertheless, 'critics of formal grammar are still questioning the legitimacy of the sorts of abstractions and idealizations that the autonomous systems view requires'. They also talk of 'formalisms for stating syntactic rules explicitly'. But it is evident that formalism is not explicitness as such. It is a level of explicitness to be achieved precisely by abstracting form or formal structure, in a Hjelmslevian or Bloomfieldian sense, from the substance with which, on a Chomskyan view, the generative semanticists had muddled it up.

In the light of such discussions it is reasonable to wonder if *formal syntax* in the Chomskyan tradition is in fact so very different from *formal grammar* as envisaged by Robins, or if the sense of *formal* as 'formalized' or 'explicit', as Lyons describes it, is truly independent of the others.

Another, though less important, problem concerns the relation of formalization to notation. In the early days of generative grammar it was stressed that notation did not, in principle, matter. According to Lees, 'a valid grammatical statement is just as valid whether it is affirmed in an abstruse algebraic notation or in plain words' (1957, 391). In the first edition of his textbook Bach remarks that 'the use of special symbols and mathematical notations is not essential'; practically, however, it is 'of great importance' and has an advantage in that 'ordinary language is often so vague' (1964, 146f.). This fits with notions of formalization outside our field (compare, for instance, Carnap 1958, 171f., on formalization and symbolization). It also fits the general requirement that statements should be explicit. For it would be absurd to suggest that something said in plain words (such as 'Two and two makes four' or 'A noun phrase can consist of an adjective followed by a noun') is for that reason less explicit than a translation into a symbolic system ('$2 + 2 = 4$' or 'NP $\rightarrow$ A + N').

But as one surveys the later literature it is hard to avoid the impression that, for many linguists, the putting of plain words into notation is at least a large part of what formalization is about. In his monograph on daughter-dependency grammar, Hudson remarks that some of the 'types of rules' he will illustrate are 'in the form of prose statements, rather than formalized rules' (1976, 20): for example, rule S.8 in his appendix reads 'Less peripheral items precede more peripheral items' (195). But the reason is simply that he is reluctant to put into notation an individual statement which is unclear. A format for sequence rules exists: for example, rule S.5 in the same section reads '[+ article] → [− article]', with the gloss 'I.e. articles precede nouns'. In the same way we could write, say, '[i peripheral] → [j peripheral], where $i < j$', which would be the corresponding notation for S.8. Now for neither rule is the prose gloss either more or less explicit, or more or less formalized in the senses we have been considering hitherto, than the other. The real problem is that Hudson did not have a definition of peripherality (95). Hence it was inappropriate to put S.8 into a format which would make it look more formal, or more precise, than it in fact was.

There is nothing objectionable in such usage. If I send someone a formal invitation, printed on a card with the customary phrasing, he is entitled to greater precision on my part than if I simply suggest to him that he might like to come to dinner some day next week. Likewise, if I write a 'formal rule', or rule in some impressive-looking notation, my reader is entitled to assume that I have a clearer idea of what its terms mean than if I simply hint at an approximate way of taking care of the problem. We must merely note that an opposition between 'formalized' and 'in prose' was not part of the basic aim of formal linguistic theory, as Lees, Bach and others conceived it. The usage does become more questionable, however, if notation as such is claimed as a virtue. For, once again, there is no advantage simply in writing '[+ article]' instead of 'an article' or an arrow instead of 'precedes', 'can consist of', 'is changed to' and so on, other than the saving of space, which holds equally for any unformalized field.

There are perhaps two grounds on which a proponent of notation might want, or might in the past have wanted, to disagree. Firstly, it might be objected that, if the notation is standard, then, pending a true formalization, it will in itself enforce a nearer approach to explicit statement than the use of ordinary language which is unconstrained. This is presumably the point of what Akmajian and Heny, for example, call a 'rough formalization' (1975, 140). In an earlier chapter they have introduced rules such as a question transformation, with a prose formulation and an illustration of its effect on a phrase-marker (86f.). But 'the formal characteristics of transformations are not as clearly understood' as those of phrase structure grammars; accordingly they give more detailed prose statements and more detailed diagrams, with a corresponding notation distinguishing different components of rules, different kinds of adjunction, and so on. A later section deals with 'Formalizing rules utilizing features' (159f.); in fact this presents a formula in which [+ Reflexive] is written underneath one term in a 'structural change' component of a transformation and this 'has the effect of placing the feature . . . on the . . . node' in question, shown by writing it underneath in a tree diagram (162f.). If there is any purpose in teaching such notations to students it must be that the corresponding prose statements, though clear enough in Akmajian and Heny's own exposition, are felt to be too dangerous a model for ordinary precision to be maintained.

In fact, it is very easy to find contributions whose 'formalizations' are even less precise than the ordinary language accompanying them. A rule such as 'Noun Phrase → Nominal + Case' is one of a set that are said to 'formalize some fundamental observations of traditional Latin grammar' (Kelly 1968; in Strunk 1973, 442): in this instance, that case is assigned 'not . . . to the noun but to the total noun phrase' (it is immaterial to ask if Latin grammars do make this observation); 'that is to say, case is determined by the larger construction in which the noun phrase is found'. In fact neither this rule nor any other says anything about how case is determined. In the following pages Kelly formulates transformations which are said, for instance, to assign case and number formatives to the noun and adjective. In fact they are written in a notation which does not show what adjunctions are intended; only the text and diagrams make clear that these formatives are not, say, prefixed to an adjective stem as well as suffixed. In this case the direct cause lies in the deficiencies of Bach's textbook (1964), which were typical of its time. But so long as 'formalizations' are just notations, and are then taught as if it was improper or unscientific to go beyond them, students will continue to have illusions about what they are doing. The result will be precision in neither mode, neither in what is shown by the notation (since one does not dare depart from what is prescribed) nor in plain language (since that is only a gloss on the 'formalization' anyway).

The second objection would have been common 10 years ago and would have had to do with Chomsky's, or perhaps more accurately Halle's, proposal for an evaluation measure. In Halle's view, it seemed 'natural' that this should be a measure of length: that is, of the number of symbols in a grammar under given notational, and especially abbreviatory, conventions (1962, 55). These had no bearing on formalization in a true sense: it is of no importance to the formal characterization of, for example, phrase structure grammar whether a pair of rules are written as 'NP → N' and 'NP → A + N', or abbreviated as 'NP → (A) N', or abbreviated with a brace instead, and so on. But they were central to Chomsky's aim of explanatory adequacy, as he himself makes clear (1965, 42f.), so long as Halle's assumption held. The study of notation had thus itself become a major topic of linguistic theory.

But does anyone still believe that Halle's assumption was justified? In his own field of phonology a straightforward count of symbols notoriously failed to deal with problems of phonetic naturalness, and the pseudo-remedy proposed by Chomsky and Halle (1968), in which symbols were counted or not counted depending on the substantive character of the rule in question, led immediately to the appreciation, by others if not openly by Halle himself, that the substance and not the form was what mattered. (See, in particular, Chen 1973, 247–8, on the 'sterility of the manipulation of formal devices'.) In my work on morphology I began by assuming that a measure was necessary; in the end I realized that the demand might be 'just as preposterous' (Matthews 1972, 395) as the search for a mechanical discovery procedure. In syntax little serious work was ever done, and in the past half-decade almost all the general discussion has been hostile (as for example, that of Smith and Wilson 1979, 245ff.). In short, this was a mistake and all we lack is a proper admission by those who made it.

Having said goodbye to the evaluation measure we can also say goodbye to the obsession with notational devices which wasted so much of our time in the 10 or 15 years after it was proposed. Notation is a practical matter and there is no longer any theoretical reason for bothering with it.

Let us therefore return to formalization in its more interesting senses. As presented by Lyons and others the notion seems, at first sight, to be unexceptionable. How could one object to making a description explicit? But then one wonders why it was thought to be new. Had not grammars always striven to be precise, and if, in practice, they often failed, is this not just as true of grammars, or fragments of grammars, from the generative school? Moreover, people have in fact objected, or at least questioned whether formalization is an urgent need. Surely they cannot mean that it is a virtue to be inexplicit?

A reaction had already begun by the time that Lyons's accounts (1968; 1970) were published. In the preface to a collection of papers covering the first dozen years of transformational grammar, Reibel and Schane remark that 'in the early studies linguists attempted to state precisely . . . the exact environmental conditions under which a particular rule applied'. But by the late 1960s they detect a 'feeling that it is premature, or even not possible, to write formal rules'; partly for that reason, and partly because of the obscurity of earlier notations, 'later studies often merely state in ordinary language what rules are supposed to do' (Reibel and Schane 1969, ix). Warnings also came from scholars outside the transformational school. In the previous year Dik wrote of the dangers of 'premature formalization'—of formalisms, that is, which are developed before a theory is adequate in material respects (Dik 1968, 5). Of his own theory Dik remarked that 'it does not seem to contain any feature which would not lend itself to a complete formalization or explicitation' (199). Nevertheless he did not give one and—or should we say 'since'?—his account is in general only partial. Such views and practices have in turn been criticized by Chomskyan fundamentalists. In particular, Postal's study of raising (1974) was open to the serious objection, if such objections are indeed serious, that in a text of over 400 pages it offered no precise statement of the (allegedly single) rule that it was advocating. The review articles devoted to it (Bresnan 1976; Lightfoot 1976; Bach 1977; Hurford 1979) are the rebuke of a man fallen from grace. In this light we must consider rather carefully both the possible objections to formalization, and what the defence of it might be.

The most obvious objection is one already implied by Reibel and Schane: namely, that the more our statements gain in formalization, the more they are apt to lose in perspicuity. It is sometimes assumed that precision and perspicuity go together; thus for Heringer, whose account in general shows a clear grasp of what formalization is about, 'die Festlegung

der Zusammenhänge und die Armut machen Beschreibungen in Formal-
sprachen übersichtlicher und expliziter' (1970, 93). But although this
'Übersichtlichkeit' may be evident to the scholar who has devised a
grammar, and has therefore spent hours checking and amending rules in
the formal metalanguage in which they appear, experience shows that it is
generally not so for the readers who have to try and use it. For example, in
Heringer's own book we are presented with a list of constituency and
lexical rules (131–8), followed by a series of explanatory notes (139–271)
taking each of the former in turn. If the formulae were as clear as they are
explicit this would be an admirable method: to find what Heringer has to
say on a specific issue, we would simply check the initial list, and then
locate and read the note in question. But in fact I could not use this chapter
until I had added page headings showing, in ordinary language, what each
section deals with. I confess that, having done that, I ignore the formulae
entirely.

In early transformational studies 'the notations were frequently cumbersome and showed much individual variation from author to author' (Reibel
and Schane 1969, ix); they may also be inexplicit, like that of the
transformations in Kelly's article (1968) cited earlier. We might suppose,
therefore, that the obscurity would vanish once they became efficient,
standard and adequate. But the problem is more fundamental and is not
confined to our field. In a paper with virtually the same title as this, Wang
(1955) refers, for example, to the different ways in which a mathematical
proof can be expounded, either formally with every minor step spelled out,
or informally so that the reader must make intuitive leaps from one
proposition to another. Since readers can in fact make intuitive leaps there
is often no point in obscuring the argument by making explicit what is
trivial as well as what requires demonstration. In such cases it is not the
notation that is 'cumbersome', but the use of an apparatus which, though
suitable for its own purposes, is too elaborate for the task in hand. As
Wang remarks, one does not take an aeroplane to visit someone else in the
same town (233).

Nevertheless there is a feeling in linguistics that informality will not do.
In a passage typical of the 1960s, Chomsky and Halle ask us to think of
rules of grammar 'as instructions that might be given to a mindless robot,
incapable of exercising any judgement or imagination in their application';
to the extent that they 'do not meet this standard of explicitness and
precision, they fail to express the linguistic facts' (1968, 60). But it is only
the familiarity of such remarks that prevents one from seeing what an odd
requirement this is. To 'express the linguistic facts' is presumably to make
them clear to whoever wants to know about them. Such persons are not in
fact 'mindless robots' and if told, for example, that in such and such a
language the verb agrees in number with its subject, will be perfectly able
to understand that number in subjects covers both inflections and coordination, that the rule may apply only to certain constructions in which the
verb is finite, and so on, without the very complex statement which a
formal exposition would require, and which might be recognizable for what
it is only because a redundant label, '$T_{agreement}$', is attached to it. The grammar will be clearer if their 'judgement and imagination' are allowed for.

In practice, no generative grammarian does make every detail explicit. But the principle that it should be so continues to inspire gratuitous obscurity. Let us take, for instance, Chomsky's formulation of what, at the time of writing, is called the 'opacity principle' (Chomsky 1980, 176). This is meant to cover a number of restrictions on the interpretation of anaphoric elements: for example, *each other* cannot be construed with *they* in *They wanted the people to like each other,* but only with the subject of its own clause, *the people.* Chomsky therefore writes that 'an anaphor α cannot be free in β (β = [e.g.] $\overline{S}$) if [e.g.] α is c-commanded by the subject of β', where by a previous definition a category α c-commands ' . . . ' in a structure $_\beta$[. . . α . . .]. Now I am willing to suspend doubts and believe that this formulation does allow the relations to be construed correctly. But it is hard to see how its sense can be grasped if it is not explained beforehand, or that it adds to our real understanding of the restriction. What point then do such formulations have?

An uncharitable answer, in this as in many other cases, including (alas) some of my own earlier work, is that they make the argument look more impressive. Alternatively precision is itself a virtue, regardless of the trouble the reader is caused. But we must also consider two specific motives, which were both attractive in the early days of formal linguistics and whose invalidity or unimportance, like that of the argument for notation based on the need for an evaluation procedure, may need to be underlined.

The first was that if theories of grammar are formalized it might be possible to prove theorems about formal languages which are in some way of interest to our field. For example, Chomsky was thought to have proved that English was not a finite state language (in Chomsky 1957, ch. 3) or, to put it more generally, that 'the classes of languages [finite-state grammars] define do not contain the class of natural languages' (Bach 1974, 203). It was then asked whether 'natural languages' were contained in the class of formal languages defined by context-free phrase structure grammars or, from what seemed at the time to be a more promising angle, what subclass of formal languages would be defined by transformational grammars, given that all 'natural languages' were to be contained in it. The latter was a live issue when the first edition of Bach's textbook (1964) was published. As he remarked, the formal study of grammars had by that time 'shown a great deal about the (weak) generative capacity of grammars that are known to be inadequate', including (on grounds then thought convincing) phrase structure grammars. 'On the other hand, a good deal has been learned about applying a more powerful model (transformational grammar) to the description of actual languages'; further research must therefore both continue the empirical investigation and study the mathematical properties of the system or systems which seemed appropriate (Bach 1964, 168).

But this is hardly a live issue now. Part of the reason is that to talk of 'natural languages' as objects that can both be studied empirically and have theorems proved about them is acknowledged nonsense. Another, more important part had to do with the discovery, apparently surprising to some scholars, that the class of languages defined by transformational grammars was effectively unconstrained (initial announcement by Peters and Ritchie

1969). In the decade following, almost no attention has been paid to generative capacity, and more and more to particular restrictions on the application of transformational or other rules, like Chomsky's opacity principle. Perhaps he and his colleagues have thought it premature to ask how far the power of their grammars might be affected. But it is not clear that the answer would matter. Suppose, for instance, that the opacity principle is correct. We might then find that the set of languages construable under it was formally restricted. Alternatively (and more probably) they might not be. But neither finding would tell us anything about the relevant constructions, or suggest any explanation for possible linguistic universals, that we did not have already. Nor would the negative result leave us dissatisfied with what had been achieved. Such questions can safely be left to scholars interested in formal systems, without grammarians having to pursue them.

If we are not going to prove theorems the point of formalization, as a mathematician would see it, disappears. But the second of our motives concerned explicitness in a more ordinary sense and, in particular, as a methodological principle. For it is only when rules are stated explicitly—so we were told—that we can begin to evaluate hypotheses about the structure of a language. Above all, a hypothesis should make predictions. When we test these we may find that they are wrong; this leads us to a better hypothesis. That may then make fresh predictions, going beyond the facts it was intended to account for; if these are right the generalization is confirmed by its fruitfulness. There was often a comparison with 'other, more developed sciences'. Discoveries could be made and problems be identified only if we too adopted their standards of precision in formulating theories.

The classic statement of this method is in the preface to *Syntactic structures* (Chomsky 1957, 5), which applied it with apparently complete success. In the years following it belonged to the stock-in-trade of any ordinary generative apologist, and had scarcely to be argued afresh until the 1970s, when the practices of scholars such as Postal (1974) clearly did not conform to it. In his late contribution to the controversy surrounding this book, Hurford (1979) agrees with Postal that there is no difficulty in seeing what effect a raising operation would have (Postal 1977, replying to Bresnan 1976). But two further problems 'beset' his work. Firstly, a precise statement of the rule requires 'a host of conditions' governing its application to particular words; the 'detailed spelling out' of these might 'prove so cumbersome that there remains no overall gain in generality' from adopting it. Secondly, the book has no 'precisely specified general framework': we can only guess at the character of other rules that Postal assumes (Hurford 1979, 112f.). Later on Hurford argues that Postal's 'methodological view . . . is . . . incoherent', in that he tries to postulate a rule without also postulating a grammar of which it forms part (117f.). But there is 'no *independent* way of establishing' it (119). In short, the validity of raising cannot be assessed unless the hypothesis as a whole is spelled out.

But it is easy enough to appreciate Postal's argument. In the first instance, what he proposed should be seen not as a rule but as an analysis—an analysis in which, for example, *him* in *I expect him to come* is shown to have properties both of the object of *expect* and (as generally assumed) the subject of *to come*. According to current models for representing the syntactic structure of sentences, that meant that it stands in different configurations at the deep and surface levels. If we accept that the former has it in the embedded clause, we must posit a transformation raising it into the main clause. It does not matter whether the rule is stated explicitly, or if stated whether it is very complex or very simple. Nor have we any interest in rules which would assign a different structural description, unless that as such could be shown to be better. Descriptions, not rules, are primary.

At this point we have to recall that an essential element in formalization, in the sense in which Chomsky took the notion over in the 1950s, was the abstraction from meaning. Postal himself said very little about meaning, and that only in a thin chapter near the end of his book (1974, 356–68). But it is crucial to his argument. To say that *him* is the object of *expected* is to say that in a certain respect it stands in its own semantic relation to it, separately from the infinitive which follows. It is this relation that is confirmed by the acceptability of a personal passive (*He was expected to come*); although there are other mechanisms by which that could be derived, by moving the pronoun directly from the structure *I expected* [*he to come*], they do not explain how it comes about that, by a partial adjustment of the valency of *expect* to that of 'Equi-' verbs like *persuade*, such a construction is possible. On the other hand, *He was expected to come* still means that something was expected to happen, whereas a sentence like *He was persuaded to come* means that an individual was persuaded to do something; it is for that reason that *expect* is not itself classed as an 'Equi-' verb, or ambiguously as either an 'Equi-' verb or one that simply takes an infinitival complement. Furthermore, it is precisely because we are concerned with the valency and meaning of particular verbs that, as Palmer (1972) had already made clear, there is so much indeterminacy in the interpretation and indeed with regard to the acceptability of examples. It is hardly surprising that a general rule requires a 'host of conditions' on its operation. To expect otherwise is to misunderstand the nature of semantic relationships.

If we ignored meaning then, of course, the argument would be different. All we could do would be to state rules for the distribution of words in sentences. Given two alternative rules we could only ask which was more general; that question could not be answered unless they were explicitly spelled out. Nor could a rule be taken in isolation: the alternatives would assume other rules which we would also have to spell out. In the end, only complete grammars could be compared—a proposition often stressed in the 1960s, until its complete unreality became evident. I have put this in the hypothetical mood because it is not clear to me that, after 30 or 40 years of dreaming about the goal of 'rigour' in linguistic analysis, anyone still believes that syntactic description should be based on distributional evidence alone, or that the aim of providing the simplest account which meets a requirement of observational adequacy should not be subordinated to that of describing individual sentences in a way which illuminates the speakers' own understanding of them. One phase of this dream was that the rules themselves could be evaluated for 'descriptive adequacy' (Chomsky 1965, 30ff.). Unless one still believes that, there is no reason why their formulation should be thought to have any special importance in deciding what treatment is right.

This does not mean that distributional criteria are not needed. But they are needed precisely as one sort of criterion for an analysis: to show that, for example, *a cat* forms a unit in *A cat miaowed* we do not have to postulate a set of rules S → NP + VP, NP → Article + N, and so on, and then go through a rigmarole of checking predictions against an alternative hypothesis S → Article + XP, XP → N + V, or others that might occur to us. Although that is one way of putting it, it is a misleading way when other criteria are also recognized as relevant.

Nor does it mean that rules should not subsequently be stated. Thus, if we accepted 'raising' as a form of discrepancy between deep and surface structures, it would then be easy to state a transformation epitomizing what is involved. But in doing so we would ignore the vagaries of individual verbs and individual collocations, which belong to the lexicon and not to the syntax. The rule would accordingly be clear, or explicit as an ordinary grammarian might see it, rather than precise in the technical sense which Postal's critics have urged. That is because it takes the analysis for granted (see already Haas 1966, 119f.), instead of itself being the pretended justification for it.

There are two further aspects of formalization, or of the reaction against formalization, with which we may end. The first concerns the specific dangers in introducing any formalism—for example, that of phrase-structure grammars—before an informal view has been justified. As Dik points out, in a passage already briefly referred to, our main task is to work out 'a theoretical framework adequate to deal with the facts of language' (1968, 5). This is what I have elsewhere called a model of description (Matthews 1974, 225). If it is satisfactory, formalization is then 'only a matter of time and ingenuity'. But a premature formalism may perpetuate errors which might otherwise have been identified and eliminated, since (still in Dik's words) 'formalized systems tend to develop into self-contained organisms, independent of the facts they were designed to account for'.

There is surely no doubt that this is so. Perhaps the simplest case is the assumption (which for mathematical reasons was quite natural in the 1950s) that a phrase structure grammar, or in general any grammar whatever, should be formalized as a rewrite system. By the end of the 1960s this had hardened into dogma: for example, in Wall's textbook (1972) the chapter on 'Grammars of formal languages' begins directly with systems of that type (207ff.). Hence it is not surprising that when, for example, Postal came to consider the construction of sentences like *I expect him to come,* the only mechanism which presented itself was one in which the role of *him* as subject was represented at one level, in terms of a structure known to be specifiable by one type of rewrite rule, and its role as object at another, in terms of a formally similar structure which could be derived by another type of rewrite rule. The natural account, that it has properties both of object and of subject at the same level, could not be formulated within the tradition of formalism in which, for purely historical reasons, Postal had to work. He has since turned to other forms of description, which seem more appropriate (for instance, in Postal and Pullum 1978). But at the time of writing only glimpses have been published. One cannot but wonder if the bugbear of providing what will be accepted as an elegant formalization has not helped to prevent relational grammar and its congeners from getting off the ground. As one of the first writers to suggest anything of the kind (Matthews 1967, 149f.), I can report that it has certainly been a drag in my case.

In fact there is no reason why even simple constituency grammars should be formalized in the way that Chomsky originally chose (see now Gazdar 1981). As new formalisms take the field, it would be better if all students of linguistics learned to balance the damage they can do against the strictly limited contribution they can make.

The final issue is whether, as Hudson put it in the introduction to the earlier of his attempts to formalize systemic grammar, 'any kind of formalism can ever encompass ALL that we should want to include in a complete description of what a native speaker must know' (1971, 7); alternatively, whether 'the assumption that a language is well-defined', which still underlies most formal and quasi-formal work in linguistics, is not 'obtained by leaving out of account *just those properties of real languages that are most important*' (Hockett 1967, 10; his emphasis). These are wide questions, which I can perhaps pretend to have dealt with in my general booklet on Chomsky's theories (Matthews 1979). But it is worth pointing to the special case of formalization in semantics. For it seems that this can only mean one of two things. One is the mere translation of sentences into logical notation, which is indeed what it often means but which is trivial. The other is that alongside the syntactic rules which constitute a calculus for grammaticality, or perhaps replacing them, there should be a calculus for some other property, typically for truth values, which is supposed to bear on meaning instead. For a philosophical critique see a recent paper by Heal (1978), which contrasts such an approach with what she calls a 'concept analysis of meaning'. But from our viewpoint it does indeed dodge every question that matters: namely, why a speaker should use this word rather than that, one construction rather than another, and so on.

It is therefore ironic that it is in this branch of linguistics—or this branch of linguistics as most people would call it—that, with the fresh encouragement of Montague's propagandists, formalization is an element in research to which a reasonable number of scholars still pay more than lip service. But perhaps my parenthesis is important. Can a true formal semanticist— not someone, as I say, who merely uses logical notations—really be in our field rather than in logic or some application of it?

References

Akmajian, A. and Heny, F. 1975: *An introduction to the principles of transformational syntax*. Cambridge, Mass.: MIT Press.

Bach, E. 1964: *An introduction to transformational grammars*. New York: Holt, Rinehart & Winston.

—1974: *Syntactic theory*. New York: Holt, Rinehart & Winston.

—1977: Review article on Postal 1974. *Lg*. **53**, 621–54.

Bloomfield, L. 1935: *Language*. London: Allen & Unwin.

Bresnan, J.W. 1976: Nonarguments for raising. *LIn*. **7**, 485–501.

Carnap, R. 1958: *Introduction to symbolic logic and its applications*. Tr. W.H. Meyer. New York: Dover.

Chen, M. 1973: On the formal expression of natural rules in phonology. *JL* **9**, 223–49.

Chomsky, N. 1957: *Syntactic structures*. The Hague: Mouton.

—1965: *Aspects of the theory of syntax*. Cambridge, Mass.: MIT Press.

—1980: *Rules and representations*. Oxford: Blackwell.

Chomsky, N. and Halle, M. 1968: *The sound pattern of English*. New York: Harper & Row.

Corneille, J.-P. 1976: *La linguistique structurale: sa portée, ses limites*. Paris: Larousse.

Culicover, P.W., Wasow, T. and Akmajian, A. (eds.) 1977: *Formal syntax*. New York: Academic Press.

Dik, S.C. 1968: *Coordination: its implications for the theory of general linguistics*. Amsterdam: North-Holland.

Dubois, J. *et al.* 1973: *Dictionnaire de linguistique*. Paris: Larousse.

Edwards, P. (ed.) 1967: *The encyclopedia of philosophy*. 8 Vols. New York: Macmillan.

Gazdar, G. 1981: Phrase structure grammar. In G. K. Pullum and P. Jacobson (eds.), *The nature of syntactic representation*. Dordrecht: Reidel.

Haas, W. 1966: Linguistic relevance. In C. E. Bazell *et al.* (eds.), *In memory of J. R. Firth*. London: Longmans.

Halle, M. 1962: Phonology in generative grammar. *Word* **18**, 54–72.

Harris, Z. S. 1951: *Methods in structural linguistics*. Chicago: University of Chicago Press.

———1954: Distributional structure. *Word* **10**, 146–62.

Heal, J. 1978: On the phrase 'theory of meaning'. *Mind* **87**, 359–75.

Heringer, H.-J. 1970: *Theorie der deutschen Syntax*. Munich: Hueber.

Hjelmslev, L. 1953: *Prolegomena to a theory of language*. Tr. F. J. Whitfield. Baltimore: Waverly Press for Indiana University.

Hockett, C. F. 1967: *Language, mathematics, and linguistics*. The Hague: Mouton.

Hudson, R. A. 1971: *English complex sentences: an introduction to systemic grammar*. Amsterdam: North-Holland.

———1976: *Arguments for a non-transformational grammar*. Chicago: University of Chicago Press.

Hurford, J. R. 1979: Review article on Postal 1974. *JL* **15**, 111–20.

Jespersen, O. 1924: *The philosophy of grammar*. London: Allen & Unwin.

Katz, J. J. and Fodor, J. A. 1963: The structure of a semantic theory. *Lg*. **39**, 170–210.

Kelly, D. H. 1968: Transformations in the Latin nominal phrase. *CPh*. **63**, 46–52. Reprinted in Strunk 1973, 440–51.

Lakoff, G. 1974: Interview in H. Parret (ed.), *Discussing language.* The Hague: Mouton.

Lees, R. B. 1957: Review of Chomsky 1957. *Lg.* **33,** 375–408.

Lightfoot, D. W. 1976: The theoretical implications of subject raising. *FL* **14,** 257–85.

Lyons, J. 1968: *Introduction to theoretical linguistics.* Cambridge: Cambridge University Press.

————1970: Introduction, In J. Lyons (ed.), *New horizons in linguistics.* Harmondsworth: Penguin.

Matthews, P. H. 1967: Review of Chomsky 1965. *JL* **3,** 119–52.

————1972: *Inflectional morphology: a theoretical study based on aspects of Latin verb conjugation.* Cambridge: Cambridge University Press.

————1974: *Morphology: an introduction to the theory of word structure.* Cambridge: Cambridge University Press.

————1979: *Generative grammar and linguistic competence.* London: Allen & Unwin.

Palmer, F. R. 1972: Noun phrase and sentence: a problem in semantics/ syntax. *TPhS,* 20–43.

Peters, P. S. and Ritchie, R. W. 1969: A note on the universal base hypothesis. *JL* **5,** 150–2.

Postal, P. M. 1974: *On raising: one rule of English grammar and its theoretical implications.* Cambridge, Mass.: MIT Press.

————1977: About a 'nonargument' for raising. *LIn.* **8,** 141–54.

Postal, P. M. and Pullum, G. K. 1978: Traces and the description of English complementizer contraction. *LIn.* **9,** 1–29.

Reibel, D. A. and Schane, S. A. (eds.) 1969: *Modern studies in English: readings in transformational grammar.* Englewood Cliffs: Prentice-Hall.

Robins, R. H. 1964: *General linguistics: an introductory survey.* London: Longmans.

Smith, N. and Wilson, D. (1979). *Modern linguistics: the results of Chomsky's revolution.* Harmondsworth: Penguin.

Strunk, K. (ed.) 1973: *Probleme der lateinischen Grammatik.* Darmstadt: Wissenschaftliche Buchgesellschaft.

Wall, R. 1972: *Introduction to mathematical linguistics.* Englewood Cliffs: Prentice-Hall.

Wang, H. 1955: On formalization. *Mind* **64,** 226–38.

2

Pseudo-controversy in linguistic theory
David Crystal

Somebody once said that a person has only to speak, to be controversial. Certainly, in linguistics there is no shortage of controversial statement: rather, the problem for researcher and supervisor is to decide which of the many controversies is worth spending time on. There is nothing worse than a 'pseudo-controversy'—one which takes us no further forward in our theoretical understanding of a subject, because it turns out to be unresolvable in our present state of knowledge, or methodologically impracticable, or trivial in its empirical consequences, or wholly speculative, or vacuous. As an illustration of 'meta-controversy', such exercises might be instructive; indeed, one can always learn from the previous dead ends of research history. But no one wants to be the first to find a dead end for himself. One of the problems of contemporary linguistics is that it is becoming increasingly difficult to tell the difference between a fruitful and a fruitless controversy. When someone made a controversial statement in the 1940s and 1950s—so senior colleagues have told me—the consequences of the various positions adopted were on the whole clearer than they are today. But as the scope of linguistics has developed, and with the inclusion of psycholinguistics and sociolinguistics in particular, it has become increasingly difficult to anticipate the empirical, methodological or theoretical consequences of a controversial statement. In a linguistics which attempts to provide an integrated account of human behaviour, such as Pike's or Chomsky's, it is often impossible to trace the implications of an apparently straightforward linguistic argument so as to take account of its psychological, sociological, neurological or other consequences. The problem is at its worst when these broader issues are introduced into linguistic reasoning at the outset, as when theoreticians debate the general conditions which a linguistic theory is supposed to meet. Such a debate is inevitably controversial—but how fruitful a controversy is it?

As a starting-point, we may consider one of Chomsky's statements about the issue (1967, 100): 'it is going to be necessary to discover conditions on

16

theory construction, coming presumably from experimental psychology or from neurology, which will resolve the alternatives that can be arrived at by the kind of speculative theory construction linguists can do on the basis of the data available to them.' It would seem that neurophysiological and neuropsychological factors are to play a major role in developing our evaluation procedures for linguistic theories. The same point is made by Katz (1964, 133–4), along with some further implications which can usefully be quoted in full:

> since the psychologist and the mentalistic linguist are constructing theories of some kind, i.e. theories with the same kind of relation to the neurophysiology of the human brain, it follows that the linguist's theory is subject to the requirement that it harmonize with the psychologist's theories dealing with other human abilities and that it be consistent with the neurophysiologist's theories concerning the type of existing brain mechanisms. . . . Further, by subjecting a linguistic theory to this requirement we make it more easily testable. For the requirement enables us to refute a linguistic theory if we can find psychological theories or facts that are inconsistent with it or neurophysiological accounts which describe brain structure in a way that precludes the linguistic theory from being isomorphic to any of the structures in the human brain.

This general view, in due course, led to the development of the so-called APHASIA PARADIGM of linguistic enquiry, which has attracted a great deal of controversy since it was first propounded by Whitaker and others in the late 1960s.[1] The main aim is to take pathological linguistic data, such as that provided by aphasic patients, and analyse it in the expectation that it will give us insight into normal linguistic behaviour and into the nature of linguistic theory in general. How fruitful is this approach, and its associated controversy, likely to be?

Whitaker gives three reasons for the linguist's interest in pathological data. Firstly, there is a direct contribution to a putative neuroscience (1969, 135):

> Someday man's understanding of the brain and its behavioral mechanisms will progress far beyond the contemporary awareness of a few biochemical properties of neurons, a rough approximation of electrical events and partially specified functions for some of the neuro-anatomic structures. And when that day arrives, the biochemist, physiologist, anatomist, neurologist and all others concerned with brain functions will suddenly be in need of a specification of behavioral units that can be correlated with their information.

Therefore, he argues, we should avoid any 'artificial dichotomy between an abstract linguistic model of [the *actual* knowledge of language] and the neurological structures and functions and events which *are* that knowledge'. Secondly, there is an associated gain, in that such studies will help to provide an explanation for the qualitative differences between human and animal communication. Species-specificity, it is argued, implies 'genetic specificity or a structural-functional uniqueness in the brain' (1969, 8).

But the third, and main justification is to provide empirical evidence

---

[1] See Whitaker (1969; 1971), Weigl and Bierwisch (1970), Schnitzer (1974).

18   *David Crystal*

bearing on linguistic hypotheses (1969, 69). Whitaker argues that we must avoid creating models of language that bear no relation to neurological reality:

> the closer we get to the brain, the more likely we are to be discussing the realities of the structure of language (1969, 135). . . . there are *a priori* grounds for bringing neurological information to bear upon linguistic theory. . . . Ultimately we have to. Certain structures and functions of the nervous system are the substrate of both our 'knowledge' and our 'use' of language (1969, 7). . . . language is a product of man's nervous system—literally . . . [it] has physical reality in the human brain (1969, 17).

The argument may be summarized as follows: linguistic hypotheses represent underlying psychological reality; therefore they are hypotheses about normal brain structure and function; abnormal brain structure produces abnormal linguistic behaviour; it is, however, the same brain which produces both the normal and the abnormal behaviour; it should therefore be possible to relate the two types of behaviour, such that the same linguistic theory can account for both; if so, we have the neurological data acting as a constraint on linguistic theory (in addition to whatever other constraints linguistic theory itself imposes, such as descriptive adequacy).

There are, however, several difficulties with this line of argument. Whitaker makes it plain (e.g. 1971, 140) that there is no reductionism involved: linguistics is not to be 'reduced' to psychological or neurological states. Rather, the aim is to establish equivalences between subject areas or categories 'at similar . . . corresponding levels of abstraction' (cf. also the use of 'harmonize' and 'consistent' in the above quotation from Katz). But it is unclear how one defines 'a similar level of abstraction' between two theories, or places the claims of different theories in correspondence— a point made by Black (1970, 457) in a critique of Chomsky (though Black was talking about the relationship between mathematical and psychological premises, not neurological ones). Is there any precise formulation that might be given to a hypothesized equivalence involving linguistic classes (such as noun), categories (such as tense) or rules (such as S → NP+VP), on the one hand, and neurological 'realities' on the other? Moreover, how appropriate is the characterization of the nervous system in such terms as 'physical reality'? There are many models of neurological activity, involving electrical, chemical, molecular, information theoretic and other bases. A phrase such as 'structures and functions of the nervous system' (cf. above) is reminiscent of traditional controversy in linguistics, concerning the best way of representing the 'reality' of these notions. Given the possibility of alternative neurological models which attach different significance to concepts such as 'structure', 'function', 'substrate', and so on, the use of the term 'reality' becomes less meaningful, and the likelihood of our being able to specify clear equivalences more remote.

Nor are the above arguments any more persuasive if we investigate particular linguistic features. Here, the aphasia paradigm maintains that if a linguistic construct can be shown to be lost after a lesion, without other aspects of language being affected, then this is evidence for the representation of such constructs in the brain and thus for their functional autonomy in linguistic theory. As Weigl and Bierwisch (1970, 13) put it, these constructs 'must be considered as relatively autonomous functional units even in normal performance'. On this basis, the 'neurological reality' of several linguistic constructs has been proposed: for instance, the distinction between the main modalities of speech/listening/reading/writing, and between the levels of phonetics/phonology/syntax/semantics (bringing together several claims from Whitaker, and Weigl and Bierwisch); also the reality of various aspects of deep structure, of semantic fields and features, and of some specific grammatical transformations and phonological contrasts, such as tense/lax (Whitaker 1969, Ch.4; Schnitzer 1974). The arguments are put both positively (e.g. Whitaker proposes a specific underlying structure for the noun phrase; Schnitzer proposes a copula-creation transformation) and negatively (one of Whitaker's patients 'does provide evidence against a linguistic theory which fails to distinguish semantic and syntactic aspects of language . . . and more significantly argues against . . . the generative semantics proposal/(1969, 100).

The trouble is, that it is possible using this rationale to hypothesize the neurological reality of far too many linguistic constructs—including several from incompatible theoretical backgrounds. It is rarely if ever going to be the case that aphasic data will unequivocably support a single linguistic analysis or theory. Even assuming that enough data has been analysed from a sufficiently large group of patients to enable a generalization about deficit to be made,[2] there would still be several alternative ways of identifying the deficit. For instance, lack of ability to use a phonological contrast still leaves open the question of whether distinctive feature theory, phonemic theory, prosodic theory, or whatever is 'correct', as all might be used to describe the lost contrast. Or again, to show that an aphasic has lost a syntactic form (e.g. the ability to use adjectives with a noun, or to use the passive) does not clarify whether a structuralist, tagmemic, transformational or other analysis of the category is going to be supported by neurological evidence. Linguistic controversy on these matters is not going to be settled by an appeal to neurological data; on the contrary, these data are quite ambivalent, as the main debate in this literature, over the competence/performance issue, demonstrated.

This debate focused on the question of whether aphasic data should be described as a disorder of competence or performance, in Chomsky's original sense. The debate now seems somewhat dated, given the criticisms that have been levelled at the usefulness of this distinction since (cf. Matthews 1979), but the issues it raised are worth reviewing (see also, Lesser 1978, 45.ff.). Weigl and Bierwisch (1970), amongst others, argued that aphasic language could be analyzed as a disorder of performance: competence was intact, the aphasia being 'a disturbance of the access to the knowledge of language' (*ibid.* 14). De Saussure (in passing) seems to have held a similar view:

---

[2] Whitaker avoids studying aphasic language behaviour statistically, preferring to use a single informant basis. But the variability between patients is such that some statistical reasoning cannot be avoided (see further below).

What is lost in all cases of aphasia or agraphia is less the faculty of producing a given sound or writing a given sign than the ability to evoke by means of an instrument, regardless of what it is, the signs of a regular system of speech. The obvious implication is that beyond the functioning of the various organs there exists a more general faculty which governs signs and which would be the linguistic faculty proper.[3]

Weigl and Bierwisch's evidence is threefold: that some modalities remain intact within aphasia (e.g. speech may be affected; reading may not be), suggesting a 'single underlying competence'; that aphasics fluctuate in their linguistic skills, suggesting variable access to their ever-present competence; and that aphasics 'de-block', i.e. devise an alternative strategy to avoid a particular linguistic difficulty, which ultimately enables them to use a linguistic feature. By contrast, Whitaker argues that aphasic data bears directly on competence: competence is the ' "core" of the central part of performance . . . equated with the representation of language in the central nervous system' (1969, 11). A linguistic feature or system, in this view, is seen as part of competence if it is central, i.e. appears in all modalities of language; if a feature/system is present in only some modalities, then it is part of performance. Using this distinction, he attacks the Weigl and Bierwisch position, on two main grounds: that there are some permanent deficits, where there is no fluctuation in ability; and some of these do cut across all modalities. How is such a debate to be resolved?

In a sense, it does not need to be resolved, for it is a pseudo-problem— an artefact of the competence/performance distinction.[4] Neither approach can in the end decide on what is competence and what is performance. Whitaker points out that Weigl and Bierwisch cannot distinguish between competence which is lost as opposed to competence which is blocked. But likewise, if the central nervous system gives rise to both competence and performance (cf. above), there will be similar difficulties for Whitaker— for example, in deciding whether a linguistic problem is due to a limitation of competence or a limitation due to memory or attention. Whitaker in fact allows at one point that a competence deficit may be variable - when there are fluctuations in all modalities (1969, 71). But this makes it impossible to say anything unambiguous about the neurological basis of the competence/ performance distinction. It is not particularly surprising, then, that one year after his 1969 publication, Whitaker stopped trying to refine the distinction; and in a later paper (1971, 145) abandoned it altogether. Likewise abandoned are such 1969 views as the proposal of a specific underlying structure for the noun phrase, the evidence for which is 'less than secure' (1971, 221), the support for the lexicalist position, which 'may have been a premature claim' (1971, 230), and the argument for the syntax v. semantics distinction—an issue which 'cannot be independently verified from this data' (i.e. the 1969 work) (1971, 215).

[3] 1916, 11 (trans. W. Baskin). Cf. also Critical Edition, Engler 3291, App. to Vol. 4.
[4] For pseudo-problems, see Abercrombie (1963). The conception of competence is in any case puzzling: on this view, any linguistic features which distinguish speech from writing would have to be considered performance features, by definition, e.g. almost the whole of intonation.

The more one reads in this literature, the more one feels that the whole theoretical debate is premature. Why should this be so? One reason is empirical. It would seem that insufficient aphasics have had their language systematically examined to warrant the generalizations which are being made about them. To take some basic empirical questions: just how much variation is there in the linguistic behaviour of aphasic patients? just how abnormal is this behaviour, compared with our everyday speech? The lack of published empirical studies has not stopped the formulation of major theoretical positions. Whitaker, for example, admits that there is some 'idiolectal variation' (1971, 168.ff.), but says that 'this fact makes the linguistic analysis of aphasia no less and no more difficult than the linguistic analysis of normal language behavior', and concludes 'aphasic language behavior is a subset of normal language behavior' (1971, 169; cf. 1969, 48–9). Yet all of this is on the basis of an analysis of only a few patient samples; and Schnitzer, similarly, bases all his claims on a few hundred judgements taken from a single speaker. One cannot assume representativeness: it is the representativeness one is trying to prove. One cannot even assume that one is dealing with an idiolect; it is the systemicness one is trying to prove.

The empirical weaknesses in the aphasia paradigm are due partly to the level of generality at which the characterization of aphasic data has been arrived at. Using only the selective and linguistically superficial criteria of the main aphasia tests, it is not too difficult to point to gross similarities across patients. But as soon as more detailed grammatical, phonological or semantic approaches are used, the similarities become far less obvious. Indeed, there are several basic aspects of aphasic language which have received hardly any study, e.g. the grammatical role of the patient's prosody, the paradigmatic or syntagmatic structure of the patient's semantic fields, and the discourse connectivity within the patient's grammar (see further, Crystal 1981). Above all there are the complex linguistic interdependencies between patient and clinician. It is a truism that the complexity of a therapist's linguistic stimulus will be a major factor in determining the nature of the patient's response—which makes it all the more surprising that systematic analysis of input and reinforcement language has not yet taken place. But until it has, theoretical conclusions such as those made above are undoubtedly premature. Failure to elicit a structure may tell us more about the limitations of our eliciting strategies than about the structure of the patient. Putting this another way, is the failure due to the patient's lack of competence, or the clinician's?

The urgent need for a meticulous linguistic analysis of patients' language behaviour is apparent, with reference both to the clinician's intervention strategies and the constraints imposed by the clinical setting in which the aphasic finds himself.[5] 'What then is a naturalistic environment for an aphasic patient?', asks J. M. Wepman appositely, in discussion following a paper of Jakobson's (1971, 326). On top of that, one might also ask what presuppositions an aphasic patient brings to the clinical setting. I am

---

[5] Cf. this point made in the context of child language disability (Crystal 1980).

reminded of the scene in *Wings*,[6] where the aviatrix recovers consciousness following her stroke to be greeted by the clinicians asking her such questions as 'Who is the President of the United States?' Only enemy intelligence officers would be asking her such questions, she reasons, and so she 'decides' to say nothing! Seeing the reason for a question is often part of the information needed in order to answer. The lack of such awareness may well account for some of the inadequacies found in patients who try to respond to question batteries in conventional tests. Putting the questions into full and motivating contexts often produces very different results. Again, we are faced with the question of whose competence we are studying—the test-designer's, in this case?

There can only be a handful of descriptions of samples of aphasic patients' language in print—linguistically sophisticated descriptions, that is, where proper attention has been paid to the need for a good transcription, involving intonation, stress, and so on, and with the analysis taken down to a depth of detail comparable to that found in other fields of descriptive linguistics. Those that I have seen, and those I have made myself, have so far indicated one major 'finding'—that the differences between patients are far more striking than the similarities. Doubtless, as more patients come to be analysed, we shall begin to see the broad outline of the wood, rather than the trees which at present take up all our attention. But it will be a far more complicated wood than has been suggested to us so far. The real controversies, perhaps, have yet to be discovered.

But it is not simply an empirical issue. Even if our aphasic data were reliable and representative, we would still be unable to use this as evidence in support of the claims of specific linguistic theories, for the evidence will logically bear any of the available alternatives. The early debate focused exclusively on issues within the transformational-generative paradigm of inquiry. More recently, other linguistic or psycholinguistic theories have been proposed as alternative candidates for neurolinguistic support. Schnitzer, for example, thinks that stratificational grammar might allow for 'greater clarity in determining whether data do or do not support a certain theoretical position' (1978, 359). He also mentions cognitive grammar (in the sense of Lakoff and Thompson (1975)) as a further alternative. Doubtless there are other neurolinguistic papers currently being written which will argue the merits of the several other theoretical positions to be found in contemporary linguistics. But one wonders if there is any point in continuing this research theme, in the absence of any principled way of resolving the competing claims. Ironically, Schnitzer's review of the uncertainty and tentativeness which has bedevilled the aphasia paradigm leads him to conclude: 'One thing is certain: if linguistics is to become a science, it will have to make use of hard data of the kind suggested, in choosing among proposed theories' (1978, 359). Yet this is precisely the conclusion which is least certain of all.

[6] This play, by Arthur Kopit, was first produced on stage at the Yale Repertory Theatre in February 1978. The play had its first production in June 1977 on American National Public Radio's *Earplay* project.

What then is the linguist, anxious to discover conditions for his construction of theories, to conclude? Whitaker, and the others, are not interested in linguistic theories which make no claims about neurological reality: 'Although linguistic theories can be abstract in this sense, as such they are not of interest to me' (Whitaker 1969, 80–1). But in our present state of knowledge (or in the foreseeable future), linguistic theories can make no testable claims about neurological reality, not simply because we do not know what neurological reality is, but because there are too many variables intervening between language and the underlying factors in a patient's behaviour. There is plenty for the linguist to do, in trying to tease apart these factors, and in attempting to think predictively about patients' linguistic behaviour. But when the linguist works in this way, he is not using aphasic data to test his theories; rather it is the other way around: he is attempting to impose some system on aphasic data using whatever theory he has been brought up to believe in. In this field of study, it is the 'hocus-pocus' linguist, and not the 'God's truth' one, who seems likely to prosper.

Are the problems raised by this debate unique to neurolinguistics? I do not think they are. Chomsky, in the above quotation, mentions experimental psychology as another source of constraints on linguistic theory construction (though he is not optimistic about the prospects (1967, 100)). One might go further than this, in searching for extra-linguistic factors with which linguistic theories might need to be in tune, and which would accordingly form part of any evaluation procedure. Why not cite sociological, semiotic, anthropological and social psychological factors, for instance? There could also be a whole range of pragmatic factors, relating to the use which the proposed theory would be put—presumably a major consideration in applied linguistics, yet by no means excluded from 'linguistics proper'. But the 'realities' underlying these other areas seem as chimerical as the neurological one, as soon as we start to investigate them. At a recent conference on physiological psychology, a psychologist colleague was bemoaning the way in which he felt contemporary psychology seemed no longer concerned with facts, but only with methods. He spoke as one bemused by the increasing statistical, computational and electronic sophistication required of him, and by the proliferation of models generated by other disciplines than his own. To go to psychology or biology for definite 'conditions' on linguistic theory is to go on a wild-goose chase: psychologists and biologists, no less than linguists, are looking for conditions on theory construction too. Indeed, ironically, these days the goose chase leads us back home again, in view of the way in which these other disciplines have constructed new models for their endeavours in which major roles are played by such notions as deep structure and competence. The moral is plain: as linguistics attempts to develop its concept of explanatory adequacy, it would do well to adopt a narrower rather than a broader frame of reference, if it is not to avoid pseudo-controversy. Evaluative criteria for linguistic theories must come from linguistics itself: there currently seems only irrelevance or ambiguity to be had from outside.

References

Abercrombie, D. 1965: Pseudo-procedures in linguistics. In D. Abercrombie (ed.), *Studies in phonetics and linguistics*. London: Oxford University Press.

Black, M. 1970: Comment on N. Chomsky's 'Problems of explanation in linguistics'. In R. Borger and F. Cioffi (eds.), *Explanation in the behavioural sciences*. Cambridge: Cambridge University Press.

Chomsky, N. 1967: Discussion of I. Pollack's 'Language as behavior'. In C.H. Millikan and F.L. Darley (eds.), *Brain mechanisms underlying speech and language*. New York: Grune & Stratton.

Crystal, D. 1980: Research trends in the study of child language disability. Paper given to the Symposium on Research in Child Language Disorders, Madison, Wisconsin.

————1981: *Clinical linguistics*. Vienna and New York: Springer.

de Saussure, F. 1916: *A course in general linguistics*. New York: Philosophical Library, 1959.

Jakobson, R. 1971: Linguistic types of aphasia. In *Selected writings 2.* The Hague: Mouton.

Katz, J.J. 1964: Mentalism in linguistics. *Lg.* **40,** 124–37.

Lesser, R. 1978: *Linguistic investigations of aphasia*. (Studies in Language Disability and Remediation **4.**) London: Edward Arnold.

Matthews, P.H. 1979: *Generative grammar and linguistic competence*. London: Allen & Unwin.

Lakoff, G. and Thompson, H. 1975: Introducing cognitive grammar. In C. Cogen, H. Thompson, G. Thurgood, K. Whistler and J. Wright (eds.), *Proc. 1st. Ann. Meet. Berkeley Ling. Soc.* Berkeley: Berkeley Linguistics Society, 295–313.

Schnitzer, M.L. 1974: Aphasiological evidence for five linguistic hypotheses. *Lg.* **50,** 300–15.

————1978: Toward a neurolinguistic theory of language. *B & L* **6,** 342–61.

Weigl, E. and Bierwisch, M. 1970: Neuropsychology and linguistics: topics of common research. *FL* **6,** 1–18.

Whitaker, H.A. 1969: On the representation of language in the human brain. Working papers in phonetics **12.** Los Angeles: University of California.

————1971: Neurolinguistics. In W.O. Dingwall (ed.), *A survey of linguistic science*. University of Maryland Linguistics Program.

3

Linguistic historiography
Giulio Lepschy

"What are historians of language writing the history of?", asked at the third International Congress of Linguists one of the most subtle practitioners of the discipline, B. A. Terracini (1933). One is tempted to extend his question today, and to ask: "What are historians of linguistics writing the history of?". These two questions are in fact more closely related than one might at first think. The historian's view of what linguistics is will inevitably be influenced by the linguist's view of what language is. According to some modern theorists, the typical object of linguistics is what people know about language (the distinction between this knowledge and language itself being problematic); from this point of view history of linguistics moves paradoxically near to history of language, and the distinction between the two sorts of awareness they refer to becomes disturbingly delicate. And, more generally, there is the basic problem of connecting history of linguistics with cultural history, or rather with history proper (Malkiel and Langdon, 1969). This has to be done making the connection so intimate that the reflections on language become intelligible as a historical phenomenon, but not so intimate that they lose their individuality and disappear within general history of culture. Recent attempts at interpreting the development of linguistics in its historical context are not too encouraging. This tangle of questions has been frequently observed, but not sorted out, in the context of discussions of Kuhn's (1962) theory of scientific revolutions (Hymes 1974; Parret 1976).

Besides, the historian of linguistics and the linguist are often the same person, in a way that might appear surprising in other disciplines. One of the results is that history of linguistics is sometimes not pursued very rigorously, but is considered a kind of undemanding hobby, which takes second place to the real business of analyzing languages or elaborating linguistic theory—a hobby which is almost a by-product of examining the literature on individual linguistic problems being studied. What comes out is expanded into an historical outline of the discipline, which in turn

25

becomes a section of, or a companion to the manual or introduction to the discipline which linguists are only too often tempted to write.

That this is so is evident from even the quickest inspection of traditional and current textbooks of linguistics. It is well known that comparative philologists used to place the origins of scientific linguistics at the beginning of the nineteenth century, with Bopp, Rask, Grimm and the other founding fathers of Indo-European comparative philology; for what came before, it was a question of establishing the real merits of Friedrich Schlegel, or of Sir William Jones, or of Wilhelm von Humboldt, or of retracing individual forerunners of the historical comparative method, through the intuitions and observations of people like Alexander Hamilton, the Jesuit G. L. Coeurdoux, Filippo Sassetti, perhaps going back to Dante. . . . For the rest one finds patronizing and often unreliable accounts of the hypothetical speculations of philosophers of language, and of the arbitrary etymologies proposed before the discovery of the comparative method.

With the development of structural linguistics and its interest in synchronic study, comparative philology appeared in a different light and the beginnings of scientific linguistics were moved nearer to Saussure, Trubeckoj and Bloomfield, and then it was a matter of looking for more immediate precursors, like Baudouin de Courtenay, Kruszewki, or J. Winteler, or for more remote ones like Pāṇini. Structural linguists, although they did not depreciate Indo-European comparative philologists, tended to underline the innovative break constituted by the onset of structuralism, with Saussure and Bloomfield. It is interesting that transformational linguistics, which originated within some of the most rigorous attempts to develop certain systematic and abstract aspects of structuralism with Z. S. Harris, has tended in turn to insist on its own originality, and to oppose structural linguistics, linking it in many respects with nineteenth-century comparative philology, and criticizing both for their reliance on a corpus of texts rather than on generative rules, and for their interest in the classification of surface phenomena rather than in generalizations concerning deeper regularities.

The most striking example in recent years of the impact which theoretical assumptions can have on linguistic historiography is of course offered by Chomsky's *Cartesian Linguistics* (1966), which revalued Port-Royal grammar and logic, in which it found the roots of several Chomskyan notions such as deep structure and even transformations, and traced the threads of rationalist linguistics, through the seventeenth and eighteenth centuries, down to Humboldt. Chomsky's book, although it was savagely attacked by some historians of linguistics, bears the marks of that genius which is evident in his theoretical works. From less vigorous hands, attempts at reinterpreting history of linguistics in the light of modern ideological preconceptions, have produced merely superficial and fanciful results.

Irrespective of whether it offers a correct and objective historical interpretation, Chomsky's work certainly throws a new, bright flash of light on texts which in previous studies of linguistic history appeared dull and unrewarding. But then, it has been suggested that the roots of generative grammar reach even farther into the past of our discipline: Chomsky's and Port-Royal's precursors are to be found in the Renaissance, in Sanctius's *Minerva,* and perhaps in the Middle Ages, with the Modistae. Here the difficulty is partly that these areas have not been investigated with the perceptiveness and originality which Chomsky devoted to what he called Cartesian linguistics, partly that not enough is known on these earlier authors and their background. Reliable modern editions, exegetic commentaries, historical interpretations are frequently lacking. No wonder that, in the absence of so much necessary preliminary work of an analytical character, the standard synthetic histories of linguistics are no substitute for a much needed full, comprehensive historical reference work, as can be seen by looking at well known examples: the work by Tagliavini (1963), rich in out of the way information, but rather flat and lacking in historical sensitivity; the clear but meagre book by Robins (1967); the more ambitious, but occasionally sectarian and unreliable texts by Mounin (1967; 1972); the uneven attempts by Coseriu (1972; 1975), etc. Koerner (1978) provides a general bibliography.

From the tricky problems of the influence of linguistic assumptions on historical perspective, we have arrived at a theoretically less intractable, although in practice just as difficult question: the lack of a large-scale, systematic history of linguistics, comparable in size and reliability to the reference works available in other fields, such as the traditional histories of literature or of philosophy.

I can perhaps illustrate the situation with two examples taken from my own recent experience. Both examples point, in their own different ways, to the poverty of available research instruments and reference works. What I am saying is of course not that I was expecting (nor was I entitled to expect) to find the specific results of my research already embodied in existing studies, but that the background information to the individual questions I was studying was not helpfully set out, and sometimes not provided at all.

In the first case, I was looking into the cooperation which Saussure gave to Théodore Flournoy, professor of psychology in Geneva at the turn of the century, in an investigation of a case of speaking in tongues (Lepschy 1974). The medium Catherine-Elise Muller (now known as Mlle Smith), when in a trance, would give her voice to characters speaking unfamiliar languages, such as Martian (the language of the planet Mars) which was studied by Victor Henry, professor in Paris, and author of the interesting *Antinomies linguistiques,* a work which has been linked with Saussure's dichotomies. Another language she used was, allegedly, Sanscrit, for the interpretation of which Saussure's help was enlisted. The book in which Flournoy (1900) published his analysis of Mlle Smith's case was at the time very famous; it is an important landmark in the history of dynamic psychology, and quotes many passages written by Saussure on the analysis of the 'Indian' texts. Saussure's procedures, in his analysis of these texts, are worth comparing with his work on anagrams; his awareness of the notions of 'unconscious' and 'subliminal', which were central to Flournoy's

work, is of course a point of the greatest interest for the interpretation of
his theories and by implication for the origin of contemporary linguistics.
Flournoy, a friend and admirer of William James, exerted a powerful
intellectual influence on his milieu, and was instrumental in acquainting
Geneva with Freud's theories. He was the mentor, as well as a relative, of
Edouard Claparède, the founder of the Institut J.-J. Rousseau where a key
figure in modern psychology, Jean Piaget, also worked. Claparède, whose
work is also highly relevant for linguistics, published a long and important
review of Saussure's *Cours*. Of all this, both from the point of view of the
evaluation of a network of intellectual and personal connections which
were obviously important for Saussure, and of the existence of actual texts,
both by and about Saussure, I could find no trace in the current literature,
although my reading included De Mauro's (1967) extensive apparatus to
his edition of the *Cours*, Koerner's comprehensive Saussurean bibliography (1972) of over 2500 items, and his large monograph on the origins and
development of Saussure's thought (1973). This example is, I think, all the
more revealing because Saussure must be one of the most actively
investigated figures in the history of linguistics. The absence of interesting
data even from the fullest accounts available is, I feel, related to the
general poverty of standard reference works for linguistic historiography.

My second example illustrates this poverty even more dramatically
(Lepschy 1980). While working on Freud's linguistics (what were his ideas
on language? how did they contribute to his general theories? and what do
these contribute to our views of language?), I tried to look into one of his
sources, Carl Abel's *Gegensinn der Urworte* (1884). Freud discovered this
work in 1909, had it reviewed by Wilhelm Stekel, published a comprehensive account of it, using the same title (Freud, 1910), and kept quoting it
afterwards, as a linguistic confirmation of his theory that, for the
unconscious, opposites are equivalent to each other. Benveniste (1956), in
an otherwise perceptive article on language and psychoanalysis, criticized
Freud for having relied on the etymological speculations of Carl Abel,
which deserve no credit: 'it is not by chance that no qualified linguist,
either at the time when Abel was writing (there already were such in 1884),
or afterwards, has taken any notice of this *Gegensinn der Urworte*, either
for its method, or for its conclusions.' This is in fact misleading, as Abel
was an interesting figure and occupies a not inconspicuous place in the
history of nineteenth-century linguistics. It is true that by the 1880s his
linguistic views had not changed since he formed them around the middle
of the century, and appeared to be superseded by those of the
Neogrammarians. Abel's positions were generally within the Humboldtian
tradition, because of their attention to the relationship between language
and world view, and partly akin to Schleicher's in their acceptance of a
distinction between an early, creative age (in which his *Gegensinn* and
Gegenlaut, i.e. the possibility of inversions of meaning and sound, found
their place), and the later historical periods (in which semantic specializa-
tion and phonetic laws found their application). It is not true, however,
that he was ignored by qualified linguists: his ideas were taken seriously by
people of the calibre of Pott, Steinthal, and Schuchardt, not to mention
scholars who were interested in the philosophy of language and in the

ethnography of speech (rather than in Indo-European comparative philology). They also aroused considerable curiosity outside academic linguistics, in the general public. Abel's early Coptic studies obtained him an honourable place in that field. He was also a journalist, acting as a correspondent for English newspapers (including *The Times*) in the 1860s and 1870s, and as such he incurred the wrath of Karl Marx (1860).

His theory on the importance and interest of words with opposite meanings (which were, he suggested, particularly frequent in the early stages of languages) finds its place in a long tradition of studies, from the Stoics' grammar and the etymologies *e contrario* (of the *lucus a non lucendo* kind; but see also the reflections on the *voces mediae*), to the chapter in Arab linguistic tradition devoted to the addād (i.e. contraries, or words of opposite meanings; cf. Charnay 1967), to the medieval Jewish grammarians' discussions on parallel phenomena in Hebrew (cf. Gordis 1936–37), to Christian biblical scholars who at least since the seventeenth century examine cases of 'enantiosemy' in the Sacred, classical, and modern languages, commenting on words like Hebrew *berekh* 'he blessed' and 'he cursed', Greek *argós* 'swift' and 'slow', Latin *altus* 'high' and 'deep', English *to skin* 'to remove the skin' and 'to grow the skin', *to let* 'to allow' and 'to prevent' (Pococke 1654, 19–21). Nearer to Abel, in the first part of the nineteenth century, we find the German romantics meditating on these opposite meanings, with J. A. Kanne elaborating a whole mystical philosophy of language around enantiosemy; and it is impossible not to remember Hegel's comments on a key term in his logic, *aufheben*, which means both 'to eliminate' and 'to preserve', illustrating a coexistence in language of opposite meanings which has great speculative import.

But of Abel and his theories I could find hardly any trace in the standard works on the history of linguistics, in spite of the fact that nineteenth-century Germany must be one of the best known and cultivated areas; nor did I find much which would help me to relate his *Gegensinn* to the long tradition of studies on *addād*, enantiosemy and antiphrasis. Perhaps, I should add, it is not quite fair to choose Abel as an example, because not only is he ignored in linguistic historiography, but even standard, general reference works offer unreliable information about him. Most encyclopaedias and biographical dictionaries give 1837 as his date of birth, but the *Grand Dictionnaire Universel Larousse* gives 1839, adding rather self-consciously that he was only 15 when he published, in 1854, his first essay on the Coptic language. Both 1837 and 1839, which make him absurdly precocious, are probably wrong, and the correct date, as I gather from the Archives of Tübingen University, where he studied in 1848–50, is 1827.

To conclude: the work which I most felt the lack of, in the course of the researches mentioned above, is a large-scale, systematic history of linguistics, from ancient times to the present day, covering the main cultural areas and periods: China, India, the ancient Middle East, Greece and Rome, the Middle Ages, Arabic, Hebrew, and vernacular; and, from the Renaissance, the various national cultures. A tall order, no doubt. Can such a history be produced? One ought at least to try, because a more worrying question, it seems to me, is the one we have to ask now: How can we do without it?

The theoretical problems I mentioned at the beginning are also relevant; but from this point of view a large enterprise of the kind I have in mind ought to be inclusive rather than exclusive in its criteria. History of linguistics ought to be taken to refer not only to what its author considers to be scientific linguistics, but also to those facts and notions which were thought to be linguistic by the people whose ideas we describe. Ideally, it ought also to include information about what, in different ages and countries, people thought and knew about language and languages.

In practice, one could proceed in two directions, aiming at (*a*) some attempts at a synthesis, using existing historiographical work and as much of the primary texts as can be collected and coherently assimilated, and (*b*) the production of as much work as possible of an analytical and monographic character, to cover important problems about which too little is known. It seems that progress will be made only as a result of collective efforts. There are recent signs of a lively interest and willingness to work in the field of linguistic historiography, as can be seen from a perusal of the journal *Historiographia Linguistica* (1974–), and from the panorama offered by the imposing twelfth volume, devoted to linguistic historiography, of *Current Trends in Linguistics* (Sebeok 1975). The general feeling one is left with is not so much a paralysing sense of awe for what has been accomplished as invigorating excitement at all the worthwhile work that remains to be done.

References

Abel, C. 1884: *Über den Gegensinn der Urworte.* Leipzig: Friedrich.
Benveniste, E. 1956: Remarques sur la fonction du langage dans la découverte freudienne. *La Psychanalyse* **1**, 3–16. Also in E. Benveniste, *Problèmes de linguistique générale* (Paris: Gallimard, 1966), 75–87.
Charnay, J.-P. (ed.) 1967: *L'ambivalence dans la culture arabe.* Paris: Anthropos.
Chomsky, N. 1966: *Cartesian linguistics. A chapter in the history of rationalist thought.* New York and London: Harper & Row.
Coseriu, E. 1972: *Die Geschichte der Sprachphilosophie von der Antike bis zur Gegenwart. Eine Übersicht. Teil II: Von Leibniz bis Rousseau.* Tübingen: Tübinger Beiträge zur Linguistik **28**.
——(1975). *Die Geschichte der Sprachphilosophie von der Antike bis zur Gegenwart. Eine Übersicht. Teil I: Von der Antike bis Leibniz.* Second edition. Tübingen: Tübinger Beiträge zur Linguistik **11**.
De Mauro, T. (ed.) 1967: F. de Saussure, *Corso di linguistica generale.* Bari: Laterza.
Flournoy, T. 1900: *Des Indes à la Planète Mars. Etude sur un cas de somnambulisme avec glossolalie.* Paris: Alcan; Geneva: Eggiman.
Freud, S. 1910: Über den Gegensinn der Urworte. *Jahrbuch für psychoanalytische und psychopathologische Forschungen* **2**, 179–84.

Also in S. Freud, *Gesammelte Werke* (Frankfurt am Main: Fischer, 1978), **8**, 213–21. English Translation in S. Freud, *Standard edition* (London: The Hogarth Press, 1957), **11**, 153–61.

Gordis, R. 1936–37: Studies in Hebrew roots of contrasted meanings. *The Jewish Quarterly Review*, n.s. **27**, 33–58.

Historiographia Linguistica (1974–). Ed. E. F. K. Koerner. Amsterdam: Benjamins.

Hymes, D. (ed.) 1974: *Studies in the history of linguistics. Traditions and paradigms*. Bloomington and London: Indiana University Press.

Koerner, E. F. K. 1972: *Bibliographia Saussureana 1870–1970*. Metuchen, NJ: The Scarecrow Press.

——1973: *Ferdinand de Saussure. Origin and development of his linguistic thought in Western studies of language. A contribution to the history and theory of linguistics*. Braunschweig: Vieweg.

——1978: *Western histories of linguistic thought. An annotated chronological bibliography 1822–1976*. Amsterdam: Benjamins.

Kuhn, T. S. 1962: *The structure of scientific revolutions*. Chicago: University of Chicago Press. (2nd edn., enlarged, 1970).

Lepschy, G. C. 1974: Saussure e gli spiriti. In *Studi saussuriani per Robert Godel*. Bologna: il Mulino, 181–200. Also in G. C. Lepschy, *Intorno a Saussure* (Turin: Stampatori, 1979), 111–138.

——1980: *Freud, Abel e gli opposti*. Paper presented to the Fondazione Rizzoli conference on *La comunicazione spiritosa* (Venice, December 1980), to appear in the proceedings of the Conference.

Malkiel, Y. and Langdon, M. 1969: History and histories of linguistics. *Romance Philology* **22**, 530–74.

Marx, K. 1860: *Herr Vogt*. London: Petsch, 144–46. Also in K. Marx and F. Engels, *Werke* (Berlin, Dietz, 1964), **14**, 602–5.

Mounin. G. 1967: *Histoire de la linguistique des origines au XXe siècle*. Paris: Presses Universitaires de France.

——1972: *La linguistique du XXe siècle*. Paris: Presses Universitaires de France.

Parret, H. (ed.) 1976: *History of linguistic thought and contemporary linguistics*. Berlin and New York: de Gruyter.

Pococke, E. 1654: *Porta Mosis. Appendix notarum miscellanea*. Oxford: Hall.

Robins, R. H. 1967: *A short history of linguistics*. London: Longman. (New ed., 1980).

Sebeok, T. A. (ed.) 1975: *Historiography of linguistics. Current trends in linguistics* **13**. The Hague: Mouton.

Tagliavini, C. 1963: Storia ed evoluzione della linguistica. In his *Introduzione alla glottologia* **1**, Bologna: Pàtron, 19–380.

Terracini, B. A. 1933: Di che cosa fanno la storia gli storici del linguaggio? In *Atti del III congresso internazionale dei linguisti* (Roma, 19–26 settembre 1933–XI). Florence: Le Monnier (1935), 354–9.

4

Constraints on coarticulatory processes
W. J. Hardcastle

It is a well attested observation that a stream of speech cannot be straightforwardly segmented, either at the articulatory or the acoustic level into a string of discrete elements corresponding to linguistic units such as phonemes, syllables, or words. This is because the articulatory and acoustic events that accompany production of a given phoneme will vary depending on the context in which it occurs, such variables as the phonetic environment (e.g. which sounds precede or follow it), the overall rate of utterance, the rhythmical structure and stress and intonation patterns being the main influencing factors. The physical consequences of these contextual effects is that articulatory movements tend to overlap or coarticulate in real time, resulting in a lack of invariance between particular phonemes and any fixed set of articulatory manoeuvres. But although the phenomenon of coarticulation itself has been relatively well described there is wide disagreement in the literature as to how one might incorporate such a concept in a model of speech production. The central theme of this paper is to take issue with those models which claim invariant phonemes as the central neural encoding units, with coarticulatory processes attributed to trivial, automatic, low-level adjustments imposed by the inherent characteristics of the peripheral speech-producing apparatus. Recent evidence suggests, rather, that at least some types of coarticulation are specified at a high level in the neural encoding stage of an utterance and thus should play a central role in any adequate model of the speech production process.

The overlapping or coarticulated movements which are the subject of this chapter can be clearly illustrated when one instrumentally monitors movements of different articulatory organs such as the tip of the tongue, the back of the tongue, the velum, mandible and lower lip simultaneously during connected speech. Instrumentation suitable for this purpose is, for example, the computer-controlled x-ray microbeam system developed at the University of Tokyo Medical School (see Fujimura, Kiritani and Ishida

1973). In this system miniature lead pellets are attached to points on the surface of the articulatory organs and the movements of these pellets can be recorded and displayed by suitable interactive software. Under conditions of normal connected speech it can easily be demonstrated that the articulatory organs are continuously moving and interact with each other. At no point will they adopt a static position. Even during the closure phase of a stop consonant such as the [k] in *keen,* the back of the tongue will be sliding along the palate towards a more anterior position (see e.g. Butcher and Weiher 1976). Thus at no point during production of a speech utterance can the speech organs be said to assume static target postures. Of course the degree of articulatory movement during production of a speech sound will vary with the type of sound itself - some fricatives (e.g. [s], [ʃ]) probably involve less articulatory movement during the formation of the lingual stricture than other sounds such as velar stops, alveolar laterals, etc.

The overlapping or coarticulation of these continuously moving speech organs becomes apparent when one records the movement of one particular articulator in relation to another. For example, in a word such as *cocktail,* the back of the tongue and the tip will normally coarticulate briefly during the [kt] stop consonant sequence. This can be illustrated by the technique of electropalatography which records spatio-temporal details of tongue contacts with the palate during continuous speech (see Hardcastle 1972). Fig. 4.1 shows a computer printout recording typical patterns of tongue contacts with the palate during the [kt] sequence. Each small diagram represents a schema of the hard palate with the alveolar ridge at the bottom and the velar region at the top. Points of tongue contact are shown as zeros, and the sequence of diagrams is read from left to right with a ten-millisecond interval between each one. The period of coarticulation can be seen in diagram numbers 75 to 78.

Another example of coarticulated gestures occurs in the word *my,* where raising of the soft palate (in anticipation of the vowel) will normally occur simultaneously with movement forward of the tongue for the second half of the diphthong. Such coarticulatory features are a ubiquitous aspect of normal connected speech and, in fact, it has been shown (e.g. by Shohara 1939) that without such overlapping of movements, speech production simply could not proceed at the normal rate of about six syllables per second.

Previous attempts to account for coarticulatory processes have been relatively unsuccessful. One approach, mentioned above, has been to attribute coarticulation to low-level mechano-inertial characteristics of the speech-producing mechanism. This approach normally assumes, at a high neural level of processing, a stored set of discrete and invariant phonemes as the basic encoding units. They are idealized, context-free, target elements which are transformed into motor commands for the appropriate speech articulators. Because of the low-level constraints on the system operating at the periphery, they become modified to varying degrees and the boundaries between them become obscured. (For a review of these phoneme-based accounts of speech production, see MacNeilage 1970). Thus, it is claimed, coarticulation will be an automatic result of these low-level adjustments.

```
      60              61              62              63              64
• • • • • • • • • •  • • • • • • • • • •  • • • • • • • • • •  • • • • • • • • • •  • O • • • • • O O •
 • • • • • • • •      • • • • • • • •      • • • • • • • •      • • • • • • • •      • • • • • • • •
 • • • • • • • •      • • • • • • • •      • • • • • • • •      • • • • • • • •      • • • • • • • •
 • • • • • • • •      • • • • • • • •      • • • • • • • •      • • • • • • • •      • • • • • • • •
 • • • • • • • •      • • • • • • • •      • • • • • • • •      • • • • • • • •      • • • • • • • •
 • • • • • • • •      • • • • • • • •      • • • • • • • •      • • • • • • • •      • • • • • • • •
 • • • • • • • •      • • • • • • • •      • • • • • • • •      • • • • • • • •      • • • • • • • •
  • • • • • •          • • • • • •          • • • • • •          • • • • • •          • • • • • •

      65              66              67              68              69
• O O • • • O O O O  O O O O • O O O O O  O O O O O O O O O O  O O O O O O O O O O  O O O O O O O O O O
 • • • • • • • •     O • • • • • • •     O • • • • • •       O O • • • • • •       O O • • • O O O
 • • • • • • • •      • • • • • • • •      • • • • • • • •     O • • • • • •       O • • • • • • •
 • • • • • • • •      • • • • • • • •      • • • • • • • •      • • • • • • • •      • • • • • • • •
 • • • • • • • •      • • • • • • • •      • • • • • • • •      • • • • • • • •      • • • • • • • •
 • • • • • • • •      • • • • • • • •      • • • • • • • •      • • • • • • • •      • • • • • • • •
 • • • • • • • •      • • • • • • • •      • • • • • • • •      • • • • • • • •      • • • • • • • •
  • • • • • •          • • • • • •          • • • • • •          • • • • • •          • • • • • •

      70              71              72              73              74
O O O O O O O O O O  O O O O O O O O O O  O O O O O O O O O O  O O O O O O O O O O  O O O O O O O O O O
O O O • • O O O     O O O • • O O O     O O O O • O O O     O O O • • O O O     O O O • • O O O
O • • • • • • O     O O • • • • • O     O O • • • • O O     O O • • • • O O     O O • • • • O O
 • • • • • • • •      • • • • • • • •     O • • • • • • O     O • • • • • • O     O O • • • • • O
 • • • • • • • •      • • • • • • • •      • • • • • • • •     O • • • • • • O     O O • • • • • O
 • • • • • • • •      • • • • • • • •      • • • • • • • •      • • • • • • • •     O O • • • • • O
 • • • • • • • •      • • • • • • • •      • • • • • • • •      • • • • • • • •     O O O • • • O O
  • • • • • •          • • • • • •          • • • • • •          • • • • • •          • • • • • •

      75              76              77              78              79
O O O O O O O O O O  O O O O O O O O O O  O O O O • O O O O O  O O O O O O O O O O  O O O O • • O O O O
O O O • • O O O     O O O • • O O O     O O O • • O O O     O O • • • O O O     O O • • • • O O
O O • • • • O O     O O • • • • O O     O O • • • • O O     O O • • • • O O     O O • • • • O O
O O • • • • • O     O O • • • • • O     O O • • • • O O     O O • • • • O O     O O • • • • O O
O O • • • • • O     O O • • • • O O     O O • • • • • O     O O • • • • O O     O O • • • • • O
O O • • • • • O     O O • • • • O O     O O • • • • • O     O O • • • • • O     O O • • • • • O
O O O O O O O O     O O O O O O O O     O O O O O O O O     O O O O O O O O     O O O O O O O O
 O O O O O O         O O O O O O         O O O O O O         O O O O O O         O O O O O O

      80              81              82              83              84
O O • O • • O O O O  O O • • • • O O O  O O • • • • • O O  O O • • • • • O O  O O • • • • • O O
O O • • • O O     O O • • • • O O     O O • • • • O O     O • • • • • O O     O • • • • O O
O O • • • • O O     O O • • • • O O     O O • • • • O O     O O • • • • O O     O • • • • • O O
O O • • • • O O     O O • • • • • O     O O • • • • • O     O O • • • • • O     O • • • • • • O
O O • • • • • O     O O • • • • • O     O O • • • • • O     O • • • • • • O     O • • • • • • O
O O • • • • • O     O O • • • • • O     O O • • • • • O     O O • • • • • O     O O • • • • • O
O O O O O O O O     O O O O O O O O     O O O O O O O O     O O O O O O O O     O O O O • O O O
 O O O O O O         O O O O O O         O O O O O O         O O O O O O         O O O O O O

      85              86              87              88
O • • • • • • O O  O • • • • • • O O  O • • • • • • O O  O • • • • • • O O
O • • • • O O     O • • • • O O     O • • • O O O     O • • • • • O
O • • • • • O     O • • • • • O     O • • • • • O     O • • • • • O
O • • • • • O     O • • • • • O     O • • • • • O     O • • • • • O
O • • • • • O     O • • • • • O     O • • • • • O     O • • • • • •
O • • • • • O     O • • • • • O     O • • • • • •     O • • • • • •
O O O • • • O O     O • • • • • O     O • • • • • •      • • • • • •
 O O O • O O         O • • • •           • • • • • •          • • • • •
```

Fig. 4.1 Computer printout from an electropalatograph showing the sequence of tongue-palate contacts during the [kt] cluster in the word *cocktail*. Sampling interval is 10 msec.

One cannot deny that mechano-inertial constraints do indeed operate at the periphery of the speech-producing mechanism. Speech production involves moving speech organs about the oral region as well as various respiratory and laryngeal gestures and these movements must have mechanical consequences. The main mechanical constraints can be broadly grouped into those related to the inherent characteristics of the speech organs themselves (e.g. their relative masses, inertias, etc.), those related to interactions between those organs which are interconnected by muscles and ligaments, and those related to characteristics of the neural pathways relaying the motor commands from the higher centres of the brain to the muscles of the various organs. It is instructive to examine these different types of constraints closely and to see how they might account for coarticulatory processes.

Firstly, as far as intrinsic anatomical characteristics are concerned, the speech organs vary greatly in mass from the relatively large mandible to the small mobile tongue tip, and thus one would expect mechanical forces related to their individual movements to be different. Also the types of muscle systems within the organs vary considerably, ranging from the sphincter-type configuration of the orbicularis oris muscle involved in closing the lips, to the strap-like superior longitudinal muscle of the tongue, responsible for rapid movements of the tip. In general, the smaller muscles in the oral region, such as the intrinsic muscles of the tongue, will have faster contraction times than the larger muscles, such as the temporalis and the extrinsic tongue muscles, and so can move the relevant speech organs appreciably faster. The variations in mass and anatomical configuration are reflected in the different velocities of movement that have been recorded in the past (see Hudgins and Stetson 1937, and, more recently Sawashima 1979; Kuehn and Moll 1976). Most agree that the tip of the tongue is the fastest of all articulators, capable of moving at a velocity of at least 220mm/sec (Sawashima 1979), and it can move relatively independently of the back of the tongue, which has a velocity slightly less. Next in order of velocity come the lips, then the soft palate (105 mm/sec) with the relatively large mandible slowest of all. Velocity of movement for a particular organ will depend also on the direction of the activity taking place. For example, velocity of lower-lip movement depends on whether it is being closed or opened (see Sussman et al. 1973). Perhaps because of the assistance from gravity the opening movement is faster.

The second main type of constraint depends on the mechanical linkages between different speech organs, particularly the articulatory organs in the oral region. The tongue, for example, is connected via the palatoglossus muscle to the soft palate and to the hyoid bone by, among others, the hyoglossus muscle, so any movement of the tongue will, potentially at least, affect the position of the soft palate and hyoid bone. Conversely, movements of the soft palate and hyoid will influence tongue position, other factors being equal. The hyoid bone, in addition to being attached to the tongue, is also attached to the thyroid cartilage of the larynx by means of muscles and ligaments, so movement of the hyoid will in fact have some effect on the state of the vocal folds. One possible consequence is that raising the hyoid and so also the thyroid cartilage will stretch the vocal folds in the vertical dimension and so increase their frequency of vibration. Thus tongue movement (through the hyoid connection) will potentially affect the rate of vibration of the vocal folds. Also the mandible and the tongue are intimately connected, so will participate in reciprocal movements. As the mandible is lowered, so too is the tongue in the oral cavity, other factors being equal. The speech apparatus, then, can be said to function as a single complex interrelating unit where the dynamics of different component parts will mutually influence each other. (For a more detailed discussion of these anatomical considerations, see Hardcastle 1976; Kaplan 1971.)

The third main type of biomechanical constraint relates to characteristics of the neural pathways relaying the motor commands to the speech muscles. Little is known of the precise details of these pathways, but some interesting possibilities have been mentioned in the literature. For example, Lenneberg (1967) draws attention to some work by Krmpotić (1959) which purports to show that the lengths of nerve fibres supplying different speech organs vary considerably. One can hypothesize that, for any given type of nerve fibre, the greater the distance the greater will be the delay in the motor command reaching the periphery (Lenneberg 1967). Thus if a set of motor commands to various speech organs appropriate for a given phoneme is issued simultaneously at the motor cortex and sent along the different nerves, such as the recurrent branch of the vagus (supplying intrinsic muscles of the larynx) and the facial (supplying muscles of the lips), the time of arrival of the impulses at the periphery will vary, the longer recurrent branch fibres causing a longer delay than the shorter facial nerve fibres. Some of the implications of this perhaps too simplistic a view of neuromuscular constraints are discussed in Kim (1971). He claims that one can account for at least some of the coarticulatory movements in the word *school* [skul] by allowing for different latencies of activation in muscles depending on different lengths of nerve fibres. Thus lip rounding will occur simultaneously with tongue back movement towards the [k] closure while the tongue front is forming the [s] configuration, because the path along the motor fibres to the lips is shorter than that along the hypoglossal nerve to the tongue. Kim goes further, to claim that frequently observed historical linguistic changes (e.g. [b] → [p] → [pʰ] in word-initial position) may be explained by the fact that motor instructions to the glottis will be received later than to the lips, leading to a relative delay in voicing onset (as in [pʰ]). This latter situation is regarded as the less 'marked' situation which will eventually prevail. However, these explanations all depend on the hypothesis that neural commands for whole words or at least sequences of sounds are issued simultaneously by the motor cortex, and there is no direct evidence substantiating this.

It is not difficult to see how these mechano-inertial constraints operating on different speech organs may account for overlapping of articulatory movements at the periphery, particularly if the mechanism is under time constraints, for example when the rate of utterance is increased. Under these circumstances, articulatory gestures for earlier phonemes may merge with articulatory gestures for later phonemes, and some gestures may be considerably 'undershot' or not fulfilled at all. In the example given earlier of soft palate movement during the word *my,* one theory would claim that the velum opening is specified at a high level as one of the necessary articulatory gestures for the initial nasal consonant and that because of inertial effects and the relatively sluggish intrinsic velocity of this organ, the opening gesture will 'carry-over' into the following vowel. Eventually the motor command for velum raising for the vowel will 'catch up' with the actual tongue movement for the vowel, but not until well after the acoustically defined onset of the vowel.

Another example of juxtaposed articulatory gestures becoming merged is the situation described by Kent *et al.* (1974) for tongue and velum coarticulation in a VNC sequence (where N = nasal consonants [n] or [m]). For sequences such as this they frequently found that the maximum velar lowering for the whole sequence occurred during the vowel rather than during the nasal, and that at the point of apical contact for the [n] the velum had already completed half its movement towards elevation. This suggests an asynchrony between tongue-tip and velum movements which may have its origin in the different mechanical characteristics of these two organs. Likewise, in the [kt] sequence mentioned above, the tongue-tip movement, being the fastest of the articulatory gestures, will overlap briefly in time with the [k] closure involving the relatively slow-moving back of the tongue.

In its simplicity and elegance the phoneme-based model of speech production discussed so far, where contextual variation is attributed to trivial low-level automatic adjustments at the periphery of the speech apparatus, has considerable intrinsic appeal. Indeed it seems feasible that many carry-over coarticulatory influences and even some anticipatory ones can conveniently be explained by low-level mechano-inertial constraints. It may well be that many more timing phenomena, particularly those involving short-term time spans, will be explained when our knowledge of the neuromuscular system of speech production becomes more complete.

But there are nevertheless serious limitations in this sort of model. One problem is that it fails to account for another type of coarticulation, the type which spreads over a considerable time scale, well beyond the span of adjacent or nearly adjacent segments. This extensive type of coarticulation process may involve two different parts of the same organ such as the tongue tip and back of tongue or it may involve different organs such as tongue and velum or tongue and lips. An example of this type of extensive coarticulation is alleged to be the tongue-backing process associated with production of the so-called 'emphatics' in Arabic (see Ghazeli 1977). In Ghazeli's study, cinefluorography was used to monitor movements of the tongue during production of meaningful Arabic words and phrases. Tracings were made from the cinefluorograms, and one measurement made was the intersection of the tongue dorsum with a reference line radiating superiorly-posteriorly from a fixed point within the tongue body. Plots were made of the changes in value of this measurement against time for words such as [bifīd] 'he(it) will be useful' and [bifī$\eth$] ([$\eth$] =emphatic [$\eth$]) 'it is going to spill' (see Fig. 4.2). It was found that the backing of the tongue root appropriate for the emphatic consonant [$\eth$] extends through-out the whole word affecting more than just adjoining segments. One

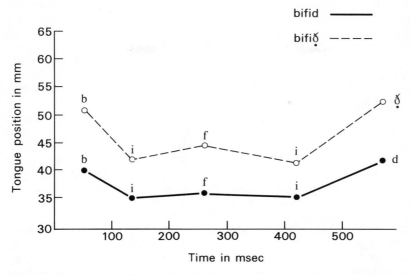

Fig. 4.2 Tongue position as measured along a tongue root reference line (in mm) during articulation of [bifīd] 'he (it) will be useful' and [bifīð] 'it is going to spill' (adapted from Ghazeli 1977, 91).

could say therefore that the emphatic [ð] has imposed an increased degree of tongue back coarticulation on the whole word. Similar extensive coarticulatory backing was found for the word [ṣimīli] 'fast for me (imper. fem.)' when compared to [limmīli] 'you (fem.) gather for me'. In [ṣimīli] coarticulated backing of the tongue root persists throughout the whole word even though front close vowels, normally involving raised forward tongue configurations, occur in intervening segments.

Extensive coarticulated nasality has also been noted. Moll and Daniloff (1971), for example, note that soft palate opening in the phrase *free Ontario* begins with the tongue constriction for the first [i] vowel and persists until the alveolar stop [t]. Although this type of extensive coarticulated nasality is typical for many speakers, it does not seem to be a universal. Kent, *et al.* (1974) found that many of their subjects showed no evidence of widespread coarticulated nasality. Some speakers had closed velum specifications for vowels even in nasal contexts such as in the sentence *many a man knows my meaning*. Labialization, also, has been found to extend over a considerable time span. For example, upper-lip protrusion in French, which normally would accompany a front rounded vowel [y] begins simultaneously with tongue constriction for the first [s] fricative in the [strstr] cluster in the utterance *un sinistre structure* (see Benguerel and Cowan 1974), and lip protrusion for the vowel [u] begins before or during the lingual contact for [n] in the sequence *since true* (Daniloff and Moll 1968).

Phonological theory traditionally has taken little account of such phenomena except for the prosodic theory developed by J.R. Firth (1948).

Here extensive coarticulation processes such as nasalization, pharyngeal-ization, etc., spreading over stretches of speech, variable in length, are accorded status as prosodies. Unfortunately a systematic statement of the type and scope of these phenomena within the framework of the prosodic approach is still lacking. Also phonologists working in the prosodic framework were not concerned with providing explanations of these phenomena in terms of physiological or other constraints on the system.

It is difficult to see how low-level mechano-inertial constraints such as those outlined above can account for the extensive type of coarticulation which spreads over a series of segments, syllables or even words. The time span of coarticulations attributable to mechano-inertial constraints would be strictly limited in scope to immediately adjacent segments only. One is tempted therefore to regard the extensive type of coarticulation as resulting not from low-level accommodatory adjustments of adjacent articulatory manoeuvres but rather from high-level specifications during the motor planning stage in the generation of a speech utterance. Evidence in support of the theory that this type of coarticulation process is imposed at a high neural level comes from an analysis of the wide range of language-specific constraints that may operate on these processes during normal speech production. Some of these constraints concern syntactic and phonological rules of the particular language but they may also have more universal application relating, for example, to perceptual demands placed on the system to ensure communicative efficiency. It seems fairly clear that these constraints operate on the system during the generation process prior to transmission of the motor commands themselves to the speech muscles. It is thus important to consider the evidence in support of the presence of these constraints and to incorporate them into a model of the speech generation process.

One type of language-specific constraint on extensive coarticulation is that imposed by the phonological rules of the language. An illustration comes from a comparison of nasalization in English and French. In English there is no phonemic distinction between nasal and oral vowels, and coarticulated nasality of both the anticipatory and carry-over types will occur freely on vowels in the presence of nasal consonants as seen above. One theory is that in English, velum lowering associated with a nasal consonant will spread as far as possible in either direction, the extent of the spreading being limited only by the presence of an 'antagonistic' articulatory manoeuvre such as a closed velum movement necessary for an oral obstruent. Thus in this view coarticulated nasality in English will frequently spread across syllable and word boundaries at will. One description of this feature-spreading process is provided by Daniloff and Moll (1968) developing earlier ideas of Henke (1966). They assume a segmental input at the level of neural processing, where each segment is associated with a set of articulatory features such as lowered velum, lip-rounding, etc. If a feature is unspecified for a particular segment the system may 'scan ahead' to subsequent units to determine the next specified value for the feature. Anticipatory coarticulation comes about when the feature is articulatorily realized earlier than its parent segment (Kent and Minifie 1977). This will happen as long as articulation of the feature does not 'contradict' the articulation of the segment currently being produced. Extensive coarticulation of labialization and nasalization have been explained by this theory although there are some problems (such as the definition of a contradictory movement).

While nasality appears to be extensive in English (at least for many speakers), in French the situation appears to be different. In this language there is a phonemic distinction between nasal and oral vowels, and this phonological feature appears to mean that the system will not be as free as in English to extensively coarticulate nasality of vowels in the presence of a nasal consonant. In an experiment carried out by Clumek (1976) using a nasograph (a photoelectric device designed to record soft-palate movement; see Ohala 1971), coarticulated nasality was found to be language specific. He looked at a number of languages including American English and French and found that the onset of velum lowering varied with the language, it being earlier in English than in French. It seems, therefore, that French does not show such freedom in the extent of coarticulated nasality as in English.

More evidence for the phonological rules of the language imposing constraints on the extent of coarticulation comes from Ghazeli's (1977) investigation of Arabic emphatics. In one part of his study, Ghazeli examined the coarticulatory effects of tongue retraction on segments adjacent to pharyngealized consonants (the emphatics) and uvular consonants. He found that emphatics caused coarticulated tongue retraction to spread throughout the whole word, the spread being far greater in extent than in the case of the uvular consonants. It seems in addition that such coarticulated backing was not blocked by a close front vowel [i]. In the examples cited above where this vowel occurred preceding an emphatic, no vowel 'undershoot' was observed to take place. However, when the vowel [ɨ] occurred in a position following an emphatic in similar circumstances, it was normally reduced or 'undershot' to [ə]. Ghazeli explains that the resistance on the part of [i] to undershoot can be accounted for by the fact that [i] and [ɨ] are separate phonemes in the particular dialect of the language under discussion; therefore the central processing unit in the brain will ensure that these remain distinct. There is no problem with reducing [ɨ] to [ə], on the other hand, as [ə] is not a phoneme in the language (see Ghazeli 1977, 185). Thus phonological rules have here also exerted a constraint on a coarticulatory process.

Grammatical features of the language can also influence the extent of coarticulation. The grammatical type of constraint has received considerable attention in the literature, as it seemed feasible that linguistically defined units such as syllable and word could at least in theory define the boundaries of coarticulatory influences. One of the earliest attempts to define the extent of coarticulatory influence was the work of Kozhevnikov and Chistovich (1965). In their model of coarticulatory processes they suggested that coarticulation might be constrained by a unit which they called an ARTICULATORY SYLLABLE with a C^nV type structure (where C^n = any number of consecutive consonants followed by a vowel). According to this theory, coarticulation will be maximal within such a unit and minimal between such units. The articulatory syllable thus defines the limit of coarticulatory spread. But while explaining cases such as coarticulated labialization beginning simultaneously with initial lingual contact in sequences such as the word [stju] *stew,* there seem to be some problems with this model. Öhman (1966) for example, in an acoustic analysis of V_1CV_2 type sequences in Swedish, found evidence of coarticulated tongue movement where the formant values of V_1 are affected by V_2, thus showing coarticulatory effects operating outside a CV-type syllable unit. Also Moll and Daniloff (1971) in an investigation of velum movement in American English showed that velar opening for a nasal consonant will frequently coarticulate with a preceding vowel belonging to a preceding syllable. There is some evidence, however, that grammatical units do constrain coarticulatory processes. In his work on Arabic, Ghazeli (1977) found that tongue-backing coarticulation for pharyngealized consonants was maximal within a word but did not extend beyond a word boundary. Thus, in a sequence [gfaṣṣ ænīs] 'Anis' cage', coarticulated backing spreads throughout the first word due to the influence of the emphatic [ṣṣ] but does not extend the 15 msec or so across the word boundary to the following word. The vowel [æ] does not change to [a], which happens elsewhere when it occurs in the same word as an emphatic consonant. One should be cautious in generalizing from Ghazeli's results because they are based on a rather limited number of cinefluorographic and acoustic measurements and a relatively small number of subjects. But the results do nevertheless seem to suggest that at least in this language grammatical constraints are overriding any mechano-inertial effects which may account for carry-over coarticulation.

There is evidence in the literature on English also for various types of grammatical junctural boundaries affecting at least certain types of coarticulation. McClean (1973) plotted the temporal onset of soft-palate coarticulation in the sequence [ri æn] as it occurs in the words *three answers.* A high-level boundary (such as a phrase, clause, or sentence boundary) was inserted between the vowels [i] and [æ]. Utterances were of the type *the three answers are wrong* (low-level word boundary) and *Andy has three? Answer him* (high-level sentence boundary), and the onset of velum lowering was plotted with reference to the onset of the tongue tip contact for the [θ] in *three.* McClean found generally that low-level word boundaries did not normally constrain coarticulation (thus agreeing in principle with other work, e.g. Moll and Daniloff 1971), but that high-level boundaries such as between phrases, clauses, or sentences did. Specifically he found that in the cases where a high-level boundary was inserted between the two vowels in the test sequence, velum lowering was delayed until the onset of the second vowel.

It seems therefore that, at least for some articulatory gestures in English, coarticulation will extend freely across 'low-level' boundaries such as between sound segments, syllables and words, but is constrained by higher-level junctures such as between clauses, tone-groups, etc. In the case of Arabic it appears that word boundaries are functioning as a high-level boundary at least as far as tongue-backing coarticulation is concerned. Evidence from another language, Finnish, seems to support the word as a primary constraining element of coarticulatory spread. Lehiste states (1965, 177, quoted by Hyman 1978): 'When the nasal consonant started the word, progressive nasalization of the vowel following the nasal consonant was always present. When a word boundary occurred between a word ending in a nasal and one beginning with a vowel, progressive nasalization was not observed'. It appears then that syntactic constraints on coarticulation may be language-specific, with units such as the grammatical word limiting coarticulatory spread in some languages but not in others. One problem in all this work is, however, the variations not only in the techniques used to register articulatory movements but also the variation in the type of articulatory movement investigated. It may well be, for example, that coarticulated nasality behaves differently from, say, coarticulated labialization in one language compared with another, at least as far as constraints imposed by grammatical structure are concerned.

Another important consideration is the role of perceptual criteria in accounting for coarticulatory patterns. Coarticulatory spread will often be blocked in those circumstances where perception would be otherwise adversely affected. Thus anticipatory coarticulation of tongue tip with tongue body or lips in cases such as *that cat* or *hot pie* lead to varying degrees of undershoot of the full articulatory gesture for the final [t] in the first word (see Hardcastle and Roach 1979). Figs. 4.3–4.5 show typical electropalatographic printouts of tongue contacts with the palate during three [tk] stop consonant sequences. In Fig. 4.3 the alveolar and velar contacts occur virtually simultaneously, whereas in Fig. 4.4 no complete alveolar contact is present but there is a more forward lateral contact than for a single [k] in similar position. In Fig. 4.5 alveolar contact occurs not as a complete stop but a short apical tap. These various manifestations of the alveolar gesture can be interpreted as varying degrees of undershoot. However undershoot will not occur when the order of the stop sequence is reversed. For example a final velar or bilabial stop will not assimilate the following alveolar. In *black tin,* articulatory gestures for both the [k] and [t] closures are completed.

This suggests there is something characteristic about alveolar articulations making them more susceptible to undershoot than others (the so-called 'instability' of alveolars is a well attested phenomenon of British English (see Gimson 1980) and also probably of German (see Kohler 1976). A possible explanation for the instability of alveolars is that the articulatory apparatus simplifies the speech process as much as possible by, for example, avoiding an articulatory gesture involving an additional system, namely the tip-blade system. This will happen as often as possible when perceptual cues for the identification of tip/blade alveolar consonants are partly obscured (e.g. in word final unexploded position); but in initial position when cues to their identity such as the frequency of the burst will be intact, the tip/blade consonants will be preserved.

Arguments in favour of coarticulation as a deliberate process imposed on the system at a high neural level come from work on the role of coarticulation in the communication situation. For instance, it is claimed that anticipatory coarticulation often seems to aid the listener in the perceptual process. For example, a lowered velum on a vowel in English will alert the speech-decoding system of the listener to the presence of a following nasal consonant. Indeed, experiments have shown that a nasal or

```
    400              401              402              403              404
..........       OO.......O       OOO...OOOO       OOOO.OOOOO       OOOOOOOOOO
 ........         O........        OO.....O         OOO..OOO         OOO.OOOO
 ........         O........        O.......         OO....OOO        OOO..OOO
 ........         ........         O.......         OO....OO         OO....OO
 ........         ........         ........         OOO....O         OOO....O
 ........         ........         ........         OOO...OO         OOO...OO
 ........         ........         OO......         OOOOOOOO         OOOOOOOO
  ......           ......           ......           OO....            OOOOOO

    405              406              407              408              409
OOOOOOOOOO       OOOOOOOOOO       OOOOOOOOOO       OOOOOOOOOO       OOOOOOOOOO
 OOOOOOOO         OOOOOOOO         OOOOOOOO         OOOOOOOO         OOOOOOOO
 OOO..OOO         OOO..OOO         OOO..OO          OOO..OOO         OOO.OOOO
 OO....OO         OOO....O         OOO...OO         OOO..OOO         OOO..OOO
 OOO....O         OOO....O         OOO....O         OOO....O         OOO....O
 OOO...OO         OOO...OO         OOO...OO         OOO...OO         OOO...OO
 OOOOOOOO         OOOOOOOO         OOOOOOOO         OOOOOOOO         OOOOOOOO
  OOOOOO           OOOOOO           OOOOOO           OOOOOO           OOOOOO

    410              411              412              413              414
OOOOOOOOOO       OOOOOOOOOO       OOOOOOOOOO       OOOOOOOOOO       OOOOOOOOOO
 OOOOOOOO         OOOOOOOO         OOOOOOOO         OOOOOOOO         OOOOOOOO
 OOOOOOOO         OOOOOOOO         OOOOOOOO         OOOOOOOO         OOOOOOOO
 OOO..OOO         OOO.OOOO         OOOOOOOO         OOOOOOOO         OOO...OO
 OOO...OO         OOO...OO         OOO...OO         OOO...OO         OOO...OO
 OOO...OO         OOOO.OOO         OOOO.OOO         OOO..OOO         OOO....O
 OOOOOOOO         OOOOOOOO         OOOO.OOO         OOOO..OO         ......
  OOO...           OO....           OO....           O.....            ......

    415              416              417              418              419
OOOOOOOOOO       OOOOOOOOOO       OOOOOOOOOO       OOOO.OOOOO       OOOO...OOO
 OOOOOOOO         OOOOOOOO         OOOOOOOO         OOO..OOO         OOO..OOO
 OOOOOOOO         OOOOOOOO         OOOOOOOO         OOO..OOO         OOO.OOOO
 OOO..OOO         OOO..OOO         OOO...OO         OO....OO         OO....OU
 OOO...OO         OOO....O         OO.....O         OO.....O         OO.....O
 OOO....O         OO.....O         OO.....O         OO......         O.......
 OOO.....         OO......         O.......         ........         ........
  ......           ......           ......           ......            ......

    420              421              422              423              424
OOO....OOO       OOO....OOO       OO.....OOO       OO......OO       OO......OO
 OO....OO         OO....OO         OO....OO         OO....OO         OO....OO
 OO....OO         OO....OO         OO....OO         OO....OO         OO....OO
 OO....OO         OO.....O         OO.....O         O......O         O......O
 OO.....O         O.......         O.......         O.......         O.......
 O.......         O.......         O.......         ........         ........
 ........         ........         ........         ........         ........
  ......           ......           ......           ......            ......
```

Fig. 4.3 Computer printout from an electropalatograph showing tongue-palate contacts during the [tk] sequence in the word *Watkins.* Sampling interval is 10 msec.

```
    193            194            195            196            197
00....000      00.....000     000...000      000...0000     000...0000
0000.000       0000.000       00000000       00000000       00000000
000..000       000..000       000..000       000.0000       000.0000
00...000       00...000       00..000        000.0000       000.0000
00....00       00...000       00...000       00...000       000..000
......0         ......0        .....00        .....00        .0....00
........        ........       ........       ........0      .......0
......         ......          ......         ......         ......


    198            199            200            201            202
00000.0000     00000.0000     00000.0000     0000000000     0000000000
00000000       00000000       00000000       00000000       00000000
000.0000       00000000       00000000       00000000       00000000
00000000       00000000       00000000       00000000       00000000
00000000       000.0000       00000000       00000000       00000000
00....00       00...000       00...000       0000.000       0000.000
0......0        0......0        0......0       0......0       0......0
........        ......         ......         ......         ......


    203            204            205            206            207
0000000000     0000000000     0000000000     0000000000     0000000000
00000000       00000000       00000000       00000000       00000000
00000000       00000000       00000000       00000000       000.0000
00000000       00000000       00000000       00000000       00000000
00000000       00000000       00000000       000..000       000..000
0000.000       00...000       00....00       .0....00       .0....00
0......0        0......0        0......0       ......0       ........
......          ......          ......         ......         ......


    208            209            210            211            212
0000000000     00000J0000     0000000000     0000000000     0000000000
00000000       0000.000       0000.000       0000.000       0000.000
000.0000       000..000       00...000       00....00       00....00
000.0000       00...000       00...00        0.....00       0......0
00....00       00....00       0......0       0......0       ........
.......0        .......0       ........       ........       ........
........        ........       ........       ........       ........
......          ......          ......         ......         ......


    213            214            215            216            217
00000.0000     00000..000     00.....00      00.....00      00.....00
0000.000       00....00       00....00       00....00       0......0
0.....00       0......0        0......0       00....00       ........
0.....0        ........        ........       ........       ........
......0         ........       ........       ........       ........
........        ........       ........       ........       ........
.........       .........      .........      .........      .........
......          ......          ......         ......         ......
```

Fig. 4.4 Computer printout showing tongue-palate contacts in the [tk] cluster in the sequence *eat cake.*

```
     86                87                88                89                90
. . . . . . . . . .   . . . . . . . . .   . . . . . . . . .   . . . . . . . . .   . . . . . . . . 0
. . . . . . . . .     . . . . . . . .     . . . . . . . . .   . . . . . . . .     . . . . . . . .
. . . . . . . . .     . . . . . . . .     . . . . . . . .     . . . . . . . .     . . . . . . . .
. . . . . . . . .     . . . . . . . .     . . . . . . . .     . . . . . . . . .   . . . . . . . .
. . . . . . . .       . . . . . . . .     . . . . . . . .     . . . . . . . .     . . . . . . . .
. . . . . . . .       . . . . . . . .     . . . . . . . .     . . . . . . . .     . . . . . . . .
. . . . . . . .       . . . . . . . .     . . . . . . . .     . . . . . . . .     . . . . . . . .
. . . . . .           . . . . . .         . . . . . .         . . . . . .         . . . . . .

     91                92                93                94                95
0 . . . . . . . . 0   0 . . . . . . . 0   00 . . . . . 00     00 . . . . . 00     0000000000
. . . . . . . 0       0 . . . . . 0       0 . . . . . 0       00 . . . 00         00 . . . 00
. . . . . . . .       . . . . . . . 0     . . . . . . 0       0 . . . . 00        0 . . . . 00
. . . . . . . .       . . . . . . . .     . . . . . . 0       . . . . . 00        0 . . . . 00
. . . . . . . .       . . . . . . . .     . . . . . . 0       . . . . . 00        0 . . . . 00
. . . . . . . .       . . . . . . . .     . . . . . . . .     . . . . . 00        . . . . . 0
. . . . . . . .       . . . . . . . .     . . . . . . . .     . 00000 . .         . 00000 . .
. . . . . .           . . . . . .         . . . . . .         . . . . . .         . . . . . .

     96                97                98                99                100
0000000000            0000000000          0000000000          0000000000          0000000000
00 . . . 00           00 . . . 00         0000 . 000          0000 . 000          0000 . 000
00 . . . 00           00 . . . 00         00 . . . 00         00 . . 000          00 . . 000
0 . . . . 00          0 . . . . 00        00 . . . 00         00 . . 000          00 . . 000
0 . . . . 00          0 . . . 000         00 . . . 000        00 . . 000          00 . . 000
. . . . . . 0         . . . . . . 0        . . . . . 00        . . . . . 00        . . . . . 00
. . . . . . . .       . . . . . . . .      . . . . . . . .      . . . . . . 0        . . . . . . 0
. . . . . .           . . . . . .          . . . . . .          . . . . . .          . . . . . .

     101               102               103               104               105
0000000000            0000000000          0000000000          0000000000          0000000000
0000 . 000            0000 . 000          0000 . 000          0000 . 000          0000 . 000
00 . . . 000          00 . . . 000        00 . . . 00         00 . . . 00         00 . . . 00
00 . . . 000          00 . . . 00         00 . . . 00         00 . . . 00         00 . . . 00
00 . . . 000          00 . . . 00         00 . . . 00         0 . . . . 00        0 . . . . 00
. . . . . 00          . . . . . 00         . . . . . 00        . . . . . 0         . . . . . 0
. . . . . . 0         . . . . . . 0         . . . . . . 0        . . . . . . . .      . . . . . . . .
. . . . . .           . . . . . .           . . . . . .          . . . . . .          . . . . . .

     106               107               108               109               110
0000000000            00000 . 0000        000 . . . 000       00 . . . . 000      00 . . . . . 00
0000 . 000            0000 . 000          0000 . 000          0000 . 000          00 . . . 00
00 . . . 00           00 . . . 00         00 . . . 00         00 . . . 00         00 . . . 00
00 . . . 00           0 . . . . 00        0 . . . . 00        0 . . . . 00        0 . . . . 00
0 . . . . 00          0 . . . . 00        0 . . . . 00        0 . . . 000        0 . . . . . 0
. . . . . . 0         . . . . . . 0         . . . . . 00        . . . . . . . .      . . . . . . . .
. . . . . . . .       . . . . . . . .       . . . . . . . .      . . . . . . . .      . . . . . . . .
. . . . . .           . . . . . .           . . . . . .          . . . . . .          . . . . . .
```

Fig. 4.5 Computer printout showing tongue-palate contacts during the [tk] sequence in the word *Watkins* spoken by a different speaker from the one shown in Fig. 4.3.

non-nasal consonant can be detected when the final consonant and transition are deleted in CVC and CVVC type utterances. Some (e.g. Ali *et al.* 1971, Ostreicher and Sharf 1976) have suggested that in conversational speech considerable functional use is made of anticipatory coarticulation by the perceptual apparatus. In the experiment of Ostreicher and Sharf (1976) subjects were asked to identify deleted portions of CV, VC, VCV and CVC type utterances. It was found that subjects determined features of deleted vowels and consonants (such as place and manner of articulation) more correctly from preceding than from following sounds. They interpreted the results in terms of the possible function of coarticulation in aiding the identification of adjacent sounds in conversational speech.

Other constraints which can operate on coarticulation are sociological and stylistic in origin. It is evident for example that many types of coarticulatory processes are speaker-specific—some speakers use extensive coarticulations more than others, use more anticipatory than carry-over effects, and so on. It has even been suggested that certain types of coarticulation, for example anticipatory coarticulation of soft-palate lowering in words such as *my* may serve a speaker identification function (Su *et al.* 1974). It is clear also that many coarticulatory processes serve a stylistic purpose; the 'assimilatory' process in the sequence /'dɪʤ ə 'gəʊ/ for the less colloquial /'dɪd jʊ 'gəʊ/ *did you go* can be easily described in coarticulatory terms. It is possible also that languages differ in general coarticulatory tendencies: some may be predominantly anticipatory while others predominantly perseverative.

It seems therefore, in summary, that all types of coarticulation, particularly the extensive long-range type, cannot conveniently be accounted for by low-level automatically imposed mechano-inertial constraints present in the speech producing apparatus. These low-level constraints do undoubtedly exist and do account for many contiguous adjustment-type coarticulations, but cannot operate over extensive stretches of speech and so cannot account for the long-range type of coarticulatory phenomena. Also it is clear from the above discussion that coarticulatory patterns are often language-specific, reflecting, and being constrained by, the phonological and syntactic rules of the language. Models of speech production such as those outlined in the early part of this paper, which regard coarticulation solely as a low-level automatic adjustment to a phoneme-sized neural encoding unit, are thus found to be inadequate.

References

Ali, L., Gallagher, T., Goldstein, J. and Daniloff, R. 1971: Perception of coarticulated nasality. *JAc.Soc.Am.* **49**, 538–40.

Benguerel, A.P. and Cowan, H.A. 1974: Coarticulation of upper lip protrusion in French. *Phonetica* **30**, 41–55.

Butcher, A. and Weiher, E. 1976: An electropalatographic investigation of coarticulation in VCV sequences. *JPhon.* **4**, 59–74.

Clumek, H. 1976: Patterns of soft palate movements in six languages. *JPhon.* **4**, 337–51.

Daniloff, R. and Moll, K. 1968: Coarticulation of lip rounding. *JSHR* **11**, 707–21.

Firth, J.R. 1948: Sounds and prosodies. *TPh.S*, 127–52.

Fujimura, O., Kiritani, S. and Ishida, H. 1973: Computer-controlled radiography for observation of movements of articulatory and other human organs. *Comput. Biol. Med.* **3**, 371–84.

Ghazeli, S. 1977: Back consonants and backing coarticulation in Arabic. Unpublished Ph.D dissertation, University of Texas at Austin.

Gimson, A.C. 1980: *An introduction to the pronunciation of English*, 3rd edn. London: Edward Arnold.

Hardcastle, W.J. 1972: The use of electropalatography in phonetic research. *Phonetica* **25**, 197–215.

———1976: *Physiology of speech production*. London: Academic Press.

Hardcastle, W.J. and Roach, P.J. 1979: An instrumental investigation of coarticulation in stop consonant sequences. In P. Hollien and H. Hollien (eds.), *Current issues in the phonetic sciences*. Amsterdam: Benjamin.

Henke, W.L. 1966: Dynamic articulatory model of speech production using computer simulation. Unpublished Ph.D dissertation, MIT, Cambridge, Mass.

Hudgins, C.V. and Stetson, R.H. 1937: Relative speed of articulatory movements. *Arch. Néerl. Phon. Exp.* **13**, 85–94.

Hyman, L.M. 1978: Word demarcation. In J.H. Greenberg (ed.), *Universals of human language 2*, 443–70.

Kaplan, H.M. 1971: *Anatomy and physiology of speech*, 2nd edn. New York: McGraw-Hill.

Kent, R., Carney, P. and Severeid, L. 1974: Velar movement and timing: evaluation of a model for binary control. *JSHR* **17**, 470–88.

Kent, R. and Minifie, F.D. 1977: Coarticulation in recent speech production models. *J Phon.* **5**, 115–17.

Kim, C-W. 1971: Experimental phonetics: retrospect and prospect. In W.D. Dingwall (ed.), *A survey of linguistic science*. University of Maryland Press.

Kohler, K. 1976: Die Instabilität wortfinaler Alveolarplosive im Deutschen: eine elektropalatographische Untersuchung. *Phonetica* **33**, 1–30.

Kozhevnikov, V.A. and Chistovich, L.A. 1965: *Speech: articulation and perception*. Moscow: Nauka. Tr. Joint Publication Res. Service, No. **30**, Washington, DC.

Kuehn, D.P. and Moll, K.L. 1976: A cineradiographic study of VC and CV articulatory velocities. *JPhon.* **4**, 303–20.

Krmpotić, J. 1959: Données anatomique et histologiques relatives aux effecteurs laryngopharyngo-buccaux. *Rev. Laryngol.* **11**, 829–48.

Lehiste, I. 1965: Juncture. *Proc. 5th Int. Cong. Ling.* Basel: S. Karger, 172–200.

Lenneberg, E.H. 1967: *Biological foundations of language*. New York: Wiley.

McClean, M. 1973: Forward coarticulation of velar movement at marked junctural boundaries. *JSHR* **16**, 286–96.

MacNeilage, P.F. 1970: Motor control of serial ordering of speech. *Psych. Rev.* **77**, 182–96.

Moll, K.L. and Daniloff, R.G. 1971: Investigation of the timing of velar movements during speech. *JAc. Soc. Am.* **50**, 678–84.

Ohala, J. J. 1971: Monitoring soft palate activity in speech. *Project on Linguistic Analysis* **13**, University of California at Berkeley. J01–J015.

Öhman, S. 1966: Coarticulation in VCV utterances: spectrographic measurements. *JAc. Soc. Am.* **39**, 151–68.

Ostreicher, H.T. and Sharf, D. J. 1976: Effects of coarticulation on the identification of deleted consonant and vowel sounds. *JPhon.* **4**, 285–301.

Sawashima, M. 1979: A supplementary report on speech production. *Proc. 9th Int. Cong. Phon. Sci.*, 49–56.

Shohara, H. 1939: Significance of overlapping movements in speech. (Proc. 2nd Bien. Cent. Zone Conf. Amer. Soc. Hard of Hearing). Repr. in E.T. McDonald (ed.) 1964, *Articulation testing and treatment: a sensory-motor approach.* Pittsburg: Stanwix Ho.

Su, L.S., Li, K.P. and Fu, K.S. 1974: Identification of speakers by use of nasal coarticulation. *JAc. Soc. Am.* **56**, 1876–82.

Sussman, H.M., MacNeilage, P.F. and Hanson, R.J. 1973: Labial and mandibular dynamics during the production of bilabial consonants: preliminary observations. *JSHR* **16**, 397–420.

5

Cardinal vowels and other problems
Andrew Butcher

Daniel Jones's system of 'fixed vowel-sounds having known acoustic qualities and known tongue and lip positions', with reference to which 'the qualities of unknown vowels' might be described, has reached retirement age. It officially first saw the light of day 65 years ago (Jones, 1917a,b), although the original use of the term 'Cardinal Vowels' is attributed to A. M. Bell (1867, 16) and the principles on which the system was based have much earlier origins (cf. Ladefoged 1967, 62–75). Since then, despite occasional criticism and suggestions for modifications, the basic notion has continued to occupy a more or less central niche in the phonetic orthodoxy. To attempt an objective review of the current status of Cardinal Vowel (CV) theory would be no easy task. Although the attitude of many academic phoneticians to Cardinal Vowels might best be described as ambivalent, students on phonetics courses in Britain will almost inevitably be introduced to the concept at an early stage and, however healthy the degree of scepticism imparted, the impression is usually given that this is still a basic element of the phonetics syllabus—an impression which could only be strengthened by the treatment afforded the topic in quite recent introductory textbooks (e.g. Ladefoged 1975, 194ff; Catford 1977, 173ff).

It is the aim of the present chapter to re-examine the major practical and theoretical shortcomings of the CV system—some of which have long been recognized. But, further than this, it is hoped to show that there are wider implications for the discipline of phonetics as a whole, and that continued use of the system has a positively dangerous effect in that it conditions phoneticians to an approach to their discipline which is theoretically inadequate and scientifically dishonest.

Aims v. claims

It is important, in all fairness to the system and its author, to distinguish claims made for it by Daniel Jones from those assumed or invented subsequently by others. And yet there is a certain lack of clarity concerning even the original purpose of the CV system. The latter is set out in *An Outline of English Phonetics* (Jones 1960, 26–8),which probably contains the fullest exposition by Jones himself (1960, 26–39). The system was considered to be the 'only . . . way of making written descriptions of vowels intelligible to a large circle of readers of different nationalities'. In other words, it was quite simply an attempt to overcome a perennial problem of language teachers in the pre-cassette era—that of teaching students to produce the vowels of a foreign language from the pages of a book. And yet it has always been a basic tenet of CV theory that the reference vowels themselves can only be learned through oral instruction. One may be forgiven for wondering why, if students must 'have access to a qualified teacher [or] to a gramophone' in order to learn the Cardinal Vowels, they could not save time by learning the vowels of the language concerned by one of these methods in the first place, without recourse to the intermediate stage of the reference sounds. Whereas Jones (1960, 35) maintains that readers without these benefits 'cannot expect to learn the values of these or any other cardinal vowels with accuracy', Abercrombie (1967, 155) casts even graver doubt on the practical usefulness of the Cardinal Vowels as a language-teaching device when he insists that 'It would not be reasonable to expect full command over their production without long training, and their successful application as a descriptive device comes only after considerable experience and practice'.

Although apparently introduced as a pedagogical device, there is no doubt that the Cardinal Vowels have been used chiefly by phoneticians in their attempts to record the vowel qualities of a language or particular accent of a language for the benefit of themselves and other phoneticians. In an age before the advent of cheap high-quality tape-recording, the ability to categorize the sounds of a language and to transcribe them by means of written symbols was a skill which it was essential for phoneticians to acquire. Consonants—i.e. sounds commonly occupying a marginal position in the syllable structure of languages—have traditionally been transcribed in 'articulatory' (in other words pseudo-physiological) terms. There was apparently, however, general agreement on the difficulty of classifying vowels—i.e. syllable nuclei—in the same way, 'since in forming many vowels the tongue is far removed from the roof of the mouth, and so cannot be guided by the sensation of touch'(Jones 1955, 6). Whether or not this is the case, there is certainly a long tradition of descriptions of vowel quality based implicitly or explicitly, wholly or in part on auditory criteria. Jones's system was also only partly an auditory one, and his criteria were in fact very mixed. The boundaries of the vowel space are defined partly physiologically and partly aerodynamically. The 'top' and 'back' of the space are defined as the most extreme articulations which can be achieved without causing turbulent air flow, whereas the 'front' and 'bottom' of the space are supposedly the physiological limits of tongue movement itself. The two 'anchor' vowels of the system, CV1 and CV5, are then positioned at the two points where the two types of boundary meet and the intermediate vowels positioned at points on these boundaries which are defined auditorily (see Fig. 5.1). Lip-rounding has always been repre-

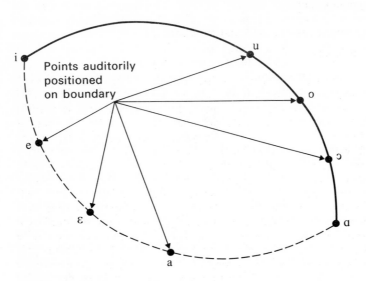

Fig. 5.1 Diagrammatic summary of basic criteria for Cardinal Vowels.

sented as a wholly physiologically defined dimension of the system. Despite subsequent claims that the model is almost entirely auditorily based, Jones himself makes it abundantly clear that this is essentially a 'tongue position' model in the tradition of Ellis (1844), Bell (1867) and Sweet (1877).

Since its inception, various modifications have been suggested to this original model. Some of these have been astoundingly trivial (e.g. Dietrich's (1969) suggestion that the continuous lines within the diagram be replaced by dotted ones) and others extraordinarily vague (e.g. Hammarström's (1973) complaint about the treatment of front rounded vowels). There have been more clearly argued contributions to this Great Debate—such as that of Kingdon (1964), recommending the reallocation of symbols within the quadrilateral in the form of a complicated dovetail pattern, or McClure (1972) insisting that the term SECONDARY cardinal vowel be dropped and separate diagrams be used for rounded and unrounded vowels—but even these ostensibly radical modifications amount to little more than a reshuffling of lines and/or symbols and reveal an implicit unquestioning reverence for the basic principles of the Jones system.

The most crucial of these principles are set out by Abercrombie (1967, 154) as follows. According to him the Cardinal Vowels are:

(*i*) arbitrarily selected
(*ii*) exactly determined and invariable

(*iii*) peripheral
(*iv*) auditorily equidistant

—to which one might further add that they are

(*v*) three dimensional.

Of these claims, the first is perhaps a little difficult to prove or disprove. The reference sounds are supposedly independent of the vowels of any language, and yet it may seem as though the somewhat mixed criteria referred to above are at least partly the result of a *post hoc* theoretical rationalization of a system arrived at on other more pragmatic (perhaps phonological?) grounds. Attention has been drawn to the similarity between the primary Cardinal Vowels and the vowels of educated early twentiety-century Parisian French and to the fact that Paul Passy had a great influence on Jones's work. Despite strong denials of any such connection (e.g. Abercrombie 1967, 152), one cannot help wondering what the Cardinal Vowels would have been like if they had been invented by a Turk or a Vietnamese. Nevertheless, point (*i*) might perhaps be seen to be the least vulnerable of the claims made for the system, perhaps because it is one of the least significant and must surely follow as a natural consequence of principles (*ii*), (*iii*) and (*iv*). The other principles, however, cannot be dismissed so lightly since they are either inaccurate, ambiguous or mutually contradictory. We shall now examine more closely the criteria upon which the dimensions and periphery of the CV model are defined and assess to what extent the Vowels can be said to be 'exactly determined and invariable'. These questions are considered firstly from the point of view of speech production, which the system was originally assumed to model, and then from the point of view of speech perception, the level at which it has subsequently been claimed to be valid.

Humps v. tubes

One aspect of the CV model which is superficially unambiguous is the correlation of its three dimensions with physiological parameters. Supposedly the FRONT-BACK dimension (left-right on the diagram) corresponds to anterior-posterior movement of the 'tongue hump', whereas the up-down dimension corresponds to its vertical position in the oral cavity. The dimension of lip-rounding might seem equally unambiguous in physiological terms. In fact matters are a great deal more complicated than they seem. The problem with the lip-rounding dimension is threefold. Firstly there is the confusion caused by having to represent three articulatory dimensions on one vowel diagram owing to the apparently illogical division into PRIMARY and SECONDARY vowel sets, which McClure (1972) is so upset about. Nor is it simply the case that 'backness' implies rounding (in the primary set). The degree of lip-rounding for the cardinal points themselves is specified by Jones (1960, 33) in the form of photographs and by Abercrombie (1967, 153) as follows: 'the posture of the lips [for CVs 1–5] is unrounded. . . . CV 6 is the least rounded, CV 7 is more rounded, and CV 8 is more rounded still'. No indication is given, however, as to the way in which this dimension behaves over the vowel space as a whole. It is not clear, for instance, when moving from front to back along the horizontal dimension of the primary diagram, at what point lip-rounding begins. In practice, when making use of the system to describe a given vowel sound, most phoneticians would take the location of a point on the vowel diagram to represent tongue position only, degree of lip-rounding being described independently. Since this would presumably have to be done, even if separate diagrams were used for rounded and unrounded Cardinal Vowels, this particular problem is, from a practical point of view, not a real one but an apparent one, and the 'improvement', proposed by Kingdon (1964) and resurrected by McClure (1972), an irrelevancy.

There is, however, a second aspect of the lip-rounding problem which does not arise from the diagrammatic representation of this dimension but from its relation at the physiological level to the TONGUE HEIGHT parameter. Descriptions of lip positions for the Cardinal Vowels such as that of Abercrombie, quoted above, seem to imply that lip-rounding is a physiologically independent parameter which becomes auditorily 'more important' as the tongue is raised. This view is illustrated by Ladefoged's (1967, 140) three-dimensional representation of the traditional articulatory vowel space (reproduced in Fig. 5.2a), which implies that the variation in lip-rounding is potentially as great for 'open' vowels as for 'close' vowels, but that, whether by accident or by design, most of the Cardinal Vowels are not peripheral with regard to this dimension (CVs 2–5 not being as spread as they might be and CVs 6 and 7 not as rounded as one could make them). In fact, as the tongue is lowered and the jaw opened, two factors have to be considered: firstly, as the oro-facial muscles become stretched, less variation is possible in the shape of the lips; secondly, as the cross-sectional area of the oral orifice increases, the same degree of movement of the lips results in proportionately less variation in that area. There is thus a physiological reason for the decreasing 'importance' of lip-rounding with more open vowels.[1] In short, a three-dimensional representation of the traditional articulatory vowel space should reflect the fact that the potential range of lip-rounding distinctions increases with increased jaw closure—i.e. the space should be wider in this dimension at the top than at the bottom (see Fig. 5.2b).

Finally, it seems clear that, within this 'close' area of the vowel space at least, lip action is not confined to changing the shape or area of the orifice. Protrusion of the lips is a partly independent parameter which alters the length of the vocal tract,[2] and could not be handled by the CV model without adding another *ad hoc* dimension.

---

[1] Indeed a symbol for CV12 (the 'front open rounded' vowel) is conspicuously absent from Jones's original exposition and from the IPA Principles (IPA 1949), presumably because of the almost negligible distinction between this vowel and CV4. Jones's pronunciation of CV12 on the commercially available recordings shows an excessively lowered F_2 (approx 1200 Hz), and he, in common with many of his pupils, habitually enhanced the distinction between CV13 and CV5 by raising the F_2 of the latter (cf. Fig. 5.9a).

[2] This additional dimension is reflected in Sweet's (1877) terms 'inner rounding' and 'outer rounding'. Although 'back' vowels are normally 'outrounded' and 'front' vowels 'inrounded', there are languages (such as Swedish) where this distinction is independent of tongue position.

(a)

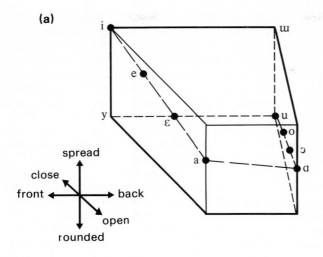

(b)

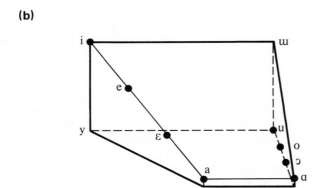

Fig. 5.2 (a) Three-dimensional vowel diagram after Ladefoged (1967, fig. 49); **(b)** Three-dimensional vowel diagram taking account of relation between lip-rounding and 'tongue height'.

There are, however, a number of other such dimensions of vowel articulation for which the basic CV system makes no provision. One such parameter of undoubted importance is NASALITY. Again there is no reason why this should not be specified separately in descriptions, but in strictly phonetic terms the state of the velopharyngeal port is not specifiable in terms of a binary feature and is, for physiological reasons, correlated with tongue height—'open' vowels being articulated, *ceteris paribus*, with a lower velum than 'close' vowels (cf. e.g. Moll 1962, Bzoch 1968). RETROFLEXION is another potentially separable articulatory dimension which has hardly been investigated. It is not clear whether different degrees of tongue blade concavity can be auditorily distinguished or even articulatorily achieved for the same basic tongue position or whether this dimension too is correlated with one or more of the others.

Probably most elusive of all articulatory vowel parameters is that of TENSENESS or WIDTH (not only is the terminology unclear but also whether two or more writers are referring to the same phenomenon). The main division of opinion on this issue seems to be whether the shape of the tongue is the main physiological correlate, or the width of the pharynx. This controversy dates back to Bell and Sweet and maybe beyond, Bell (1867) believing in the pharynx and Sweet (1877) favouring the tongue. An additional complication was introduced by Sievers (1901) and Meyer (1910) who believed that the tension (or lack of it) extended to the vocal folds and that the major difference was one of sub-glottal pressure. All three parameters were considered by Jakobson, Fant and Halle (1952, 38) and later Chomsky and Halle (1968, 324) to be contributory, although they felt the main factor to be 'the muscular strain which affects the tongue, the walls of the vocal tract and the glottis. The higher tension is associated with a greater deformation of the vocal tract from its neutral position.' Chiba and Kajiyama (1958), however, are quite sure that 'the flaccidity of the walls of the vocal organs produces no great effect on the vowel quality.' If the physiological correlate is 'deviation from the neutral position', then no extra dimension is needed since this can be handled by the existing TONGUE POSITION parameters (the only problem being 'first find your neutral position'). Many phoneticians remain convinced, however, of the reality of a separate tenseness or width dimension, although they continue to differ in their views as to its physiological correlates. Catford (1977, 205) refers to a separate dimension of PHARYNGEALIZATION and, while dubious about the whole concept of tenseness, equates Sweet's 'narrow/wide' dimension with degree of convexity of the tongue in both sagittal and coronal planes. TENSE vowels are therefore 'narrow'. Ladefoged (1975, 203), on the other hand, while recognizing the importance of 'tongue bunching', singles out pharynx width as being the deciding factor. TENSE vowels are therefore 'wide'. The whole issue is obviously a very difficult one to accommodate in terms of traditional vowel theory and if it is to be regarded as a factor independent of tongue height and tongue advancement, then it can plainly only be catered for by the addition of yet another *ad hoc* parameter or two.

At first sight, criteria for defining the boundaries of the space upon which the Cardinal Vowels are located seem more straightforward. Indeed there can be little doubt that a LOWER boundary can be quite unequivocally defined (at least for a given speaker) in terms of the limit to which the tongue can be flattened and the jaw lowered (whether or not these limits are commonly reached by phoneticians when pronouncing CVs 4 and 5 is another matter). As for the FRONT boundary, however, it would seem to be equally clear that the tongue may be stretched forward considerably further than the position usually assumed for front Cardinal Vowels—even to the extent that part of the front of the tongue lies beneath the upper lip—and that, with any desired degree of jaw opening, a sound may be produced which by most purely phonetic definitions must be considered a vowel (or VOCOID)—i.e. no obstruction or diversion of the air flow, steady state formant structure, etc. Fig. 5.3 shows a sound spectrogram of such a 'dorso-labial approximant'. It is doubtful whether this kind of sound occurs in any language as a syllable nucleus and it is obvious that it is not meant to

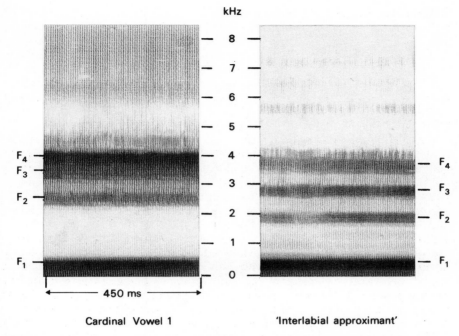

Fig. 5.3 Sound spectrograms of CV1 and an approximant articulated with the tongue fully extended between the lips (speaker AB).

be included within the CV space.[3] There is, nevertheless, a considerable area 'forward' of this space—that is between the normally accepted boundary and the actual limit of extension of the tongue—in which vowel-like articulations may be made, with no physiologically definable watershed between them and 'acceptable' front CV articulations.

The aerodynamic criteria defining the other two boundaries of the vowel space are not much less ambiguous. Unfortunately the size of constriction is not the only factor governing the occurrence of turbulence: the volume velocity of the air flow is equally important. It is therefore meaningless to define tongue positions for vowels in terms such as: 'If the tongue were raised higher/retracted further, the breath pressure remaining constant, the result would be a fricative' (Jones: 1960, 31, fn.), since the degree to which the constriction may be narrowed depends upon what the 'breath pressure' is in the first place, and this is not specified.[4] As Fig. 5.4 shows, it

---

[3] Catford (1977, 166) explicitly restricts the use of the term VOWEL to sounds with 'dorso-domal or linguo-pharyngeal articulation' and a similar restriction is implicit in all accounts of the CV system, but this is hardly as unambiguous a boundary as the 'physical limit of tongue movement' criterion. The example given here is of course an extreme one, but there are less extreme examples from natural languages. Fant (1980, 82), for instance, points out that 'the standard Swedish pronunciation of [ʉ] . . . , contrary to traditional classifications, has a constriction somewhat anterior to that of [i].'

[4] Catford's (1977, 174) *caveat* 'at normal operational volume velocities' is again hardly rigorous enough.

kHz

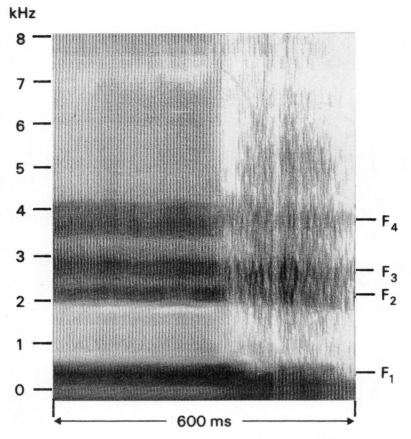

Fig. 5.4 Sound spectrogram of CV2 pronounced with stationary articulators but increasing air-flow rate. Air-flow becomes turbulent after approx. 340 ms (speaker AB).

is perfectly possible, if volume velocity is high enough, to produce a fricative with the tongue in the position normally associated with a vowel of CV2 quality.

One issue which might have been assumed to be settled at a comparatively early stage is the question of equidistance of adjacent CVs in physiological terms. A certain amount of confusion still arises from the kind of diagram originally used to represent the relations between the Cardinal Vowels (Fig. 5.5a). This figure, said to be a 'compromise between scientific accuracy and the requirements of the practical language teacher' (Jones 1960, 37), and often assumed to represent an AUDITORY space, shows the cardinal points to be by no means equidistant from one another, and indeed is not apparently intended to represent auditory distances at all but 'indicates with very considerable accuracy the relative TONGUE POSITIONS of the vowels' (*ibid.*, my emphasis). Even on the trapezoid

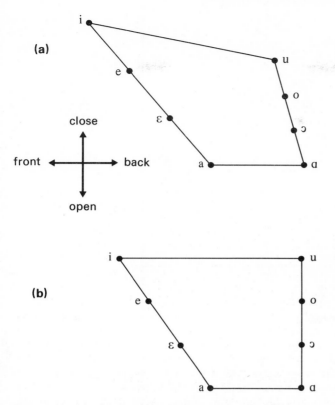

Fig. 5.5 Original **(a)** and 'simplified' **(b)** diagrams 'illustrating the tongue positions of the eight primary Cardinal Vowels' (e.g. Jones 1960, figs. 23 and 23a).

diagram subsequently favoured by the vast majority of phoneticians (Fig. 5.5b), FRONT vowels, BACK vowels and OPEN vowels are all differently spaced. The logical inference must be that to produce equidistant steps between auditory impressions of adjacent Cardinal Vowels, different distances between tongue positions are required, depending on the location of the vowels within the space. The reason given by Jones (1960, 34) for this is the 'greater importance of lip position for back vowels'. But any notion, however limited, of equidistant tongue positions between adjacent vowels should have been thoroughly discredited by Russell's (1928) largely ignored x-ray study, by S.Jones's (1929) x-ray photos of D.Jones himself (data from which are reproduced in Fig. 5.6), and by a host of subsequent radiographic investigations. Quite clearly even relative tongue positions are not as predicted by the CV model. Not only this, but it has also been quite clearly shown that there can be no question of invariability in these or any other tongue positions in the production of a given set of vowels. Ladefoged *et al.* (1972), for example, have published x-ray tracings of various speakers articulating American English vowels,

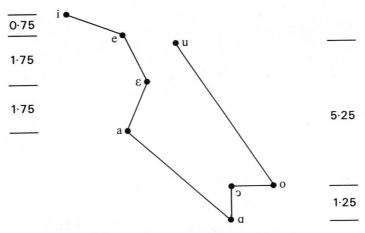

Fig. 5.6 Approximate positions of the highest points of the tongue and differences between tongue heights (in mm) measured from the only published X-ray photos of Cardinal Vowels as produced by Daniel Jones (1929). The diagram is an amalgamation of Ladefoged (1967, fig. 30) and Ladefoged (1975, fig. 9.3).

which show convincingly that widely differing articulatory strategies may be used to produce what are perceived as identical sounds.

In fact, it has been quite obvious for many years that most of the problems discussed above stem from the basic misconception that the physiological correlates of vowel quality are the height and horizontal position of the 'tongue hump'. At least since the acoustic modelling studies of the 1950s (cf. especially Stevens and House 1955), culminating in the classic work of Fant (1960), it has become abundantly clear that this is not the case. The crucial factor in the determination of vowel quality is the total supralaryngeal vocal tract area function—in other words the cross-sectional area of the tube as a function of distance from the larynx. Traditional vowel classification has ignored the fact that the vocal tract bends through 90° at the velum and, in spite of the definition of CV5 as 'almost a fricative', has continued to label this vowel type as 'open'. In fact, as the tongue is lowered the pharynx tends to be narrowed, so that the most open vowels in terms of maximum overall width of the vocal tract are (for most speakers) those of a CV3 type quality. Nevertheless, it might well be argued that the CV model would be on safe physiological ground if the area function could be specified unambiguously by the height and frontness of the tongue and whether or not the lips are rounded. The data from Russell (1928) to Ladefoged *et al.* (1972) show conclusively that this is not the case. Small adjustments in the cross-sectional area of the lip opening, or in the degree of protrusion of the lips, or in pharynx width or larynx height are equally as important as the sagittal contour of the tongue. Various studies (e.g. Lindblom and Sundberg 1971, Perkell 1969, Wood 1977) have confirmed that three basic tongue contours are necessary to distinguish three classes of vowels (see Fig. 5.7): [i]-type palatals, [u]-type labiovelars and [ɑ]-type pharyngeals (Wood (1977) further distinguishes

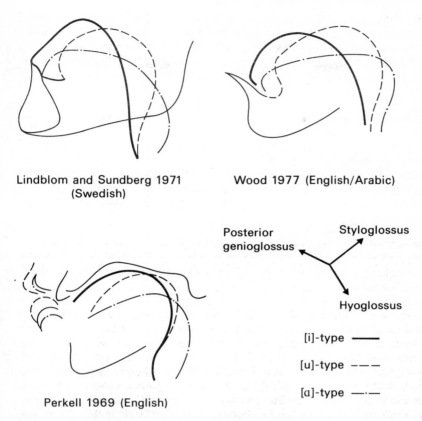

Lindblom and Sundberg 1971   Wood 1977 (English/Arabic)
(Swedish)

Perkell 1969 (English)

Fig. 5.7 X-ray tracings from three different studies showing tongue contours for three basic vowel types.

high and low pharyngeals). It has, furthermore, been pointed out that each of these three basic constrictions of the tube would be achieved mainly (but not exclusively) by the action of one single pair of the main extrinsic muscles of the tongue—namely the posterior genioglossi for the palatals, the styloglossi for the labiovelars and the hyoglossi for the pharyngeals. Any differentiation within these classes would be achieved mainly by adjustments of lip opening and larynx height. As Lieberman (1976, 93) says: 'Human speakers thus in general do not generate vowels in accordance with traditional phonetic theory.'

Nevertheless, as a last resort it might be claimed that, since a particular vocal tract area function will always result in one particular vowel quality, a CV-type approach would still be descriptively adequate, providing one could specify a sufficient number of articulatory parameters with sufficient accuracy. Unfortunately, however, as acoustic studies from Stevens and House (1955) onwards have made clear, two or more different area functions may generate an identical formant frequency pattern. In other words, articulatory specifications are not a realistic basis for vowel description, for as Lindau, Jacobson and Ladefoged (1972, 93) conclude: 'The nature of some vowel targets is much more likely to be auditory than articulatory. The particular articulatory mechanism that a speaker makes use of to attain a vowel target is of secondary importance only.'

Factors v. formants

Many phoneticians are at pains to emphasize the essentially auditory nature of the CV model—a view reflected in several recent text books (e.g. O'Connor 1973, 108ff; Ladefoged 1975, 194ff; Kohler 1977, 68ff). It seems an attractive notion to suppose that the dimensions of the CV model are articulatory in name only, and in fact represent the dimensions of variation in vowel quality at a psychophysical level. A variety of procedures are available to test this kind of assumption, usually involving the use of similarity (or dissimilarity) judgements or perceptual errors to estimate psychophysical 'distances' between vowel stimuli. Studies of subjects with similar linguistic backgrounds often yield dimensions which correlate quite well with acoustic measures such as formant frequencies (e.g. Pols *et al.* 1969; Hanson 1967; Butcher 1974). Cross-linguistic studies, however, have indicated that the dimensionality of vowel perception is one of the factors which may vary according to the mother tongue of the listener. Terbeek and Harshman (1971, 37), for example, concluded from their study of English, German and Thai listeners: 'it appears to be the case that there is no universal perceptual space. Speakers of different native languages respond to the same stimuli in different ways. Neither the number of dimensions nor the interpretation of the dimensions is consistent.' Butcher (1976) also found that perceptual spaces differed markedly, not only between English, French and German speaking groups (see Fig. 5.8), but also between age groups—children tended to hear in three dimensions and adults in two.

It has been suggested that problems with the dimensionality of the perceptual space for vowels may be due to unwarranted assumptions made about the model (cf.Terbeek and Harshman 1972). There is, for example, no basis for assuming that such a space should obey the laws of Euclidean geometry, as the CV model does. If a set of vowels are perceived by a subject in terms of two variables, for example, those vowels may be represented on a two dimensional plane, but that plane will only be flat if perceived distances between vowels conform to the Pythagorean theorem—and there is no evidence to show that they do. If, for example, distances between vowels at the periphery of the plane were estimated to be further apart than Pythagoras would predict from distances at the centre of the plane, then the surface of the plane would be 'dished' and a model based on Euclidean geometry would produce a third spurious dimension to account for the distance of the stimuli from the flat surface which such a model must assume. This dimension would correspond to no real perceptual variable and the positions of vowels on it would be predictable from their positions on the other two dimensions. Equally unfounded is the

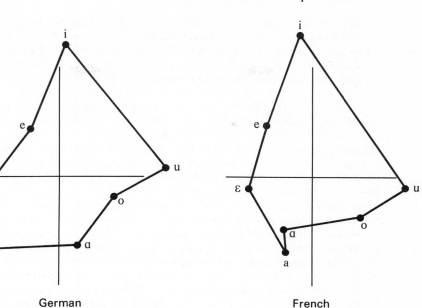

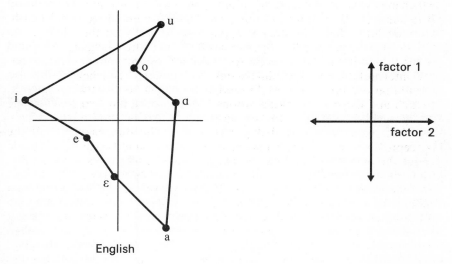

Fig. 5.8 Two-dimensional perceptual spaces for a subset of the Cardinal Vowels (speaker ACG) as perceived by speakers of three different languages.

assumption that the axes of the perceptual dimensions should, as in a CV-type model, be orthogonal to one another. Angles other than the 90° required by Descartes between dimensions would arise if perceptual distances in one quadrant were compressed and distances in a neighbouring quadrant correspondingly expanded. The former could happen where a listener's linguistic experience leads him to expect certain values to co-occur. If, for example, back vowels are always rounded and front vowels unrounded, distances between back rounded vowels might be compressed compared with distances between front rounded vowels. On the other hand, distances might be expanded in a quadrant which contains a large proportion of phonologically distinct vowels in the subjects' language, since their perception with regard to that region of the space might be expected to be more acute.

Perceptual dimensions for CVs seem, according to Butcher (1976), to run more or less diagonally across the dimensions that would be predicted from a CV- or formant frequency-based model (cf. Fig. 8). The two most important dimensions could nevertheless be regarded as a DIFFUSE/COMPACT or PALATAL/PHARYNGEAL factor and a GRAVE/ACUTE or possibly OPEN/CLOSE factor. It is notable that the configurations vary quite widely according to the native language of the subjects—but in no case could the points be said to be auditorily equidistant. Ladefoged (1967, 99) takes the view that nobody apart from Jones ever really believed in auditory equidistance anyway, which, he says, 'may be a property ascribed to cardinal vowels solely by their originator'. Apparently most of the phoneticians taking part in his study agreed that the auditory distances between CVs 1–5 were greater than those between CVs 5–8, an opinion borne out by the data shown in Fig. 5.8. Comparing the perception of native subjects of different mother tongues is perhaps the extreme case, but on the other hand there is plenty of evidence to show that a group of English-speaking phoneticians can vary widely in their perception of vowels, especially 'non-peripheral' vowels (Ladefoged 1967, 135) and even that individuals trained in the CV tradition vary within their own perception over short periods of time (Laver 1965).[5]

Thus it seems more fruitful, in the search for invariance and precision, to return to the vocal tract area function and to the acoustic parameters of vowel quality normally derived from the frequencies of the lower formants. After all, as long ago as the early 1950s, Delattre *et al.* (1952) were able to synthesize a set of 16 two-formant sounds which were 'rather highly identifiable' with the first 16 primary and secondary CVs (and acoustically equidistant to boot). It was already clear from this work, however, that the correlation of F_1 with the CV TONGUE HEIGHT dimension and (more

---

[5] It should be pointed out that both these authors draw extremely generous conclusions about the variability of their subjects' perception in view of the nature of their results *and the claims made by CV users*. Ladefoged (1967, 14), for example, concludes that the system 'allows phoneticians to make adequate judgements of at least those vowels which are judged as having lip positions like those of similar primary cardinal vowels', and Laver (1965, 120) that 'As a technique applied over a period of time, to data which is continually re-examined, the system is very efficient indeed. As a short-term technique, for use on one occasion at a time, it is less efficient.'

especially) of F_2 with TONGUE ADVANCEMENT was a simplistic one. Acceptable HIGH BACK vowels, in particular, could easily be synthesized from single formants, whereas later work showed that for HIGH FRONT vowels important information was carried by formants higher than the first two. Since then a great deal of research has been done into the nature of the 'effective' second formant frequency (or F_2'). Ladefoged (1975, 173) is satisfied that it is equivalent to the separation between the first two formant frequencies—i.e. for him $F_2' = F_2 - F_1$. On the other hand one of the latest studies, matching two-formant sounds with a set of 18 four-formant 'synthetic cardinal vowels' (Bladon and Fant 1978) concludes that

$$F_2' = \frac{F_2 + c^2(F_3 \cdot F_4)^{1/2}}{1 + c}$$

$$\text{where } c = K(f) \cdot \frac{B_2 \cdot F_2(1 - F_1^2/F_2^2)(1 - F_2^2/F_3^2)(1 - F_2^2/F_4^2)}{(F_4 - F_3)^2\left(\dfrac{F_3 \cdot F_4}{F_2^2} - 1\right)}$$

and there is no reason to suppose that this is the last word on the subject. Recent work such as this, then, emphasizes the complex nature of the relationship between acoustic and perceptual measures. Whatever model is employed, however, one would be hard put to find either invariance or equidistance of the CV points at the acoustic level. That even a small group of phoneticians, all trained in the same tradition, may vary quite widely in their production of the Cardinal Vowels has been well demonstrated by Ladefoged's (1967, 75ff) exhaustive study. Fig. 5.9a shows an F_1/F_2 plot of primary Cardinal Vowels as pronounced by Daniel Jones and more recent recordings of three of his pupils, all of whom took part in the Ladefoged study. A fair spread of values is evident, although no overlapping of adjacent vowels. Equidistance is not to be found: OPEN vowels are often more widely spaced than CLOSE vowels and FRONT vowels more widely spaced than BACK vowels. Even a more sophisticated model, taking third-formant frequency and second-formant amplitude into account (Bernstein 1975) does not show the points to be acoustically equidistant (Fig. 5.9b) (although it does show the proportions of the acoustic space when defined in this way to be much more similar to those of the perceptual spaces (cf. Fig. 5.8) than when defined simply by F_1 and F_2). As Ladefoged (1975, 197) says: 'no one has yet been able to show how acoustic analyses of the cardinal vowels recorded by Daniel Jones himself can be reconciled with his definition of auditory equidistance'.

The question of individual variation in the formant frequencies of natural Cardinal Vowels is no less problematic. Obviously only part of this variation is due to inaccurate imitation of the original sounds. A substantial part of the variation is due to variation in vocal tract size (a fact pointed out by Joos as long ago as 1948). Extreme cases of such variation are, of course, male/female differences and adult/child differences[6] as illustrated in Fig. 5.10, and, as Fant (1980, 97) remarks, although it seems probable that

[6] Fant (1980, 101) even suggests that, in view of the vast differences in relative pharynx length between adult and child, 'the relative role of front and back parts of the vocal tract could be reversed for a small child, i.e. that F_2 of the vowel [i] would be a front cavity formant, whilst F_3 is more dependent on the shorter back cavity.'

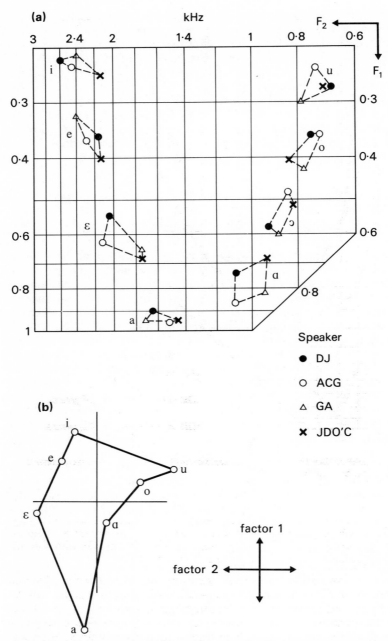

Fig. 5.9(a) F_1/F_2 plot of Cardinal Vowels as spoken by Daniel Jones and three adult male pupils; **(b)** Two-dimensional acoustic space for a subset of these vowels (speaker ACG), taking into account F_3 and A_2.

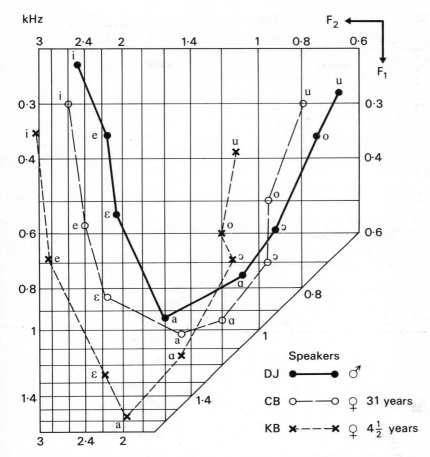

Fig. 5.10 $F_1//F_2$ plot of Cardinal Vowels as spoken by Daniel Jones and as imitated by a woman and by a child.

differences in perceptually important formants may. . . . be minimized by compensations in terms of place of articulation and in the extent of the area function narrowing [Fig. 5.11] such compensations are not possible for all formants and cannot be achieved in more open articulations.

A number of methods have been devised for normalizing formant frequencies so as to average out inter-individual variation. One simple method, for instance, assumes that the fourth-formant frequency is a good index of vocal tract size and expresses the lower formant frequencies as percentages of the mean F_4. Disner (1978) reviews a number of such methods and finds that none of them was able to remove inter-speaker differences without distorting inter-language distinctions.

It is not therefore to be expected that any two speakers articulating 'auditorily perfect' imitations of the Cardinal Vowels will produce identical

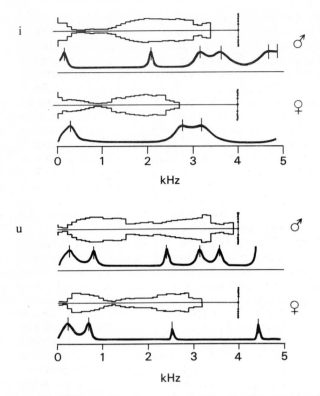

Fig. 5.11 Male and female vocal tracts (equivalent tube representation) and corresponding F-patterns, from the tomographic studies of Fant (1965). Note that, although female formants are more widely spaced because of shorter vocal tract, F_1 and F_2 of [u] and F_3 of [i] are close to those of the male.

formant frequencies for each vowel. Thus the Cardinal Vowels cannot be described in terms of physiological configurations or in terms of acoustic measures, since two different speakers may use two different vocal tract shapes to produce two sounds with different formant frequencies for them to be perceived (by a given listener) as the same vowel. Furthermore, although they may be described auditorily in terms of relative distance from one another in a psychophysical space, that space will only be valid for a particular linguistically homogeneous set of listeners—listeners with other linguistic backgrounds will perceive different distances and quite possibly different dimensions.

Measuring v. imitating

Thus the CV system is a system of reference sounds which are not uniquely specifiable in terms of any measures currently available. In other words, the Cardinal Vowels are not in any objectively demonstrable way exactly determined, invariable, peripheral or equidistant, and the only valid definition is that given by Ladefoged (1967:76) as: 'any sound(s) produced by Daniel Jones and stated by him to be cardinal vowel(s) or any sound(s) produced by any other speaker which are considered by competent observers to be equivalent in phonetic quality to the corresponding cardinal vowels produced by Daniel Jones.' The question is whether this is a scientifically useful, or even acceptable concept. It would perhaps be more so if it could be shown that 'competent observers' agree in their perception of vowel quality. Certainly from a purely phonetic point of view the precise and detailed notation of vowel (and for that matter consonant) sounds is nowadays largely redundant. It is no longer necessary as a device for transcribing the sounds of a language for subsequent reproduction. The days of the phonetician as human tape-recorder are over: magnetic tape does the job far more efficiently and does it for the dialectologist and for the speech pathologist as well as for the language teacher, for whom the Cardinal Vowels were originally intended.

There are, nevertheless, at least two purposes for which those working in these or allied disciplines still find phonetic notation useful if not essential: firstly as a kind of shorthand to remind themselves of or to communicate in writing to others the approximate nature of a sound; and secondly as a preliminary to phonological analysis. For neither of these purposes, however, is anything more than a reasonably fine *categorization* of sounds required. Distinctions as fine as those promised by the CV system are not only unnecessary in the context of inter-individual variation among speakers, but also totally spurious in the light of the degree of latitude demonstrated both in the production of the Cardinal Vowels by phoneticians and in their 'placing' of sounds with reference to them. The 'infallible precision' demanded by Abercrombie (1967, 155) is just not forthcoming.

The assignment of a vowel sound to a category based on acoustic criteria such as relative frequency of first formant and separation of first and second-formant frequencies should be quite sufficient for all practical purposes. It would no doubt be preferable to keep to labels for these categories which reflected the criteria by which they were set up— GRAVE/ACUTE and DIFFUSE/COMPACT would perhaps be appropriate if it were not for the association of these terms with a particular phonological school of thought. HIGH/LOW and BACK/FRONT will no doubt remain with us, however.[7] The labelling is unimportant so long as the twin fictions of auditory precision and invariability are abandoned along with the great sacred cow of transcription as an end in itself.

Most phoneticians are now aware that, in order for their descriptions of speech sounds to have any scientific validity at all, they must formulate those descriptions in terms of objectively measurable and independently motivated parameters. This applies not only to the description of the idiolect of a single normal speaker, but equally in the fields of language variation and language pathology. One of Lindblom's (1980, 4) essential requirements for a scientifically adequate explanation is that 'it presup-

---

[7] Only one text book author (Kohler 1977) has had the courage to apply the terms HIGH and LOW in a logical manner—i.e. to vowels with high and low F_1 respectively.

poses a theory that is completely formalized and leaves no room for the intelligence of the person using it'. A system such as that of the Cardinal Vowels, based on parameters which are difficult to justify externally and relying on the considerable imitative skill of its users, demonstrably does not fall into this category of adequate explanations.

But far more dangerous than this, and far more crucial for the future development of phonetics as a scientific discipline, is that such a system purports to be something which it is not. It masquerades as something more than a convenient labelling technique: it pretends to describe sounds in terms of the physiological and psychological processes underlying their production and perception. For Abercrombie (1967, 156), 'the location of any given vowel relative to the cardinal vowels *is* its description' (my emphasis). CV theory may no longer perpetuate the myth of the 'highest point of the tongue' as a direct physiological correlate of vowel quality, but it still perpetuates in many quarters something just as insidious : the myth of the universal auditory space and the mystique of the infallibly objective and accurate phonetician able to pinpoint a sound within it. Such a non-existent figure is not only unnecessary but also undesirable. Oral and aural acrobatics, though sometimes still useful, are no longer sufficient or even essential requirements in phonetics. One wishes the acrobats (and their flying trapezoids) a long and happy retirement.

References

Abercrombie, D. 1967: *Elements of general phonetics*. Edinburgh: Edinburgh University Press.
Bell, A.M. 1867: *Visible speech*. Washington: Volta Bureau.
Bernstein, J.C. 1975: Phonetic distance. Paper given at 8th Int. Cong. Phon. Sci., Leeds.
Bladon, R.A.W. and Fant, G. 1978: Two-formant models of vowel perception and the cardinal vowels. Paper given at the Colloquium of British Academic Phoneticians, Reading.
Butcher, A.R. 1974: 'Brightness', 'darkness' and the dimensionality of vowel perception. *J Phon.* **2**, 153–60.
————1976: The influence of the native language on the perception of vowel quality. M Phil. thesis, University of London. Also as *Arbeitsberichte* **6**, Institut für Phonetik, Universität Kiel.
Bzoch, K. 1968: Variations in velopharyngeal valving: the factor of vowel changes. *Cleft Palate Journal* **5**, 211–18.
Catford, J.C. 1977: *Fundamental problems in phonetics*. Edinburgh: Edinburgh University Press.
Chiba, T. and Kajiyama, M. 1958: *The vowel: its nature and structure*. Tokyo: Phonetic Society of Japan.
Chomsky, N. and Halle, M. 1968: *The sound pattern of English*. New York: Harper & Row.
Delattre, P., Liberman, A.M., Cooper, F.S. and Gerstman, L.J. 1952: An experimental study of the acoustic determinants of vowel color; observations on one- and two-formant vowels synthesized from spectrographic patterns. *Word* **8**, 195–210.

Dietrich, G. 1969: A suggestion for an improvement on the vowel diagram. *Le Maître Phonétique* **131**, 8–9.
Disner, S. 1978: Vowels in Germanic languages. *UCLA Working Papers in Phonetics* **40**, 1–79.
Ellis, A.J. 1844: *The alphabet of nature*. Bath.
Fant, G. 1960: *Acoustic theory of speech production*. The Hague: Mouton.
———1965: Formants and cavities. *Proc. 5th Int. Cong. Phon. Sci.,* 120–141.
———1980: The relations between area functions and the acoustic signal. *Proc. 9th Int. Cong. Phon. Sci.,* 79–108.
Hammarström, G. 1973: Revision of cardinal vowels, and some other problems. *JIPA* **3**, 22–8.
Hanson, G. 1967: Dimensions in speech sound perception: an experimental study of vowel perception. *Ericsson Technics* **23**, 1–175.
International Phonetic Association 1949: *The principles of the International Phonetic Association*. London: IPA.
Jakobson, R., Fant, G. and Halle, M. 1952: *Preliminaries to speech analysis*. Cambridge, Mass.: MIT Press.
Jones, D. 1917a: *An English pronouncing dictionary*. London: Dent.
———1917b: *Cardinal vowels* (on gramophone record) B 804. London: HMV.
———1955: *Cardinal vowels* (on gramophone record) ENG 252–5. London:Linguaphone.
———1960: *An outline of English phonetics* 9th edn. Cambridge: Heffer.
Jones, S. 1929: Radiography and pronunciation. *BJ Radiology* **2**, 149–50.
Joos, M. 1948, *Acoustic phonetics*. Baltimore: Waverly Press.
Kingdon, R. 1964: The representation of vowels. In D. Abercrombie *et al.* (eds.), *In honour of Daniel Jones*. London: Longmans.
Kohler, K.J. 1977: *Einführung in die Phonetik des Deutschen*. Berlin: Schmidt.
Ladefoged, P. 1967: The nature of vowel quality. In *Three areas of experimental phonetics*. London: OUP.
———1975: *A course in phonetics*. New York: Harcourt Brace.
Ladefoged, P., De Clerk, J., Lindau, M. and Papçun, G. 1972: An auditory-motor theory of speech production. *UCLA Working Papers in Phonetics* **22**, 48–75.
Laver, J.D.M.H. 1965: Variability in vowel perception. *L & S* **8**, 95–121.
Lieberman, P. 1976: Phonetic features and physiology: a reappraisal. *JPhon.* **4**, 91–112.
Lindau, M., Jacobson, L., and Ladefoged, P. 1972: The feature advanced tongue root. *UCLA Working Papers in Phonetics* **22**, 76–94.
Lindblom, B.E.F. 1980: The goal of phonetics, its unification and application. *Proc. 9th Int. Cong. Phon. Sci.,* 3–18.
Lindblom, B.E.F. and Sundberg, J.E.F. 1971: Acoustical consequences of lip, tongue, jaw, and larynx movement. *JAc. Soc. Am.* **50**, 1166–79.
Meyer, E.A. 1910: Untersuchung über Lautbildung. In *Festschrift Wilhelm Viëtor*. Marburg: Reisland.
Moll, K.L. 1962: Velopharyngeal closure in vowels. *JSHR* **5**, 30–7.

McClure, J.D. 1972: A suggested revision for the Cardinal Vowel system. *JIPA* **2**, 20–5.
O'Connor, J.D. 1973: *Phonetics.* Harmondsworth: Penguin.
Perkell, J.S. 1969: *Physiology of speech production: results and implications of a quantitative cineradiographic study.* Cambridge, Mass.: MIT Press.
Pols, L.C.W., van der Kamp, L.J.T. and Plomp, R. 1969: Perceptual and physical space of vowel sounds. *JAc. Soc. Am.* **46**, 458–67.
Russell, G.O. 1928: *The vowel.* Columbus: Ohio State University Press.
Sievers, E. 1901: *Grundzüge der Phonetik.* Leipzig: Breitkopf & Härtel.
Stevens, K.N. and House, A.S. 1955: Development of a quantitative description of vowel articulation. *JAc. Soc. Am.* **27**, 484–93.
Sweet, H. 1877: *Handbook of phonetics.* Oxford: Clarendon Press.
Terbeek, D. and Harshman, R. 1971: Cross-language differences in the perception of natural vowel sounds. *UCLA Working Papers in Phonetics* **19**, 26–38.
————1972: Is vowel perception non-Euclidean? *UCLA Working Papers in Phonetics* **22**, 13–19.
Wood, S. 1977: A radiographic analysis of constriction locations for vowels. *Working Papers* **15**, Phonetics Laboratory, Department of General Linguistics, Lund University. 101–31.

6

On the distinction between 'stress-timed' and 'syllable-timed' languages[1]

Peter Roach

One of the most familiar distinctions in phonetics is that between STRESS-TIMED and SYLLABLE-TIMED languages. Many textbooks refer to this, but nowhere is the distinction as explicitly made as in Abercrombie (1967, 97), who writes: 'As far as is known, every language in the world is spoken with one kind of rhythm or with the other . . . French, Telugu and Yoruba . . . are syllable-timed languages, . . . English, Russian and Arabic . . . are stress-timed languages'. Most teachers of phonetics are used to being asked by students how one can tell if a particular language is syllable-timed or stress-timed; it is easy enough to construct and perform examples, such as a comparison between an English sentence:

'this is the 'house that 'Jack 'built

and a French one:

c'est absolument ridicule.

However, it is much more difficult to set out clear rules for assigning a language to one of the two categories. Within the traditional way of teaching phonetics such a question does not necessarily need to be answered with a statement that can be tested experimentally. The question might be answered in the same way as others such as 'how can you tell if a vowel is centralized?', by saying that the ability to make such decisions comes through undergoing a certain amount of training with an expert phonetician. Consequently Abercrombie's statement that the phonetician needs 'empathy with the speaker' to apprehend speech rhythm, and his claim that 'it is necessary to learn to listen differently in order to be able to analyse speech rhythm, whether of one's mother tongue or another

[1] I am grateful to the Joint Speech Research Unit for their support of the research work on which this paper is based (G.C.H.Q. Agreement No. F7T/291/79) and to Helen Roach for her assistance in the work.

73

language, and to describe it in general terms' suggest that the distinction between stress-timed and syllable-timed languages may rest entirely on perceptual skills acquired through training. It can be objected to this that there is an infinite regression involved in saying that one can only decide whether X should be assigned to Category A or to Category B when one has been trained by someone who knows how to do this.

Is it possible to establish some experimental test, based on instrumental techniques, which would make it possible to assign a language to one category or the other? Two claims made by Abercrombie in the same work appear to offer some chance of this (*ibid.*, 98):

(*i*) 'there is considerable variation in syllable length in a language spoken with stress-timed rhythm whereas in a language spoken with a syllable-timed rhythm the syllables tend to be equal in length'.

(*ii*) 'in syllable-timed languages, stress pulses are unevenly spaced'.

In the experimental work described below, tape-recordings of the six languages listed by Abercrombie (French, Telugu and Yoruba as syllable-timed and English, Russian and Arabic as stress-timed) were examined to see if it was possible to assign languages to one of the two categories by means of tests based on the above claims. If such tests could be devised they would be useful not only in the study of rhythm but also in the broader study of phonetic differences between languages. Intensity meter traces were made from the tape-recordings and were segmented by hand. This is very time-consuming work and only one speaker of each language was studied. It was felt that it would be most suitable to examine spontaneous, unscripted speech, so speakers were given simple pictures to talk about but left free to say what they wanted. About two minutes of this speech was measured for each speaker.

Claim (*i*), that syllable length is more variable in stress-timed languages, is easy enough to test. However, it is not easy to see *why* syllable length should tend to be equal in a syllable-timed language. It is possible to imagine a language in which realizations of vowel phonemes displayed little variability, but which contained phonemically long and phonemically short vowels. This language would then contain syllables that differed considerably from each other in length, but it would not as a consequence have to have the 'regular stress beat' that is commonly ascribed to stress-timed rhythm.

A simple measure of variability in this case is the standard deviation of the syllable durations (measured in milliseconds). The measures from the six speakers are given below:

French:	75.5	English:	86
Telugu:	66	Russian:	77
Yoruba:	81	Arabic:	76

This set of figures does not appear to support claim (*i*).

Claim (*ii*) is a more complex matter. This relates to the 'regular stress beat' that is said to be characteristic of English, and to be characteristically absent in languages such as French. It is necessary in the first place to distinguish between the subjective impression of regular stress beats as perceived by the listener, and the information about time intervals that can be derived instrumentally from an acoustic signal. Considerable attention has been given recently to ISOCHRONY in English speech (i.e. the occurrence of regular stress beats), and it has been shown that the regularity of the stresses is more apparent than real, in that listeners tend to perceive isochrony even in sequences of inter-stress intervals that are manifestly far from equal (Allen 1975; 1979; Lehiste 1977; 1979; Donovan and Darwin 1979). This finding does not invalidate the claim that some languages *sound* 'stress-timed', but it suggests that finding isochrony in measurements of speech is unlikely to be straightforward. A test based on native speakers' responses to auditorily presented material would not be a practical means to providing an answer to the question 'how can you tell whether a language is stress-timed or syllable-timed?'. The only objective way of answering this question must be one based on measurements derived from acoustic or articulatory information.

Information about the perceptual reality of stress-timed rhythm has been produced mainly in relation to English, and there is no comparable information about syllable-timed languages. A few languages, however, have been investigated with measurements of inter-stress intervals, including some reputedly syllable-timed languages. The best-known study of English based on the acoustic signal is Uldall (1971), in which the material measured was a recording of a passage of written English read by Abercrombie. The measured inter-stress intervals did not show marked regularity. Spanish is claimed by, among others, Pike (1945) and Hockett (1955) to be syllable-timed; doubt is cast on this claim by Pointon (1973, 1980) and a detailed study of Chilean Spanish by Alvarez de Ruf (1978) showed that for this variety of Spanish at least, the label 'syllable-timed' is not appropriate. A similar conclusion is reached for Tamil by Balasubramanian (1980). Such information is, however, hard to find and often carried out on rather disparate material. Abercrombie's claim (*ii*) needs to be tested on several languages under conditions as nearly as possible identical. This was attempted with the recordings mentioned above (French, Telugu, Yoruba, English, Russian and Arabic).

Considerable problems arise in designing a measurement-based test of the kind envisaged. The first of these is the identification of stresses; clearly, if the phonetician were unable to identify which syllables in a speech recording were to be counted as stressed and which as unstressed there would be no possibility of measuring inter-stress intervals. Since no instrumental technique for identifying stressed syllables automatically has yet been devised, it appears that syllable and stress identification must be done auditorily, presumably by the phonetician since it would be impossibly difficult to use native speaker reactions in a coordinated way in a test involving a number of different languages. Several of the speakers recorded were, in fact, asked for their opinions on stress placement when the material was being analysed, but appeared to find it an impossibly difficult task. (This is no doubt partly the result of using spontaneous speech instead of the reading of carefully constructed sentences.) As is well known, disagreements arise among phoneticians about syllabification even of their native language; such disagreements occur more frequently over stress and even more so over the division of speech into intonation units. In analysing foreign languages the phonetician is subject to a variety of influences. His native-language intuitions may influence decisions, as may experience with other languages. Judgements of stress may be influenced by various prosodic characteristics such as vowel length and pitch height that may be relevant in his own language but irrelevant in the language being examined. It could, for example, happen that in analysing a tone language an unwary phonetician might judge all high-tone syllables to be stressed. An additional problem is that in working with an informant one may be unwittingly influenced by the informant's idealized view of what he thought he said on the tape, or by his mental picture of how what he said would appear in his orthography. In spite of these difficulties, it was felt to be worth persisting in attempting to measure inter-stress intervals for the six languages, and the recordings were therefore transcribed with stress-marks placed on those syllables which sounded stressed (i.e. which constituted peaks of prominence).

The next problems arise in measuring inter-stress intervals. First, from where should one measure the beginning of an inter-stress interval? Some researchers have measured from the intensity peak of the vowel in the stressed syllable to the corresponding following peak. If it were possible to identify what have been called P-centres (Morton *et al.* 1976) from the production side of speech (something that may be theoretically possible) there would be much to be said for measuring from these. However, in the present state of our knowledge it is felt to be intuitively more satisfying to aim to measure as nearly as possible from the PHONOLOGICAL beginning of the syllable which carries the stress, so that if the syllable begins with a consonant cluster, one measures from the beginning of that cluster.

A further problem is that measurements carried out over long stretches of spontaneous speech are likely to be heavily influenced by tempo variations. To take an extreme example, if one had a recording of a speaker of English repeating the sentence *This is the house that Jack built* many times over with perfectly regular rhythm and timing, one would expect that the variance in inter-stress intervals would be very low. However, if in another recording the speaker continued to produce the sentence with perfectly regular rhythm but changed the tempo from each repetition to the next, the inter-stress intervals would exhibit a quite misleadingly high variance. It seems reasonable to suppose that the kind of temporal regularity being discussed is a property of a unit of speech smaller than the entire text, the tone-unit; this is proposed by Rees (1975). Hence it is assumed that tempo changes will usually be manifested in terms of differences between the tempo of one tone-unit and another, and will not usually be found within the tone-unit (though since Crystal and Quirk (1964) have pointed out the phenomena of ACCELERANDO and RALLENTANDO we must accept that this does sometimes happen). Some way therefore has to be found of removing the effect of tempo differences between one tone-unit and another.

The beginnings and ends of tone-units create measurement problems. Tone-units often begin with unstressed syllables that could only be counted as belonging to an inter-stress interval if the implausible notion were adopted that they were preceded by a 'silent stress' (Abercrombie 1968) or 'silent ictus' (Halliday 1967). These 'pre-head' syllables were discarded in the present work. Syllables which are final in the tone-unit are commonly lengthened considerably, both in English and in other languages (Oller 1979), so if one included the interval between the last stress and the end of the tone-unit in the measurements one would often be introducing values that were unusually large in comparison with other intervals. Syllables between the last stressed syllable and the end of the tone-unit were therefore discarded.

The list of problems involved in setting up a procedure for measuring inter-stress intervals in a controlled way would not be complete without mention of the problem of identifying tone-unit boundaries, which is difficult enough even for English (Brown *et al.* 1980); as far as possible, pauses were taken as the most reliable boundary points. However, the identification problem raised here constitutes another serious weakness in any procedure for measuring aspects of rhythm in continuous speech.

The procedure that was tried for eliminating tempo effects was to look at durational differences and irregularities in percentage terms (expressed as a percentage of the inter-stress interval) rather than in absolute terms. Each tone-unit (minus any discarded syllables at the beginning and end) was measured, and this measurement was divided by the number of inter-stress intervals it contained. This gives a hypothetical figure for each inter-stress interval that would be expected in a perfectly stress-timed language, in that every inter-stress interval would be of the same duration irrespective of the number of syllables it contained. Such regularity is not, of course, expected in natural speech but it is now possible to compare the measured duration of each inter-stress interval with its predicted value and calculate the percentage deviation. We must hypothesize that syllable-timed languages would exhibit a wider range of percentage deviations in inter-stress intervals than would stress-timed (the latter being more nearly isochronous), and this can be tested by calculating the variance of the percentage deviation figures for each language. The variance figures are given below:

French:	617	English:	1267
Telugu:	870	Russian:	917
Yoruba:	726	Arabic:	874

It can be seen that the right-hand column (the stress-timed languages) has *higher* values than the left-hand, which is contradictory to the hypothesis. It seems likely that the English figure is an extreme value resulting from studying a single speaker, and that the figures as a whole are better taken just as grounds for rejecting the hypothesis, rather than as proof that stress-timed languages typically have greater variance in their inter-stress intervals. The significance of the difference between individual languages in terms of their variance can be tested by the Variance-Ratio (F) test (Robson 1973). This show the English data to have a significantly higher variance ($P < .05$) than French, Telugu, Yoruba and Arabic (the last-named being a stress-timed language), but apart from these the only other difference reaching the 5 percent significance level is that between Russian and French.

Another test can be tried, again bearing on Abercrombie's claim (*ii*): it can be hypothesized that in syllable-timed languages inter-stress intervals will tend to be longer in proportion to the number of syllables they contain, whereas such a tendency should be absent (or weaker) in stress-timed languages. This hypothesis can be tested by calculating a Pearson correlation coefficient for the association between percentage deviation (as set out above) and the number of syllables per inter-stress interval for each language. The results of this calculation are set out below:

French:	.41	English:	.53
Telugu:	.61	Russian:	.61
Yoruba:	.62	Arabic:	.57

It is not possible to separate the two groups of languages on this basis.

The results reported here give no support to the idea that one could assign a language to one of the two categories on the basis of measurement of time intervals in speech. Consequently one is obliged to conclude that the basis for the distinction is auditory and subjective—a language is syllable-timed if it *sounds* syllable-timed. A thorough examination of the factors that might be responsible for languages sounding syllable-timed or stress-timed would be beyond the scope of this chapter, but clearly it would be necessary to consider possibilities such as that languages classed as syllable-timed may tend to have simpler syllable structure (Smith (1976) suggests this as a factor in the case of Japanese and of French), and that languages classed as stress-timed may be more likely to exhibit vowel reduction in unstressed syllables.

It seems reasonable to conclude with the following claims, though these go beyond what may legitimately be concluded from the small experiment reported above. Firstly, as suggested by Mitchell (1969), there is no language which is totally syllable-timed or totally stress-timed—all languages display both sorts of timing; languages will, however, differ in which type of timing predominates. Secondly, different types of timing will be exhibited by the same speaker on different occasions and in different contexts; attention is drawn to this by Crystal and Quirk (1964) and Crystal (1969) with the introduction of the prosodic feature RHYTHMICALITY, which may well be relevant in languages other than English. Finally, the stress-timed/syllable-timed distinction seems at the present to depend mainly on the intuitions of speakers of various Germanic languages all of which are said to be stress-timed; examination of the subjective feelings of speakers of languages usually classed as syllable-timed should be carefully studied if the distinction is to be maintained as a respectable part of phonetic theory.

References

Abercrombie, D. 1967: *Elements of general phonetics*. Edinburgh: Edinburgh University Press.

———1968: Some functions of silent stress. *Work in Progress* **2**, Edinburgh University Department of Linguistics.

Allen, G.D. 1975: Speech rhythm: its relation to performance universals and articulatory timing. *J Phon.* **3**, 75–86.

———1979: Formal and statistical models of timing: past, present and future. *Proc. 9th Int. Cong. Phon. Sci.* **II**.

Alvarez de Ruf, H. 1978: *A comparative study of the rhythm of English and Spanish.* MPhil. thesis, Department of Phonetics, University of Leeds.

Balasubramanian, T. 1980: Timing in Tamil. *J Phon.* **8**, 449–68.

Brown, G., Currie, K.L. and Kenworthy, J. 1980: *Questions of intonation.* London: Croom Helm.

Crystal, D. 1969: *Prosodic systems and intonation in English.* Cambridge: Cambridge University Press.

Crystal, D. and Quirk, R. 1964: *Systems of prosodic and paralinguistic features in English.* The Hague: Mouton.

Donovan, A. and Darwin, C.J. 1979: The perceived rhythm of speech. *Proc. 9th Int. Cong. Phon. Sci.* **II**.

Halliday, M.A.K. 1967: *Intonation and grammar in British English.* The Hague: Mouton.

Hockett, C.F. 1955: A manual of phonology. *Memoir* **11**, *IJAL*.

Lehiste, I. 1977: Isochrony reconsidered. *J Phon.* **5**, 253–63.

———1979: Temporal relations within speech units. *Proc. 9th Int. Cong. Phon. Sci.* **III**.

Mitchell, T.F. 1969: Review of Abercrombie 1967. *JL* **5**, 153–64.

Morton, J., Marcus, S.M. and Frankish, C.R. 1976: Perceptual centers (P-centers). *Psych. Rev.* **83**, 405–8.

Oller, D.K. 1979: Syllable timing in Spanish, English and Finnish. In H.H. Hollien and P. Hollien (eds.), *Current issues in the phonetic sciences.* Amsterdam: Benjamins.

Pike, K.L. 1945: *The intonation of American English.* Ann Arbor: University of Michigan Press.

Pointon, G. 1973: Preliminaries to the study of rhythm in Spanish. *Work in Progress* **6**, 58–9. Edinburgh University Department of Linguistics.

———1980: Is Spanish really syllable-timed? *J Phon.* **8**, 293–305.

Rees, M. 1975: The domain of isochrony. *Work in Progress* **8**, 14–28. Edinburgh University Department of Linguistics.

Robson, C. 1973: *Experiment, design and statistics in psychology.* Harmondsworth: Penguin.

Smith, A. 1976: The timing of French, with reflections on syllable timing. *Work in Progress* **9**, 97–108. Edinburgh University Department of Linguistics.

Uldall, E.T. 1971: Isochronous stresses in RP. In E. Hammerich (ed.), *Form and substance.* Copenhagen.

Part III
Phonology, grammar, semantics

7

Markedness, strength and position
R. W. P. Brasington

Markedness

By the time that Chomsky and Halle's work on English phonology in the 1960s had reached a comprehensive enough stage to appear in print as *The sound pattern of English* (1968), it was becoming apparent, not least to Chomsky and Halle themselves, that something was seriously amiss with the (to quote them) 'overly formal' approach to sound pattern that had by then developed into standard generative phonology. In the 10 years or so which have followed, some of the most interesting work in phonology has been concerned to put this situation to rights. Not unexpectedly, of course, more than one problem loomed as the focus of attention was shifted. But it was perhaps fitting that, in their own attempts to remedy what seemed to them one of the most important of these problems, Chomsky and Halle should restimulate an interest in the Praguian notion of markedness and thus offer recognition to the tradition on which in large part they had built.

One of the guiding principles motivating the early development of the notational conventions used by generative phonologists was the view that, given two descriptions of a language expressed by means of these conventions, it should be possible to establish mechanically which of the two was 'the better'. One of the main functions of the conventions was in other words to provide a basis on which an evaluation measure could be constructed. Now what Chomsky and Halle—along with Postal (1968)—had discovered by the end of the 1960s was that the notational system so far developed was unable to differentiate consistently between rules that were phonologically natural (that is to say, expected in a language) and those that were not, between systems that were natural and those that were not, between segments that were natural and those that were not, and so on. If this was so, and if a description of a language was to be preferred over another description of the same language to the extent that it expressed the regularities of the language in a more natural fashion, then it seemed necessary to conclude that the current notational conventions required modification to guarantee the success of any mechanical evaluation metric.

Of course, other conclusions might have been drawn. It might have been questioned, for example, whether a mechanical evaluation procedure was after all a reasonable goal. Or, less radically, whether it was reasonable to expect that one single measure could be used to assign a value to descriptions which would reflect both the degree of 'naturalness' and at the same time the 'linguistically significant generalization' achieved. After all, although we can measure a person's height using a metre rule, we are not inclined to expect that, using that same rule, we can establish his weight, his temperature or the colour of his eyes. It might also have been asked whether it was appropriate for a descriptive framework which was established primarily to handle rule-governed patterning to be expected directly to accomodate naturalness, which is a matter of tendencies rather than rules.

Fortunately, in one sense at least, Chomsky and Halle were not disturbed by any of these questions. For by pursuing their original goal they succeeded in encouraging a fresh interest in those aspects of general phonology which are the concern of all phonologists regardless of their theoretical persuasions—namely, phonological typology and phonological universals.

We noted earlier that it was to the Praguian notion of MARKEDNESS that Chomsky and Halle turned in order to make good what they considered the defects in their descriptive framework. But terms do not survive unchanged in the passage from one theory to another. They are adopted because in some (rather than in all) aspects of their use they provide a new tool or offer a new insight. What was particularly attractive about the terms MARKED and UNMARKED to Chomsky and Halle was, in the first place, the possibility of a simple literal interpretation. UNMARKED could quite literally mean 'not marked', and in the context of the evaluation metric which they had devised, 'not marked' could mean 'not counted'. And secondly, as to the semantics of UNMARKED, it was not a great step from earlier Praguian interpretations such as 'the most common' or 'having the widest distributional range' to the newly required glosses 'expected', 'typical' and 'natural'. Jakobson had already widened the domain of application of such uses from individual languages to language in general. Taken together, then, these two interpretations of UNMARKED as (a) 'uncounted' and (b) 'natural' opened the way for an adaptation of the notational conventions which would automatically lead to natural accounts of language being less costly in terms of symbol counting, and thus more highly valued, than unnatural ones.

But the introduction of the terms MARKED and UNMARKED into a framework in which features are the primes raised difficulties which had not beset the advocates of the phoneme or even those who had thought of the distinction essentially as an ink-saving device. With features as the basic units, it was at once clear that the terms MARKED and UNMARKED could not be used to refer directly and absolutely to phonetic properties. It was clearly not possible to claim, for example, that all feature values formerly noted as PLUS should henceforth be noted as MARKED. Nor was it even possible to claim that the value PLUS for some one feature, say voice, was once and for all marked as against the feature value MINUS. Rather what had to be claimed was that for some feature the value PLUS was marked in some environments (e.g. for voice in combination with [−sonorant]) while in others (e.g. for voice in combination with [+nasal]) the marked value of that same feature was MINUS. Markedness of phonetic features was, in other words, patently context-sensitive, and if the evaluation metric required features to be assigned the values MARKED and UNMARKED, then clearly a set of general rules or conventions of some sort was also required as part of the theory to relate such assignments to the polar phonetic values identified by PLUS or MINUS. Chomsky and Halle's own contribution to this task was the sketch of universal marking conventions which forms the conclusion to *The sound pattern of English*.

Since this book, interest in mechanical evaluation procedures has waned. But the substantial question which motivated the attempt to construct a set of marking conventions remains, viz. under what conditions is a given value of a phonetic feature most (or least) likely to occur? Answers to this question continue to be sought not only by advocates of markedness (both within and without the standard generative camp) but also by members of the various splinter groups which emerged as the standard framework was challenged.

One of the most interesting deviations from the standard position, though still clearly within the framework of markedness, can be found in the work of Gamkrelidze. In a number of recent papers (e.g. 1975, 1979), Gamkrelidze has been investigating and clarifying the pattern of marking in stop and fricative systems, basing his account on a wide-ranging survey of languages. And in doing this, he appears at first glance to have neatly sidestepped the problem of the context-sensitivity of marking assignments. For although he insists on the primacy of features as phonological units, Gamkrelidze claims that, as far as the features of a segment are concerned, if any one feature is marked then all other features of that segment are also marked; or, to put it differently, markedness is—as it was for the Praguians—primarily a property of segments as wholes and of features only indirectly. Thus, on the basis of Gamkrelidze's survey, although we cannot say that [+voice] is marked in absolute terms, we can say that [+voice] is marked along with all other features in the combination [+velar, +stop, +voice]—or, more simply, that the bundle of features which we identify conventionally as /g/ is marked as a unit. In this way Gamkrelidze is able to base his investigations of markedness within phonological systems to all intents and purposes on the phoneme, and is able to present the results of these investigations with admirable force and concision in tables such as Table 7.1 in which the arrows point from the most- to the least-marked segments (or, to use his more recent terminology, from RECESSIVE to DOMINANT units in the system). Markedness, it is to be noted, has become in this scheme not merely a property of the segment but also a matter of degree.

There is no denying the interest of these results, nor the strength of the evidence on which they are based, but the context-dependency of markedness unfortunately does not disappear as soon as we declare

Table 7.1 Marking relations in stops
following Gamkrelidze.

p	→	t	→	k
b	←	d	←	g

markedness to be a property of segments as wholes. The reason is not hard
to see. In assigning a relative markedness value to a particular segment
type we say, of course, that we are predicting the likelihood of such a
segment 'occurring' in a language. But left unqualified this notion of
'occurrence' is very vague. What we find in the course of analysing a
number of languages is that the likelihood of a segment occurring as a
contrastive unit in a phonological system (or as an element in a sample of
running speech) can indeed be related to the phonetic features which
characterize it. But the likelihood of finding such a segment depends also,
on closer inspection, on where within the structure of words (or within the
stream of speech) we choose to look. The segment types we are most likely
to find at the beginnings of utterances are quite different, for example,
from those which we typically find at the ends. The likelihood of
occurrence of a segment is, in detail, as much a function of position as of
composition.

This aspect of the subject has unfortunately received comparatively little
coverage, particularly in the generative camp, by those who have adopted
markedness as their approach. The evidence for marking assignments has
commonly been drawn from comparative studies of phonological systems
set up in monosystemic fashion for languages as wholes, or from surveys of
linguistic change (and acquisition) in which the syntagmatic context is quite
often ignored, or (more rarely) from simple overall frequency counts of
vocabularies or texts. Gamkrelidze does, to be fair, mention that markedness of feature values depends on the sequential as well as the
simultaneous context, but no examples of this type of dependency figure in
his results. Table 7.1 ignores sequential context. Chomsky and Halle, also
to be fair, do recognize in their general discussion (1968, 412) the effect of
the sequential environment in determining marking, but in their sketch of
marking conventions they pay the point little attention beyond covering
such gross phonotactic tendencies as the dominance of CV syllable
structuring. Indeed, relying purely on the type of evidence we have just
mentioned, they are quite ready without more ado to commit themselves
to absolute markedness values for nasals,. They consider it a fact 'that the
unmarked nasal must be /n/' (*ibid.*, 413). As we shall see, an analysis of the
phonotactics of a variety of languages makes it clear that, as far as nasals
are concerned, such a once-and-for-all labelling grossly oversimplifies the
relationship between the differently articulated members of this series. The
'fact' so readily accepted is no more than a half-truth.

Perhaps the standard generative phonologists' lack of interest in
syntagmatic phonological structuring (inherited from their phonemic
predecessors) is in part to blame for this restriction of the field of enquiry
to the segment and the paradigmatic system, and perhaps it is an innate
dislike of probabilities rather than rules which has led in methodology to

the avoidance of statistical data. Greenberg (1965, 1966), who has paid considerable attention to frequency data and to phonotactic universals, stands aside from the mainstream, despite his use of markedness terminology, as if to prove the point. Whatever the reason, this neglect constitutes a clear weakness in the standard approach to naturalness.

Strength

Rather than rectify these omissions, it is possible, of course, to take a more radical view of the situation. From the fact (which we have seen conceded though little exploited) that markedness is not a property which we can assign absolutely to phonetic features, nor even to particular simultaneous complexes of features (i.e. segments), it is clearly possible to conclude, for example, that markedness is shown in this way to be merely an observational notion, and that our attention should in fact be directed towards establishing the *constants* which conspire to regulate the occurrence of particular phonetic features in particular environments.

Now while it may not be perhaps entirely accurate historically, it is with hindsight useful to consider the notions of PHONOLOGICAL SCALE or PHONOLOGICAL HIERARCHY which a number of phonologists have been developing since the late 1960s as the prime elements in just such an extension of the programme of research. Within this approach (see, for example, Foley (1977), Hooper (1976) and Vennemann (1972)), phonological units—regularly segments or segment classes—are considered to be arrayed on some scale, generally called STRENGTH. The behaviour of particular segments in diachronic or synchronic processes is then claimed to be simply derivable from their rank on the scale. For instance, the observation that, in the historical development of Spanish, voiced velar stops spirantize (or open) to a greater extent than voiced labials, would be said to be accounted for by /g/ being assigned a lower rank on the strength scale (i.e. being 'weaker') than /b/, given that spirantization and effacement can reasonably be said to be a case of weakening, and that weak segments are more likely to weaken than strong. It goes without saying, of course, that unless the postulated strength scale can be shown to be universal, such a statement is quite empty. For this reason, Foley's strength scale for stops, which we present in Table 7.2, is shown in his discussion to be supported by the occurrence of parallel phonological processes in a number of languages.

Before we look more closely at the way in which such strength scales are relevant to statements of distribution, it is difficult to ignore the obvious similarities between Gamkrelidze's diagram of the marking relationships in stop systems (Table 7.1) and the strength scale for stops proposed by Foley (Table 7.2). In fact, one might be forgiven for supposing, at first, that any choice we might make between the two apparently competing approaches would be more a choice of terminology than of substance. Such a confusion is not surprising, since Gamkrelidze establishes patterns of marking in abstraction from the sequential context, and thus a segment can, it seems, be said to be MARKED (expected, natural) in just the same way as a segment can be said to be STRONG. However, the likelihood of a segment occurring

Table 7.2 A strength scale for stops
following Foley.

b	d	g

(and hence its markedness value) is found to vary, as we noted earlier, as
the environment varies, while by contrast the strength of a segment in
relation to others in the system is held to be constant no matter what the
environment. In more detailed analyses, as we shall have occasion to note,
the treatment of stops and other segment types would very clearly diverge.
The similarity is thus deceptive and the choice is real. The precise terms
used in the two schools are in fact quite appropriately suggestive of the
different aims and methods. STRENGTH seeks to be explanatory, while
MARKED, NATURAL, EXPECTED and even Gamkrelidze's more recent DOMI-
NANT and RECESSIVE are essentially descriptive terms.

In these circumstances, then, if it can be shown, as some members of the
strength school propose, that the likelihood of a phonological unit
occurring in some context is automatically derivable from its position on
some scale called STRENGTH—i.e. if given a strength scale and also some
universally established characterization of structural positions, it is possible
to determine mechanically on the basis of these constants the relative
probability of any segment occurring in any position—then clearly the
strength-scale approach can legitimately claim, as far as phonotactics is
concerned, to be more fundamentally directed towards explanation and
thus to offer the more comprehensive theory, in that the terms MARKED and
UNMARKED can be simply absorbed. After all, outside the context of the
evaluation metric, these terms are no more than convenient abbreviations
for 'unlikely (or likely) to occur'.

But before opting for strength, it has to be said that this purportedly
explanatory notion is by no means uncontroversial, and one or two
questions concerning interpretation and method are certainly in order. Just
what—we might ask—is strength? Is there only one such scale for
segments and how is a scale established? How, and in how many ways, do
we characterize positions in phonological structure?

As to the *content* of the term STRENGTH, the obvious assumption would
be that such scales are simply phonetic parameters. Indeed, the gross
character of the strength scale suggested by Hooper (1972), amongst
others, in which segments are ranked from obstruent through nasal, liquid
and glide to vowel, related obviously to a traditional phonetic parameter,
and it is difficult to doubt that it was the realization that such a phonetic
parameter correlated to some degree with patterns of distribution, as
de Saussure (1916) had observed, which motivated early work in this field.
And even if more detailed investigations tended soon to leave the phonetic
ground—as with Foley (1977), who combines a productive interest in
strength scales with a desire to divorce phonology from phonetics which is
hard to comprehend—the phonologist must surely work on the assumption
that an explanation for the patterning which he finds will be discovered in
the articulatory and perceptual properties of the sounds concerned.
Languages (individually) may have crazy rules, but the idea that language

(universally) should exhibit phonetically unprincipled patterning is unten-able. Of course, more detailed scales established by reference to phonological patterning have turned out not to relate in a simple fashion to any single phonetic parameter. They are, on that account, no less real nor any less a matter for phonetic explanation, as some would suggest. No one would doubt that the ability of organisms to survive in desert environments is a matter for biological explanation even if different organisms achieve this end by different means.

As far as the *number* of scales is concerned, it seems, on the face of it, improbable that with only one strength scale (or one system of interrelated strength scales) we can handle every type of phonological patterning. But we are interested particularly in distributional patterning. Whether the data adduced in support of strength scales, or explained by reference to them, is synchronic or diachronic, the patterning is always ultimately (even if not explicitly or overtly) a matter of occurrence of sounds in environments—a matter of phonotactics. To that extent, the parallel with the occurrence—i.e. survivability—of biological organisms in geographi-cally characterized environments was quite appropriate. But even granted that our attention is for the moment restricted to patterns of distribution, if we pursue the analogy further we might still suspect that the overall distributional pattern (the raw data) is a complex function of different features of the environment. We might expect in other words that, if we could establish for phonological environments characterizations based on a variety of features comparable (say) to temperature, altitude and humidity, then we would discover an equivalent variety of classifications (or scales) of segments directly related to these features of the environ-ment. To postulate only one scale of segments in terms of strength would seem to imply that there is one (and only one) phonologically relevant characterization of structural positions.

At this stage we should perhaps note that to characterize a position in some relevant fashion is not simply to identify it, as our analogy makes clear. The conventional identification of an environment may indirectly relate to relevant properties of the environment—as latitude, for example, relates to some extent to temperature; but it is just as likely to be no more than a convenient labelling—as is, to take a more local case, the national grid reference of some location. We should be prepared to find that our conventional identifications of phonological environments by reference to positions in a hierarchically structured set of units (syllables, words . . .) or positions within some string of segment types are in the present context also no more than useful labelling systems.

Turning finally to the methodological questions, it is clear that we could proceed in two directions, categorizing segments by their compatibility with given orderings of structural positions, or alternatively categorizing structural positions by their compatibility with some given ordering of segments. That is to say, given the possibility of ranking a set of ENVIRONMENTS with respect to some property, we could establish the relative compatibility of various segments with degrees of that property by examining the relative likelihood of their occurrence, emergence or disappearance in that set of environments. On the other hand, given the possibility of ranking a set of SEGMENTS with respect to some property, we could assess the relative compatibility of various structural positions with degrees of that property by observing the relative likelihood of members of that set of segments occurring (emerging, disappearing) in those positions. In either event we assume that the phonetician would enter the scene in the final stage to tell us precisely what are the characteristics of segments which lead them to be ranked as they are with respect to a particular property of environments, or what precisely are the properties of structural positions which the examination of segment patterning has brought to light. (Naturally, the phonetician might wish to turn this methodology on its head, but we are restricting attention to a phonological approach.)

Although we have just distinguished two techniques, it is obvious that in practice they need not be treated as mutually exclusive. It may be, of course, that one tactic has fewer problems than the other. We might feel, for example, that there is less danger in working from an ordering of segments to the characterization of positions than in proceeding in the opposite direction, given that a useful ordering of segments (even though we may not know in terms of what property) is directly derivable from an examination of the pattern of distribution of segments in some one structural position, whereas orderings of environments are by no means so obviously available. But in principle an attack on both fronts is possible.

Those advocates of strength scales who have shown an interest in predicting distribution from strength have, in fact, tended to work simultaneously in both directions, and for the necessary characterization of structural positions they have turned to an earlier terminology. It was not uncommon—they note—in pre-structural days to refer to syllable- and word-initial positions as 'strong' positions by contrast with syllable- and word-final positions which were termed 'weak'. Now clearly, if it is possible to talk of positions as 'strong' and 'weak', and if linear orderings of segments can be found in these positions, and if, in particular, reversed orderings are found in strong versus weak positions, then it is a short step to propose that the link between segment and position is as common sense might suggest, viz. that it is strong segments which prefer strong positions and weak which prefer weak—in other words that the orderings of segments are orderings in strength. From this point on, in the less clear cases, positions can be identified as 'strong' insofar as strong segments dominate in them, and conversely segments can be identified as 'strong' insofar as they dominate in positions known to be strong (*mutatis mutandis* for 'weak'). The basic proposition will itself be considered to be supported to the extent that the results obtained by this dual approach converge on an overall coherent picture.

The strength school proposes, then, at the most general level that there is a universal strength scale (or perhaps set of related scales) for segments, that there is a universal strength scale also for structural positions, and that patterns of distribution can be derived automatically given some precise version of the rule 'Strong segments dominate in strong positions and weak in weak.' It is in this sense that the approach is concerned with the constants which underly the varying patterns of markedness merely *described* by the other school. (The term MARKED can obviously be applied straightforwardly to strong items in weak positions and weak in strong.)

Position

Unfortunately, within the strength framework, there has been a tendency to confine explicit interest in phonotactics to the domain of the syllable, and in fact more attention has been devoted to the establishment of the details of strength scales for segments than has been spent on the elaboration of comparable scales for structural positions. Coupled with this, in the search for supporting evidence, there has been a tendency, just as in the markedness school, to avoid the statistical analysis of vocabularies or texts (sometimes as a matter of principle).

As some sort of counterbalance to both of these biases, it seems appropriate, in this last section, to examine the possibility of making more systematic use of the relative frequency of occurrence of segments in various environments within texts and vocabularies, as a means of providing more detailed rankings of structural positions than have so far been offered. Since any such relative rankings are interesting to the extent that they are not language specific, this very preliminary exploration of the method is, albeit on a small scale, comparative.

Now, if we are to use the relative frequency of occurrence of segment types as diagnostic of scalar environmental properties, then clearly it is sensible in the first instance to select some segment types which seem noticeably susceptible to positional changes. In this respect nasal consonants appear to be particularly useful. For example, in a paper appearing not long after *The sound pattern of English,* Chen used evidence of sound change in Chinese to draw attention to the reversal of markedness values for nasal (and stop) consonants as we move from initial to final position in syllables, suggesting in fact that we might 'more fully exploit the notion of context-sensitive marking conventions and assign increasingly higher degrees of markedness to syllable initial consonants [p/m, t/n, k/n] in that order, and reverse the markedness scale for the same consonants in syllable-final positions. Such context-sensitive marking conventions would reflect both the relative change resistance and direction of merging of these consonants as manifested in a number of Chinese dialects and other unrelated languages' (1973, 230).

It is, of course, the facts of distribution which interest us here, rather than any particular consequences for marking conventions. And turning from details of linguistic change to an analysis of the frequency of occurrence of nasal consonant types in texts and vocabularies in a number of unrelated languages, we find indeed synchronically a similar pattern to that exposed by Chen. Table 7.3 provides figures for the occurrence of labial and apical nasal consonants in word-initial and word-final position in a Marshallese lexicon (Abo *et al.* 1976) and in sample texts from English, Cambodian (Jacob 1968) and Parji (Burrow and Bhattacharya 1953). It is clear from these figures that, taking both initial and final position together, the apical nasal dominates, hence the unmarked status of /n/ in Chomsky and Halle (1968). But, if word-initial position is taken alone, the labial nasal is obviously the most common ('most expected', 'least marked'), while in word-final position the apical outranks the labial. The frequency of occurrence pattern changes dramatically as we change environments.

Table 7.3 Frequency of occurrence of labial and apical
nasals in word initial and word final positions.

English	194	139	115	255
Cambodian	290	221	143	225
Parji	98	25	15	95
Marshallese	66	15	12	60
	m	n	m	n
		initial		final

(Cf. for a similar variation the root-initial and root-final statistics for nasals in Dixon (1977).)

Some interesting observations and hypotheses could be built even on such simple facts as these. For example, if labial nasals are the most common word-initially, then we would predict that any language with no labial nasals has no nasals at all, or has no nasals word-initially (perhaps has nasals only finally), or has for some reason other than a simple phonetic one no labials at all. Take also a problem of acquisition. While there is an apparent paradox in developmental phonology (on the assumption that unmarked sound types are acquired before marked) if /n/ is once and for all taken as the unmarked nasal, as soon as we have an account which takes note of syntagmatic position the paradox disappears. If the typical syllable (and word) structure in early speech is CV(CV) then the earliest expected nasal would naturally be labial. If we proceed to add to these facts of nasal distribution the further fact that nasals as a class tend to favour final position while stops favour initial position, we can also now see why Gamkrelidze's overall pattern of expectancy for voiced stops would tend to coincide with the initial (i.e. strong position) pattern for stops, and hence why Tables 7.1 and 7.2 above are so similar. By contrast, an overall pattern for nasals would give a picture quite unlike the strong initial pattern, showing the labials as recessive, so that a Gamkrelidze diagram and a strength scale would in this case diverge.

What interests us more particularly at this stage, however, is the possibility that, if the occurrence patterns of /m/ and /n/ differ so markedly in initial and final position, then the pattern of occurrence of these consonants can itself be turned into an indicator in other phonological positions of whatever property is so revealed. To be more precise, the ratio 'frequency n/frequency m' in some position in structure can be taken to provide us with a measure of that structural position with respect to some property, and naturally an ordering of positions so established for one language can in turn be simply checked for cross-linguistic validity. Obviously, there is no necessity at this point to identify the relationship between /m/ and /n/ as being one of strength, nor to consider that the positions ordered by such a measure are ordered in strength. Although perhaps a convenience, such terminology adds nothing to the basic facts.

In order to explore the possibilities of such a method, no more is now needed than to choose some set of readily identifiable positions and some set of texts and/or vocabularies from some reasonably unrelated languages. It should be no surprise that neither of these simple tasks is completely without problems. What follows is therefore no more than a quick tentative step (or stumble) into the dark.

The positions chosen for examination here are word initial (unstressed syllable), word initial (stressed syllable), word internal (unstressed syllable), word internal (stressed syllable) and word final. They will be symbolized respectively as #—V̆ , #—V́ , ..—V̆ , ..—V́ and —#. Given the variety of means of *identifying* (not characterizing) positions, such a choice was to a large extent arbitrary and in the event not ideal, though the intention was that the identification should be straightforward in the languages selected. Some environments were, of course, excluded automatically by the impossibility of nasals occurring in them or by the neutralization of the contrast in them.

Any decision to base the analysis on running texts rather than vocabularies (or vice versa) is difficult to justify, and no doubt analyses of both the total lexical stock and running texts are relevant in different ways. But if the assumption is that the frequency patterns found tend primarily to reflect the compatibility of the phonetic properties of segments with properties of positions in structure, then it is perhaps more natural to select texts, since presumably the words occurring most frequently in texts are likely to be those which exhibit best the relationship between segment and position. In this pilot study, it was therefore intended that texts should provide the basic source material. But it was quickly apparent that in the absence of a more refined treatment of stress there were in fact problems in distinguishing the positions #—V̆ and #—V́ in the case of monosyllabic, especially grammatical, words. Since most vocabularies, aside from those dictionaries which aim at complete coverage, represent only a selection of the word stock of the language concerned, and since such selections (even if not explicitly) are largely determined by frequency considerations, it seemed in the circumstances appropriate to attempt a second trial using a number of short vocabularies, and as a further precaution to restrict attention entirely to polysyllables. The lexical figures provided below are to that extent less infected by perhaps arbitrary analytical decisions.

The text data for English and Catalan was based on random extracts from modern detective novels, for Arabic on selected conversations from Mitchell (1956) and for Aymara on the texts in Tschopik (1948). As the survey was purely exploratory, no attempt was made to standardize the length of the texts used. Analysis was simply continued until it seemed clear that a stable pattern had emerged or, in the case of Aymara, until the materials were exhausted. The vocabulary data for Catalan were derived from the frequency-based basic vocabulary in Llobera i Ramon (1968), for Welsh from the glossary in Jones (1926) supplemented for initial positions by the Collins-Spurrell Welsh Dictionary, and for Arabic from Mitchell (1956). Figures for English were abstracted from Trnka (1966), whose analysis is based on the Pocket Oxford Dictionary of Current English. The results of the analyses are tabulated below in Table 7.4 (text data) and Table 7.5 (lexical data).

On the basis of this analysis, it does seem possible to conclude that an ordering can be established for the selected structural positions which holds constant over the languages examined. The ordering of the columns

Table 7.4 Ratio n/m in running texts

English	0	0.73	0.79	1.5	2.2
Arabic	0.25	0.27	0.55	1.75	2.4
Catalan	0.1	0.7	1.44	2.2	3.4
Aymara	0.44	1.5	2.92	2.91	α
	#—V̆	#—V́	..—V̆	..—V̆	—#

Table 7.5 Ratio n/m in lexical data: polysyllables only.

English	0	0.36	0.54	1.26	5.28
Arabic	0.1	0.42	1.15	1.3	1.6
Catalan	0.29	0.34	1.0	1.31	3.8
Welsh	0.17	0.28	1.1	6.45	15.25
	#—V̆	#—V́	..—V́	..—V̆	—#

in Tables 7.4 and 7.5 has been arranged in fact to correspond to just this ranking of positions. The ratio n/m increases consistently as we move from #—V̆ through #—V́, ..—V̆ to —#. But before we hasten to track down the nearest phonetician (or change hats), two *caveats* at least are in order. *Caveat 1.* There is clearly no guarantee that such an ordering of positions is anything more than a reflection of the degree of compatibility of the given positions with the segment /m/ versus the segment /n/. This in itself is, of course, by no means uninteresting if the scale is universal, but it would naturally be rather more interesting if we could establish which particular features or combinations of features of these consonants are responsible for the distribution—or, to put it differently, whether precisely the same ordering of positions would be revealed using other pairs of segments. For this, the same or a similar procedure should be repeated with the necessary variations. In the meantime we might note that a closer inspection of the Marshallese nasal figures, provided in Table 7.3, is perhaps suggestive. The nasals in this language are usually in fact further distinguished as 'dark' and 'light' and it turns out that not only do the labials tend to 'dark' and the dentals by contrast to 'light' but also the proportion of 'dark' as against 'light' dentals is higher initially than finally.

Caveat 2. There is no guarantee that the ordering of positions is an ordering with respect to just one property, just as there is no guarantee that if a number of steps on a cliff are ordered in height they are necessarily members of the same flight. It is quite conceivable that the distribution of the nasals in one of these environments is determined by a quite different property of the environment (reacting to quite different distinguishing properties of the nasals) from that which determines their distribution in some other environment.

We can, perhaps, despite these uncertainties, reach two reasonably safe conclusions. Firstly, we noted earlier that as far as segments were concerned both MARKEDNESS and STRENGTH were scalar rather than polar properties. We do not say of segments that they are 'marked' or 'strong' but rather that they are 'more' or 'less' marked or 'more' or 'less' strong. Now, whether or not the details of the ranking of structural positions found here will survive a larger-scale study, it does seem clear enough that properties of positions are no less scalar than those of segments. With respect to the distribution of /m/ and /n/, positions in structure cannot be said simply to favour one or the other segment, rather one or the other segment is favoured to a certain degree. The frequency data provided in N'Diaye (1970), though related to differently identified structural positions and not introduced for such a purpose, would also support this view. Secondly, it seems also clear enough that in examining natural patterns of distribution, our horizons must extend beyond the syllable. The compatibility of a particular syllabic position with /m/ rather than /n/ is itself not absolute but depends in turn on the position of the syllable in the larger structure. It is obviously no less clear that to tease out with more certainty the details of these scalar properties of structural positions, a great deal more data and investigation are required.

It was fashionable in the 1960s and 1970s to claim that linguistics suffered not from lack of data but from a lack of theory capable of handling the rich supply of data already available. Of course, it is inevitable that there will always be data which evade the current theoretical grasp, and in that sense we will always have too much. But it is equally obvious that there will always be areas in which our needs by far outstrip the supply, and in that sense the data we have will always be too little. To those interested in the relationship between phonetic features and structural positions—a group which must include proponents of both markedness and strength—it should be painfully obvious that in this area statistical data in particular are minimal. We have suffered in this case not so much from lack of data as from positive disinterest. Perhaps it is time to make amends. This too would raise a smile in Prague.

References

Abo, T., Bender, B.W., Capelle, A. and De Brum, T. 1976: *Marshallese-English dictionary*. Honolulu: University of Hawaii Press.

Burrow, T. and Bhattacharya, S. 1953: *The Parji language*. Hertford: Austin.

Chen, M. 1973: On the formal expression of natural rules in phonology. *JL* **9,** 223–49.

Chomsky, N. and Halle, M. 1968: *The sound pattern of English*. New York: Harper & Row.

Dixon, R.M.W. 1977: *A grammar of Yidiɲ*. Cambridge: Cambridge University Press.

Foley, J. 1977: *Foundations of theoretical phonology*. Cambridge: Cambridge University Press.

Gamkrelidze, T.V. 1975: On the correlation of stops and fricatives in a phonological system. *Lingua* **35,** 231–61.

———1979: Hierarchical relations among phonemic units as phonological universals. *Proc. 9th Int. Cong. Phon. Sci.* **II,** 9–15.

Greenberg, J. 1965: Some generalizations concerning initial and final consonant sequences. *Linguistics* **18,** 5–34.

————1966: *Language universals*. The Hague: Mouton. Also in T. Sebeok 1966 (ed.): *Current trends in linguistics* **3** (The Hague: Mouton, 1966).

Hooper, J.B. 1976: *An introduction to natural generative phonology*. New York: Academic Press.

Jacob, J.M. 1968: *Introduction to Cambodian*. London: Oxford University Press.

Jones, S. 1926: *A Welsh phonetic reader*. London: University of London Press.

Llobera i Ramon, J. 1968: *El català bàsic*. Barcelona: Teide.

Mitchell, T.F. 1956: *An introduction to Egyptian colloquial Arabic*. Oxford: Clarendon Press.

N'Diaye, G. 1970: *Structure du dialecte basque de Maya*. The Hague: Mouton.

Postal, P. 1968: *Aspects of phonological theory*. New York: Harper & Row.

Saussure, F. de 1916: *Cours de linguistique générale*. Paris: Payot.

Trnka, B. 1966: *A phonological analysis of present-day standard English*. Tokyo: Hokuou Publishing Company.

Tschopik, H. 1948: Aymara texts: Lupaca dialect. *IJAL* **14**, 108–14.

Vennemann, T. 1972: On the theory of syllabic phonology. *Linguistische Berichte* **18**, 1–18.

8

Constraints on rules of grammar as universals

Irene Philippaki Warburton

One of the most persistent controversies in linguistics has been the issue of UNIVERSALS. The two poles of this controversy can be exemplified by on the one hand Joos's (1957, 96) often-quoted statement, 'languages can differ from each other without limit and in unpredictable ways', and on the other by Chomsky's (1965, 30), 'The existence of deep seated formal universals, . . . implies that all languages are cut to the same pattern'.

Although on the face of it these two positions seem diametrically opposite to each other, one can, in fact, accept them both. Thus we can say that languages have some basic characteristics in common but they differ greatly in their details. The controversy would thus appear as one of terminology or of emphasis rather than one of substance. The dispute however, has acquired both substance and importance since 1957 within the tradition which started with Chomsky, and which is continued just as vigorously today through him and his students. They claim that the study of linguistic theory will contribute to the understanding of the human mental processes, because according to Chomsky (1965, 51): *'the form of a language,* the schema for its grammar, is to a large extent given'. This is, of course, a very strong claim whose credibility depends wholly on the degree to which the proposed universals are (*a*) restrictive enough so as to reduce the number of conceivable natural languages and (*b*) explicit enough to be refutable by evidence from a variety of languages.

In the last 20 years various proposals have been put forward as to what constitutes universals, but without much success. Since Chomsky (1973), the universals have taken the form of conditions on the form and function of the rules of grammar. My purpose in this paper is to consider some of the conditions proposed and to examine whether or not they are supported by evidence from Modern Greek (MG). I will be concerned mainly with the so called TENSED-S condition first proposed in 1973. It was modified and renamed PIC (Propositional Island Constraint) in Chomsky and Lasnik

95

(1977) and more recently (Chomsky 1980) it was reformulated as NIC (Nominative Island Constraint).

The earlier formulation of this condition is as follows: 'No rule can involve X, Y in the structure: . . . X . . . [α . . . Y . . .] where α is a tensed sentence' (Chomsky 1973, 238).

This condition was intended to do two things: (*i*) to prevent a transformation from either raising item Y to position X or lowering item X to position Y if α was a tensed clause, and (*ii*) to prevent an interpretive rule of anaphora from relating X and Y if Y was inside a tensed clause. Thus the Tensed-S condition had a function in both the transformational and the semantic component. The following example, which also appears in Chomsky (1973, 237), illustrates its application to a transformational raising rule:

(1)   I believe the dog is hungry.
(2)   I believe the dog to be hungry.
*(3)   The dog is believed is hungry.
(4)   The dog is believed to be hungry.

The difference between *(3) and (4) is that the former involves movement of the NP *the dog* out of a finite (tensed) clause, thus violating the Tensed-S condition, while the latter does not. I have presented this example to illustrate the condition because it is closely related to the MG cases I will consider. Examples of the application of this condition to lowering transformational rules as well as to interpretive rules of anaphora can be found in Chomsky (1973, 1975, 1977 and elsewhere).

The universality of the Tensed-S condition is put into doubt by evidence from MG. Consider the following examples:

(5)   perimenun   to jani.
      are-expecting-they   the-acc John-acc
      'They are expecting John.'

(6)   perimenun   na fiɣi o janis.
      are-expecting-they   that leaves the-nom John-nom
      'They are expecting that John will leave.'

(7)   perimenun   to jani   na fiɣi.
      are-expecting-they   the-acc John-acc   that leaves
      'They are expecting John to leave.'

(8)   kserun   to jani.
      know-they   the-acc John-acc
      'They know John.'

(9)   kserun   pos lei psemata o janis.
      know-they   that tells lies the-nom John-nom
      'They know that John lies.'

(10) kserun   to jani   pos lei psemata.
      know-they   the-acc John-acc   that tells lies
      'They know John that he lies.'

The verbs *perimeno* and *ksero* can be followed either by a direct object (*DO*) NP as in (5) and (8), or by an object complement clause as in (6) and

(9). The complement clause after *perimeno* is introduced by the morpheme *na*[1] whereas that following *ksero* is introduced by the complementizer *pos*, which in this environment is equivalent to the English complementizer *that*. MG complement clauses differ from English complement clauses in one important respect: whereas in English there is a formal distinction between finite (tensed) and non-finite (non-tensed) clauses, in MG all clauses including all complement clauses are finite (tensed). Thus the verbs in both *na* and *pos* clauses can show morphological differences corresponding to tense differences although the choice of tense in a *na* clause is restricted by the tense of the higher verb, but not determined by it.

The structures which we will be concerned with are those of (7) and (10). Our first observation about them is that the NP *to jani* which follows the main verb has all the characteristics of a DO. It is marked with accusative case like all DOs and furthermore it can be accompanied by its clitic pronoun as is shown in (11) and (12):

(11) ton perimenun   to jani   na fiyi.
      him are-expecting-they the-acc John-acc that leaves-he
      'Him they are expecting John to leave.'

(12) ton kserun   to jani   pos lei psemata.
      him know-they   the-acc John-acc that tells lies
      'Him they know John that he lies.'

In (11) and (12), *ton* is a clitic pronoun agreeing in number, case and gender with the DO *to jani* to which it refers. Furthermore, since clitic pronouns are proclitic to the governing verb, the NP *to jani* is not only a DO but a DO of the main verb. However, there is another aspect of the sentences (7) and (10) which is in opposition to this conclusion. (7) and (10) are semantically similar to (6) and (9) respectively. In both (6) and (7) the subjects of the main clause expect something to happen, and in both (9) and (10) the subject of the higher verb knows that something is the case. To put it in another way the NP *to jani*, in spite of its DO characteristics, is understood as the subject of the subordinate verb. Furthermore, it is understood as having the thematic function of agent in the complement clause. This thematic function can be accounted for only if we consider it to be the subject of the embedded verb in the deep structure (Chomsky 1977, 84; Chomsky and Lasnik 1977, 428–9), whereas its DO syntactic characteristics can be accounted for if we assume that structures (7) and (10) have been derived transformationally via a subject-to-object raising rule. Further evidence for this interpretation is provided by other similar paradigms:

(13) fovume   to jani.
      fear-I   the-acc John-acc
      'I ⎰ fear   ⎱ John.'
        ⎱ am afraid of ⎰

---

[1] In Warburton and Christides (forthcoming) it is argued that *na* is not a complementizer in MG but a modality marker, and that complement clauses introduced with *na* have a zero complementizer.

(14) fovume   pos θa mas γelasi o janis.
      fear-I   that will us cheat the-nom John-nom
      'I fear that John will cheat us.'

(15) (ton) fovume   to jani   pos θa mas γelasi.
      (him) fear-I   the-acc John-acc that will us cheat-he
      'Him I fear John that he will cheat us.'

In (13) the NP to *jani* has the thematic function of CAUSE or SOURCE since it is the DO of a verb of fear. In (14) the NP *o janis* has the thematic function of AGENT, since it is the animate subject of an action verb. In (15), however, the NP *to jani* is both the agent of the embedded verb and the cause or source of fear of the main verb. Sentence (15) therefore indicates that the NP *to jani* constitutes a blend of the thematic properties of structures (13) and (14). This functional blending can be accounted for if we assume that (14) is the deep structure (DS) source of (15). Semantic rules which now apply to the surface structures where traces (t) mark the DS position of a moved element can assign to the NP *to jani* both its AGENT function (from the position of its trace) and its SOURCE or CAUSE function, from its surface structure status as a DO of the main verb.

Another argument which suggests that (7), (10) and (15) are transformationally derived rather than base-generated is the following. Sentences (16) and•(17) are base-generated structures:

(16) episan   to jani   na fiγi.
      persuaded-they   the-acc John-acc that leaves-he
      'They persuaded John to leave.'

(17) episan   to jani   pos lei psemata.
      persuaded-they   the-acc John-acc that tells-he[2] lies
      'They persuaded John that he lies.'

Sentences (7), (10) and (15) are superficially the same as those in (16) and (17). However, there are important differences between the two sets as can be seen by forming the cleft sentences corresponding to them. Compare (18)–(21) to (22)–(25):

(18) afto pu perimenun   ine   na fiγi o janis.
      that which they-expect is   that leaves John
      'What they are expecting is for John to leave.'

(19) afto pu kserun   ine   pos lei psemata o janis.
      that which they-know   is   that tells lies John
      'What they know is that John lies.'

*(20) afto pu perimenun   *to jani*   ine   na fiγi.
       that which they-expect John-acc   is   to leave

*(21) afto pu kserun   *to jani*   ine   pos lei psemata.
       that which they-know   John-acc   is   that tells he lies

In the cleft sentences corresponding to (7) and (10), the NP *to jani* cannot appear in main clause DO position—only in the subject position of the

2 Where the *he* could be either *o janis* or someone else.

embedded clause. This suggests that it is not really a true, deep structure object of these verbs. Consider now the following:

(22) afto pu episan   *to jani*   ine   na fiɣi.
      that which they-persuaded the-acc John-acc is   to leave
      'What they persuaded John is to leave.'

(23) afto pu episan   *to jani*   ine   pos lei psemata.
      that which they-persuaded the-acc John-acc is   that he-lies
      'What they persuaded John is that he lies.'

*(24) afto pu episan   ine   na fiɣi o janis.
      that which they-persuaded   is   to leave the-nom John-nom

*(25) afto pu episan   ine   pos lei psemata o janis.
      that which they-persuaded   is   that tells lies the-nom John-nom

Unlike the clefts of (7) and (10) those of (16) and (17) must have the NP *to jani* in main clause DO position.

The above discussion of the characteristics of sentences like (7) (10) and (15) reinforces the hypothesis that they are derived transformationally from (6) (9) and (14) respectively via a rule of subject-to-object raising. However, such a solution would violate the Tensed-S condition, since the movement of the embedded subject NP will have to take place out of a tensed clause. We are faced, therefore, with a conflict: either the raising analysis is wrong or the Tensed-S condition is contradicted by MG and must, therefore, be rejected as a universal.

Chomsky (1976, 316 fn.) adds a proviso to the Tensed-S condition, which might at first sight be thought to resolve our conflict. He says: 'it might be that the condition holds for α finite only in languages that distinguish finite from infinitive complements.' MG is said to have lost the category infinitive and, as our examples show, all complement clauses are finite. Therefore, perhaps, MG is immune to the Tensed-S condition. Consequently we can retain both the raising analysis and the Tensed-S condition as universal, but for languages other than those like MG.

This conclusion is not satisfactory for the following reasons.

(*a*) A universal which defines 'islands' (clauses out of which elements cannot escape) in terms of the category of tense should be making the opposite prediction for a language like MG. Since all complement clauses contain tense it should be the case that all complement clauses in MG are islands. Instead, Chomsky's proviso seems to be saying, at the worst, the opposite—i.e. that there are no islands in a language when all clauses have tense—or, at best, that the purported universal makes no prediction at all about such languages.

(*b*) The proviso is contradicted by evidence from Classical Greek, where there is a clear distinction between finite and non-finite clauses and where we find structures similar to those of (7) (10) and (15). The following examples are from Jannaris (1897, 452) (my transliteration):

(26) Soph. Ai 118
      Horās Odysseu, *tēn tōn theōn ischȳn, hosē* (estin)
      You-see Odysseus the-acc of the gods power-acc, how-great-nom (it is)

The accusative *tēn ischȳn* appears as the DO of the main verb *horās* but it is understood as the subject of the indirect question starting with *hosē*.

(27)   Isocr. 4, 78
   Tous nomous eskopoun hopōs akribōs kai kalōs heksousin.
   The-acc laws-acc I-saw that accurately and well they-are-held

In this example, the underlined NP *tous nomous* is in the accusative and ıs the DO of the main verb *eskopoun* ('see to it that'), while it is understood as the missing subject of the complement clause verb, i.e. *heksousin*. Sentences like (26) and (27) have been described by traditional grammarians as involving PROLEPSIS (anticipation) and have been attributed to attraction of the lower subject by the higher verb, rendering it DO on the matrix.

I conclude from this that Chomsky's proviso is both counterintuitive and contradicted by evidence from Classical Greek, and consequently we are still faced with the dilemma created between accepting the raising analysis for the MG data and rejecting the universality of the Tensed-S condition or vice-versa. However, since the Tensed-S condition was modified in subsequent work we must consider it in the new formulations.

In Chomsky (1977) the Tensed-S condition was named PIC (Propositional Island Constraint) and it was modified in two respects. Firstly it and its complementary Specified Subject Constraint (SSC) no longer apply to constrain transformations. Transformations, in fact, apply freely, but movement transformations leave a trace (t) in the position out of which an item has been moved. The constraints PIC and SSC apply at the semantic level—more specifically they constrain rules of construal whose function is to bind anaphors to their antecedents. According to PIC, an anaphoric element including trace, if it is located inside a Propositional Island (previously Tensed-clause), cannot be properly bound to an item outside the island. A not-properly-bound trace creates an ungrammatical sentence. In this manner, a structure which was created by a transformation which moved an item out of a tensed clause leaving a trace behind will violate PIC at the level of construal and it will be filtered out.

Another aspect in which PIC differs from its predecessor Tensed-S condition is that, whereas in the latter the α of its environment was defined in terms of the category tense, in the case of PIC what constitutes an island can be defined differently in various languages (Chomsky 1977, 75). Thus formulated, PIC can now cover the case of Korean reported in Kim (1976) and discussed in Chomsky (1977, 75). Korean does not draw a formal distinction between finite and non-finite clauses, and all clauses are islands with the exception of the complement clauses of certain assertive predicates. In Korean, then, Propositional Island or the α of PIC is defined in terms of these assertive higher verbs.

Perhaps we can consider a similar solution for MG. Here too all complement clauses are finite, and in general they are all islands, with the exception of the complement clauses of verbs such as *θelo* ('want'), *perimeno* ('expect'), *ksero* ('know'), *forume* ('fear'), *vlepo* ('see'), *fantazome* ('imagine'), etc. As in Korean, we can define island as any complement clause except those following the relevant verbs. In this way we could perhaps now adopt the raising analysis without rejecting PIC.

However, this solution too is unsatisfactory because in the MG case at least, PIC becomes completely circular. Notice that the verbs that define a non-island do not belong to an independently definable class either syntactically or semantically. Thus *θelo* takes a *na, perimeno* both a *na* and a *pos,* and the raising *forume* only a *pos* complement clause. *θelo* and *perimeno* with *na* are non-assertive, whereas *ksero* and *fantazome* with *pos* are weak-assertive. Therefore, it would seem that the only characteristic that they have in common is the hypothesis that their complements are not islands. Now if what constitutes an island is defined by inspecting which clauses behave as islands, the concept Propositional Island is not an empirical one, and consequently cannot be entertained as a possible universal.[3]

This potential circularity of PIC has been avoided by the more recent formulation of this condition, namely NIC (Nominative Island Constraint) discussed in Chomsky (1980, 36). NIC is stated thus: 'A nominative anaphor cannot be free in S̄.' Nominative is the case assigned to the subject of a tensed clause; therefore if an anaphoric element like PRO, trace, and others constitute the subject of a finite sentence, then NIC stipulates that they cannot be properly bound to antecedents outside this clause. The result of the failure of a construal rule to bind a nominative anaphor is an ungrammatical string which is filtered out.

Let us now return to the MG sentences (7) (10) and (15). If we propose a raising analysis, their DSs will be something like (6) (9) and (14) respectively, where the NP *o janis* is the subject of the complement clause. As this clause is tensed, its subject will be assigned nominative case, and when the subject-to-object rule applies, the trace that it will leave behind will inherit the nominative case. At the level of rules of construal, this trace will constitute a nominative anaphor which should but cannot be properly bound to its antecedent since the latter is outside the S̄ of the nominative trace. This trace will be free in S̄, and therefore the structure will be considered ungrammatical by NIC.

We see, therefore, that NIC and a raising analysis for the MG data are incompatible and, therefore, we are still faced with the same dilemma. Either the raising analysis is wrong or MG provides a counter example for the universality of NIC. Before we reject NIC as universal we should perhaps try to explore alternative (non-raising) analyses for our data.

One possibility is to adopt a solution which assumes that structures like (7) (10) and (15) are not transformationally derived but base-generated. Under this interpretation we would still require some rule which will account for the identity between the matrix DO *to jani* and the missing (or null) subject of the complement clause. Our first step towards this will be to decide on the formal status of the missing element.

There are three types of null anaphoric elements in complement subject position: trace, PRO, and PRO-self. Trace is produced by a movement rule,

---

[3] See also Bach's (1977) comments on the circularity of PIC.

which we have considered earlier but rejected because such a solution will violate NIC. Therefore we may now explore the possibility whether the missing subject is either a PRO or a PRO-self. The difference between these two elements, in the specific context of subject of a complement clause is that PRO is used after main verbs of obligatory subject or object control (see e.g. Chomsky & Lasnik 1977, 433–40). For example, the English verb *try* is a subject control verb because it requires that the subject of its complement clause be identical to the matrix subject; *force*, on the other hand, is an object control verb since it requires that the subject of its complement clause be identical to its DO. Thus, complement clauses whose subjects are controlled have a PRO in subject position. PRO-self, on the other hand is the subject of a complement clause which is not controlled by the matrix verb. An example of a non-control verb is *want*, whose complement subject need not be identical to its subject. PRO-self is used in cases where, not by necessity but by coincidence, the subject of *want* is identical to the subject of the complement. PRO-self therefore marks the site of traditional Equi-NP structures.

One aspect of the MG examples that might justify the use of PRO in their complement subject position is the fact that the identity of the matrix DO and the missing subject is obligatory. Sentences like the following are not possible:

*(28)   perimenun   to jani na fiɣi i maria.
        They-are-expecting John   that leaves Mary

*(29)   kserun   to jani pos lei psemata i maria.
        they-know   John   that tells lies Mary

However, other main verbs which can take both a DO and a complement clause do not necessarily require this identitiy of matrix DO to complement subject. Consider (30) and (31):

(30)   episan   to jani pos lei psemata i maria.
       they persuaded   John   that tells lies Mary
       'They persuaded John that Mary lies.'

(31)   episan   to jani   na fiɣi i maria.
       they-persuaded   John   that leaves Mary
       'They persuaded John that Mary (should) leave.'

The object control property of structures (7) (10) and (15) can be captured by the use of PRO. But this solution also runs into problems. Firstly, a PRO is said to be the subject of non-finite clauses, and our complement clauses are finite. Secondly, a control verb must be marked in the lexicon as such. This means that we must mark verbs such as *θelo, ksero, perimeno, fovume*, etc. as [+ CONTROL]. But this is wrong, because when these verbs are followed only by a complement clause as in (6), (9) and (14) they must be marked as [− CONTROL] since they do not impose any restriction on their embedded subject. Furthermore, their exercising control on the embedded subject when they are followed by a DO cannot be attributed to a general property of all verbs that take NP DO along with a complement clause, as our examples (30) and (31) show. It would seem, therefore, that the generalization for these verbs is that they are

[− CONTROL] but that they become [+ OBJECT CONTROL] if in the syntactic context [− NP S]. Their control property seems to be derived rather than basic. Thirdly, PRO is an anaphor, like trace, and it must be properly bound by a rule of construal. Since its antecedent is outside its own clause and since its own clause is a tensed clause, NIC will prevent this binding, leaving PRO a nominative anaphor free in its S̄. Therefore, our result again will be an ungrammatical structure.

Let us now consider the possibility of interpreting the embedded missing subject as a PRO-self, i.e. interpret our complement clauses as cases of Equi-NP. This too creates problems. Firstly PRO-self is supposed to occur in places where any other NP including lexical NPs and other pronouns could occur. However, as pointed out, the structures under consideration show obligatory identity of matrix object and embedded subject. Not only is it impossible to have a lexical NP in the place of the missing subject, as examples (28) and (29) show, but even pronouns coreferential to the matrix DO are excluded, as can be seen from (32) and (33).

*(32) (ton) perimenun   to jani   na fiɣi *aftos.*
       They-are-expecting   John   that leaves he

*(33) (ton) kserun to jani   pos lei psemata *aftos.*
       They know   John   that tells lies he

Furthermore, PRO-self is said to occur in non-finite clauses, and our data have finite complement clauses, which in turn will make it impossible to bind PRO-self, which according to case-marking conventions will be nominative, to an antecedent outside its S̄. Therefore, in addition to its other problems, this solution too runs up against NIC.

I conclude that none of the three null elements offered is suitable as the missing subject of our complement clauses. There is one other suggestion made by Chomsky (1980, 24) to the effect that some non-control verbs such as *believe* 'are permitted to govern objective case across a clause boundary.' This will account for structures like (34):

(34) They believe (him to be a nice fellow).

The pronoun *him,* while it is still the subject of the embedded clause and derives its thematic function from it, has the morphology of a matrix object due to this idiosyncratic property of *believe.*

Can we attempt a similar interpretation from the MG examples (7), (10) and (15)? The answer is negative due to the fact that the NP *to jani* has not only changed its case marking from nominative to accusative, but it has also moved outside its clause over the complementizer as seen clearly in (10) and (15). Besides, for MG these accusative NPs trigger cliticization, and this cannot be defined in terms of the accusative case marking, since other accusative NPs following verbs (adverbial accusative and accusative of a predicate (see Warburton 1977)) do not cliticize—only object NPs do.

It would seem, therefore, that we have explored all the possibilities and that we have not resolved the conflict between MG and the condition NIC. However, the impasse can perhaps be resolved by another proviso offered in Chomsky and Lasnik (1977, 451–2). This proviso is attributed to Perlmutter (1971), according to which if a language allows simple

104 *Irene Philippaki Warburton*

subjectless sentences then it will also allow extraction of a post-comple-
mentizer subject (see also Kayne 1980, 83). MG allows for subjectless
sentences as the following examples show:

(35) ksero.
      'I know'.

(36) erxonde.
      'They are coming.'

MG therefore qualifies as a language which is immune to NIC.
Consequently we could now adopt the raising analysis which seemed to be
the most satisfactory among those considered, and also retain NIC.

In spite of the fact that Perlmutter's generalization has resolved our
conflict, it does not seem to be completely satisfactory. This proviso simply
draws a correlation between two characteristics of these languages—
namely the possibility of the absence of a subject from a simple sentence
and the possibility of a movement of a complement subject out of a tensed
clause—but it offers no explanation as to why these phenomena coincide.
Secondly, unless we can find a deeper principle which will unite these two
phenomena, languages like Spanish (see Perlmutter 1971) and Greek make
no contribution to Chomsky's constraints. In fact, it would be possible,
theoretically at least, to absolve some other language from the constraints
if we could point to some other unique characteristic of this language. Only
if we could relate the two aspects of the behaviour of subjects in Greek and
only if this behaviour can be accommodated within the theory of
constraints can we say that the constraints have some universal validity.

I would like to pursue this question further by examining the other type
of raised structure existing in MG, namely structures which involve the so
called TOUGH MOVEMENT, exemplified in (37) and (38):

(37) ineðiskolo na katalavun   ta peðja   to jani.
      is difficult that they-understand the-nom children-nom the-acc John-acc
      'It is difficult for the children to understand John.'

(38) o janis   ine ðiskolos   na ton katalavun
      the-nom John-nom is difficult-nom   that him they-understand
      ta peðja
      the-nom children-nom
      'John is difficult for the children to understand.'

In (37) the adjective *diskolo* is neuter, nom, sing, and the NP *to jani* is
the DO of the embedded verb. In (38) the NP *o janis* not only appears at
the beginning of the complex sentence but it is now in nominative case,
which suggests that it has acquired the status of matrix subject. This is
further supported by the fact that the adjective *diskolos* has changed from
neuter to masc, nom, sing in agreement with its new subject. Paradigms
like this are not very common, but they exist for a very small number of
adjectives. Joseph (1980) has argued, convincingly, that the structure of
(38) is derived from (37) by the rule of TOUGH MOVEMENT (i.e.
object-to-subject raising) which, however, is implemented not by a
movement leaving an invisible trace behind, but by a copying process

which leaves a clitic pronoun in the complement clause. Following Perlmutter he calls these clitics SHADOW PRONOUNS.

This analysis seems satisfactory in that it captures the obligatory identity between the matrix subject and the clitic pronoun. However, such a solution is not allowed in Chomsky's framework for two reasons. Firstly, at the level of construal we will need to use a rule which will bind the clitic pronoun to its antecedent. However, the SSC will prevent such a binding. The reason for this is that since the complement clause is tensed, its subject will be given the nominative case, and this renders the clause opaque to any rule which would need to relate an item inside it to an item outside it. Secondly, clitics are pronouns in MG, and according to Chomsky (1977, 80–1 and fn. 12) pronouns cannot be derived transformationally, but must be base-generated. In accordance with this claim, our sentence (38) should be generated by the base with the clitic pronoun in place. The question that remains, however, is what kind of rules will capture the coreference relation between the matrix subject and the clitic of the complement. Chomsky's answer is that we cannot appeal to rules of construal for this, because connections between pronouns and their antecedents will often violate the constraints on construal (NIC and SSC). Therefore, he concludes, pronouns will be related to antecedents by some other kind of interpretive rules which fall outside the domain of sentence grammar, and which he refers to as RULES OF PREDICATION. If we accept Chomsky's position on pronouns we must conclude that (38) is base-generated and that the connection between matrix and clitic is handled by these rules of predication.

We have, thus, reached the following state of affairs. Subject-to-object raising is a transformational rule of MG grammar. It applies to structures like (6), (9), (14) and derives (7), (10) and (15) respectively by moving the subject of the complement clause to DO position of the matrix and leaving a trace in the vacated site. Rules of construal will bind this trace to the raised NP, in violation of NIC. This however is permitted since NIC does not apply to languages like MG. However, structures like (38) are base-generated, and their coreference properties are handled outside of the grammar proper by a different set of interpretive rules. This conclusion is counterintuitive, because it treats the two types of raising structures as completely unrelated, and yet there are, one feels, important relationships between them. In both types of sentences we have a matrix and a complement clause, and one of the arguments of the matrix is obligatorily identical with a missing argument of the complement.

Secondly, it can be argued that the absence of an explicit subject in (7) (10) and (15), and the presence of a minimal object in (38), are not conflicting phenomena but reflexes of the same requirement of the language. In both cases we have a clause which is reduced by one argument, but because it is a finite clause the loss cannot be complete but must be compensated by a minimally visible trace. This minimally visible trace appears in the agreement of the verb in the case of subject, and in the clitic object pronoun in the case of object. This interpretation of our data would involve Joseph's copying rules which move a NP but leave a shadow pronominal copy in the source sentence. The shadow subject pronoun, marked with nominative case, either attaches itself as agreement on the verb or, if the verb has the agreement marking already, it deletes, while the clitic object pronoun remains. This solution captures the relationship which exists between the two raising processes, and it captures the obligatoriness of the identity between the matrix DO to complement subjects in the first case and that between the matrix subject and the clitic object in the second. However, even this otherwise very satisfactory solution violates NIC and SSC when at the level of construal we will have to bind the shadow pronouns to their antecedents.

Once again we seem to be faced with two conflicting alternatives. Either we adopt the solution involving copying rules and 'shadow' pronouns and reject NIC and SSC as universals, or we sacrifice a descriptively satisfying account for MG in order to preserve the conditions. But if the hypothesis that these conditions are universal is to have any empirical import, we must opt for the first of the two alternatives and reject the conditions.

And yet, although we have seen that the conditions cannot be accepted as linguistic universals, the evidence from MG reveals that there is probably universal validity to the concept of ISLAND which they are intended to define. The properties of the MG-raised structures show that tensed clauses do constitute islands, because even in cases where extraction of an argument must take place, the tensed complement clause out of which it moves must retain some minimal evidence (trace?) of the removed argument. This evidence is in the form of agreement in the case of subject-to-object raising, and in the form of object clitic pronoun in the case of object-to-subject raising. Therefore rather than rejecting the conditions altogether, we could perhaps amend them so as to accommodate the notion of 'shadow' pronoun. What seems to be needed is an extension of the theory so as to allow not only for transparent (infinitive) clauses and opaque (tensed) ones, but also for cases of translucency involving elements which are not completely null, inaudible and invisible, but which are nevertheless even weaker than true pronouns, as are the agreement markers and the clitic object pronouns.

We may therefore return to our original controversy of the universal validity of Chomsky's constraints, and say that on the one hand MG offers positive evidence for the universality of the concept of ISLAND (the traditional concept of clause); on the other hand, however, it constitutes a clear challenge to the purported universality of the conditions as they are currently formulated.

References

Bach, E. 1977: Comments on the paper by Chomsky. In P. Culicover, T. Wasow and A. Akmajian (eds.), *Formal syntax*. London: Academic Press.

Chomsky, N. 1965: *Aspects of the theory of syntax*. Cambridge, Mass.: MIT Press.

———1973: Conditions on transformations. In S.R. Anderson and P. Kiparsky (eds.), *A festschrift for Morris Halle*. New York: Holt, Rinehart & Winston.

————1975: *Reflections on language*. New York: Pantheon.
————1976: Conditions on rules of grammar. *Linguistic Analysis* **2**, 303–51.
————1977: On Wh-movement. In P. Culicover, T. Wasow and A. Akmajian (eds.), *Formal syntax*. London: Academic Press.
————1980: On binding. *LIn*. **11**, 1–46.
Chomsky, N. and Lasnik, H. 1977: Filters and control. *LIn*. **8**, 425–504.
Jannaris, A.N. 1897: *An historical Greek grammar*. Hildesheim: Georg Olms.
Joos, M. 1957: *Readings in linguistics*. New York: American Council of Learned Societies.
Joseph, B. 1980: Linguistic universals and syntactic change. *Lg*. **56**, 345–70.
Kayne, R. 1980: Extensions of binding and case-marking. *LIn*. **11**, 75–96.
Kim, W.C. 1976: *The theory of anaphora in Korean syntax*. Doctoral dissertation, Massachusetts Institute of Technology.
Perlmutter, D. 1971: *Deep and surface structure constraints in syntax*. New York: Holt, Rinehart & Winston.
Warburton, I.P. 1977: Modern Greek clitic pronouns and the surface structure constraints hypothesis. *JL* **13**, 259–81.
Warburton, I.P. and Christides, A. (in press): The syntax and semantics of Modern Greek complementizers.

9

In a word, meaning[1]
Colin Biggs

'The complexity of semantics is merely one aspect of the complexity of human language. What we can say will be unprecise and often controversial. There are no easy answers.' With these crisp sentences Frank Palmer ends his well known introduction to semantics. There are, indeed, *so many* controversial issues in semantics that one might be tempted to suppose that semantics itself is somehow controversial as an area of academic enquiry; to a degree that syntax, for example, is not. Bloomfield was highly pessimistic about the general prospect of developing an explicit account of meaning in a language. Quine even argued, forcefully, that linguists who discussed meaning were literally in the position of 'not knowing what they are talking about' (Quine, 1953, 47). Other philosophers, whilst not accepting Quine's dismissal of the whole notion of meaning, have, in a partisan way, supposed semantics to be the concern of philosophy of language, not linguistics. In a no less partisan manner many linguists find themselves in sympathy with the statement on the cover of Geoffrey Leech's (1974) paperback *Semantics* that whilst philosophy, psychology and anthropology all have a stake in it, 'semantics rightly belongs to the newer discipline of linguistics, since meaning is inextricably a part of the language through which it is expressed'.

Even where there is agreement that linguistics has something of value to say about meaning, there have been those who have questioned the extent to which discussion of meaning has anything to do with the language faculty as such. As one linguist has recently put it: 'My own speculation is that only a bare framework of semantic properties, altogether insufficient for characterizing what is ordinarily called "the meaning of a linguistic expression", can be associated correctly with the idealization "language". '

[1] An earlier version of this chapter was presented in a paper at Brown University, April 1980. I am most grateful to the Department of Linguistics at Brown for having given me an opportunity to air some of these ideas, and for their hospitality on that occasion.

The reader may or may not be surprised that the linguist in question is Chomsky (1979, 143).

These are matters of controversy at the most general possible level: about whether semantics is possible, and, if it is, about what it is and who should practise it. Were these matters to be resolved there remain a myriad other issues at various more or less general levels: is there a reasonably clear borderline to be drawn between semantics and syntax, semantics and pragmatics? is there a semantic relation of presupposition? can meanings be atomized? . . . Faced with such a field where discord and controversy have seemed the rule, and agreement rare, professional linguists and students alike have been dismayed and disillusioned about the prospect of ever developing a semantic component for a grammar. A measure of how strong this feeling has been, and how persuasive the arguments that lie behind it, is given by the fact that in the final pages of his introduction to semantics, from which we have already quoted, Frank Palmer was led to remark: 'One conclusion that will be drawn from reading this book is that semantics is not a single, well-integrated discipline. It is not a clearly defined level of linguistics, not even comparable to phonology or grammar' (1976, 154).

This is, as I understand it, a rather sombre conclusion, comparable at a general level to that of Chomsky (1979). All the more so since it is the outcome of a careful and detailed attempt to sift through so many of the controversial issues and to get to the heart of what semantics is about. It prompts the exasperated question: where do we go from here?

One response at this point would be to accept that semantics is multi-faceted and simultaneously to look for an enduring character behind the many appearances. This is not, I believe, a programme to which Palmer himself would object, although he and I might disagree as to the likelihood of actually finding any such enduring character amidst so many controversial issues. This chapter is concerned with one important part of such a programme: developing a plausible general theory of word meaning.

There is an issue at the outset, of course, about the propriety of parcelling off a domain of word semantics. Bazell once claimed that 'to seek a semantic unit within the boundaries of the word simply because these boundaries are clearer than others is like looking for a lost ball on the lawn simply because the thicket provides poor ground for such a search' (Bazell, 1954, 339). Certainly there are problems on occasion about establishing the word as a semantic unit (and some of these problems are problems about what counts as a word in any particular language) but we hardly end up with the mindless, pointless search implied by Bazell's analogy. To take just one allegedly problematic area: it is often pointed out that idioms, such as *kick the bucket, bury the hatchet,* function as single units from a semantic point of view, whose meaning is not predictable from the meanings of the words themselves. So here at least the level of the individual word is not the appropriate level of analysis. Yet this very way in which the problem is characterized reveals its marginal status: for idioms are commonly identified, as here, by their failure to conform to the normal semantic pattern, where the meaning of the whole is a function of the meaning of the parts, and those parts are words. This is one issue which we can, perhaps, tentatively assign *non*-controversial status.

Some recent controversial issues in word semantics

It may be useful at this point to review briefly some of the more controversial and problematic issues raised in the recent history of word semantics, beginning with Bloomfield. Close on half a century ago Bloomfield wrote, in a passage which is now famous, perhaps infamous, that 'in order to give a scientifically accurate description of meaning for every form of a language, we should have to have to have a scientifically accurate knowledge of everything in the speakers' world' (1933, 139). It is appropriate to begin our historical review with Bloomfield for he represents an extreme position against which many subsequently reacted.

Two such were Katz and Fodor, who in their 1963 paper 'The structure of a semantic theory' argued that the first major step to be taken in freeing ourselves from Bloomfield's discouraging conclusion is to recognize that there is a fundamental distinction to be drawn between *dictionary knowledge* and *encyclopaedic knowledge,* and *knowledge of language* and *knowledge of the world.* The domain of a semantic theory is language; and knowledge of the world, whatever else it is, is not knowledge about the language-system.

With hindsight we can see very clearly both why it is so important to draw the distinction which Katz and Fodor wanted to draw, and also why it is quite impossible to draw the distinction in the manner they suggest. It was, perhaps, Bolinger in his insightful and incisive paper 'The atomization of meaning' (1965), who best captured the nature of the problem. He pointed out that on Katz and Fodor's analysis it is most plausibly an encyclopaedic fact about alligators that they do not, and about horses that under certain conditions of domesticity they do, wear shoes (in much the same way that it is an encyclopaedic rather than a semantic fact that under certain distressing conditions of domesticity rather small dogs wear cosy red coats with 'Snuffles' embroidered on them). But if encyclopaedic information is to be excluded from semantics, how do we account for the quite different semantic interpretation which we assign to *Our store sells alligator shoes* v. *Our store sells horse shoes?*

Is the answer then to say that it is part of the meaning of *horse* that horses wear shoes, of a non-leather variety, in certain states of domesticity, in the same way that it is presumably part of the meaning of *horse* that horses are typically quadruped? The import of Bolinger's criticism is that there is no principled way of answering questions of this type, since there is no principled way of drawing a distinction between knowledge of the language and knowledge of the world.

Now if this conclusion is correct it seems but a short step back to 1933 and to pessimism about the entire enterprise of developing a theory of word semantics rather than settling for necessarily partial descriptions (barring omniscience, that is). It is just this latter type of work, invariably conducted on a piecemeal basis, that Austin once dismissed as 'myth-eaten description'. I shall discuss presently what would be required of a theory of word semantics, but I think we have sufficient of an intuitive grasp of the notion to see already that unless we *can* offer a principled way of making the fundamental distinction between knowledge of the language and knowledge of the world then it looks as if it will not be possible to construct any such theory.

This distinction has assumed an even greater importance in more recent writings on semantics. For example, in *Reflections on Language* Chomsky (1975) has distinguished between a 'system of language' (which he calls a GRAMMAR) and a 'system of beliefs and expectations about the nature and behaviour of objects' (which he calls COMMON SENSE). One of Chomsky's aims—in some ways perhaps the main aim—has always been to establish the INDEPENDENT existence of the language faculty as an Autonomous Republic of the Mind. There are signs in his new book *Rules and representations* (1980) that he may be prepared to allow that this republic has border disputes, and these, interestingly, concerning the representation of the meanings of words. In Chapter 2 he writes (p. 62):

> Do the 'semantic rules' of natural language that are alleged to give the meanings of words belong to the language faculty strictly speaking, or should they be regarded perhaps as centrally embedded parts of a conceptual or belief system, or do they subdivide in some way? Much of the debate about these matters has been inconclusive. It turns on dubious intuitions as to whether we would still call our pets 'cats' if we learned that they are descended from robots controlled by Martians.

The real question is not, of course, whether we would continue to *call* Felix a cat if we discover that he is extraterrestrial—nor even what a robot has been doing with all that milk and catfood—but whether we would revise our dictionary entry to signal a change in meaning of the word *cat* contingent upon a change in our beliefs about these creatures. Whether we would continue to call them cats is a different matter, dependent on a number of psychological factors. Children who discover that their parents are foster-parents do not typically cease to call them *Mummy* and *Daddy*.

Examples such as these had already been discussed in works by Katz and Putnam and Fodor in the mid 1970s. In such an admittedly highly unlikely but still possible case, our beliefs about cats would be quite shattered. At this stage we would have to choose either to revise radically our assessment of the meaning of the word *cat* or, as in Katz (1975), to decide that it had now turned out that there were not, and never had been, any cats in the world, but only things which superficially resembled cats. I am inclined to agree with Chomsky that our intuitions are not up to it.

Consider, by contrast, a less extreme case. I believe that beavers build dams. Suppose that I also believe that they only build dams during the daylight hours. Later, I come to learn that beavers being beavers they also go in for a bit of nocturnal dam-building. Here no radical reassessment is required: I am likely simply to revise slightly one of my beliefs about beavers. What this case would seem to highlight is that not *every* belief counts, as it were, when it comes to assessing whether a change in meaning has occurred. Some beliefs about the objects referred to by expressions of the language simply represent personal attitudes and expectations on the part of individual speakers; other beliefs are integral to the very meanings of the expressions involved. This two-class system of beliefs is perhaps what Chomsky had in mind when he suggested, in the passage we quoted earlier, that it was possible that 'the semantic rules of natural language . . . subdivide in some way'.

But the idea of a rigid two-class system of beliefs is a myth. It is no more possible to sort beliefs neatly and categorically into semantically relevant vs. semantically irrelevant than it proved possible to sort knowledge into two discrete epistemic sets: knowledge of the language and knowledge of the world—although it may be an improvement to talk about *beliefs about* the world, rather than knowledge of the world. What we have, as so often in language, is a cline: at one extreme there are beliefs whose centrality is relatively unimpeachable, like the belief that cats are domestic pets not alien animaloids; at the other, there are beliefs about the dam-building of beavers. No theory of world semantics which fails to recognize the existence of this cline can possibly succeed. As yet, however, we still have to show that a theory of word semantics which does recognize the existence of this cline can possibly succeed.

Before we go any further it will be as well to draw a distinction between *conventional* beliefs and *personal* beliefs. It is clear that our beliefs that cats are domestic pets not alien animaloids is a conventional belief. My belief about when beavers build dams would be, I presume, a personal rather than a conventional belief. It is the conventional beliefs, if any, which are semantically relevant. Precisely how they may be relevant, given the objection to the two-class system of beliefs, we leave until later in the chapter, but it may be as well to anticipate in part a further point. Conventionally held beliefs are never totally unrevisable. No matter how central a belief is, however much it is a matter of convention, it can be changed. There is no slide here into that analyticity which Quine rightly discredited.

The alleged impossibility of a theory of word semantics

It is a fact, perhaps a quite remarkable fact, that some of us do communicate with one another at least some of the time. It is clearly a crude oversimplication—and indeed an insult to the creative abilities of speakers—to suppose the communication between A and B in English simply amounts to A's uttering certain words of English with a certain meaning and B's recognizing the meaning of A's words, whereupon B utters certain other words having certain other meanings, . . . and so on. But at the core of the oversimplification is an important truth: if linguistic communication is to succeed there must be conventions. And some of these constitute agreements about what a word is to mean. None of this is to deny that speakers may use a word on occasion, perhaps even predominantly, in an *extended* sense, or metaphorically, but merely to assert that at a fundamental level there are—there must be—conventions. Now speakers of, say, English intuit that there are certain relations of meaning between chunks of their language. And whilst there may often be far from complete agreement amongst speakers as to whether such-and-such a relation of meaning does or does not hold between two chunks of English, there is, in general, broad agreement about these relations. This is only to say that language, and more particularly those aspects concerned with meaning, form a conventional *system*, not a conventional *taxonomy*. A theory of word semantics will need:

(i) to explicate the nature of these conventions, and to represent them in a formal, testable way;

(ii) to provide explicit procedures for checking out the predictions made by the explications as to the relations of meaning which may hold between units of the language.

All of this may seem reasonably familiar. What I have tried to do, however, is to phrase the requirement on a theory in a way which is as neutral as possible with respect to existing accounts of word meaning. Later I shall argue for a particular theory.

First, however, we need to consider some further, fundamental objections to the whole enterprise of providing a theory of word semantics. The objections in question come in a recent book by Geoffrey Sampson, *Making sense* (1980). Approximately half of the book is given over to arguing *against* the view that a theory of word semantics is possible. The attack is part of a larger rejection of the entire conceptual framework of contemporary Theoretical Linguistics.

Sampson makes his points with what one reviewer of an earlier book of his (Anthony Quinton) calls 'an open and breezy aggressiveness'. He argues that semantic description cannot be scientific and that therefore 'so far as I can see the complex apparatus of formal symbolism used by Linguistic Semantics serves little purpose'. He continues (p. 103): 'The job of giving approximate historical accounts of the most conventional usage of words at particular times does not require esoteric formalisms. It was already done, about as well as it could be done, decades before Linguistic Semantics was heard of—in the columns of the *Oxford English Dictionary* and its counterparts in other nations.' The 'open and breezy aggressiveness' comes across perhaps most clearly on the last page (211) of his book when he writes about those who actually *teach* semantics.

For a don in a Linguistics Department who finds himself responsible for lectures on semantics it is much easier, psychologically, to take his class through the contemporary literature on formal semantic analysis with the attitude that 'there must be something in it' than to spend the term or year insisting that the readings are as valuable as so many patents for perpetual-motion machines.

These are colourful conclusions, but Sampson does not draw his conclusion hastily. The book as a whole is very closely and carefully argued, and we cannot possibly consider his theses in any great detail here, but there are two central objections which are relevant here. Both are objections to a theory of word semantics on the grounds that it ignores our role as speakers in *creating*. This is creativity not in the Chomskyan sense, but in the sense in which an artist may be creative.

The first point concerns semantic indeterminacy arising in precisely the sort of case Chomsky envisaged. Sampson considers the word *father*. We believe, I think, that fathers are male parents. But what, Sampson asks, of the man who fathers children and then has a sex-change operation. This might prompt the children to say 'That's no lady; that's my father' but we as linguists must decide whether *she* remains the children's father, or becomes their second mother; or whether neither word is now applicable. Sampson thinks that the first of these three usages—where *she* remains father—is 'becoming standard'. I had not realized that such situations were now sufficiently frequent for us to talk of standard practice, but the important point anyway is that we need to amend the semantic definition in some way: in this case to something like 'parent who *was* male at the time of conception'.

Can we not say, then, simply that *father* has changed its meaning? That our set of conventional beliefs about fathers has been revised? Yes indeed; but for Sampson the matter does not rest there. He is interested in semantic change because he believes that a rigorous semantic analysis of the language, if *per impossibile* it *were* possible, would need to *predict* the direction in which change would take place—to predict the new convention. He rightly remarks that there can be no such predictive device; and wrongly concludes that a theory of word semantics is not possible.

Wrongly, because it is not a requirement on a semantic theory that it make predictions about potential changes in meaning. Of course any theory must be in principle falsifiable, as Popper has rightly argued; and for a theory to be falsifiable it must make testable predictions. Granted also that theories in some of the paradigm 'hard sciences' make predictions about changes which occur through time. But a semantic theory makes predictions of a different kind: it predicts that native speakers will judge *a* to be synonymous with *b,* opposite in meaning to *c,* included in the meaning of *d,* and outside the meaning of *e.* These predictions are eminently testable, although considerably more sophistication is necessary in devising the tests than has been sometimes evinced in the past. To deny that we can develop a theory about some aspect of language unless it is possible to make predictions about changes that are to occur over an indefinitely long time span is absurd. We may consider phonology. The worth of a phonological theory is not reduced to nil by its inability to make full and accurate predictions about sound changes. (These remarks are not, however, intended to suggest—far from it—that diachronic studies are never relevant to phonological theory. This is a separate issue.)

The second point of Sampson's which I wish to consider concerns metaphor. Here too speakers are creative. For Sampson there is no sharp contrast between figurative and literal usage, only a cline where one shades into the other. As he puts it (p. 76): 'All of us are using language somewhat metaphorically all the time; the thing about poets is simply that they take this tendency further than most of us.' Given the open-endedness of metaphor, and the alleged lack of a sharp contrast between the literal and the metaphorical we find that suddenly the very subject matter of a theory of word meaning becomes unbounded, unstable and impossibly complex.

Now it is true, as Sampson complains, that linguists' discussion of metaphor has more often than not been programmatic (and I am not about to carry out the programme), but we can perhaps scotch this idea that there is no clear distinction to be drawn between the literal and the metaphorical. If there were no clearly distinct literal meaning there would be no metaphor (except, perhaps, for the so-called 'frozen' metaphors). Unless we know the literal meaning of *drink* then the sentence *My car just drinks petrol* is not interpretable. The figurative use of language represents an exploitation of the non-figurative. It is only because we are acquainted with such literal and pedestrian phrases as *a week ago* and *a month ago* that Dylan Thomas's *a grief ago* has the impact that it does. It is with the literal and pedestrian and conventional that a theory of word semantics is first of all concerned.

Three contemporary approaches to word semantics

In the remaining part of this chapter I want to consider the three major contemporary attempts from within linguistics to characterize the literal and pedestrian and conventional, and to consider to what extent any of them offer us a theory in the sense we have been considering. We shall reject the first two (field theory and componential analysis) and argue that the third (the meaning-postulate approach), whilst it scarcely constitutes a theory as it is normally presented, furnishes us with appropriate machinery for a genuine theory of word semantics.

First, field theory. This is very much a European product. The basic ideas are easily stated and well-known. For present purposes we can restrict ourselves to paradigmatic relations, though, of course, field theorists have had much to say about syntagmatic relations too. Semantic space—what Trier called conceptual space—can be divided into semantic fields. To give the meaning of a word is first to locate it in the appropriate semantic field and then to show how it differs in meaning from the other words in the same semantic field. (I present the approach in a very informal way: we shall see presently that no other way is realistically possible.) To take a familiar example, we can capture the sense of *red* by first locating the term in the appropriate semantic field—in this case the field of colour terms—and then showing how the sense of *red* differs from the sense of the other lexemes of the same field. (This approach is more than a little anticipated in Aristotle's notion of definition *per genus et differentiam*, although it is debatable whether we could consider him European.)

Whilst field theory has produced much careful and detailed work on particular fields such as the field of colour terms, especially in diachronic semantics, it has never in fact reached the status of a genuine theory. John Lyons, one of the best known contemporary presenters of field theory, has remarked (1977, 267) that:

> Most authors who have written recently on the subject of semantic fields have conceded that the majority of lexical fields are not so neatly structured or as clearly separated from one another as Trier originally suggested; and this concession of a point that has been constantly urged against field theory by its critics may be held to detract from its value as a general theory of semantic structure, for it necessarily makes the theory *more difficult to formalize*. On the other hand, vaguely formulated though it has been, field theory has proved its

worth as a general guide for research in *descriptive* semantics over the last 40 years. (my emphasis)

We can, I think, accept Lyons's concluding remarks, but it would be wrong also to accept that field theory is merely difficult to formalize. We can, I would argue, show that field theory taken now as a general theory about word meaning is fundamentally incoherent.

To see the nature of the problem we need to recognize at the outset the vicious circularity of field theory: semantic space is partitioned into lexical fields on the basis that each and every member has more in common semantically with the other members than with any element outside the field. But there is ultimately no way of characterizing this notion of 'having something in common semantically' in a manner which does not appeal to semantic fields. Once we recognize this we can see that semantic field theory licenses a potentially infinite number of fields. For there is a potentially infinite number of partitions of the vocabulary, depending on which package of semantic features—I use this term in a neutral, pre-theoretical way—we elect to consider. What we would like, of course, is a way of coming up with the 'good' partitions and rejecting the 'bad' partitions. Field theory contains, however, no procedure—actual or potential—for sorting the good from the bad partitions, for the very simple reason that there is no principled independent way of sorting partitions. The real problem with semantic field theory, then, is not, *pace* Lyons, that we cannot define semantic fields (except perhaps such highly conventional ones as the colour field) with sufficient accuracy, but rather that we can define all too many semantic fields. One of the consequences of this, is that we shall have to admit fields within fields within fields.

The problems are even more endemic, however, for semantic features cross-classify. Hence pairs, triples, *n*-tuples of semantic fields will intersect. Not only will we get circles within circles within circles, but also endless intersections. Suddenly our semantic space is becoming multi-dimensional. And for every multi-dimensional complex we come up with there is an alternative complex of partitions which is no more and no less justified.

Field theory, then, fails to offer, even potentially, a general theory about word meaning. If, however, we can see the meaning of words as molecular structures whose atomic composition can be rigorously specified by word scientists then we shall indeed be able to formulate a predictive theory of word semantics, as Katz, for example, has clearly envisaged. But in practice and in principle such componential analysis has proved impossible.

Volumes have been written about the shortcomings of componential analysis, but the fundamental difficulty with this theory is rarely discussed. It is that componential analysis is by its very nature committed to writing definitions giving necessary and sufficient conditions. Now, as has often been pointed out, the meaning of most words (Russell argued *all* words) is to some extent vague. But as Jonathan Cohen (1962) argued in a book published a year before the presentation of componential analysis in Katz and Fodor's 'The structure of a semantic theory', if we can conceive a borderline case for the applicability of a word whose meaning is vague then we must also be able to conceive a standard case. But 'the borderline case must resemble the standard one in satisfying some sufficient condition of the word's applying, and differ from it in not satisfying some necessary condition' (Cohen 1962, 270). This, though, means that the word must have at least two criteria of application; the one for the standard case, the other for the borderline case. But then any theory such as componential analysis which is committed to a unique decomposition of the meaning of any (non-ambiguous) word is bound to fail. Nor is it in any way obvious that one could amend componential analysis in order to escape this consequence.

The final approach to word semantics we shall consider, that via meaning postulates, avoids this fundamental difficulty. A meaning postulate is an explicit statement about set-inclusion or, if you prefer, hyponomy. The set of tulips in the world is included in the set of flowers, and *tulip* is a hyponym of *flower*. We can capture this in a meaning postulate of the form

(x) $(Tx \to Fx)$ where 'T' and 'F' are predicate letters.

Typically any given word will have a sizeable set of meaning postulates associated with it. Thus *bachelor* would have associated with it

(x) $(Bx \to Mx)$
(x) $(Bx \to Ax)$
(x) $(Bx \to Ux)$,

which we can then collapse to yield (x) $(Bx \to Mx \ \& \ Ax \ \& \ Ux)$. What is attractive about the meaning postulate approach here is, paradoxically, that compared with componential analysis it is much less ambitious. In particular there is no claim to have provided the complete atomic structure of *bachelor*. As normally conceived, what the meaning-postulate approach yields are necessary properties of, in this case, bachelors; but there is no claim that the list is closed. The properties may be necessary (in a sense to be made clear) but are not necessarily sufficient: no definition as such is given; merely a specification of those lexical relations which it is felt are sufficiently conventional to be captured by postulates.

Yet some have argued that too little ambition is a bad thing. Thus Kempson, in her book on semantic theory, remarks: 'Meaning postulates are language specific: so unless some extra formulation is included within the theory, there is no way of relating the meaning postulates for English to corresponding meaning postulates in other languages' (1977, 190). Since we wish for an account of semantics as part of a universal linguistic theory, she continues, we must supply this extra formulation. This can only take the form of semantic components. Hence (*ibid.*, 191): 'Despite the superficial contrast between a meaning-postulate approach and a semantic-representation approach [here she has in mind a version of componential analysis], the difference is not so great.' Essentially the same point has been made by Manfred Bierwisch.

But there is a confusion here about how to interpret the predicate letters 'F', 'G' etc. Kempson wishes to interpret them in terms of semantic components. But the language of semantic components is itself notoriously uninterpreted. It would be far better to see meaning postulates as simply stating relations between lexical items. Thus:

(x) If x is a bachelor then x is male, adult and unmarried.

Or even:

All bachelors are male, adult and unmarried.

Here the meaning postulates are couched in English and we can then go on to consider how best to give a semantic interpretation to the meaning postulate just as if it were any other sentence of English. Our object-language and metalanguage are as one, and we avoid an infinite regress. But now the problem which Kempson posed of how to make cross-linguistic remarks about word meanings is reduced to the problem of translation at the level of the sentence.[2]

We are able, then, to characterize at least the conventional aspect of the meaning of a word in terms of a set of meaning postulates couched in English. It might well appear at this point as if we have come full circle: for we set out to devise a theory which would explicate the semantic relations holding between units of the language, and we are now considering explications which are themselves couched in units of the self-same language whose semantic relations we sought to explicate. There is indeed a circularity here, but one which merely points up the systematic nature of language. The circularity will be prevented from becoming vicious if we can *ultimately* appeal in our explications to a notion which takes us outside the linguistic plane. A notion of this kind will also take us outside the columns of the OED, however salutary it may be, as Sampson urges, to linger there. Such a notion is the notion of truth.

The notion of truth establishes a relation between the linguistic and the non-linguistic plane, between language and the world. Moreover, one who knows the conditions under which a sentence would be true knows what that sentence means. Donald Davidson has suggested, in Davidson (1967) and numerous other publications, that herein lies the hope that we may be able to establish a theory of meaning *via* a theory of truth. Our theory of truth will yield, for every sentence of the language, an instantiation of the schema

'*S*' is true iff *p*,

where for simplex sentences the semantic rules will specify directly the conditions under which '*S*' is true, as in the celebrated

'Snow is white' is true iff snow is white,

and where for complex sentences the rules will recursively specify the conditions under which a sentence is true as a function of the way the sentence is built up from simplex sentences, so that, to take a simple example, if we consider the complex sentence (S_1 & S_2), then this is true if

---

[2] Some writers have, of course, suggested that translation is best effected via componential analysis, or some other system of semantic primitives. The arguments are, however, far from compelling.

and only if S_1 is true and S_2 is true. The semantic rules which specify the truth-conditions for simplex sentences will exhibit the meaning of the sentences by revealing the systematic contribution which the parts of sentences make to determining the truth-conditions of the whole. So *John loves Mary* differs in meaning from *Mary loves John* since although these two sentences are composed of the same parts these parts make differing systematic contributions to the determining of truth-conditions in the two sentences. This difference in contribution brings out the fundamental difference in meaning between the two sentences. In just the same way meaning postulates will be assigned a semantic interpretation via a specification of their truth-conditions.

If we have now allayed the suspicion of vicious circularity the reader may well be entertaining a further doubt: that these proposals about meaning postulates covertly reintroduce analyticity. After all, do not meaning postulates in effect specify a set of entailments, so that *Fred is a bachelor* entails 'Fred is male' and 'Fred is adult' and 'Fred is unmarried'? Yes, but the entailments in question are of a *probabilistic* kind. For the entailments are merely a device for capturing the conventional usage of a word, and the conventional beliefs that underlie that usage. These conventional beliefs have a status which in no way approximates to analytic truth, for they are mutable. Furthermore, for us to call something a horse it suffices that some representative cluster of conventionally held beliefs about horses be satisfied. A three-legged horse is still a horse, a tail-less horse is still a horse. *A horse is a quadruped* is not analytically true; rather it represents a prominent and central convention about horses, but one which is open to exceptions, or even to permanent revision.[3]

To this extent, then, all entailments are probabilistic.[4] What probability we assign to any particular set of entailments for any particular lexical item will depend upon the centrality of the conventional belief in the linguistic culture. Thus in our present culture the set of conventional beliefs about *father* may well be moving away from a highly central position, as Sampson's example would indicate. A plausible representation for the meaning of *father,* which will serve as a simple example of the approach we are proposing, would be:

x is a father $p \rightarrow x$ is male & x is a parent.

[3] Our approach here has affinities with that of Putnam in a number of publications (e.g. Putnam 1975), where he develops the notion of a *stereotype*. He, however, rejects the notion of meaning postulates as such, for reasons which are not persuasive.
[4] Although there have been a number of publications on probabilistic rules since Bar-Hillel (1969, 205) drew the attention of the linguistic community at large to 'the probabilistic status of the semantic and pragmatic rules of natural languages', much work remains to be done on devising effective procedures for *testing* theories involving probabilistic rules. To this extent, then, any theory which we may devise along the lines indicated in this chapter is not yet falsifiable. This is a temporal, not a fundamental, problem: we simply lack sufficiently refined techniques at present to carry out such tests. Such work as has already been done on probabilistic rules has, with some notable exceptions, been concerned with *sociolinguistic* data. For a recent detailed discussion of some of the central issues involved, with extensive bibliographic references, see Kay and McDaniel (1979) and, in response to this, Sankoff and Labov (1979).

What Sampson's discussion suggests is that the value of p, the probability of the entailment from 'x is a father' to 'x is male' and 'x is a parent', is considerably lower in 1980s English than in, say, 1880s English. It is also possible, and plausible, to argue that of the two entailments 'x is male' and 'x is a parent' the latter has a much higher value for p than the former. This reflects the relative centrality of our belief that fathers are parents as against our increasing awareness that this does not always mean that they are male.

Our task in word semantics is, then, to identify the conventionally held beliefs associated with each lexical item. That these are to be represented by a set of probabilistic entailments simply reflects the extent to which words are, as we noted in discussing componential analysis, open-textured, or vague. The greater part of all linguistic communication involves vagueness within quite precise limits, where the *degree* of precision is dictated by the centrality of the beliefs concerning the lexical item, and our central task in word semantics is to devise a theory of the kind indicated here in which we can precisely characterize the vagueness of language in a way which is demonstrably nonparadoxical.[5]

References

Bar-Hillel, Y. 1970: Argumentation in natural languages. In Y. Bar-Hillel, *Aspects of language.* Amsterdam: North-Holland.

Bazell, C. 1954: The sememe. Reprinted in E. Hamp, F. Householder and R. Austerlitz (eds.), *Readings in linguistics* **II.** Chicago: University of Chicago Press.

Bloomfield, L. 1933: *Language.* New York: Holt.

Bolinger, D. 1965: The atomization of language. *Lg.* **41,** 555–73.

Chomsky, N. 1975: *Reflections on language.* London: Temple Smith.

—— 1979: *Language and responsibility.* Hassocks: Harvester.

—— 1980: *Rules and representations.* New York: Columbia University Press.

Cohen, J. 1962: *The diversity of meaning.* London: Methuen.

Davidson, D. 1967: Truth and meaning. *Synthese* **17,** 304–23.

Katz, J. 1975: Logic and language: a defense of intentionalism. *Minnesota Studies in the Philosophy of Science,* **8,** 36–130.

Kay, P. and McDaniel, C. 1979: On the logic of variable rules. *Lang. Soc.* **8,** 151–87.

Kempson, R. 1977: *Semantic theory.* Cambridge: Cambridge University Press.

Leech, G. 1974: *Semantics.* Harmondsworth: Penguin.

Lyons, J. 1977: *Semantics.* 2 vols. Cambridge: Cambridge University Press.

[5] After completing this chapter I came across McCawley's (1980) review of Sampson (1979), a work in which, as McCawley notes, essentially similar arguments are raised to those of Sampson (1980) (though in considerably less detail). McCawley's discussion specifically of Sampson's arguments about semantics is fairly brief, but the overall conclusions have much in common with some of those reached in this chapter, although McCawley remains convinced that semantic primitives have an important role to play.

McCawley, J. 1980: Review of Sampson 1979: *Lg.* **56,** 639–47.

Palmer, F.R. 1976: *Semantics: a new outline.* Cambridge: Cambridge University Press.

Putnam, H. 1975: *Mind, language and reality.* 2 vols. Cambridge: Cambridge University Press.

Quine, W.V.O. 1953: The problem of meaning in linguistics. In W.V.O. Quine, *From a logical point of view.* New York: Harper.

Sampson, G. 1975: *The form of language.* London: Weidenfeld & Nicolson.

————1979: *Liberty and language.* London: Oxford University Press.

————1980: *Making sense.* London: Oxford University Press.

Sankoff, D. and Labov, W. 1979: On the uses of variable rules. *Lang. Soc.* **8,** 189–222.

10

Russian *takže* and *tože* revisited[1]
Roland Sussex

The Russian words *takže* and *tože* 'also, too' pose a constant difficulty for linguists, teachers and students of Russian. The explanations offered for the choice between these two words have sometimes been based on stylistics (Kovačeva 1964), sometimes on foreign-language equivalents (Bogusławski 1969), and, more recently, on Functional Sentence Perspective (Gundel 1975; Baker 1977; Nakhimovsky and Leed 1980). Linguists and native speakers do not agree on the stylistic properties of the two Russian 'also' words. In so far as there is any consensus, *takže* is regarded as more formal, literary or technical:

(1a) My čitaem Tolstogo, i Solženicyna takže (*more formal*)
(1b) My čitaem Tolstogo, i Solženicyna tože (*less formal*)
       'We read Tolstoy, and Solzhenitsyn also.'[2]

But informal questioning of sophisticated native speakers has not yielded results which are statistically consistent enough to establish this stylistic criterion as the central property distinguishing *takže* and *tože*. Furthermore, a stylistic criterion could be the determining factor only if there were always a genuine choice between alternative forms. The problem is that there are some sentences where one of the two words is clearly preferable to the other. Informed native speakers agree closely enough as to which word is preferable in a given construction, but differ over whether the less favoured form is absolutely ungrammatical, or merely marked or substandard:

(2a) Miša igraet na klarnete. Miša takže (? tože) igraet na skripke.
       'Misha plays the clarinet. Misha also plays the violin.'

[1] I am grateful to Grev Corbett, Paul Cubberley, Zhanna Dolgopolova and R.T. Sussex for comments on an earlier version of this paper.
[2] The English versions given with the Russian example sentences are not so much translations as translation-glosses, which are designed to illustrate the meaning of individual words in Russian where appropriate.

(2*b*)   Miša igraet na klarnete. Sergej tože (? takže) igraet na klarnete.
'Misha plays the clarinet. Sergej also plays the clarinet.'

So what is the rationale behind the exclusion of one or the other of the two 'also' words?

One line of approach, which is particularly favoured by language teachers, is through cross-language comparisons (Bogusławski 1969). There are some examples where English *also* appears to be parallel to Russian *takže,* and *too* to Russian *tože:*

(3*a*)   John likes honey. I too like honey.
(3*b*)   Ivan ljubit mëd. Ja tože ljublju mëd.

(4*a*)   John likes honey. He also likes jam.
(4*b*)   Ivan ljubit mëd. On takže ljubit varen'e.

But substituting the alternative form has different effects in the two languages:

(5*a*)   John likes honey. I also like honey.
(5*b*)?   Ivan ljubit mëd. Ja takže ljublju mëd.

(6*a*)??John likes honey. He too likes jam.
(6*b*)??Ivan ljubit mëd. On tože ljubit varen'e.

English *also* is obviously less restrictive than *too,* as we can see by comparing (3*a*) and (5*a*) with (4*a*) and (6*a*). But Russian *takže* and *tože* are much more closely controlled by their grammatical-semantic context—except at the end of a sentence, where all four 'also' words may occur. The parallelism of *also-takže* and *too-tože* consequently breaks down, though the *too-tože* pair is stylistically preferable:

(7*a*)   John likes honey. I like honey too/also.
(7*b*)   Ivan ljubit mëd. Ja ljublju mëd takže/tože.

(8*a*)   John likes honey. He likes jam too/also.
(8*b*)   Ivan ljubit mëd. On ljubit varen'e takže/tože.

We cannot hope, therefore, to explain the use of Russian *takže/tože* by reference to English. In spite of the measure of help which it may offer the foreign language learner, this approach to the problem of *takže/tože* has internal inconsistencies, and in any case it does not provide a rigorous explanation in terms of the internal grammar or semantics of Russian.

These example sentences, however, do bring out several important aspects of the *takže/tože* problem. The unacceptability of the sentences with 'misplaced' *takže/tože* is not as categorical as errors of morphology or syntax, like

(9)   *On čitaeš' gazeti. 'He reads (2sg.) the newspaper.' (gen. sg.)

So we are presumably dealing with a matter of semantic acceptability, perhaps with some variation in usage. Furthermore, the examples clearly involve two sentences, and the communication of certain types of information within the scope of *takže/tože*. Both of these considerations lend weight to the most promising explanation of *takže/tože* offered so far:

that the choice between them is linked to the old/new information structure of the sentence in terms of Functional Sentence Perspective.

The argument is presented most fully in Gundel (1975). She claims that *takže* occurs with new information (RHEME, COMMENT), while *tože* occurs with old information (THEME, TOPIC). Her principal set of examples includes:

(10*a*) Ivan vzjal v biblioteke žurnal. Maša tože vzjala žurnal.
'Ivan took a periodical from the library. Masha also took a periodical.'
(10*b*) Ivan vzjal v biblioteke žurnal. On vzjal tam takže knigu.
'Ivan took a periodical from the library. He also took a book there.'

(11*a*) Ivan ljubit igrat' na gitare, i Maša tože.
'Ivan likes to play the guitar, and so does Masha.'
(11*b*) Ivan tancuet, poët, a takže ljubit igrat' na gitare.
'Ivan dances, sings, and also likes playing the guitar.'

(12*a*) V Moskve est' istoričeskij muzej, i v Leningrade tože.
'In Moscow there is a historical museum, and (there is one) in Leningrad too.'
(12*b*) V Moskve est' istoričeskij muzej. V Moskve takže est' literaturnyj muzej. 'In Moscow there is a historical museum. In Moscow there is also a literary museum.'

(13*a*) Vy ne spite? A ja vot tože nikak ne mogu zasnut'.
'You can't sleep? And I also can't get to sleep at all.'
(13*b*) Ja ne mogu est', a takže ne mogu spat'.
'I cannot eat, and also cannot sleep.'

So far, it looks as if all we need is a rule: 'if same subject, use *takže;* if different subject, use *tože'. But this is clearly too simplistic:*

(14*a*) Ja očen' ljublju Čexova. Tolstogo tože ljublju.
'I very much like Chekhov. Tolstoy I also like.'
(14*b*) Ja očen' ljublju Čexova. Ja takže ljublju Tolstogo.
'I very much like Chekhov. I also like Tolstoy.'

Gundel claims that the examples show *tože* is used when it refers to (or 'has within its scope') the topic of the sentence, while *takže* is used to refer to the comment. She is able to adduce several important pieces of evidence to support this claim. Subjectless sentences, for instance, often consist totally of comment, and lack a topic; the Gundel hypothesis correctly predicts the appearance of *takže:*

(15*a*) Takže prodajut jabloki i gruški. 'They also sell apples and pears.'
(15*b*) Takže torgujut korovami i vsjakim skotom.
'They also trade in cows and all kinds of cattle.' (Grigorovič)

Furthermore, she is able to refer to 'a special class of sentences which typically begin with a verb and have a reading where the comment is either the whole sentence or an identification of some description as the noun phrase that follows the verb' (*ibid.*, 179). These examples predictably show *takže:*

(16*a*) Ispol'zovalis' takže drugie instrumenty.
'There were used also other instruments.'

(16*b*) Takže ne ostalos' vina.
     'Also there was no wine left.'
(16c) Vošla takže devuška.
     'There came in also a girl.' ('A girl also came in.')

But she is forced to qualify the generalization: 'with a different word order, when the grammatical subject of the sentence is also the topic, *tože* is more commonly used' (*ibid.*), as is seen in

(17*a*) Drugie instrumenty tože ispol'zovalis'.
     'Other instruments too were used.'
(17*b*) Vina tože ne ostalos'.
     'There also wasn't any wine left.' (i.e. the wine too ran out)
(17c) Devuška tože vošla.
     'The girl too came in.'

And finally, there are parallels of stress with English, where Gundel claims that *also/tože* take primary stress when referring to the topic, and *also/takže* take secondary stress when referring to the comment:

(18*a*) Mary passed the exam, and Bill also passed.
     (*Primary stress*)
(18*b*) Mary passed the exam, and she also got the job.
     (*Secondary stress*)

(19*a*) Maša kupila plastinku, i Pëtr tože kupil plastinku.
     'Masha bought a record, and Peter also bought a record.' (*Primary stress*)
(19*b*) Maša kupila plastinku, i ona takže kupila plat'e.
     'Masha bought a record, and she also bought a dress.' (*Secondary stress*)

    Gundel's analysis is adopted by Nakhimovsky and Leed (1980), with several additions. They claim that *takže* is always usable, while *tože* can only occur with new topics, and not with new comments. The evidence of (5-6) would seem to support this view. They also claim that with fronted comments—that is, with the comment occurring in sentence-initial position in inverted word-order—*tože* can be used instead of *takže;* this is an extension of Gundel's 'special class of sentences':

(20*a*) Ja xoču xleba. Masla ja tože xoču.
     'I want some bread. Butter I also want.'

though this sentence can also be expressed by

(20*b*) Ja xoču xleba. Ja xoču i masla.
(20c) Ja xoču xleba. Ja i masla xoču.

using the emphatic particle *i*.

    I would like to suggest an alternative explanation of the distribution of *takže/tože*. It is not inconsistent with most of the FSP-based analyses of Gundel and Nakhimovsky and Leed (and others!), but relies on simpler criteria, and is able to explain certain aspects of the distribution of *takže/tože* which they are either unable to handle, or handle only by means of special exceptions and sub-rules. In our analysis, the behaviour of *takže/tože* is not dictated by topics and comments at all, though the FSP structure of the sentence, as we shall see, is in fact correctly predicted by *takže/tože* themselves in most cases. We require only the notion of SCOPE, which finds ample independent justification in syntax and semantics (Jackendoff 1972); and the observation that *tože* refers (= 'has as its scope') the major constituent to its LEFT, and *takže* to the major constituent to its RIGHT. This rule is consistent with all the examples given so far, with the one exception of the examples with inverted word-order (20), to which we shall return below. We can now see why *tože* is so unusual at the beginning of the sentence (except marginally in elliptical constructions in conversation): a sentence-initial *tože* has nothing to attach itself to, no leftwards constituent which could fall within its scope:

> (21)   Takže ne vedaeš' ničego pro syna-to svoego . . . (Grigorovič)
> 'You also know nothing about your son . . . '

Tože is possible, but stylistically marked, in such constructions. What is more important is the fact that the occurence of *takže* in a structure like (21) does not depend on the topic/comment structure of the sentence.

The occurrence of *takže/tože* in sentence-final position is less straightforward. Russian, like English, has a stylistic bias against sentence-final 'also'. But both *takže* and *tože* occur in sentence-final position, and in a way which again does not depend on the topic/comment structure of the sentence:

> (22*a*) Včera Maša byla v kino. Ona byla na lekcii tože (takže).
> 'Yesterday Masha went to the cinema. She went to the lecture also.'
> (22*b*) Včera Maša byla v kino. Na lekcii byla ona tože (takže).
> 'Yesterday Masha went to the cinema. At the lecture she was also.' (she also went to the lecture)

Notice that these examples have the 'also' word referring to the whole sentence, as can be seen from the paraphrase:

> (22*c*) Včera Maša byla v kino. Takže pravda, čto ona pobyvala i na lekcii.
> 'Yesterday Masha went to the cinema. It is also true that she went to the lecture too.'

The appearance of *takže* in some sentence-final 'also' statements suggests that in this position it is not exclusively right-referring. *Tože* is also found, though rather seldom, in sentence-initial position, which suggests that here at least it is not exclusively left-referring. In both instances the sentence can be paraphrased as 'SENTENCE also happened', which separates *takže/tože* from reference to individual constituents, arguments, or information-components within the sentence. This phenomenon with sentence-initial and sentence-final position is not restricted to *takže/tože*. Time adverbs like *vsegda* 'always' can also have an adjective within their scope, and in medial position in the sentence this adjective is always to the right of the *vsegda:*

> (23*a*) Aleksandr smotrel v eë vsegda očarovatel'nye glaza.
> 'Alexander gazed into her always enchanting eyes.'

And *vsedga,* in referring to the Verb Phrase, regularly occurs to its left:

> (23*b*) Aleksandr vsegda slušaet radio posle obeda.
> 'Alexander always listens to the radio after dinner.'

But *vsegda* can occur in sentence-final position—and, very emphatically and somewhat marginally—in sentence-initial position:

(23*c*) Aleksandr slušaet radio posle obeda vsegda.
(23*d*) Vsegda Aleksandr slušaet radio posle obeda.

There is, then, precedent for right-scope words to occur at the beginning or end of sentences. There are rather few left-scope words like *tože* in Russian, however, and their freedom of occurrence at the beginning of the sentence is restricted. *Tože* in this position principally occurs with exclamations:

(24*a*) Tože xoroš! 'You're a fine one!'
(24*b*) Tože mne ešče. { 'Do you expect me to take that seriously?' 'Try pulling the other leg!'

Nevertheless, there is obvious precedent for right- and left-scope words to occur in both sentence-initial and sentence-final position, and for their left/right referring powers to be modified when they refer to whole sentences rather than to individual arguments.

The most common position for *takže/tože*, however, is after the first major constituent in the sentence. This fact at once suggests Wackernagel's (1892) law for the placement of enclitics, in the first unaccented position in the sentence. *Tože*, in fact, is also like an enclitic in attaching itself to the next leftwards constituent semantically—though it does not follow the usual practice of enclitics in being unstressed. *Takže*, though it is also primarily a second-place word, is PROCLITIC in the same semantic sense in which *tože* is ENCLITIC. We can follow this difference in meaning through the usual tests of paraphrase:

(25*a*) Segodnja Maša byla v kino. Ona takže (??tože) byla na lekcii.
'Today Masha went to the cinema. She also went to the lecture.' (where else did she go?)
(25*b*) Segodnja Maša byla v kino. Sergej tože (??takže) byl v kino (tam).
'Today Masha went to the cinema. Sergej also went to the cinema (there).' (who else went to the cinema?)

The left/right scope of *tože/takže* can be shown by altering the word order with the same topic/comment structure in the sentence. This demonstrates that the crucial fact in choosing *tože* or *takže* is not the association of *tože/takže* with topic/comment, but with the surface ordering of these elements with respect to *tože/takže:*

(26*a*) Segodnja Maša byla v kino. Na lekcii (*comment*) tože (??tažke) byla ona (*topic*).
'Today Masha went to the cinema. To the lecture also went she.'
(26*b*) Segodnja Maša byla v kino. V kino (*topic*) takže (??tože) byl Sergej (*comment*).
'Today Masha went to the cinema. To the cinema also went Sergej.' (i.e. it was also Sergej who . . .)[3]

---

[3] Note that these sentences are stylistically marked. To be fully acceptable they require appropriate intonation, together with a pause after *tože/takže*.

The use of *tože* in examples like (26*a*) poses a difficulty for Gundel's theory. Nakhimovsky and Leed propose a special set of sentences with 'fronted comments', and Gundel has a special class of verb-initial sentences for comparable problems of topic/comment structure (15). Both sets of exceptions are handled automatically by the left/right scope of *tože/takže.*

There are, however, some difficulties. The most serious concerns examples quoted by Nakhimovsky and Leed in their special class of fronted comments:

>(27*a*) Ja xodil v teatr. V kino ja tože xodil.
>   'I went to the theatre. To the cinema I also went.'
>(27*b*) Ja xoču xleba. Masla ja tože xoču.
>   'I want some bread (Partitive genitive). Some butter I also want.'

Here we find that *tože* does not occur directly to the right of the constituent(s) which are within its scope. One can, of course, say

>(28*a*) . . . V kino tože ja xodil.   (cf. 27*a*)
>(28*b*) . . . Masla tože ja xoču.   (cf. 27*b*)

But these are stylistically marked, and Nakhimovsky and Leed are correct in claiming that Russians prefer to avoid such structures, especially by means of the emphatic particle *i* 'too, even':

>(29*a*) Ja xodil i v kino.
>   Ja i v kino xodil.
>   I v kino ja xodil.
>(29*b*) Ja i masla xoču.
>   I masla ja xoču.

Before tackling this difficulty with *tože,* however, it is useful to investigate *takže,* which also need not occur immediately next to the constituent within its scope (we return later to the constructions like (27) where *takže* can replace *tože*). If we reorder the last sentence of (27*a*) we find

>(30*a*) . . . Ja takže xodil (xodil takže) v kino.
>(30*b*) . . . Ja takže xoču (xoču takže) masla.

In transformational terms, *takže* would originally occur next to the constituent(s) within its scope, and would then be optionally moved leftwards across *xodil/xoču.* Such a solution would seriously weaken the left/right scope analysis of *tože/takže* if it were not possible to find other words which can move in a comparable way, or to define the constituents across which *takže* can move in some independently motivated way. Happily, there are good reasons for supposing that both these difficulties can be overcome.

To begin with, the Negative particle in both Russian and English is right-scope, like *takže.* This Negative particle in both Russian and English can be moved leftwards—or 'raised' by the NEG-RAISING transformation—from the embedded to the superordinate sentence:

>(31*a*) Ja xoču ne kurit'.
>   'I want not to smoke.'
>(31*b*) Ja ne xoču kurit'.
>   'I don't want to smoke.'

(32*a*) Ja dumaju, čto ona ne ljubit menja.
'I think that she doesn't love me.'
(32*b*) Ja ne dumaju, čto ona ljubit menja.
'I don't think that she loves me.'

In both sets of examples the Negative can occur at the leftmost margin of the Verb Phrase. The same mobility is shown by Russian *tol'ko* 'only' and English *only*. These are also right-scope words, and are much closer semantically to Russian *takže:*

(33*a*) Ja xoču tol'ko masla.
'I want only butter.'
(33*b*) Ja tol'ko xoču masla.
'I only want butter.'

(34*a*) Ja xoču tol'ko pet'.
'I want only to sing.'
(34*b*) Ja tol'ko xoču pet'.
'I only want to sing.'

All these examples lend credibility to the right-scope analysis of Russian *takže,* and its restricted but distinct capacity for leftwards movement to the leftmost margin of the Verb Phrase. This movement can only occur if the verb is the same (or, within certain tolerances, semantically a near-synonym) in both sentences:

(34) Včera ja byl v gostjax u Larinyx. Ja takže posetil Mašu.
'Yesterday I was at the Larins. I also visited Masha.'

If the verbs are different, or semantically far apart, the 'also' word would have to occur in any case at the leftmost margin of the Verb Phrase, since the verb constitutes new information:

(36*a*) Včera ja napisal operu. Ja takže perevël *Vojnu i Mir.*
'Yesterday I wrote an opera. I also translated *War and Peace.*'

cf. (36*b*) . . . . . . *Ja perevël takže *Vojnu i Mir.*

Let us now return to *tože,* and the difficulties presented by examples (27*a, b*). These sentences are potentially ambiguous. The *tože* may refer either to *ja* 'I'—that is, 'I too was going to the cinema . . . ', except that 'I' is already identified in the first sentence, which transfers the scope of *tože* to the preceding constituent. Here the subject intervenes between *tože* and the constituent within its scope. The examples of (28*a, b*) show a predictable left-scope use of *tože,* but one which is rejected on stylistic grounds in favour of (27). The parallel English use of *also* (with primary stress in Gundel's sense (18–19)), is more restricted by the marginal status of OSV word-order in English:

(37*a*) Honey I detest. Bread I also detest.
(37*b*) Honey I detest. Bread also I detest.

But this provides reassurance rather than explanation. In terms of Functional Sentence Perspective, the Object-Subject-*tože* or Adverbial-Subject-*tože* order can be explained by having *tože* refer to the nearest leftwards constituent which constitutes new information. This is a mirror image of the displaced *takže* (30), which refers to the nearest RIGHTWARDS constituent which constitutes new information. It would, of course, be more satisfactory to avoid the introduction of Functional Sentence Perspective into a problem which we have been attempting to handle in terms of syntax and scope-semantics. I believe that the explanation we have offered for *takže* is convincing. I suspect, reluctantly, that the FSP explanation for this aspect of *tože* is the best that we can do; but it is at least worth while considering the arguments that can be brought to support a syntactic and scope-semantic explanation of *tože*.

The worst aspect of the problem is that Russian has relatively few left-scope words. Most of them are strictly enclitic, and so cannot be displaced rightwards. It is therefore difficult to refer the displaced *tože* to other precedents, as we can with *takže* and its similarities to NEGATIVE and *only*. The evidence that we do have is more suggestive than decisive, and is based mainly on word order. In spite of the often cited variability of Russian word order, the Subject-initial order predominates in 75 percent of Subject-Predicate, and 79 percent of Subject-Predicate-Complement structures (Bivon 1971, 30 and 42). This allows us to predict that *tože* in second position will follow the subject in precisely this proportion of instances, which must therefore be counted as the unmarked order for the location of *tože* with respect to subject and verb in medial position. Furthermore, there is an even stronger tendency in Russian—and one which Bivon does not quantify—to keep noun subjects and objects on opposite sides of the verb (pronoun objects precede the verb in SOV structures in about 50 percent of cases (Svedstedt 1976)):

(38*a*) Nikita Sergeevič udaril stol.
     'Nikita Sergeevich struck the table.'
(38*b*) Stol udaril Nikita Sergeevič.   (OVS)

The other orders strongly prefer to have the subject before the object and their acceptability depends on special emphatic information patterns:

(38*c*)   Nikita Sergeevič stol udaril.   (SOV)

(38*d*)   Udaril Nikita Sergeevič stol.   (VSO)

(38*e*)?   Stol Nikita Sergeevič udaril.   (OSV)

(38*f*)??   Udaril stol Nikita Sergeevič.   (VOS)

With intransitive verbs of motion the subject and direction adverbial also tend to bracket the verb in the large majority of cases:

(39*a*) Nikita Sergeevič priexal v N'ju Jork.
     'Nikita Sergeevich arrived in New York.'
(39*b*) V N'ju Jork priexal Nikita Sergeevič.

And when the subject and adverbial occur on the same side of the verb, there is again a strong preference to have the subject first:

(39c) Nikita Sergeevič v N'ju Jork priexal. (SAV)
(39d) Priexal Nikita Sergeevič v N'ju Jork. (VSA)
(39e)? V N'ju Jork Nikita Sergeevič priexal. (ASV)
(39f)? Priexal v N'ju Jork Nikita Sergeevič. (VAS)

(though adverbials are markedly more flexible than objects in variations of word order). The acceptability of the more marginal word-orders depends on the weight of the subject and object. A 'heavy' constituent, containing complex constructions or marked word-order, makes the whole construction significantly less acceptable, whether it functions as subject or object. Clitics *can* be added without weighing down constituents unduly:

(40a) Nikita Sergeevič i stol udaril.
'Nikita Sergeevich struck the table too.'
(40b) Priexal v N'ju Jork i Nikita Sergeevič.
'Nikita Sergeevich too arrived in New York.'

But practically any other kind of constituent or modifier attached to a subject, object or adverbial makes it stylistically heavy, particularly in the least favoured orders with object before subject.

(41a)?? Derevjannyj stol Nikita Sergeevič udaril.
'Nikita Sergeevich struck the wooden table.'

(41b)?? Udaril derevjannyj stol Nikita Sergeevič.

On the other hand, pronouns count as light subjects or objects. In structures like (27), where the pronoun *ja* repeats a stated subject in the preceding sentence, the pronoun subject reaches probably its 'lightest' point—the next lighter stage being the deletion of the pronoun altogether. Now *tože,* although semantically a clitic, does not function as a phonological clitic; it is regularly stressed. If it were attached to *v kino* or *masla* it would increase the stylistic weight of the sentence. Consequently it reverts to its unmarked stylistic position after the ('light') pronoun subject, as in (27). This conclusion is supported by the fact that the heavier the subject, the less acceptable is the displaced *tože:*

(42a) . . . V kino vse učeniki pervogo klassa tože byli.
'At the cinema all the students of the first class also were.'
(42b) . . . Masla vysokij čelovek s širokimi plečami tože xočet.
'Butter the tall man with the broad shoulders also wants.'

Both these sentences are only marginally able to carry the interpretation where *tože* refers to *v kino* or *masla;* it is more natural to interpret them as if the *tože* were in sentence-final position, with the paraphrase 'it is also the case that + SENTENCE'. But notice that even with sentences like (27) there is no possibility of misunderstanding the reference of *tože,* since *ja* has been mentioned in the previous sentence, and therefore cannot be the comment.

The general lines of our argument for the left/right scope analysis of *tože/takže* are confirmed by a variety of evidence. The first important confirmation concerns the notion of left/right scope itself. We have already seen how other right-scope words function somewhat like *takže,* particularly NEGATIVE and 'only'. Two further crucial examples of scope are the particles *i* 'and, also' and *že* 'but, however'. These particles resemble *takže* and *tože* respectively, since *i* has as its scope the following constituent (i.e. is proclitic), and *že* has as its scope the preceding constituent (i.e. is enclitic). These particles differ from *tože/takže,* however, in that *že* is a Wackernagel-type sentence enclitic, while *i* is a word-clitic, and can attach itself to major constituents in many positions in the sentence:

> (43*a*) Maša byla v kino. Sergej že byl na lekcii.
> 'Masha was at the cinema. But Sergej was at the lecture.'
> (43*b*) Maša byla v kino. Potom ona byla i na lekcii.
> 'Masha was at the cinema. Later she even went (went even) to the lecture.'

(and here, incidentally, English *even* shows the same leftwards movement that we saw in (30–33), so providing further correlation for our analysis.) The correlation of Russian *i* and *že* with *takže* and *tože* is also evident in that they are sometimes found in pairs:

> (44*a*) Maša igraet na klarnete. U neë est' i goboj tože.
> 'Masha plays the clarinet. She has an oboe too.'
> (44*b*) Maša igraet na klarnete. U neë est' takže i goboj.

and this also shows why *takže* can be replaced by *i,* since both are right-scope (the corollary does not apply to *že* and *tože,* because of their semantic differences).

The examples with *i* and *že* raise the more general question of where *tože* and *takže* belong with respect to clitic systems on the one hand, and syntactic left- and right- modifying systems, on the other hand. The Slavonic languages in general, and Russian in particular, show a variety of clitic-like structures. There are genuine phonological unstressed clitics, like *i* and *že;* Wackernagel-type second-place enclitics (*že*); and syntactic-semantic clitics, which may be stressed, but still have right/left scope. *Tože* and *takže* are predominantly second-place words, like French *donc* 'therefore' and German *aber* 'however'; they may be stressed, and they may occur in sentence-initial and sentence-final position. Their capacity for left/right scope links them to more clitic-like elements of the *i* and *že* type, as well as to broader syntactic structures like left-modifying relative clauses and right-modifying strings of adjectives in Noun Phrase. Their indeterminate position in Russian word-classes, and this diversity of affiliations, have probably been among the more important factors which have delayed a proper understanding of their place in the syntax and semantics of modern Russian.

Furthermore, their semantic-pragmatic functions, as we have described them, are in all cases consistent with Functional Sentence Perspective. Not that the Gundel analysis is wholly correct. We have been able to point out some factual errors, and some instances of *ad hoc* adaptations of the theory to fit the facts. The Gundel approach, indeed, sees *takže* and *tože* partly through the wrong end of the telescope. Topics and comments, and their association with subjects and predicates, do not primarily dictate the choice of *takže* and *tože*. Instead, *takže* and *tože* themselves function as markers of the FSP structure of the sentence, by having the comment within their scope respectively to right and left. This claim may sound odd. Why should it be that only the comment occurs within the scope of an 'also' word? The answer lies in the pragmatic and functional construction of the sentence. An 'also' word marks new information (comment) as being of special interest or relevance. Especially with contrastive intonation, it may even signal information which runs counter to the presuppositions, implications and conversational expectations of a given discourse. This is why Gundel's association of *tože/takže* with topics/comments is semantically misleading. 'Also' statements about topics are usually pragmatically infelicitous: there is no point in marking known information for special attention if it is already known.

A check through the three major modern dictionaries of Russian (*AN* 4, *AN* 17, *Ušakov*) shows that our proposed analysis is confirmed in all the quoted examples, with one significant but systematic exception. This occurs when the expectations of the discourse are violated, and the 'also' word highlights a piece of information about, and including, the topic. The traditional view of topic-comment structure concentrates on explicit information, and relatively less attention has been directed to the status of implication in the structuring of new/old information and the formation of grammatical constructions. The data of *tože/takže*, however, clearly show how comments are associated with overt as well as implied information. Perhaps the clearest indication of this parallelism occurs when what is apparently the wrong 'also' word occurs—'wrong', that is, with respect to the topic/comment structure of the sentence as it would normally be expected:

(45a)?Ivan znaet Mašu. Ivan tože znaet Ol'gu . . .
    'Ivan knows Masha. Ivan too knows Olga . . . '

The second sentence is marginally acceptable, and would normally be expected after a sentence like

(45b) Petja znaet Mašu. Ivan tože znaet Mašu . . .
    'Pete knows Masha. Ivan too knows Masha . . . '

Conversely, the structure of (45a) would normally show *takže:*

(45c) Ivan znaet Mašu. Ivan takže znaet Ol'gu (znaet takže . . .)
    'Ivan knows Masha. Ivan knows Olga too . . . '

What (45a) suggests is that, contrary to implications and expectations (expressed within or outside the text), Ivan knows Olga. In such sentences it is not easy to determine what is the topic. 'Ivan' certainly constitutes known information, but the connection between the two sentences of (45a) is irregular: it suggests that what was thought to be established information about Ivan can no longer be assumed. In such sentences there is a strong tendency for the whole sentence to be interpreted as new information, as can be seen from the paraphrase test. Whereas (45b) answers the question 'Who else knows Masha?', and (45c) the question 'Who else does Ivan know?', (45a) has no immediately obvious trigger question, and the best paraphrase available is something like 'And it is also the case that (previous evidence notwithstanding) Ivan knows Olga'.

It is precisely in such instances—when the whole sentence can be interpreted as new information or comment—that we find a choice between *tože* and *takže,* particularly at the sentence's margins, and especially sentence-finally:

> (46*a*) U Ivana est' klarnet, i u Peti est' flejta. U Ivana est' flejta takže/tože.
> 'Ivan has a clarinet, and Pete has a flute. Ivan has a flute too.'

Such data do not destroy our argument, but they do introduce an important but plausible modification. In all the Russian dictionary corpus (see above), *tože* is strictly left-scope when it occurs in medial position. *Takže* is predominantly right-scope in medial position, though it does show a few uses which are apparently left-scope. One such example is

> (46*b*) U Ivana est' klarnet, i u Peti est' flejta. U Ivana takže est' flejta.
> 'Ivan has a clarinet and Pete has a flute. Ivan also has a flute.'

—which incidentally shows the left/right scope ambivalence of English *also*. There is also the question of the replacement of *tože* by *takže* in (27), which we foreshadowed:

> (47*a*) Ja xodil v teatr. V kino ja takže xodil.
> 'I went to the theatre. To the cinema I also went.'
> (47*b*) Ja xoču xleba. Masla ja takže xoču.
> 'I want some bread. Some butter I also want.'

All these structures confirm the observation of Nakhimovsky and Leed that *takže* is less restricted than *tože*. But structures like (47) are stylistically marked, and native speakers prefer to place the *takže* (or *tože*) in final position:

> (48*a*) Ja xodil v teatr. V kino ja xodil takže/tože.
> (48*b*) Ja xoču xleba. Masla ja xoču takže/tože.

With *tože/takže* in sentence-final position, the rules of left/right scope, and the association of 'also' with comments as individual constituents of the sentence, break down; the principal residue of the left/right scope rule is the preference for *takže* over *tože* in sentence-initial position, and for *tože* over *takže* in sentence-final position.

There are two difficulties here: the relation between medial and sentence-margin *tože/takže,* and the issue of why *takže* can apparently have left scope. The difference of medial/non-medial *tože/takže* finds parallels in other types of constituent: we have already seen one example with *vsegda* 'always' (23*a*), and there are many other examples of adverbs which modify individual constituents in medial position, but whole sentences in non-medial position:

> (49*a*) V Avstralii muzykanty často igrajut na didžeridu.
> 'In Australia musicians often play the didgeridoo.'
> (49*b*) Muzykanty v Avstralii často igrajut na didžeridu.
> 'Musicians in Australia often play the didgeridoo.'

The sentence-margin positions therefore weaken the association of 'also' ('always', 'only', adverbs, etc.) with individual constituents, and suggest paraphrases like 'it is also/always/etc. the case that + SENTENCE'. But the association of 'also' with comments still holds. In sentences with sentence-margin 'also' the linguistic context and the word order mark the identity of the comment, as in ordinary sentences which do not contain 'also'.

So what has happened in sentences like (46), where *takže* is apparently violating the rule of comment identification to its right? Like *tože*, *takže* in medial position may be displaced, as we have seen (27, 30, 35, 36). But while *tože* is strictly left-scope, *takže* need not be strictly right-scope. The examples where this occurs are (*i*) with *takže* at the end of the sentence, which we have already discussed; (*ii*) in examples like (46*b*), where there is some doubt about exactly what is the topic; and (*iii*) in cases like (27, 47), with the displaced *tože*. (46*b*) can, I think, be handled naturally within the analysis already presented. Native speakers sometimes object to such structures, but agree that, if anything, (47*b*) suggests that Ivan, in addition to having a clarinet, also has a flute. The reading which assigns the 'also' to Ivan is unnatural—that Ivan is another person who possesses a flute, as Pete does. This ambivalence in the topic/comment structure arises from the occurrence of both 'Ivan' and 'flute' in the preceding sentence, and from the resulting indeterminacy in the topic/comment structure of (46*b*). The left/right scope properties of *tože/takže*, far from being thrown into doubt, actually serve to mark what is to be interpreted as topic and comment in the continuing discourse.

But (27) and (47) require closer attention, since they seem to show *takže* with left scope. There are several possible explanations for this phenomenon. It might be argued that the underlying structure of (47*b*)—for the sake of argument—in the neutral word order, is

(50*a*) . . . Ja xoču takže masla.
'I want butter too.'

which gives

(50*b*) Ja takže xoču masla.

by some rule like 'ALSO-displacement' (see 31–34). Sentence (47*b*) is then derived by COMMENT-FRONTING, a common and well established rule of all Slavonic languages. But why should the comment leave behind its 'also' marker, producing a potentially ambiguous sentence, or at least a violation of the right-scope rule for *takže*? There is no obvious answer to this objection. Nor do we find good reason to relax the right-scope rule for *takže* just to accommodate (47), even if this occurs only in the slot where displaced *tože* is expected.

One of the strongest confirmations of our analysis is that it provides a rationale for this apparently aberrant behaviour of *takže*. The explanation hinges on the semantax of 'also'. All sentences with constituent-'also', where *tože/takže* refers to a single constituent, logically include the same sentence with sentence-'also', where the 'also' refers to the whole sentence, and is paraphrasable by 'it is also the case that + SENTENCE':

(51*a*) Ivan ljubit mëd. Ja tože ljublju mëd. (=7*a*)
        'Ivan likes honey. I too like honey.'
(51*b*) Ivan ljubit mëd. Ja ljublju mëd tože/takže.
        'Ivan likes honey. I like honey too/also.'

The reverse does not hold, since the sentence-'also' structure (51*b*) need not imply the explicit association of the 'also' with any one constituent. Now let us return to (47*a*, *b*). Both sentences contain *takže* in a position where the constituents to its right cannot be the comment, and where the comment is a constituent to its left, but not immediately to its left. This 'irregular' *takže* occurs only with fronted comments (which is, incidentally, quite the reverse of Nakhimovsky and Leed's special rule for *tože* with fronted comments!). The fronted comment is always emphatic, since it violates the regular topic-comment, Subject-Verb-Object neutral order of the Russian sentence. And 'also' apparently attaches itself automatically to any emphatic component of a sentence: as we remarked, 'also' has the comment within its semantic scope, and emphasis always marks a comment—either a constituent-comment or a sentence-comment. This association can be seen in other examples, where the emphatic constituent and the 'also' are not adjacent:

(50*c*) Masla ja xoču takže/tože.
        'Butter I want also/too.'

The association of 'also' and 'butter' is shown by the paraphrase test suggested by Gundel: 'what else do you want?', which triggers (50*a–c*) as well as (27*b*).

This suggests the following conclusion. *Tože/takže* mark comments to left and right respectively, in sentences with neutral word-order. They may be displaced medially, and they may appear sentence-initially and sentence-finally. In these positions *tože/takže* may have within their scope either individual constituents or the whole sentence. Furthermore, in these positions the strict left/right scope rule is weakened, a phenomenon which is confirmed by the behaviour of other constituents of the sentence in medial and non-medial position. *Tože*, however, remains left-scope, even if the comment is not immediately to its left, except in its rather marginal ability to occur at the beginning of a sentence. *Takže* is more flexible, and occurs both sentence-initially, sentence-finally, and medially. It only replaces *tože* medially, however, when the word-order of the sentence marks the comment independently of the 'also' word, which is thus allowed to occur in any of its regular positions, but now without strict right-scope. This explanation, of course, may also hold for the displaced *tože*. Instead of having it refer to the next leftwards possible constituent able to function as a comment, it is just as plausible to transfer the comment-identifying function to word order, and leave *tože* free to choose its location in the sentence on stylistic grounds. Either way, we find confirmation for the central claim of this paper: that *tože/takže* are one of the basic markers of comments in the FSP structure of the sentence.

This problem, and this style of analysis, leave several loose ends untied. It would be encouraging, for instance, if the stylistic aspect of *tože/takže* turned out to be illuminated by, or at least consistent with, our Scope+ FSP approach (Sussex, in prep.). There are also, however, more far-reaching problems with the data themselves. As we have seen, there is no absolute division between the two 'also' words in their areas of application in the sentence. In some instances it is simply not clear where topics and comments are divided, which leads to indeterminacy in the choice of *tože/takže*. And there are some types of sentence where both the 'also' words may occur. It is likely that this possibility of choice has something to do with their misuse elsewhere in the sentence, and with the difficulty in eliciting from native informants responses which are statistically consistent enough to use as a solid basis for generalization. A lot depends on intonation and on felicity conditions; and while some of these may be explicit enough in terms of the functional structure of the sentence and its extra-linguistic context, other factors remain inexplicit and sometimes inaccessible to objective testing. In such cases the predictive power of the proposed explanation is itself a vital heuristic tool. It allows the investigator to test the limits of the hypothesis, and to identify, if not always solve, some of the hitherto undiscovered or uncontrolled variables. And finally, it lends some support to the notion that the best explanation, *ceteris paribus,* is the least costly in terms of descriptive machinery. As a matter of theoretical principle, as well as heuristic practice, we are therefore bound to try the scope theory to the limits before adding to the explanation the more costly apparatus of Functional Sentence Perspective.

References

AN SSSR. Institut Russkogo Jazyka, 1957–1961: *Slovar' russkogo jazyka.* 4 vols. Moscow: GIINS.

AN SSSR. Institut Russkogo Jazyka, 1950–1965: *Slovar' sovremennogo russkogo literaturnogo jazyka.* 17 vols. M–L., Izd-vo AN SSSR.

Baker, R.L. 1977: *Mastering Russian: a workbook for use with 'Russian for everybody'.* Laconia, New Hampshire: Andre Pacquette Associates.

Bivon, R. 1971: *Element order.* Cambridge: Cambridge University Press.

Bogusław ski, A. (Boguslavskij) 1969: K voprosu o vtoričnom oboznačenii opredelënnogo soderžanija v russkom svjaznom tekste. *Filologičeskie nauki* **12,** 115–20.

Gundel, J.K. 1975: Topic-comment structure and the use of *tože* and *takže. Slavic & East European J* **17,** 174–81.

Jackendoff, R.S. 1972: *Semantic interpretation in generative grammar.* Cambridge, Mass.: MIT Press.

Kovačeva, N.N. 1964: O nekotoryx slučajax upotreblenija *tože* i *takže. Očerki po metodike prepodavanija russkogo jazyka inostrancam.* Moscow: Universitet Družby Narodov, 91–107.

Nakhimovsky, A. and Leed, R. 1980: *Advanced Russian.* Columbus: Slavica.

Sussex, R. (in prep.). *Clisis and clitics in Slavic.*

Svedstedt, D. 1976: *The position of objective personal pronouns: a study of word order in Modern Russian.* Stockholm Slavic Studies.

Ušakov, D.N. 1935–1940: *Tolkovyj slovar' sovremennogo russkogo jazyka.* Moscow: OGIZ.

Wackernagel, J. 1892: Über ein Gesetz der indogermanischen Wortstellung. *IF* **1,** 333–436.

11

On grammars and language acquisition
Paul Fletcher

Introduction

To a linguist, the assumption of a close relationship between linguistic theory and description, on the one hand, and language acquisition, on the other, comes so naturally as to be unquestioned. In particular, the notion that language-learning is rule-learning maintains a powerful appeal. The link between grammars and language acquisition is established in two related ways: first, via a specific innateness hypothesis, which holds that the child's language learning is determined by a set of principles which also serve as limits to the construction of grammars by linguists; and secondly, via empirical studies of language development which interpret certain features of children's productions as evidence for the dependence of those productions on grammatical rules. It will be contended here that the assumption that language-learning is rule-learning is unhelpful and distorting. In order to establish this we will begin by taking seriously the view that assumes an isomorphism between the grammar constructed by the linguist and the grammar constructed by the child. It will then be useful to examine the consequences of this view in some detail in relation to one area of English grammar (the learning of verb forms[1]), to show that rule-based accounts both oversimplify the learning process, and overestimate the young child's potential for productivity. This will then provide a platform for a more realistic assessment of the relationship between the linguist's constructs and the investigation of language development.

---

[1] The general term VERB FORM is used for any modification of a main verb by inflection, auxiliary or auxiliary plus inflection. This inevitably (and appropriately, for this volume) maintains the traditional view of *be, have, do, can,* etc. as auxiliaries and not main verbs.

Rule-learning: the case for

The innateness hypothesis

For some linguists, the relationship between linguistics and language acquisition remains much as it has been since Chomsky's first formulation. Those whose main concern is the elaboration of linguistic theory continue to contemplate a specific innateness hypothesis to explain the rather narrowly constrained forms of 'humanly accessible grammars' (for example Chomsky 1975, 13ff.; 1979, 35ff.; Lightfoot 1979, 16–17; Smith and Wilson 1979, 27–31). Such approaches rarely consider child language data systematically, but argue back from characteristics of adult language (rather, grammars of adult language) to innate principles. An argument presented by Chomsky (1975, 30–3) in relation to the principle of structure-dependence will serve as an example. He points out that one way of explaining the child's ability to form questions such as (1*a*) and (2*a*), corresponding to the declarative sentences (1*b*) and (2*b*), would be in terms of a rule constructed by the child of preposing the first occurrence of *is* in the declarative string:

(1*a*) Is the man tall.   (1*b*)   The man is tall.
(2*a*) Is the book on the table. (2*b*)   The book is on the table.

A similar strategy would work, in general, for the formation of other *yes-no* questions with auxiliary *is* and other auxiliaries from declarative sentences. There would therefore be a good deal of evidence which did not conflict with this explanation. An example like (3*a*) from the child, however, would indicate that the hypothesis was wrong:

(3*a*) Is the man who is tall in the room.
(3*b*) The man who is tall is in the room.

Here the strategy of preposing the first occurrence of *is* in (3*a*) would result in the ungrammatical string, (4):

*(4)   Is the man who tall is in the room.

The fact that children, at some point in their language development, produce sentences like (3*a*), but never (Chomsky asserts) make mistakes like (4), leads him to propose a hypothesis which credits the child with an analysis of declarative sentences like (1*b*)–(3*b*) into abstract phrases, as a preliminary to successful question-formation:

(1*b*)   NP [the man] VP [is tall]
(2*b*)   NP [the book] VP [is on the table]
(3*b*)   NP [the man who is tall] VP [is in the room]

It is on the analysis into abstract phrases (particularly the correct identification of subject NP in these examples) that appropriate question-formation depends, and not on word-by-word scanning for the first occurrence of *is* or auxiliary forms. The crucial difference between these rules is that the one which relies on an analysis into abstract phrases is structure-dependent, while the scanning rule is structure-independent. Structure-dependence is a grammatical universal; it is this, and the relative complexity of the structure-dependent question-formation rule (the word-by-word scanning hypothesis is much simpler, but the child, Chomsky claims, plumps for the less straightforward abstract analysis) that leads to the conclusion that: 'the child's mind . . . contains the instruction: construct a structure-dependent rule, ignoring all structure-independent rules. The principle of structure-dependence is not learned, but forms part of the conditions for language-learning' (Chomsky 1975, 32–3).

Transformations and langage learning. A theory of the kind outlined does not purport to provide a programme for language acquisition research. While in itself perhaps unexceptionable, nevertheless the theory continues to have regrettable effects on that research. A natural complement to arguments which establish innate principles for language learning on essentially rationalist grounds is empirical study which investigates in detail the extent to which structure-dependent rules—transformations—govern children's language-learning. At one time, language acquisition research was dominated by the search for grammatical rules. While this is no longer the case, there are still a number of recent examples of this genre (Hurford 1975; Fay 1978; Mayer *et al.* 1978), which by happy coincidence tend to focus on the area Chomsky uses for his structure-dependent rule example—verb forms and question formation. The most detailed and most recent study of this area is that by Erreich *et al.* (1980). Their argument begins from the interpretation of children's errors within a grammatical framework. Here are three examples cited (160):

(5) Did you came home?
(6) What did you bought?
(7) What shall we shall have?

These sentences have in common that they are all questions, and that they all contain, in addition to the appropriately pre-positioned auxiliary (*did/shall*) either an inappropriate tense marker (*came, bought*) or a wrongly positioned auxiliary before main verb (*shall*). The explanation given for these errors is that they 'result from an incorrect formulation of subject-aux inversion'. That is, they are the result of the incorrect formulation by the child of a transformational rule. There is nothing vague about this claim, which is elaborated in terms of a specific structural description, and certain basic operations on that description. The SD is the familiar *Aspects* type,[2] incorporating a Q-marker, as follows:

$$Q \quad NP \quad Tns \quad \left\{ \begin{array}{c} \text{Modal} \\ \textit{have} \\ \textit{be} \end{array} \right\} \quad Y$$

The question-formation rule involves two 'basic operations' on this structure; one of COPYING, which copies the relevant categories of Tns (present or past) and auxiliary into pre-subject NP position, and one of DELETION, which removes the pre-main verb Tns and auxiliary categories once copied. The child's (or children's) mistakes, in these terms, with

---

[2] Erreich *et al.* use an *Aspects* formulation 'because it is most widely known', not because their arguments specifically depend on that formulation of a transformational grammar. Their errors, they claim, 'could be accounted for within any of the more current candidate grammars'. It is convenient to follow their lead here.

reference to (5)–(7), involve failing to apply DELETION to the Tns and auxiliary categories after COPYING has taken place. Since the explanation of errors is so specifically in terms of constituent structure and rules that operate on this structure, it is worth examining the proposed account, for one of the errors, in a little more detail. In (5), the basis for the error in the child's production may be presumed to be as follows: if we take (5a) as the underlying structure[3],

(5a)

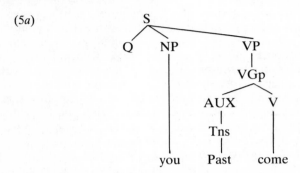

the child should convert this to (5b) (the correct structure) by COPYING Past to sentence initial position and then DELETING Past from its pre-main verb position. The Past formative in initial position then triggers *do*-SUPPORT.

(5b)

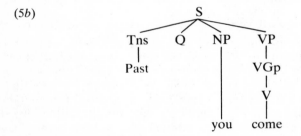

Instead, the child has formulated something like (5c):

(5c)

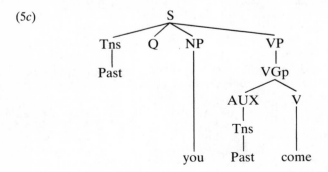

[3] Again for convenience, a VP expansion rule used by Huddleston (1976, 70) is applied here.

This arises, supposedly, because, after the basic operation of COPYING Past to sentence-initial position, DELETION of the pre-verb Past formative fails to take place. The structure (5c) meets the structural description for *do*-SUPPORT, in the same way as (5b) (hence sentence initial *did*), but in addition the second Past formative is available for affix-hopping—hence *came* in (5). Similar explanations, in terms of constituent structure configurations and operations on them, hold for the errors in (6) and (7) also. More generally, the child's syntax-learning is accounted for in terms of a hypothesis-testing model, where the child's hypotheses consist of candidate rules. Crucial evidence for these rules is errors that the child makes: 'incorrect hypotheses on the part of the child's device about the structural description, the basic operations, or the structural change of any transformation should result in characteristic errors in the child's errors in the child's speech' (Erreich *et al.* 1979, 160).

This is an attractive explanation of the errors we have seen, both because it might be seen as providing plausibility arguments for the specific innateness hypothesis, and because it appears to provide a principled and well-defined account of grammatical learning. It should be noted however that the data base for the account is limited to a rather selective range of errors, and that widening the range of data the theory has to account for presents problems for this and similar accounts of language-learning. Among these problems are:

(*i*) errors which could not be accounted for in terms of plausible candidate rules, or a range of error types which result in a proliferation of candidate rules;

(*ii*) the *absence* of errors predicted by the kind of rule proposed to account for correct instances;

(*iii*) distributional gaps which suggest arbitrary restrictions on rule application, or require non-syntactic factors for their explanation;

(*iv*) evidence of a 'lexical dimension' to the development of syntax, which suggests that acquisition is gradual and piecemeal (by being limited at some points to certain verbs or classes of verbs, in the case of verb-forms, for example).

We will consider examples of each of these problems in turn (though to a certain extent they overlap). Generally, we will use examples under the headings (*i*)–(*iv*) to argue that the Chomskyan view and that of his legatees is of limited value in accounting for the development of verb-forms.

Rule-learning: the case against

Errors and non-errors

There is a class of errors which British English children have been observed to make (see Fletcher 1981) which are not so straightforwardly explicable in terms of mistakes in basic operations. These are some examples:

(8)　Is it got a name?
(9)　Is our put the cake in?
(10)　Is you got the top off?

Indeed, such examples might not be the result of structure-dependent rules at all. They could equally well be accounted for by a strategy on the child's part which might be summarised as: 'to form a *yes-no* question, put *is* at the beginning of a declarative sentence'. If however (for the sake of generality), we want to account for these errors in the same way as (5)–(7), in terms of a transformation preposing *is* in each case, we have to assume that an underlying structure for (8), for example would resemble (8*a*):[4]

(8*a*)

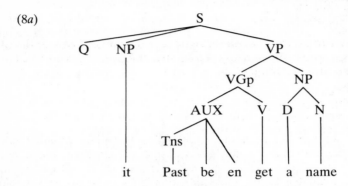

In these terms, (8) results from an *appropriate* transformation on an *inappropriate* constituent structure—*be* + *en* not being an allowable constituent for active sentences in English. Such an analysis by the child is of course not at all surprising (if we may widen the perspective for a moment) given the nature of the language of his environment. The child will hear sentences like (9)–(11), in which *have* forms contract to *'s*:

(9) It's got a name.
(10) He's put the cake in.
(11) She's got the top off.

In addition, there will be cases like (12)–(14), where *is* also contracts to *'s*:

(12) She's pretty.
(13) He's singing the song.
(14) It's taking the biscuit.

And finally, there will be questions, like (15)–(17), which have *is* in sentence-initial position:

(15) Is he singing?
(16) Is he tired?
(17) Is he happy?

In the face of these features of the child's language environment, the kind of error we see in (8)–(10) is not too surprising. Further, since it is attributable to an incorrect phrase-structure rule, and since Erreich *et al.* specifically allow for this possibility ('incorrect structural description') why

---

[4] One of the assumptions here, for the sake of the argument, is that it is reasonable to analyse *got* in (8) as *get* + past participle. For discussion of the status of (*have*) *got* see Fodor and Smith (1978), Fletcher (1981).

are such errors problematical? Seen individually, or as a set of similar items (often culled from different children), most errors can be explained away in terms of some inadequate formulation at some level of the grammar.[5] It is when these errors are examined in relation to the other errors and correct instances from the *same* child that difficulties emerge. Examples (18)–(20) are instances of sentences produced by a British English child at 2;6:

    (18)   He's broken that.
    (19)   Can you help me?
    (20)   Is you broken that?

If we attempt to account for these sentences in similar terms to the other examples, we would presumably set up structural descriptions like (18a)–(20a) for the three examples:

    (18a) N Pres have en V NP
    (19a) Q NP Pres can V NP
    (20a) Q NP Pres be en V NP

From (18) we are led to assume that *have + en* is a possible phrase structure rule outcome; from (19) (a type of sentence which occurs frequently—see Table 11.1) we can assume that subject-auxiliary inversion is available to the child. On this basis, it seems reasonable to conclude that a plausible underlying structure for (20) is (20a). Unfortunately this suggests that both *have + en* and *be + en* are possible phrase-structure rule expansions. While there is no reason why the child should not have 'competing hypotheses' at certain points in his development, a proliferation of candidate rules makes us at the least uncomfortable. Rules imply productivity, and a high positive correlation between error-proliferation and the number of candidate rules proposed might well shake our faith in the value of the proposed explanation. Further, even if we take the notion of competing hypotheses at face value, the theory provides few constraints on candidate hypotheses nor does it explain how the appropriate rules emerge from the conflict.

    As a postscript to this discussion we can briefly consider errors which do *not* turn up (see also Maratsos 1978; Pinker 1980). The Erreich *et al.* formulation of AUX structure, along with a number of recent accounts of the structure of English (e.g. Akmajian and Heny 1975, Brown and Miller 1980) accounts for the discontinuity of surface verb forms by positing some level of representation at which the constituents *have + en* and *be + ing* are contiguous. A transformation of affix-hopping is then responsible for the correct surface structure sequence. If it is the case that the child 'has' a representation in these terms, which is used to explain certain errors, then one might reasonably expect mistakes which involve, for instance 'hanging' affixes. There is no obvious reason why, if the child is working with this kind of representation, (18) and (19) should not occur:

    (18)   he is ing sing
    (19)   ing he being sing

[5] For discussion of this issue in relation to errors in second language learning, see Hughes (1978).

In (18) (we may say) affix-hopping has occurred once (to provide the appropriate form of *be*), but has failed to iterate and postpose *ing* to *sing;* in (19) only partial copying to sentence-initial position has taken place. Needless to say, such examples are not attested. But there is nothing in the theory to prevent them.

Distributional restrictions. As should by now be apparent, the fundamental problem with any account of acquisition in terms solely of rule-learning is that while rules imply productivity, early language-learning is character-ized by restrictions, constraints and exceptions with respect to syntactic patterns. This will be clear if, instead of considering individual errors or non-errors we look more generally at the distribution of the verb-forms in a sample (of approximately 150 utterances) from a child of 2;6. This structural profile, using the categories relevant to the inversion transforma-tion discussed above, appears in Table 11.1.[6] In looking at the sample as a whole we see (*a*) that the majority of lexical verbs have no inflection or auxiliary (these are the 78 forms listed as UVF, the unmarked verb); (*b*) that apart from the two *is* forms, the only inversion is with *can,* and *can* is much more likely to appear inverted than in pre-verb position; (*c*) all other verb-forms are inflected only, with auxiliaries *be* and *have* omitted in obligatory contexts. To attempt to explain this heavily restricted use of verb-forms in terms of rule-learning seems perverse. What seems to require explanations are questions relating for example to the child's selection of *can* as her only modal at this point. Why are other modals not represented? To extend the questions diachronically: when and in what order do other modals occur? When is *have* represented in the child's output? Does it tend to appear like *can,* predominantly in sentence-initial position? Rule-learning has little to say about the selectivity, in relation to category members and their distribution across sentence-types, repre-sented in this sample, or by extension the order in which restrictions on either are lifted.

The picture of distributional asymmetries and restrictions indicated in Table 11.1 is reinforced in Table 2, which is a summary of present and perfect and related forms in the spontaneous speech of 32 children aged 3;3. Table 11.2 gives the categories used in the analysis, examples of each category, and their frequency.[7] A wide range of analytical categories is used here because the term PRESENT PERFECT subsumes a set of rather disparate items which are classed together on distributional grounds for the adult language. If we assume that the child initially uses phonetic resemblances as a heuristic for classifying forms, then the existence of either phonetically disparate forms in a class, or homonymy between members of this class and members of some other class, are potential problems to the construction of generalizations. Hence Table 2 distin-guishes, for example, between full and contracted auxiliaries, between regular and irregular past participles, and includes past tense as a separate

[6] The research from which this data emerges was supported by SSRC grant HR-6974.
[7] I am grateful to Gordon Wells for permission to publish data derived from his transcripts (Wells 1975).

Table 11.1 Distribution of some verb-forms in a sample from a British English child aged 2;6.15

	UVF	Modal	Have + PP	Be + ing	Past irreg.	Past reg.	Other
Inverted in question	—	*can* 24	—	—	—	—	*is* 2
Before verb in Declarative Negative Non-inverted question	78	*can* 3	PP 4	*ing* 17	11	4	—

category. (A full account of Table 11.2 appears in Fletcher 1981.) On the basis of a comparison of the two tables, we would expect the British English child to have a wider range of forms available at 3;3 than at 2;6. For example, it appears that some children at 3;3 are using *have* + PP forms. (In fact, this development is paralleled by the appearance of *do*-SUPPORT and auxiliary *be*.) But the differential frequencies of the forms in Table 2 (with contracted forms more frequent than full forms) together with analyses of individual children (see Fletcher 1981), which show that a number of children use contracted *have* forms but not full forms suggest once again a gradual and slow development to mastery rather than the sudden change that a rule hypothesis would predict.

There is another distributional feature of one child's data in this group which deserves mention, because it suggests that we have to take function into account in explaining the child's formal behaviour at this point. One child in the sample who used both *have* + *PP* forms and past tenses had them in complementary distribution across sentence types:

Questions	Negatives	Declaratives
have + PP	haven't + PP	Past or PP only

Questions and negative statements about recent past events use *have* forms, while past tenses and some past participles (without either full or contracted auxiliary) appear in positive statements referring to recent past events. The data is not extensive enough to warrant certainty; but it is tempting to conclude that for this child past and perfect were not functionally differentiated. On the evidence of the homonymy of most past tenses and past participles, the tendency for full forms of *have* to appear in only questions and negatives in input, and functional similarity of perfects and past (which both tend to be used to refer to recent past in motherese, without temporal specification), the child could be led to an analysis which (albeit temporarily) fails to maintain an adult grammatical distinction. This kind of distributional asymmetry in a synchronic analysis may reflect a functional merger. The nature of the restrictions on the distribution of the auxiliary here, and the semantic reasons which may account for it, seem difficult to reconcile with an explanation solely in terms of candidate rules.

Table 11.2 Present perfect and other relevant forms, with examples, and frequencies, in a sample of 32 British English children at 3;3.

		Frequency
1. has/have + -en	I have taken	12
2. -en	taken	19
3. 'aux + -en (trans.)	they've taken the bus[1]	19
4. has/have + -ed	he has stopped	9
5. -ed	it stopped	78
6. 'aux + -ed (trans.)	I've stopped the bus[2]	3
7. 's + past participle (intrans.)	it's broken[3] he's hidden he's finished	44
8. tag/have (no past part.)	hasn't he?/I have	6
9. has/have got	I have got	26
10. 'aux got	we've got	37
11. got	they got	47

[1]This category includes any contracted auxiliary occurring with a verb used transitively *and* in irregular past participle form.
[2]This category includes any contracted auxiliary occurring with a verb used transitively *and* in regular past participle form.
[3]This category includes any third person singular contraction occurring with a verb used transitively and in *either* irregular *or* regular past participle form.

The lexical dimension. The last three categories of Table 11.2 (9–11) separate *got* forms, with and without auxiliary, from the other categories in the Table. Why single out one lexical verb for special attention? The major part of the profile in Table 11.2, while rather more detailed than is customary, nevertheless maintains the custom of treating syntactic development in terms of syntactic categories. And since we have no satisfactory criterion for when a particular form is acquired,[8] we tend to rely on the frequency of occurrence of an item as a rough guide to its mastery. This practice (in relation to verb-forms) has to be considered in the light of a type-token ratio for lexical verbs. If we are hoping to use frequency as a guide to the productivity of a form, then a high frequency distributed over a number of different lexical verbs has to be interpreted differently to the same form frequency limited to one or two verbs. It is in this connection that the figures in Table 11.2 relating to *got* forms are relevant. It will be seen that the got forms with auxiliary, contracted and uncontracted, are as frequent as the full and contracted forms of *have* appearing in categories 1–4 (i.e. with all other lexical verbs). In addition an individual analysis of the children's samples (see Fletcher 1981, 100) shows that some children use full and contracted forms of *have* with *got* but with no other lexical verb. Data of this kind suggests that, in parallel to structural profiles of verb-forms, a longitudinal analysis of the diffusion of these forms across lexical verbs is essential, both in terms of individual lexical verbs and possible semantic classes. One of the questions raised by Brown (1973) concerned the variability with which verb-forms for which

[8] Brown's criterion (1973; 255) for the acquisition of grammatical morphemes—appearance in 90 per cent of obligatory contexts—is difficult if not impossible to apply to many past/present perfect forms. *He called*, for example, may be a correct past tense or a present perfect with auxiliary omitted. It would not be easy to set up satisfactory criteria for a decision.

obligatory contexts could be identified were used, up to the time at which they were acquired. Acquisition was not sudden, but a gradual matter over a relatively long period of time. One recent type of explanation adduced for this variability is in terms of semantic classifications of verbs made by the child. Antinucci and Miller 1976 (see also Bloom *et al.* 1980), for example, suggest that variability in early past-tense marking depends on whether or not a particular verb is a CHANGE-OF-STATE verb. Those verbs which are change-of-state, which describe a situation in which some end-state comes into existence as a result of a process, will be marked for past, whereas other verbs (state verbs, and activity verbs without result) will not. Whatever one's view of this specific analysis, it is undeniable that the gradual development of forms cannot be seen independently of verbs, and that much more attention needs to be paid to lexis in this area of syntax learning than has been so far.

Reappraisal

We began by looking at an influential theoretical position that, from the standpoint of adult grammars, asserts an intimate link between the principles on which those grammars are constructed, and language acquisition. An empirical interpretation of the theory, however, appears to be presented with considerable difficulties once the data-base for its evaluation is extended beyond selected examples. At best the Erreich, *et al.* analysis (and all similar analyses in terms of rule-learning) is a partial account of what the child does in learning syntax (in that it provides descriptive summaries at the points in acquisition at which the child constructs rules, after a long process of gradual learning). At worst, their assumption of rule-based creativity is drastically at odds with the actual course of acquisition, whose slow and gradual development over time, both of the range of forms and their productivity, is reflected synchronically in distributional asymmetries and constraints, and lexical restrictions. Does this mean that linguistics has no relevance for language acquisition, and that this is a domain best left to other disciplines? A positive reply here would be unduly pessimistic; nevertheless it is important to be realistic, and to admit our limitations. It may well be the case that rule-based theories constructed for adult language (or indeed any such theories) are either inapplicable, or unduly restrictive, with respect to the child's language development, particularly in its earlier stages. But it is not of course true that the rejection of 'adult-based' theories leaves us with no possible contribution.[9] It is not the case (*pace* Erreich, *et al.* 1979, 176) that any theory is better than no theory, and there is no shame in admitting, with Campbell (1979, 419) that 'what is both desirable and possible in the study of language development at the present time is more facts, more flower-picking natural history.'

The first requirement here is a realistic data-base, which ideally means

[9] See however Pinker (1980) for an outline of a lexical-interpretive grammar, which may allow for the kind of gradualism we have outlined here with less strain than the standard theory model.

150   *Paul Fletcher*

longitudinal records with much more frequent sampling intervals than are customary. It should be apparent from the discussion above that we require a holistic approach to grammatical systems both cross-sectionally and over time. An example of the preferred approach which is a massive (but generally ignored) demonstration of just how gradual language learning is, is the study by Labov and Labov, of their daughter's development of *wh*-questions. This is based on a daily record totalling about 25,000 questions over two and a half years. The conclusion that they reach on the basis of this evidence could serve as an epitaph for all attempts to show that rule-learning is the essence of language-learning, rather than its final outcome:

> The notion that children learn syntactic regularities with great ease and rapidity does not find support in these data. We are dealing with a period of two and a half years, and an enormous volume of questions. The problem then is not to ask, how does the child learn the syntactic rule [auxiliary inversion] so quickly, but rather: why does it take so much time and so many trials? (1978, 7).

Given a realistic data base, the linguist's contribution at the present time becomes the provision of realistic descriptions to serve as the basis for explanation. In this way we have provided in Table 11.2 a structural profile for present perfect and other relevant forms which treats a number of items in the (heterogeneous) adult *have + en* class as potentially distinct, since we have no reason to suppose that the child will class them together from the beginning. The contribution to be made will not only be a refinement of syntactic categories. The child does not separate form from function, and has always to consider the contexts in which forms occur. A more seriously considered functional perspective is therefore a priority. And the focus on meaning will not end at the functions verb-forms have, for both children and their conversational partners, but will also encompass the semantics of the verbs themselves.

In sum, the relationship between linguistics and language learning has to be more diffuse than Chomsky and his followers would have us believe—learning, after all, is a psychological process which linguistic theories are not equipped to cope with. But the linguist's contribution, both to the picking of the flowers and their arrangement, is both serious and essential.

References

Akmajian, A. and Heny, F. 1975: *An introduction to the principles of transformational grammar.* Cambridge, Mass.: MIT Press.

Antinucci, F. and Miller, R. 1976: How children talk about what happened. *J Ch. Lang.* **3**, 167–89.

Bloom, L., Lifter, K. and Hafitz, J. 1980: Semantics of verbs and the development of verb inflection in child language. *Lg.* **56**, 386–411.

Brown, R. 1973: *A first language.* Cambridge, Mass.: Harvard University Press.

Brown, E.K. and Miller, J.E. 1980: *Syntax: a linguistic introduction to sentence structure.* London: Hutchinson.

Campbell, R.N. 1979: Cognitive development and child language. In

Fletcher, P. and Garman, M. (eds.), *Language acquisition: studies in first language development.* Cambridge: Cambridge University Press.

Chomsky, N. 1975: *Reflections on language.* New York: Pantheon.

————1979: On cognitive structures and their development: a reply to Piaget. In M. Piatelli-Palmarini (ed.), *Language and learning: the debate between Jean Piaget and Noam Chomsky.* London: Routledge & Kegan Paul.

Erreich, A., Valian, V. and Winzemer, J. 1980: Aspects of a theory of language acquisition. *J Ch. Lang.* **7**, 157–79.

Fay, D. 1978: Transformations as mental operations: a reply to Kuczaj. *J Ch. Lang.* **5**, 143–50.

Fletcher, P. 1981: Description and explanation in the acquisition of verb-forms. *J Ch. Lang.* **8**, 93–108.

Fodor, J.D. and Smith, M.R. 1978: What kind of an exception is 'have got'? *LI* **9**, 45–65.

Huddleston, R. 1976: *An introduction to English transformational syntax.* London: Longman.

Hughes, A. 1978: Problems in contrastive analysis and error analysis. Paper presented at the 6th National Conference on Language Teaching, Stellenbosch University.

Hurford, J. 1975: A child and the English question-formation rule. *J Ch. Lang.* **2**, 299–301.

Lightfoot, D. 1979: *Principles of diachronic syntax.* Cambridge: Cambridge University Press.

Labov, W. and Labov T. 1978: Learning the syntax of questions. In R.N. Campbell and P.T. Smith (eds.), *Recent advances in the psychology of language* **4B.** New York and London: Plenum.

Maratsos, M. 1978: New models in linguistics and language acquisition. In M. Halle, J. Bresnan, and G. Miller (eds.), *Linguistic theory and psychological reality.* Cambridge, Mass.: MIT Press.

Mayer, J., Winzemer, J., Erreich, A. and Valian, V. 1978: Transformations, basic operations and language acquisition. *Cognition* **6**, 1–13.

Pinker, S. 1980: A theory of the acquisition of lexical-interpretive grammars. In J. Bresnan (ed.), *The mental representation of grammatical relations.* Cambridge, Mass.: MIT Press.

Smith, N. and Wilson, D. 1979: *Modern linguistics: the results of Chomsky's revolution.* Harmondsworth: Penguin.

Wells, G. 1975: Language development in pre-school children: transcripts of children aged 39 months. Mimeo, University of Bristol School of Education.

12

Is Broca's aphasia a phonological deficit?
Michael Garman

According to a recent argument (Kean 1977, 1978, 1979), Broca's aphasia is to be interpreted as the result of a purely phonological deficit. This runs counter to the traditional view, which many still subscribe to, which sees in this syndrome a multiple deficit involving not just phonology but morphology, syntax, lexis and semantics.[1] Clearly, if the phonological hypothesis is sound, it represents a distinct advance in our understanding of the syndrome, and demonstrates the validity of a particular type of psycholinguistic approach to the study of language disorders—in this case, an approach which is based on 'substantive universals of grammatical structure' (Kean 1977, 9). However, the argument originally put forward in Kean (1977) has been criticized (Kolk 1978; Klosek 1979), and subsequently defended (Kean 1979): there is every indication that the 'phonological deficit hypothesis' is currently both influential and controversial in this area of psycholinguistics, particularly since it is presented as a model for future work (as 'an example of this type of enquiry', Kean 1977, 13). In this chapter, we shall attempt to assess its merits, and to draw some conclusions regarding the linguistic analysis of Broca's aphasia.[2]

---

[1] Broca's own observations (1861, 1865) were directed towards the relation between articulatory difficulties and the left hemisphere, in what he called 'aphemia'; see Critchley (1973), Hécaen (1972, 620). The presence of other deficits, in what has become known as Broca's aphasia, is part of later tradition. See Mohr (1976) for a balanced review of the clinical syndrome.

[2] At some points, the discussion in this chapter will touch on issues that Kolk (1978) and Klosek (1979) have already raised; Kean (1979) rejects some of their criticisms, but modifies her approach in two respects (she accepts that the phonological deficit is not distributed throughout the whole phonological component, and amends her treatment of inflections v. derivational affixes). In this chapter we shall for the most part concentrate on other issues.

Agrammatism

We must first outline the traditional view, and we may start this by referring to a typical case involving Broca's aphasia. Mr J., still in his forties, suffered a stroke while on holiday with his family. At first totally paralysed on the right side of his body (the result of damage to the left hemisphere of the brain) and with no apparent ability to produce or understand language, he showed some spontaneous recovery over the next few months to the point where he could walk unassisted using a stick, but still had little use of his right arm. His right visual field was also impaired. His comprehension of language gradually improved, but, as the following extract shows (more than two years after the stroke), his productive language was severely affected (— = unit length pause, . = brief pause, / = tone unit boundary; see Crystal *et al.* 1976, Ch. 8, for further details):

Therapist. 'what's thìs/—	Showing picture of
Patient. erm—	cowboys lassooing horse
T mhm̀/—	
P 'cowboys 'and—	
T mhm̀/— —	soft, slow
P 'cowboy 'and wréstler/—	
'wrestler 'and—	
T wèll/.	
the 'horse is 'tied with a rópe/. išn't it/	
P a ròpe/.	
'ah 'yes yès/	
T 'what are they 'doing with the ròpe/—	
'what are they 'doing with the ròpe/	soft
P strīng/	difficulty with *str-* cluster
T m̀hm/	
P yēs/— —	
strīng/. strìng/	difficulty with *str-*
T mhm̀/.	
'they're pùlling it/	
P pūl'ling it/. 'ah yès/'pu [whispers]	
T pùlling it/	
pùlling it/	
P yès yes/	

Faced with this sort of patient, the traditional view has recognized, among other deficits, a morphosyntactic disability referred to as 'agrammatism'. Goodglass (1976) provides a representative introduction to this concept, and Marshall (1977) contains a succinct review which we may follow here:

(*i*) it occurs frequently in patients who have lesions in the frontal area of the brain yielding what is often referred to, more specifically, as EXPRESSIVE AGRAMMATISM);

(*ii*) it is characterized by a small active vocabulary, mainly of nouns, main verbs and adjectives;

(*iii*) it shows widespread omission of grammatical formatives, both free forms (e.g. articles) and bound forms (inflectional affixes);

(*iv*) in extreme cases, 'all expression is reduced to nominal form'

(Marshall 1977, 132).

These four characteristics together define what we may call the restricted view of agrammatism. However, as Marshall points out, there are other associated disorders, including laboured articulation, phonological 'paraphasias' (segmental substitutions and transpositions) and suprasegmental difficulties with stress-placement, pitch and loudness control. These conspire to reduce the output of speech, giving rise to a 'nonfluent' class of disorders. Marshall notes that 'it is not surprising that, although agrammatism can obviously be *described* in syntactic terms, most scholars have emphasized a combination of phonologic and semantic variables in their explanations of the condition' (1977, 132). We may discern here a (representative) tendency to widen the scope of the term AGRAMMATISM to refer to a multiple deficit which includes a significant morphosyntactic disorder, along with other disorders. In this wider sense the term is frequently used of Broca's aphasia as a whole.

If we now turn to consider a few details, we find, not surprisingly, that there are no simple boundaries between levels (e.g. phonological, syntactic) of disorder in language. For example, Goodglass and Berko (1960) noted that in agrammatic speech certain inflectional morphemes were more likely to occur appropriately than others, depending on phonological factors such as phonotactic patterning (consonantal suffixes are more likely to occur on a stem ending in a vowel than a consonant) and syllabic structure (syllabic suffixes are more likely to be produced than nonsyllabic ones). Such phonological conditioning yields a hierarchy of 'likelihood of production' for these morphemes. However, on either side, as it were, of these interactive phenomena, we find (*i*) purely phonological substitutions such as /kəunin/ for *combing*, and (*ii*) apparently purely grammatical phenomena, as where differential ability is exhibited in encoding morphemes that have identical phonological form. Such instances are at the heart of the concept of agrammatism, of course, and are well illustrated in the case cited by Myerson and Goodglass (1972), of a patient who successfully marks regular plural nouns with -/s/~-/z/~-/əz/ but fails to mark third person singlar present tense (*3s*) forms of verbs. As far as this patient is concerned, moreover, phonological and grammatical hierarchies of difficulty interact, yielding the situation as set out in Fig. 12.1. Similarly, Jakobson (1964) proposes that, in general, noun inflections are easier to produce than verb inflections; and that low-level (word-structure) affixes, such as plural and past tense, are easier than possessive (phrase-structure) and *3s* (clause-level) affixes. Putting these observations together with those of Fig. 12.1, we have the picture set out in Fig. 12.2.

Obviously, this understanding of agrammatism is quite weak. Empirically, it is vulnerable to such observations as those of Myerson and Goodglass (1972) and de Villiers (1974), reporting that progressive -*ing* is produced with much greater ease than this model would suggest.[3] And

---

[3] Marshall (1977) makes some pertinent observations in this connection; in particular, it seems that progressive -*ing* might benefit from homophony with a nominalising suffix, as in *the lending of books,* and that it frequently might be reported through occurring at word level, as in *John going,* rather than in phrase level construction with the auxiliary verb *be.*

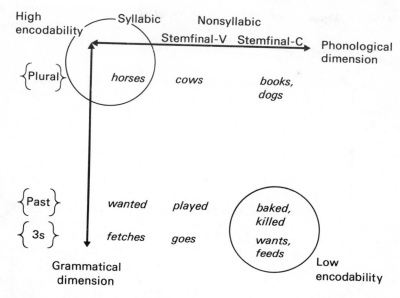

Fig. 12.1 Interaction of phonological and grammatical determinants of encodability for three English morphemes in agrammatism.

there is more to agrammatism than this model captures, since omission of the copula, auxiliary verbs, articles, pronouns, prepositions and other elements are reported frequently in the literature; and Schnitzer (1974) has data to suggest that fluctuating control of such elements may be bound up in the concept of redundancy, which figures nowhere in the model. From a theoretical point of view, also, the traditional concept of agrammatism is less than satisfactory; it tends, for instance, to rely on the notion of 'telegraphic'/'telegrammatic' speech (Caramazza and Zurif 1978) which is probably as ill-conceived in relation to adult disorder as it is in emerging grammatical abilities (Brown 1973, 403).[4]

All in all, then, it seems that we badly need a better model. More radically, what Kean offers is an entirely new approach:

> recent characterizations of [Broca's aphasia] as a language deficit involving the compromise of phonetic, phonological, syntactic, and semantic functions is [sic] untenable. It is our hypothesis that the manifested linguistic deficits of Broca's aphasics can only be accounted for in terms of the interaction between an impaired phonological capacity and otherwise intact linguistic capacities (1977, 10).

---

[4] We should, however, note the possibility of arguing that there may be a parallel between the aphasic's attempt to compensate for a linguistic deficit and the non-aphasic adult's strategy in composing a telegram message; Caramazza and Zurif (1978) cite Lenneberg (1973) and Fodor, Bever and Garrett (1974) in connection with one version of this argument, but they conclude that it is of doubtful validity.

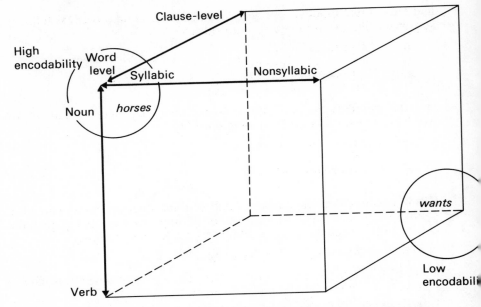

Fig. 12.2 Three-dimensional model of the interaction of phonological (syllabic structure) and grammatical determinants of encodability of inflectional morphemes in agrammatism.

Broca's aphasia as a phonological deficit

The argument

In this section, the presentation of the argument basically follows Kean (1977) and the order therein, but, for ease of reference, it is set out in five steps. Reference is also made to Kean (1979) where necessary, but page numbers are those in Kean (1977), unless otherwise specified.[5]

Step 1 (pp. 18–21). The purpose of the first step is to show a similarity between what Kean calls WORD-BOUNDARY morphemes such as -*ing* in progressive verbs and -*ness* in de-adjectival nominals, etc. on the one hand and cliticized copula and auxiliary verb forms as in (1)–(3) on the other:

(1)   Liz's cooking dinner
(2)   He's out tonight
(3)   Pat's intelligent.

Kean calls these cliticized forms DERIVED WORD BOUNDARY elements, since like -*ing*, -*ness*, etc., they attach to a unit of analysis called the word (we shall look at her definition of this unit presently). Following the Chomsky

---

[5] Kean (1978) hardly concerns us here, as it contains what is basically a restatement of Kean (1977), plus some further general remarks.

and Halle (1968) model, she describes the cliticization process as follows: substrings like (4) are mapped onto substrings like (5),

(4) . . . [#Tom#] [is] . . .
        N   N Aux Aux
(5) . . . [#[#Tom#] is#] [*] . . . ,
      N N   N   N Aux Aux

and this parallels the way that true word-boundary elements attach to words, as illustrated in (6) mapping onto (7):

(6) . . . [boy, +*pl*] . . . [6]
       N
(7) . . . [#[#boy#] s#] . . .
      N N   N N

Kean concedes that 'it may seem odd to think of *is* becoming part of a noun' (p. 18); but, since cliticization forms, appearing as [s]~[z]~[əz], do not, as in (8), occur across word boundaries (Kean's example):

(8) * Children are [z]usceptible to colds,

'there is strong *prima facie* evidence that when *is* is contracted, it becomes a suffix of the immediately preceding word' (p. 20).

There are, then, distinct sources in grammar (cliticization, plural affixation, and word formation processes as involved in forms such as *definiteness*) for one and the same phonological output, which may be represented as (9):

(9) [#[# . . . #] Aff#]
     L L   L   L

where L denotes some lexical category and Aff represents a word-boundary (suffixal, in this illustration) morpheme.

There is, however, a different structural pattern, found in forms such as *permit, object, subjective, definitive*, etc. Kean calls the affixes *per-, ob-, sub-,* and *-ive* in these forms NON WORD-BOUNDARY ELEMENTS, since they attach to items that are not in themselves words. The boundary symbol she uses for these forms is +.

Finally, Kean underlines the importance of the distinction thus made between word-boundary (#) elements and non word-boundary (+) elements, by proposing that # affixes are those 'which Broca's aphasics are typically most likely to omit', while + affixes 'typically are not omitted' (p. 21).

Step 2 (pp. 22–3). This step seeks to clarify the linguistic nature of the distinction between # affixes and + affixes: 'If the hypothesis that Broca's aphasia is a phonological deficit is to be maintained, we must establish that there is . . . a phonological motivation for the notational distinction

---

[6] The example here comes from (Kean 1979, 72); the notation is slightly different, but the structural pattern is to be interpreted as essentially the same as (4). Note, however, that '+' here is NOT the 'non word-boundary' symbol + that Kean introduces in her (1977) discussion, and which we encounter a little later on in this step.

between + and #, and we must find this distinction realised . . . in the speech of Broca's aphasics' (p. 22). Kean finds the phonological motivation in stress assignment; this underlies her concept of the word: 'the notion of "word" we are using here is, of course, not the ordinary usage of that term; a phonological "word" is the string of segments, marked by boundaries, which function in the assignment of stress to a word (in English)' (p. 22), and distinguishes the # affix form in (11) from the + affix form in (12), although both are linked to the form in (10):

(10)   'definite
(11)   'definite # ness
(12)   de'finit + ive.

Note that (11) preserves the stress pattern of (10), while (12) does not; Kean takes this to be the fundamental difference between all # affixes and all + affixes, and leads us to the following conclusion of step 2: 'Therefore we can say of English-speaking Broca's aphasics that they have a tendency to omit those affixes which do not play a role in the assignment of stress to words' (p. 21).

Step 3 (p. 23). This is not really a distinct step forward in the argument, so much as a pause in order to highlight the two complementary aspects which constitute the hypothesis thus far:

(*i*) *Convergence*—because # affixes have more than one source in the grammar, the only level at which a generalized statement may be made about them is the phonological. Therefore, if it is the case that # affixes as a class tend to be omitted in the speech of Broca's aphasics, then this fact is most economically captured at the level of phonology.

(*ii*) *Divergence*—because + affixes and (some) # affixes come from the same source in grammar, namely, the word-formation (WF) rules, yet have distinct phonological representations, the only discriminating statement to be made about them has to be at the phonological level. Therefore, if it is the case that + affixes are differentiated from # affixes in the speech of Broca's aphasics (tend to be retained, rather than omitted), this fact also has to be captured at the phonological level.

In other words, there is just one level that will correctly partition elements that Broca's aphasics usually omit from those that they usually retain, and that is the level of phonology.

Step 4 (pp. 23–5). This step extends, and thereby strengthens, the hypothesis, by noting that the substring (13),

(13)   . . . [# [the]   [#boy#]#] . . . .
         NP Det Det   N   N NP

may be considered 'the mirror image of the structure of the plural "boys" [see (7) above]: in both cases we have a noun, *boy*, flanked by [# and #], to which an element not flanked by [#and#] is attached' (p. 24). Thus the force of step 3(*i*) is increased; it is not just affixes, as conventionally conceived, that fit the phonological pattern defined by [#and#], but elements such as the definite article as well. This makes the phonological generalization all the more potent, if it is the case that Broca's aphasics tend to omit the definite article in spontaneous speech. Of course, it is observed that they do; and Kean accordingly simplifies her hypothesis: 'Items which are not phonological words tend to be omitted in the language of Broca's aphasics' (p. 25).

It is convenient to suspend the presentation of the argument for a while at this point, in order to consider what has been achieved. Thus far, Kean has managed to use a phonological criterion, stress-assignment, to define a unit of analysis, the phonological word, which allows us to incorporate an apparently grammatical phenomenon, article-omission, within a unified account at the phonological level for a range of Broca's aphasic data. This certainly is the stuff of which a phonological hypothesis might be made, and at this stage we might simply await the outcome of adequate testing of the hypothesis. Before proceeding to this, however, we should also note additional supporting details from Kean (1979), where the following distinct sources of # morphemes (apart from cliticized forms) are recognized:

(14) (*i*) pure inflectional morphemes, such as nominalizing *-'s* in *the city's destruction*
(*ii*) morphemes introduced by PS rules:
    (*a*) abstract formatives, such as *pl, past* in *boys, played;*
    (*b*) formatives having phonological form, such as *the* in *the boy;*[7]
(*iii*) morphemes introduced by lexical insertion rules, such as *on* in *on the bank;*
(*iv*) morphemes introduced by WF rules, such as *-ness* in *definiteness*.

In respect of (*iii*) above, Kean (1979, 72) draws our attention to the sentence (15):

(15) The boys played on the bank.

Assuming the sentence (16) to be a typical Broca's aphasic version of this:

(16) boy play bank,

Kean argues that, while prepositions (like nouns and verbs) are 'both the syntactic heads of phrases[8] and items inserted by lexical rule', they are unlike nouns and verbs in being frequently omitted in Broca's aphasic speech. Our only safe generalization, then, concerning which items tend to be omitted, has to be set at the phonological level; at this level, argues Kean, prepositions are clitics like *the*, the plural affix, the past tense affix, and so on. All other items (nonclitics, or phonological words) tend to be retained (Kean 1979, 79).

---

[7] As Kean (1979, 72) notes, the article could be represented as a set of abstract features at this level, but this does not affect the issue.
[8] Kean apparently believes this to be the case in the example (15), although *on* is actually exocentric with respect to the phrase *on the bank*. However, we can note instances which are endocentric, as in *The boys climbed up (the bank)*, and which are therefore compatible with her argument here.

If this were the end of the argument, we might conclude that a *prima facie* case had been made out for recognizing stress-defined phonological words as the primes of language production in Broca's aphasia. The way would seem to be open to an investigation of a whole range of apparently morphosyntactic phenomena to determine whether they too could be brought within the scope of the phonological hypothesis (we shall consider this briefly below, pp. 166–9). To the extent that this might be achieved, the demise of AGRAMMATISM in an account of this syndrome would be correspondingly certain.

However, there is one further step in the argument.

Step 5 (pp 25–8). The position thus far elaborated has a major embarrassment: 'it is empirically falsified by the fact that suffixes such as *-ive* are deleted [in the speech of Broca's aphasics], in spite of the fact that there is not typically an analogous truncation of words like *object*' (p. 25). This rather astonishing reversal of the direction of the argument thus far involves Kean in a radical restructuring of her hypothesis. The problem is set out in Fig. 12.3: we find that the phonological distinction of + elements v. # elements now *fails* to partition the data in the way stated in step 3(*ii*). Kean therefore has to modify her hypothesis in such a way as to be able to distinguish between the subclass of + affixes in forms like *object* and the subclass of + affixes in forms like *de'finitive*. But, as we have seen, the phonological fact is that no such subclasses can be recognized. Kean therefore has to appeal to a NONPHONOLOGICAL concept, of 'lexical construal', by which *de'finit-* is to be set apart from *-ject* by virtue of the fact that it has a lexical relationship with a *word*, *'definite*, while *-ject* has none. This gives us the final form of Kean's hypothesis:

(17)   A Broca's aphasic tends to reduce the structure of a sentence to the minimal string of elements which can be lexically construed as phonological words in his language (p. 25).

But, since this hypothesis makes appeal to a nonphonological concept, the question we must ask is: is it still a purely phonological hypothesis?

Kean is at pains to show that it is. She sets about doing this by referring to lexical construal as part of intact language capacity; therefore, the fact that it is nonphonological leaves her phonological hypothesis unscathed, since lexical construal is not part of the deficit: the *deficit* is purely *phonological*. It is in this sense that her hypothesis is an interactional one: it functions 'by assuming all aspects of the language faculty to be intact, save for the phonological' (p. 10), and relates observable features of Broca's aphasic speech to the interactive operation of intact and impaired levels of language ability. We shall now examine this step in the argument a little more closely.

Kean seeks to establish lexical construal as part of intact language capacity by looking at normal speech errors: 'The structure of the mechanisms of language production (above the level of phonetics) is studied through the analysis of the spontaneous speech errors of normal

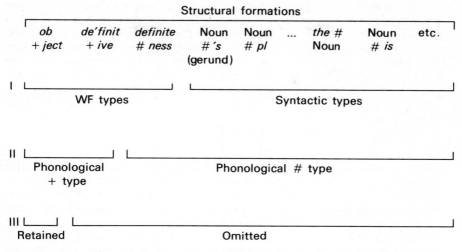

Fig. 12.3 Partitioning of structural formations, according to (I) grammatical type, (II) phonological type, (III) two categories of likelihood of encoding in Broca's aphasia.

individuals' (pp. 25–6).[9] Referring to work done in this area (Fromkin 1971; 1973, Garret 1975; 1976), she concludes that the notion of lexical construal is required in order to distinguish between the possible error of (18) and the 'impossible' (p. 26) error of (19):

(18) I'm not in a read for mooding
      (. . . [#mood#] . . . [#[#read#] ing#])
(19) *They papermitted the subs
      (. . . [#[#sub + mit#] ed#] . . . [#[#paper#] s#])

By this notion, *sub* is not available for transposition, because it does not occur in a [# . . . #] environment. But in fact lexical construal is a fairly abstract concept which is a stage removed from the observation regarding (18) and (19). The immediately relevant concept is that of a HIERARCHY OF AFFIXAL ADHESION/SEPARABILITY, concerning which the pertinent quotation comes a few pages further on: 'There is a hierarchy of the degree to which a bound morpheme adheres to the item to which it is attached. The degree of separability is, first, determined by whether the morpheme is inflectional or derivational . . . Among the derivational affixes themselves there is a hierarchy' (p. 31). Throughout Kean's discussion, this hierarchy is taken to be identical with the concept of lexical construal. As such, it is hypothesized to be part of the Broca's aphasic's unimpaired linguistic resources. The situation is set out in Fig. 12.4, where D represents a phonological deficit and C some unimpaired linguistic concept, in this case

[9] It is unfortunate that this statement, which looks like a comprehensive assertion, gives no indication of the fact that this is by no means the only way of carrying out investigations of the mechanisms of language production. Indeed, it is a highly problematic way, for reasons which will become apparent (pp. 164–5 below).

Total linguistic capacities

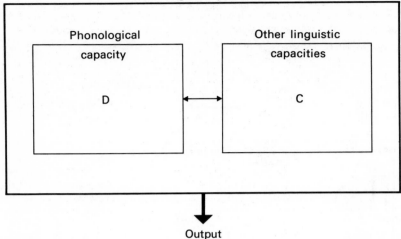

Fig. 12.4 The phonological deficit hypothesis, final version.

lexical construal. Alternatively, we could go back to Fig. 12.3 and simply replace the label 'retained' by 'not lexically construable', and 'omitted' by 'lexically construable'. By doing this, Kean argues, we should not be destroying the phonological nature of the hypothesis, since the only deficit that is recognized is at the phonological level. We may conclude our presentation of her argument here.

At this stage, we should briefly consider the implications that Kean sees in her hypothesis. She first (pp. 28–33) looks at some further observations concerning the speech of Broca's aphasics, in English, and then turns (pp. 33–9) to review some predictions made from her hypothesis for other languages. Since these predictions are tested only against observations which are inadequate for the purpose (e.g. Luria 1970 for Russian, Jakobson 1973 for Japanese), they prove unfruitful, and will not be pursued further here. Her consideration of further English data, however, serves usefully to extend the illustration of her hypothesis, and we may summarize the outcome at this point in the form of six questions, all of which attract the same general answer in terms of her hypothesis:

i. Why should Broca's aphasics retain (in comprehension) *plural -s* better than *possessive/3s -s?* (Goodglass and Hunt 1958) (p. 28)

ii. Why should they retain derivational affixes in preference to inflectional affixes and function words? (pp. 31–2)

iii. Why should they retain non-productive derivational affixes in preference to productive ones? (p. 32)

iv. Why should syllabic suffixes like *-ing* be retained in preference to non-syllabic ones? (p. 32)

v. Why should progressive *-ing* be retained in preference to gerundive *-ing?* (p. 32)

vi. Why should Broca's aphasics show evidence of dysprosody? (pp. 32–3)
The general answer to all these questions is: because these features derive
from intact linguistic capacity—they are not part of the deficit as such. The
precise form of the answer is (for *i* to *v*): 'Given that there is a hierarchy in
normal production of the degree to which an affix is attached to a word, it
must be predicted that this hierarchy will be retained under the conditions
of any deficit which is not a direct deficit to that aspect of the language
system of which the hierarchy is a part' (p. 32), and (for *vi*): 'A normal
speaker who pauses between words in a sentence, like the hesitating
Broca's aphasic, speaks dysprosodically … . ' (p. 33).

Evaluation

In our critical evaluation of this hypothesis, we shall first look more closely
at certain aspects of the hypothesis itself, and then turn to consider further
observable features of Broca's aphasic data.

The hypothesis

In a sense, we have two quite different hypotheses to consider. The first
has emerged by the end of step 4 above, and is in this form ready to be
tested empirically. The fact that it fails to survive such testing (in step 5)
need not be a reason for our dismissing it out of hand; it may still tell us
much about the nature of Broca's aphasia. But clearly it is out of court as a
purely phonological account of the syndrome. Let us simply recognize here
that it may contribute something worthwhile to a multiple deficit view of
Broca's aphasia (e.g. in sharpening our perception of where the boundary
between phonological and grammatical deficits may lie),[10] and pass on to
consider the final hypothesis. As we have seen, this is characterized by
three features:

(*i*) it involves an interaction between a specific phonological deficit and
otherwise intact linguistic capacity;
(*ii*) it views Broca's aphasia as involving a purely phonological deficit;
(*iii*) it claims to cover all aspects of the data.

There is a logical dependency here; if (*i*) is correct, then (*ii*) follows
automatically, and vice-versa (given an interactionist view of language
processing). How far (*iii*) is correct remains to be seen. We shall first look
more closely at (*i*). Consider the following statement: 'It is our argument
that by assuming all aspects of the language faculty to be *intact,* save for the
phonological, we can predict that there will be systematic variation in the
likelihood of omission of function words and grammatical morphemes
which parallels the variation in the way these elements are treated within
the *normal* language processing system' (p. 10; my emphasis). Here we can
see that Kean uses both 'intact' and 'normal' in referring to what we may

[10] Further, since the phonological generalization on which it is based concerns stress, which is
a prosodic feature, the implication would be that there is a type of dysprosody in Broca's
aphasia (differently defined, of course, from the dysprosody that is traditionally recognized in
the syndrome, and which Kean specifically excludes by her final hypothesis).

call the standard language abilities and behaviour of the non-aphasic adult. As far as her discussion is concerned, then, we have a single opposition, between intact/normal on the one hand, and impaired/abnormal on the other.

However, it may be argued that there are really two oppositions to be recognized: the first, INTACT V. IMPAIRED, most appropriately relates to the assumed language capacity of classes of language user (aphasic, non-aphasic), while the second, NORMAL V. ABNORMAL, characterizes the type of language behaviour that individuals actually exhibit. In terms of this approach, it makes sense to talk of an intact language capacity even in certain contexts of abnormal language behaviour—indeed, that is precisely the way we should wish to characterize the situation where a non-aphasic adult produces errorful speech. If the occasion of the errorful speech is transient, one does not wish to alter one's assumption of the intact nature of the individual's language capacity (e.g. where a fleeting spoonerism appears, for no apparent reason). If errorful speech is at all prolonged, however, and especially if an aetiology is apparent (as when an individual's speech is affected by alcohol) one *may* wish to alter one's assumption regarding the language capacity, perhaps describing the situation in terms of a temporary impairment. Whatever one decides, the point at issue seems quite clear: normality or otherwise of speech is 'given', observable, and ranges over a scale, while intact or impaired status of language capacity is inferred, not directly testable, and to a degree is independent of the scale of (ab)normality. It would seem to be important not to lose sight of this distinction. There is also the inescapable fact that certain aspects of an aphasic's speech may be observed to be normal; not *all* typically omissible elements are actually omitted, and we continually find references in the literature to *tendencies,* to what is *regularly* the case, and to what is *typical.* Thus, our two oppositions are logically independent of each other, although of course there is a strong association between intact capacity and normal behaviour, and between impaired capacity and abnormal behaviour. The situation is set out in Fig. 12.5, from which it will also be seen that the terms APHASIC and NONAPHASIC range from capacity to behaviour, without discrimination: this seems to be how they are used in the literature, and there is a certain advantage in having a set of terms which neutralise the distinction we have recognized, as long as they are used with caution.

Let us now return, armed with these considerations, to Kean's argument that not only is lexical construal involved in Broca's aphasics' treatment of forms such as *de'finitive* but it is also a part of intact/normal language systems. As we have already noted, her discussion of lexical construal is actually concerned with the specific hierarchy of affixal adhesion that she sees arising out of the study of 'normal speech errors'. Our problem with this is that we must, according to our approach, talk instead of abnormal speech errors. After all, what is observed in normal speech is that there is no *degree* of affixal adhesion at all, all affixes being normally attached to their stems; degrees creep in when speech departs from the norm (in language-processing terms; of course there are degrees also in the domain

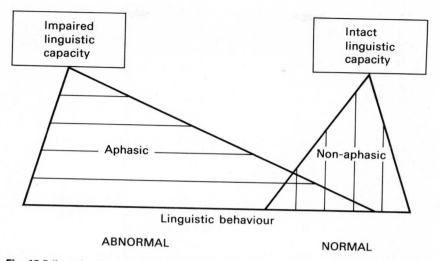

Fig. 12.5 'Impaired' v. 'intact' linguistic capacity, and 'abnormal' v. 'normal' linguistic behaviour.

of linguistic description, where they reflect distributional patterns of grammatical elements, and may bear some relation to what is observed in language use). Now, if it turns out that Broca's and non-aphasic speech errors reveal the same sort of differential-adhesiveness pattern, then this is certainly interesting (though not unexpected, in terms of Fig. 12.5). But of course, it in no way forces us to say that the hierarchy in Broca's aphasic speech errors proceeds from intact linguistic capacity: indeed, given the very much more frequent instantiation of this error hierarchy in Broca's aphasia over non-aphasic speech (an important feature which does not appear in Fig. 12.5), such a conclusion would fly in the face of the observable facts. We must bear in mind that 'intact' v. 'impaired' linguistic capacity are inferential notions and a theory of language processing (aphasic or non-aphasic) which rests on them will carry no logical conviction by itself; it will stand only insofar as it is empirically validated. In advance of such validation, all we can say is that it is not necessary that the deficit involved in Broca's aphasia is phonological (as in (*ii*) above); for all we know, the syndrome might result from an impaired capacity to control structural formations, affixal and nonaffixal, lexical and syntactic. If this latter view seems less than well defined, let us remind ourselves that Kean's (final) hypothesis is also not well defined, in the following important respect: because her phonological generalization (steps 1 to 4) *fails* to predict what is typically retained/omitted in Broca's aphasia, her hypothesis appeals to an *open-ended* set of intact linguistic capacities, which may interact in mysterious ways with her assumed phonological deficit (see further below). There is little well-definedness here. Accordingly, we must turn to an evaluation which is founded on a wider data base.

Further features of Broca's aphasia

We may start with the following list of features, as a first approximation to what is commonly recognised in Broca's aphasia (cf. pp. 152–5 above):

(*i*) non-fluency;
(*ii*) segmental substitutions;
(*iii*) dysprosody;
(*iv*) omission of affixes, determiners, auxiliary verbs and prepositions;
(*v*) word-finding difficulties.

The thrust of Kean's proposals has been to extend a phonological account to cover (*iv*), and, to the extent that this attempt is successful, it represents a considerable achievement. But there is a substantial weakness, in that category (*v*) is not seriously mentioned in her discussion; and even a cursory glance at data from Broca's aphasics will reveal many features that are not included either in Kean's discussion or in our list above. We shall first consider two of the items that Kean does mention, and then turn to those she does not.

She mentions DETERMINERS and PREPOSITIONS. Determiners are illustrated in her discussion by the definite article, subsumed under clitics and brought into line with affixal word-boundary elements (steps 1 to 4). What of the other determiners? Some, like the indefinite article and unstressed *some*, are also clitics in the same sense, but others are not so clear. How should we define a clitic? The answer, for English at least, is not obvious. Let us consider the following forms:

(*i*) -'s (as in *John's coming*)
(*ii*) *is* (as in *John is coming*)
(*iii*) *the* (as in *the boy left*)
(*iv*) *these* (as in *these boys left*)
(*v*) *these* (as in *these have come*).

We might wish to restrict our definition of a clitic to type (*i*) alone; indeed, the name of the process involved in the derivation of this type, CLITICIZATION, suggests that *is* is not a clitic, while -'s is. One could, of course, define the term less narrowly, so as to include type (*ii*), whereupon it may be convenient to treat type (*iii*) similarly; this is what Kean does. But it is perfectly correct to point to the distinction between (*ii*), which can be reduced to a type (*i*) form, and (*iii*), which cannot; and arguably the boundary between clitic and non-clitic lies here. Surely (*v*) is not a clitic, since it carries the noun-phrase stress; but what of (*iv*), which may also carry stress, in contrastive function? Should we perhaps say that it is a clitic just when it is unstressed, and not otherwise? If so, this interpretation should also apply to types (*ii*) and (*iii*). Let us consider this possibility. We shall say that element X—regardless of which grammatical form class it belongs to—is a clitic in context Y if it is unstressed in that context. Thus *'this boy* and *this 'boy* will represent the patterns 'non-clitic + clitic' and 'clitic + non-clitic' respectively. Now, if we start from a stress-marked transcript of data, we shall encounter problems in answering the question 'Do Broca's aphasics tend to omit clitics?'. For, if *'boy* turns up, it may represent *this 'boy* (clitic omission), or *'this boy* (with the first element omitted and stress falling now on the second element). And if *'this* turns up, what right have we to assume that a clitic noun has been omitted? We may also find, as with Mr J. (above), that there is a tendency for almost every word, even syllable, to be stressed (part of what is usually referred to as 'effortful articulation'); but of course this is far from saying that 'those items which are typically unexploited are clitics' (1979, 79). So there is little comfort for Kean's approach here. If we take another view of clitic status, in terms of which clitic and non-clitic elements can be reliably identified *independently* of their utterance context, then we shall find Kean's simple opposition, between 'two classes of items, *clitics* and *non-clitics* (the latter also being called phonological words)' (1979, 77) to be woefully inadequate. What we shall find in the data is a range of more or less word-like elements which have to be treated on their own terms.[11] Such an approach calls for a fine-grained linguistic analysis of a great deal of Broca's data, which is no easy task. But at least it would entail analysing what is present rather than what is left out; and we really cannot go on arguing about Broca's aphasia until such analysis has been done.

Kean's discussion of prepositions is similarly selective and incomplete. In example (15) above, *on* is taken to be a clitic in the phrase *on the bank;* and certainly we can say that it is the unmarked prepositional form in that construction. It turns up similarly in other constructions such as *on the wall* and even *on the ceiling.* As such it has what Lyons calls 'abstract' or 'grammatical' function (1968, 303), and this is bound up in its phonological status as a clitic. However, not all prepositions are like this, nor even all instances of the preposition *on:* in (20),

(20)   You'll find the milk money   in   the newspaper,
                                     on
                                  under

the prepositions serve what Lyons calls 'local' or 'concrete' function, and are accordingly much closer to full lexical items. Are they clitics for Kean? Presumably so, since they tend to be omitted in Broca's aphasic speech, and her hypothesis says that it is clitics that tend to be omitted; but we have no independent definition of a clitic provided for us, to avoid the circularity here. If we follow her guideline, 'In positive active declarative sentences, clitics do not participate [sic] or contribute to the stress pattern of the sentence' (1979, 78), we should treat *on* as not being a clitic in (21)

(21)   I 'found it 'on the tàble,

and we should expect it to occur in a Broca's aphasic version of this sentence (but not in (15) where it is unstressed). Is our expectation well founded? Again, we need more information than Kean provides: she simply says that 'prepositions, particularly short ones, tend to be unexploited . . . ' (1979, 73).

Similar considerations hold for elements that Kean does not mention. For instance, some auxiliary verbs have clitic status:

[11] Matthews (1974, 168–9) provides a brief but helpful discussion of clitics in English and some other languages.

(22)   I've seen the boys
(23)   I'll be back tomorrow,

but others are quite different:

(24)   I must tell you . . .
(25)   I ought to inform you . . .

and many others. Here again we are dealing with elements that are much closer to lexical verbs (though this is not to say that auxiliaries should be treated as main verbs; see Palmer 1979, 178–85). To this extent, they should be retained in Broca's aphasic speech, according to Kean's hypothesis; but are they?

This is not the place to elaborate such points further. But we should explicitly draw attention to an implicit feature of this discussion, namely, the fact that the clitic/non-clitic status of grammatical elements is not independent of their role in what we may most generally characterize as 'message structure'. As a result, phonological facts may prove to be facts about more than phonology; and, while it may be possible to make a 'significant linguistic generalization' at the phonological level of description, it would be most unwise to assume that phonology thereby was shown to be the only level of language description involved, or to conclude that the 'significance' of the statement extends beyond the model into the domain of human language processing. Yet it is a misunderstanding of this order to conclude that a purely phonological hypothesis relating to Broca's aphasia (let us grant for the moment that such could exist) supports the view that the 'LRCS [language responsible cognitive structure] is neuroanatomically uniform' (p. 41).

Quite apart from this consideration, however, it quickly becomes apparent that, in any assessment of Broca's aphasia that tries to be reasonably comprehensive, serious areas of weakness will emerge that certainly elude a purely phonological explanation. One sort of morphosyntactic assessment is illustrated in Crystal, Fletcher and Garman (1976), of which Chapter 8 contains a fairly full discussion of a half-hour sample extracted from a longer unstructured exploratory session with a Broca's aphasic (Mr J.). Clearly, we cannot repeat that discussion here, but it will suffice to mention such features as low incidence of verbs as opposed to nouns, weakness of clause structure, and total absence of complex sentence types. We must ask how far a purely phonological account could plausibly handle such features. For instance, as far as lack of complex sentences is concerned, Kean's first hypothesis would predict that it is at the phonological level, and no other, that the class of complex sentences is differentiated from the class of simple sentences in English; and it would be disconfirmed. However, when we turn to consider her final hypothesis in this context, its ill-defined status (p. 165 above) is revealed most devastatingly: for it effortlessly 'accounts for' lack of complex sentences by appeal to some phonological deficit (D, in Fig. 12.4) interacting with some yet-to-be-determined aspect of intact linguistic capacity (C, in Fig. 12.4). In this case, we could 'define' this capacity by reference to the observation that non-aphasics can be shown to have greater difficulty in producing and comprehending complex as opposed to simple sentences. Hey, presto! But, of course, this analogue of Kean's argument in step 5 merely serves as a *reductio ad absurdum*.[12] Her hypothesis turns out, as we suspected, to be untestable.

Conclusions

We started by reviewing the concept of agrammatism, and we recognized that it badly needed linguistic refinement. Kean's earlier arguments (steps 1 to 4) seem to suggest that certain phonological factors are of prime importance in correctly interpreting some aspects of Broca's aphasia which, at first sight, appear to be morphosyntactic in nature. However, she misguidedly seeks to establish a uniquely phonological deficit hypothesis, and so abandons her earlier arguments which have some merit, in order to take up a final position (step 5) which has much less to recommend it. We cannot, of course, simply conclude that our criticisms of Kean's work establish the case for agrammatism; there is a real possibility that a specific morphosyntactic disability exists in Broca's aphasia, but much careful analysis is needed before we can say much more than this. In our present state of knowledge, attempts to provide unitary hypotheses, of universal validity, are certainly premature. We must, for instance, look in much more detail at the statistical patterns of omission and retention of grammatical elements in a wide range of aphasic patients, and interpret these patterns in terms of a much more sophisticated linguistic classification than that which Kean attempts to apply. There is no grammatical model available 'off the shelf' for the interpretation of the data of human language processing: we already know this, as far as 'non-aphasic psycholinguistics' is concerned, and it would be a great pity to think that we had to learn that lesson over again in the context of language pathology.

References

Broca, P. 1861: Remarques sur le siège de la faculté du langage articulé, suivies d'une observation d'aphémie (perte de la parole). *Bulletin de la Societé d'Anatomie de Paris* **6**, 330–57.

———1865: Sur le siège de la faculté du langage articulé. *Bulletin de la Societé d'Anthropologie* **6**, 377–93. Reprinted in H. Hécaen and J. Dubois (eds.), *La naissance de la neuropsychologie du langage (1825–1965)* (Paris: Flammarion, 1969).

Brown, R. 1973: *A first language: the early stages.* Cambridge, Mass.: Harvard University Press.

Caramazza, A. and Zurif, E. 1978: Comprehension of complex sentences in children and aphasics: a test of the regression hypothesis. In A. Caramazza and E. Zurif (eds.), *Language acquisition and language breakdown: parallels and divergencies.* Baltimore: Johns Hopkins University Press.

[12] This is more than a rhetorical point: as far as comprehension of relative clause patterns by Broca's aphasics is concerned, Kean (1978, 126–7) seems to be willing to advance this line of argument (but she does not go into details).

Chomsky, N. and Halle, M. 1968: *The sound pattern of English.* New York: Harper & Row.
Critchley, M. 1973: Articulatory defects in aphasia: the problem of Broca's aphemia. In H. Goodglass and S. Blumstein (eds.), *Psycholinguistics and aphasia.* Baltimore: Johns Hopkins University Press.
Crystal, D., Fletcher, P. and Garman, M. 1976: *The grammatical analysis of language disability.* (Studies in Language Disability and Remediation **1.**) London: Edward Arnold.
de Villiers, J. 1974: Quantitative aspects of agrammatism in aphasia. *Cortex* **10,** 36–54.
Fodor, J., Bever, T. and Garrett, M. 1974: *The psychology of language: an introduction to psycholinguistics and generative grammar.* New York: McGraw-Hill.
Fromkin, V. 1971: The nonanomalous nature of anomalous utterances. *Lg.* **47,** 27–52.
———(ed.) 1973: *Speech errors as linguistic evidence.* The Hague: Mouton.
Garrett, M. 1975: The analysis of sentence production. In G. Bower (ed.), *The psychology of language and motivation: advances in research and theory* **9.** New York: Academic Press.
———1976: Syntactic processes in sentence production. In G. Walker and R. Wales (eds.), *New approaches to language mechanisms.* Amsterdam: North-Holland.
Goodglass, H. 1976: Agrammatism. In H. Whitaker and H.A. Whitaker (eds.), *Studies in neurolinguistics* **1.** New York: Academic Press.
Goodglass, H. and Berko, J. 1960: Aphasia and inflectional morphology in English. *JSHR* **3,** 257–67.
Goodglass, H. and Hunt, J. 1958: Grammatical complexity and aphasic speech. *Word* **14,** 197–207.
Hécaen, H. 1972: Studies of language pathology. In T. Sebeok (ed.), *Current trends in linguistics* **9.** The Hague: Mouton.
Jakobson, R. 1964: Towards a linguistic typology of aphasic impairments. In A. de Reuck and M. O'Connor (eds.), *Disorders of language.* London: Churchill.
———1973: Toward a linguistic classification of aphasic impairments. In H. Goodglass and S. Blumstein (eds.), *Psycholinguistics and aphasia.* Baltimore: Johns Hopkins University Press.
Kean, M.-L. 1977: The linguistic interpretation of aphasic syndromes: agrammatism in Broca's aphasia, an example. *Cognition* **5,** 9–46.
———1978: The linguistic interpretation of aphasic syndromes. In E. Walker (ed.), *Explorations in the biology of language.* Hassocks, Sussex: Harvester.
———1979: Agrammatism: a phonological deficit? *Cognition* **7,** 69–83.
Klosek, J. 1979: Two unargued assumptions in Kean's 'phonological' interpretation of agrammatism. *Cognition* **7,** 61–8.
Kolk, H. 1978: The linguistic interpretation of Broca's aphasia: a reply to M.-L. Kean. *Cognition* **6,** 353–61.
Lenneberg, E. 1973: The neurology of language. *Daedalus* **102,** 115–33.
Luria, A. 1970: *Traumatic aphasia.* The Hague: Mouton.

Lyons, J. 1968: *Introduction to theoretical linguistics.* Cambridge: Cambridge University Press.

Marshall, J. 1977: Disorders in the expression of language. In J. Morton and J. Marshall (eds.), *Psycholinguistics series* **1**, Developmental and pathological. London: Elek.

Matthews, P. 1974: *Morphology: an introduction to the theory of word-structure.* Cambridge: Cambridge University Press.

Mohr, J. 1976: Broca's area and Broca's aphasia. In H. Whitaker and H.A. Whitaker (eds.), *Studies in neurolinguistics* **1.** New York: Academic Press.

Myerson, R. and Goodglass, H. 1972: Transformational grammars of three agrammatic patients. *L & S* **15,** 40–50.

Palmer, F. 1979: *Modality and the English modals.* London: Longman.

Schnitzer, M. 1974: Aphasiological evidence for five linguistic hypotheses. *Lg.* **50,** 300–15.

13

On the limits of passive 'competence': sociolinguistics and the polylectal grammar controversy

Peter Trudgill

The term SOCIOLINGUISTICS is itself somewhat controversial and confusing, since it appears to mean many different things to many different people (see Trudgill 1978a).[1] It is therefore useful to indicate what exactly one means by the label on any particular occasion. In the title of this chapter, for instance, I have used the term in the sense of studies that are 'based on empirical work on language as it is spoken in its social context, and are intended to answer questions and deal with topics of central interest to linguists' (Trudgill 1978b). In other words, the label is being used to refer to a methodology—to sociolinguistics as a way of doing linguistics. The role of this type of sociolinguistics in linguistic controversies is to shed empirical light on these controversies, and to help in their resolution, by concentrating on the linguistic behaviour and capabilities of speakers of languages, rather than on the intuitions of a single linguist.

Polylectal grammars

The controversial area which this chapter attempts to address, by means of data-based studies of various types, is that of the POLYLECTAL GRAMMAR. Following Weinreich's (1954) attempt to reconcile structural linguistics with dialectology, a number of linguists sought to incorporate more than one variety of the same language into a single description or grammar. Structural diasystems of the Weinreich type (e.g. Cochrane, 1959; Wölck 1965) were followed by generative treatments which attempted to show that dialects may differ principally through the ordering or addition of rules (e.g. Newton 1972). Most often, works of this type dealt with only a small number of varieties of a language; and they were justified by their authors on the grounds that they provided a good

---

[1] I am very grateful to the following for their comments on previous versions of this paper: C.-J. Bailey, Jean Hannah, William Labov and F.R. Palmer.

way of demonstrating and investigating the degree and nature of the relatedness of different dialects.

Subsequently, however, a rather stronger thesis was mooted—that of the PANDIALECTAL or PANLECTAL grammar. A panlectal grammar was intended to incorporate not simply a few but all the varieties of a particular language; and it was justified, not as a descriptive device, but in terms of the model it was said to provide of the adult native speaker's 'competence'. Associated particularly with the work of C.-J. Bailey (e.g. Bailey 1972; 1973), the rationale behind work on panlectal grammars was summarized by Labov (1973) as follows:

> We can and should write a single grammar to encompass all (or nearly all) of the dialects of a language, since the competence of the (fully adult) native speaker reaches far beyond the dialect he uses himself. Bailey argues for such grammars on the ground that (*a*) as native speakers become older, they become familiar with an increasingly large number of other dialects; (*b*) they have the ability to understand and interpret the productions of those other dialect speakers, analysing their rules as extensions of limitations of their own rules; and (*c*) they can even extrapolate from their own rules and predict the existence of dialects which they have never heard.

After some initial work in this area, however, it gradually came to be recognized that attempting to incorporate *all* the varieties of one language in a single grammar was an unreasonable endeavour. (One obvious argument against panlectal grammars is the well known fact that languages are not discrete objects: no one would want to compose a panlectal grammar encompassing all varieties of French, Occitan, Catalan, Spanish, Portuguese and Italian, and yet these varieties form a dialect continuum without sharp boundaries.) Early work on panlectal grammars was therefore followed by work on a more limited hypothesis—that of the POLYLECTAL grammar.

As the name indicates, the polylectal grammar seeks to include many, rather than all, of the varieties of a particular language. The notion of the polylectal grammar thus raises two interesting and challenging questions: (*a*) is it in fact legitimate to include more than one variety of language in a grammar? and (*b*) if it is, how many varieties may one include?

If the grammar is intended to be a model of native speakers' linguistic 'competence', then it should be possible to answer these questions by investigating empirically the extent of a native speaker's competence in another dialect. Labov's paper *Where do grammars stop?* is an attempt of this type to answer question (*b*). The present chapter, on the other hand, is an attempt to answer question (*a*). Labov points out that while 'the competence of native English speakers ranges far beyond their own use', it is also true that 'there are limits to its reach'. In this chapter, I shall argue that these limits are in some respects so severe that it may not be legitimate to attempt to model this 'competence' by means of a grammar. Drawing on empirical evidence from a number of sources, I will also argue that, while a grammar of rules may or may not be the correct way to model a native speaker's productive or active competence (cf. Matthews, 1979), speakers' receptive or passive competence may well rest on irregular and *ad hoc* types of procedures to such an extent that the best way of explicating this sort of ability may well not be in terms of extensions of and extrapolations from rules at all.

It is of course undoubtedly true that native speakers of a language can, in some sense, cope with varieties of their language other than the one they speak themselves. It is also well known that passive 'competence' greatly exceeds (and, in language learning, usually precedes) active 'competence'. However, if we examine the claim that this passive 'competence' ranges 'far beyond' a speaker's own dialect, it emerges that we should not exaggerate the extent of this ability nor, in particular, its regularity.

We proceed now to a comparison of the abilities speakers have with respect to their own dialects and those that they have with respect to dialects other than their own.

Production of other dialects

The strongest claim that one could logically make about the nature of passive 'competence' would be that it is *potentially* the same as productive 'competence', i.e. speakers *could* speak other dialects if they wanted to or if it became necessary for some reason—although they do not normally do so. This is, at its most extreme, an absurd view, and one that has never been advanced in support of the notion of the polylectal grammar. It is of interest, nevertheless, to look at those situations where speakers do attempt to turn passive competence into active competence—where they do attempt to speak other varieties—since this may shed valuable light on the nature of passive competence, and on its limitations.

The most obvious attempts to turn passive into active competence involve imitation. Some people, of course, are very good at imitating other accents and dialects; most others are not. It is, of course, not surprising if speakers older than adolescence have difficulties with the phonetics of a different accent. It can be no criticism of the polylectal grammar hypothesis if older speakers are less than successful at adjusting the automatic neurological and physiological habits involved in the production of speech sounds. This lack of imitative ability, however, extends also to grammar and, especially, phonology. Typically, errors in imitation reflect an inaccurate analysis of the imitated dialect and therefore, presumably, a mismatch between active and passive competence. Very many examples could be given, but the most obvious involve the extension of forms to environments where they do not belong, as in hypercorrection:

(*i*) A well known case of hypercorrection in British English is the 'correcting' of North of England /ʊ/ to South of England /ʌ/ not only in *cut* /kʊt/>/kʌt/ but also in *foot* /fʊt/>/fʌt/. (Not all examples of hypercorrection of this type, however, can be said to represent an inadequacy in passive competence. As Knowles (1978) points out, some cases of hypercorrection are due not to inaccurate knowledge but to inability to produce the correct form, as it were, in the heat of the moment, i.e. performance error.)

(*ii*) When imitating American accents, British speakers, including especially pop-singers (see Trudgill 1980) and actors, often reveal quite clearly that they have misanalysed some aspects of American English phonology. This is particularly true in the case of HYPER-AMERICAN /r/—the insertion of preconsonantal /r/ not only in words like *born* but also in words like *dawn*. Even excellent mimics such as Peter Sellers may be guilty of this, but less skilled mimics in the world of popular music are particularly likely to produce hyper-American /r/:

(a)   Cliff Richard, *Bachelor Boy* (1961)
      'You'll be *a bachelor boy* . . . ' /ər bæčələr bɔi/
(b)   Kinks, *Sunny Afternoon* (1966)
      ' . . . *Ma and Pa*' /ma:r ən pa:r/
(c)   Paul McCartney, *Till There Was You* (1963)
      'I never *saw them* at all' /sɔ:r ðɛm/.

Incorrect insertion of /r/ also occurs in the imitation of southwestern English English accents.

(*iii*) In Trudgill (1973), I argued for a single grammar for the English spoken in the city of Norwich on the grounds that, *inter alia,* 'Norwich speakers are . . . able to imitate without error types of Norwich English other than those they normally use, for humorous or other similar purposes'. Outsiders, it was argued, could not do this accurately, tending to produce 'hyper-Norwichisms', cf. (*ii*) above. However, I am now persuaded that this is not necessarily the case and that even members of the same speech community do not always have accurate passive competence of other varieties spoken in that community.

Older Norwich English has a distinction between *daze* /de:z/< M.E. ā and *days* /dæɪz/< M.E. ai. Younger speakers have merged these two vowels as /æɪ/. Further work (Trudgill 1978c) has now uncovered a number of Norwich speakers who, noting but analysing incorrectly the older Norwich distinction, produce not only *daze* as /de:z/ but also *days* as /de:z/ when attempting to imitate older speakers or simply trying to speak in a more local manner. We can perhaps refer to forms such as *days* /de:z/ as HYPERDIALECTISMS. Hyperdialectisms are not perpetrated by especially many Norwich speakers, but the fact that they occur at all is significant.

(*iv*) As we noted above, misanalysis of other dialects is not confined to phonology. For example, hyper-Americanisms in the speech of British people imitating American English occur also in grammatical forms:

American English:	*I've gotten one*	(=I've acquired one)
	I've got one	(=I have one)
British English:	*I've got one*	(=both meanings)
Hyper-American English:	*I've gotten one*	(=both meanings)

(*v*) The failure to imitate another variety correctly may extend also to the level of language use and communicative competence. Speakers not only have an incorrect analysis of the phonology and grammar of other dialects, they also have an inadequate appreciation of how they are employed in social interaction. As an illustration of this, observe the following:

The Canadian linguist J.K. Chambers, after some months in Britain, walks into my room at Reading University and says 'Cheers!'.

This incorrect usage was based on the correct observation that in certain forms of British English (see Trudgill 1978*b*) *Cheers* can function as a greeting. The error lay in the extension of this greeting to a situation where it was not appropriate. *Cheers,* it seems, can be employed as a greeting only between people who are passing each other at some distance, say in the street, and where it functions as 'hello and goodbye'.

Many other examples could be cited. One can, for instance, readily observe that even after several months residence in Britain, some speakers of American English have failed to acquire a correct appreciation of the strength of the swear-word *bloody* and use it in social contexts where it may cause offence.

None of the linguistic forms dealt with in this section is likely to cause any difficulty in comprehension or interpretation. British speakers readily understand the American pronunciation of *born* with an /r/ and the use of *gotten* as a past participle. Northerners know perfectly well that when southerners say /kʌt/ they mean *cut*. However, the behaviour of British people and of northerners when they actually attempt to imitate the other varieties shows that this comprehension is not due to accurate or rule-governed knowledge of how these varieties are structured. When passive competence is employed in speech production—if this is indeed what actually happens in imitation—it is shown to fall far short of the active competence speakers have in their own variety.

It is not only in imitation that we can observe the attempted use of passive competence in actual speech production. Speakers who at some stage in their lives change to another variety or acquire an additional dialect, as a result of social or geographical mobility, perform the same kind of operation and over a much longer period.

Casual observation of speakers who have changed dialects indicates that, while there are large differences between individuals in their ability (as well as desire) to effect a successful change, it is a very rare adult that successfully masters the speaking of a new dialect in all its details. Children, of course, as is well known, are much better at acquiring new varieties. However, there is reason to suppose that even the ability of children in this respect should not be exaggerated. Payne (n.d.), for example, has shown that children who have lived most of their lives in an area of Philadelphia, but who have out-of-town parents, have not acquired some of the detailed phonological constraints of the local accent in the same way as indigenous children, although this fact is apparent only after careful linguistic analysis.

As another example of this, my current research in Norwich shows that even adults who have lived all their lives in Norwich and who otherwise have perfect Norwich accents may not, if their parents were from some other dialect area, have mastered successfully the Norwich distinction between /uː/ and /ʌu/ (see Trudgill 1974):

/uː/	/ʌu/	
moan	mown	
nose	knows	etc.

Even after a lifetime's exposure to this distinction, they neither produce it nor imitate it correctly.[2] (This is further evidence against the single speech-community grammar discussed above, of course.)

Examples such as these indicate that while (particularly younger) speakers can be reasonably successful at acquiring a new variety of their language, the respects in which they fall short of total success suggest that any passive competence they may have had in the new variety before beginning its acquisition was inaccurate and insufficient.

Grammaticality judgements

One important ability that speakers have with respect to their own dialect is that they are able to make grammaticality judgements about it. Drawing upon their native linguistic competence, they are usually able to state whether particular grammatical constructions are or are not possible in their variety. The extent to which speakers' competence in their own dialect differs from their passive competence with respect to other dialects can therefore be tested by asking speakers to make grammaticality judgements about forms that occur in dialects other than their own. In doing this, we are interested in people's knowledge of other dialects, but we are particularly concerned with their ability to judge the grammaticality of forms that they are not aware of having heard before. If they are truly able to 'predict the existence of dialects which they have never heard', they should be able to do this.

In a study carried out at Reading University, a group of subjects were presented with a number of sentences, on paper, which they were asked to label as follows:

A.   I use this kind of grammatical construction myself.
B.   I don't use this grammatical construction, but other English speakers do.
C.   I've never heard anyone use a construction like this, but I would guess that some native speakers do use it.
D.   The sort of thing only a foreigner (non-native speaker) would say.
E.   Nobody would say this—not even a foreigner.

Answers A and B demonstrate first-hand knowledge of a particular construction by the subject; answers C, D and E demonstrate genuine predictive ability and are thus the crucial ones for this experiment.

The subjects fell into three groups: 20 non-native speakers, most of them teachers of English, studying at Reading University; 80 first-year undergraduate students of linguistics (with about 40 hours of linguistics teaching, average age 19); and 11 lecturers and research students from the Department of Linguistic Science.[3] To select subjects of this type, of course, is to bias results in favour of the polylectal grammar hypothesis, since one can assume that linguists will have more extensive passive

---

[2] I am very grateful to the following for their collaboration in this research: Neil Brummage, Tom Geddes, Adrian Hannah, Douglas Howes, John Sandford, Sue Sandford, Eric Trudgill, Stephen Trudgill, Colin Wills.

[3] Including the well known and highly respected author of *The English Verb*, *Grammar*, and *Modality and the English Modals*.

competence and be better able to predict the existence of forms in other dialects than the rest of the population. The results show, however, that while the lecturers were somewhat better in their predictive abilities than the first-year students, both groups were very bad indeed and were in some cases actually worse than the foreigners. The eight sentences used in the test include constructions which are all current in British dialects, and it is a remarkable fact that some subjects were totally unable to predict the occurrence of forms used only a few miles from their own homes.

The first sentence to be evaluated was:

   (*a*)   *Look—is that a man stand there?*

This is an entirely normal, grammatical sentence in many East Anglian dialects, and corresponds to the form *is that a man standing there* in most other dialects.

This is probably the most difficult sentence to handle, since at least according to one interpretation it varies from other dialects in two ways. First, non-continuous aspect is employed: *stands* rather than *standing* (this is a feature of a number of conservative English dialects; see Wakelin 1972). Secondly, there is no third-person *-s* marker: *stand* rather than *stands*. The results given in Table 13.1 show that the accuracy of speakers of other dialects in predicting the grammaticality of this East Anglian construction is very low indeed. The most striking feature of these results is that around half of the native speakers could not imagine that *anyone* could possibly say such a thing, let alone other native speakers. And the overwhelming majority of subjects categorized this sentence as something that no native speaker would ever say. One academic linguist was prepared to concede that this construction might be a possibility in English—and so we have one actual prediction of grammaticality out of the 87 native speakers who responded. Otherwise, only two students recognized that it was a possibility, but both claimed to use the form themselves—so theirs was a grammaticality judgement about their own dialect and not some other. (One of these students came from East Anglia. The other may have given the answer A in error.)

These figures are very damaging to any polylectal grammar hypothesis. Even native speakers who, as linguists, supposedly know more about English than most, are for the most part totally unable to predict the grammaticality of this construction. The native speakers as a whole, moreover, are no better than the non-native speakers (who are presumably not assumed to have access to any polylectal grammar in their predictive ability).

The second sentence was the following:

(*b*) *My hair needs washed.*

This construction is the one normally employed in Scotland as well as in some areas immediately to the south of the border and in some parts of the USA, and it corresponds to the sentence *My hair needs washing* found elsewhere. A rough guess suggests that perhaps 4 to 5 million native speakers of British English normally use this construction. Subjects' reactions to this sentence are given in Table 13.2.

Table 13.1 Grammaticality judgements for sentence (*a*).

Label	% (N) Lecturers	Students	Foreigners
A	0	3(2)	0
B	0	0	0
C	9(1)	0	5(1)
D	45(5)	45(34)	47(8)
E	45(5)	52(40)	47(8)

Table 13.2 Grammaticality judgements for sentence (*b*).

Label	% (N) Lecturers	Students	Foreigners
A	0	4(3)	6(1)
B	18(2)	4(3)	0
C	9(1)	3(2)	6(1)
D	45(5)	38(29)	28(5)
E	27(3)	52(40)	61(11)

Of the lecturers, two knew that the form was Scots and labelled the sentence accordingly; and one made a genuine prediction that the construction could occur in other dialects. The remaining eight could only predict that either foreigners or no one at all would say this.

The students fared even worse. More than half could not imagine anybody saying this, and altogether 90 percent believed that no native speaker could say it. The three students who gave A were all Scots themselves, and one of the three who gave B labelled the sentence 'Scots'. We can therefore say that between two and four of the students made a genuine and correct prediction—a very low level of success.

The third sentence was:

(*c*) *I'm not sure—I might could do it.*

This double modal construction, as well as being current in a number of American dialects (see Butters 1973), is a normal grammatical form in the northwest and northeast of England and in parts of Scotland. Reactions to this sentence were as in Table 13.3.

Once again, 44 of the native speakers were unable to predict that any speaker could say this, and altogether 74 out of the 85 native speakers who responded could not conceive of any other native speaker using it. Of the remaining eleven, four of the lecturers gave the response B with the label 'Geordie' (northeastern), while one student from Cumberland (in the northwest) used the form herself. There were thus five apparently genuine correct predictions amongst the students—or possibly six if we count the one (unlabelled) B response. This is somewhat better than the results for

Table 13.3 Grammaticality judgements for sentence (*c*).

Label	%(N)		
	Lecturers	Students	Foreigners
A	0	1(1)	0
B	36(4)	1(1)	0
C	0	7(5)	5(1)
D	36(4)	35(26)	21(4)
E	27(3)	55(41)	74(14)

the previous two sentences, but still represents a low percentage of correct predictions.

The next sentence to be tested was:

(*d*) *She love him very much.*

The lack of the third-person singular -*s* is a feature of East Anglian (and other) British dialects (see Trudgill 1974) as well as of a number of American varieties. The number of speakers of English who commonly use this grammatical form must be in the order of several millions. The reactions to this sentence were as in Table 13.4.

The lecturers did very well here, but once again it is clear that this was as a result of their *knowledge* of this linguistic form rather than of any predictive ability. (Interestingly enough, moreover, only two of the lecturers' B answers were labelled 'East Anglian'. The others mentioned 'Black American', 'West Indian', or something similar. British linguists, in other words, know about this form but, for the most part, only from non-British dialects.) As can be seen from Table 13.4, one correct prediction occurred amongst the lecturers. As far as the students were concerned, the vast majority thought that only a foreigner would employ this grammatical pattern. Eight were familiar with this kind of verb form (although only two from British dialects), and four correct predictions took place—although even this figure must be in doubt in view of the large number of rock and pop-music lyrics, which most students have undoubtedly heard, which contain verbs of this sort.

We already have, so far, a certain amount of evidence to suggest that native speakers—including even linguists—either have first-hand knowledge of a particular grammatical form or can imagine that only foreigners (or even no one at all) would use it: very few genuine correct predictions appear to take place. This picture is confirmed by the remaining four sentences. These were:

(*e*)   *Where's my book?—Ah, here it's.*

This form—which presents perhaps as much of a phonological as a grammatical problem—is current in the West Highlands of Scotland. (It causes great difficulties, incidentally, for Labov's (1969) thesis on copula deletion and reduction in English.) Post-experimental questioning showed that A responses to this sentence were all the result of misreadings.

Table 13.4 Grammaticality judgements for sentence (*d*).

Label	% (N) Lecturers	Students	Foreigners
A	0	0	0
B	91(10)	14(8)	17(3)
C	9(1)	5(4)	6(1)
D	0	83(64)	50(9)
E	0	1(1)	28(5)

    (*f*)   *Wait a minute—I'm now coming.*

This form occurs in East Anglia in the sense of *I'm just coming.*

    (*g*)   *Had you a good time last night?*

This is normal in Scottish and some northern dialects.

    (*h*)   *It's dangerous to smoke at a petrol station without causing an explosion: petrol is very inflammable.*

This construction is found in parts of South Wales with the meaning *in case of* or *because you might cause an explosion*. Discussion of this sentence with the students after the test revealed that the A and B responders had all misinterpreted this sentence, ignored what to them was a semantic anomaly, or supposed it to have the meaning *even if you don't cause an explosion*. Results for sentences (*e*)–(*h*) are given in Table 13.5.

The conclusion to be drawn from the results of this test is that native speakers of English are not able to employ their passive competence in making grammaticality judgements about forms that they do not use themselves but that are habitually used by speakers elsewhere in the country—or, in the case of the student subjects, by members of the same class: sentence (*b*), for example, obtained student responses ranging from A to E. It could be claimed that these results are not conclusive, since only a small number of grammatical forms were employed, and since 'difficult' and out-of-the-way constructions were deliberately selected. Against this argument, we can say that there *are* only a small number of grammatical differences within British English; and that it is useless to select more familiar examples, since we would then obtain a large number of A and B responses. Subjects cannot exhibit their predictive prowess if they are presented with a form already known to them.

It should be noted, however, that speakers are able to extend their passive competence somewhat, *if they are given help*. Labov (1973) takes as an example of this phenomenon the grammatical construction:

John's smoking a lot anymore.

This construction is employed with the meaning 'John's smoking a lot nowadays' in the 'positive *anymore* dialects' of the American Midwest. In a series of tests, Labov discovered that speakers from other American

Table 13.5 Grammaticality judgements for sentences
(e)–(h).

Label	(e)	(f)	(g)	(h)
(i) Lecturers — %				
A	0	0	0	0
B	0	0	27	0
C	0	18	18	17
D	55	82	55	17
E	45	0	0	67
(ii) Students — %				
A	4	1	9	14
B	5	11	27	19
C	15	21	18	28
D	33	60	38	10
E	42	6	8	28

dialect areas found this construction to be totally ungrammatical and indeed incomprehensible. However, Labov also administered a further test to non-Midwesterners in which the function of positive *anymore* was explained. The test began:

> *Anymore* actually means 'nowadays' in these sentences, the way it's used in the Midwest. Would you guess that if someone says *John smokes anymore,* meaning 'John smokes nowadays', that he would also say . . . .

and then subjects were asked to make predictions about a number of sentences. It emerged that, given this degree of help, speakers are rather good at acquiring the right sorts of intuitions. All subjects, for example, correctly rejected sentences such as:

> *When would you rather live, in 1920 or anymore?*

as being ungrammatical, even in the Midwest.

This should not, however, lead us to be too optimistic about native speakers' abilities. It is not often that one is given such overt help with new dialects, and exposure of the normal type to positive *anymore* does not inevitably lead to a correct analysis: Labov notes that outsiders who had spent years in the Midwest and were familiar with positive *anymore* were inclined to interpret it incorrectly as meaning 'still' rather than 'nowadays'. And positive *anymore* speakers themselves, when apprised of the fact that Easterners do not use *anymore* in the same way as themselves, 'seem to find it very difficult to know which of these forms would be used by Easterners' (Labov 1973); that is, they were not sure in which contexts Easterners would use *anymore*. Thus, even given overt guidance with or long-term exposure to new forms, there are severe limits to the extent to which speakers are able to extend their passive competence to include those forms.

Comprehension of other dialects

To what extent can speakers understand forms and constructions from other dialects? If they have internalized some form of polylectal grammar, one would not expect there to be many serious difficulties. And indeed it is obvious that speakers of different dialects of English can nearly always understand one another.

However, I want to suggest here that comprehension of other dialects does not take place by means of extensions of rule systems, or anything similar. Rather, comprehension occurs in a very *ad hoc* manner that relies heavily on linguistic and extra-linguistic context. Context, that is, plays a much greater role in the comprehension of other varieties than it does in the comprehension of one's own.

The importance of context is particularly obvious in the case of phonetics and phonology. If, when in the USA, I ask for a *pair of jeans* [ʤeɪ-inz], no American fails to understand me. However, if I say I am going to see *Jean* [ʤeɪ-in], many Americans want to know who *Jane* is. Similarly, when, employing my Norwich accent, I tell someone that I've bought a new *coat* /ku:t/, no one assumes I have bought a *coot*. If, on the other hand, I mention my friend *Joan* /ʤu:n/, people tend not to be sure whether her name is *Joan* or *June*. Thus, lexical predictability is of considerable importance.

To test this point of view further, however, we need also to see how difficult speakers find it to comprehend different *grammatical* forms out of context. The argument will go as follows. Speakers comprehend forms from their own dialect even out of context. They comprehend forms from other dialects in context. Are they also able to comprehend forms from other dialects out of context? If not, then it can be argued that these forms have not become part of any polylectal grammar that the speaker has internalized and is therefore able to call upon in the passive interpretation of utterances.

A test that was intended to examine the extent of speakers' ability to comprehend such forms was carried out in the following way. A set of sentences containing grammatical forms known to be restricted to particular varieties of English was presented, on paper, to a group of 47 subjects. The subjects consisted of 21 students at Reading University who were native speakers of languages other than English, and 26 British students (second year undergraduate, and MA—beginning postgraduates) of linguistics. The sentences were introduced as follows:

If you heard someone you supposed to be a native speaker of English say the following things, what would you think he meant? Please tick one of the interpretations under each sentence, or write in one of your own.

In each case, interpretation (*a*) was 'nonsense', and (*e*) was left blank for the subject to fill in if desired. The sentences, with accompanying interpretations, were the following:

(1)   *Don't jump off while the bus stops.*
    (*b*)   . . . when the bus stops
    (*c*)   . . . while the bus is stopping
    (*d*)   . . . until the bus stops

In parts of northern England, including Yorkshire, this construction is grammatical in the sense of (*d*). It was felt that, in the test, the bias would be towards subjects comprehending this sentence in the 'correct' *while=until* interpretation, since (*b*) is not particularly plausible semantically—or at least not as plausible as (*d*)—and (*c*) is fairly unlikely to be equivalent to (1) on grammatical grounds. Results, however, are as given in Table 13.6.

Interestingly enough, the non-native speakers were very much better than the native speakers at getting the 'right' answer. Of the natives, nearly a quarter, far from being able to understand this construction, thought it was nonsense. And only 15 percent (four individuals) actually got it right. Of these four, two had lived in Yorkshire. In other words, it seems that only two genuine acts of comprehension of a new dialect form out of context took place—although even in these cases we cannot be certain that the people in question had not been regularly exposed to northern dialects at some time.

We therefore have one piece of evidence to show that most speakers are unable to comprehend a dialect form in widespread use, in some cases as little as 25 miles from their own homes—not apparently a very good justification for positing polylectal competence. Now it could be argued that lack of comprehension of a form occurring in isolation, in an artificial testing situation, is not a fair test. However, it is precisely this sort of ability that speakers ought to have if they comprehend by means of rule extension. With this sort of ability, they should not require any context to help them—particularly when they are presented with the right answer in a multiple-choice test. The thesis of this chapter is that when speakers from elsewhere in the English-speaking world hear a Yorkshireman use *while* in this way, they generally understand what he means; but as the above results show, they are not able to do this by drawing on the resources of any polylectal grammar they have internalized. Rather, they depend on the context to make it clear what is meant. Bailey (cf. 1972) might have wished to argue that it is precisely this kind of process—the use of context—which speakers use in the *development* of their polylectal grammars. But we have cited evidence above (see the discussion of sentence (*d*), *She love him very much*) that even where speakers have certainly been exposed to forms from different dialects, and have presumably employed context to help in comprehending them, they are still unable to 'predict' their occurrence. We prefer to argue here that it is possible for *ad hoc* contextual comprehension processes to be employed many times without any 'internalization' of the rule in question taking place.[4]

It could also perhaps be claimed that alternatives (*b*) and (*c*) to sentence (1) are too plausible and gave subjects too much encouragement to select

---

[4] It could be argued that in this, and subsequent sentences, it is lexical rather than grammatical differences which cause comprehension difficulties, i.e. it is simply the meaning of the word *while* that differs. It is, however, clear that differences in the function of grammatical words such as *while* are not the same order of phenomenon as differences in lexical meaning between, say, American and British *pants*.

Table 13.6 Comprehension judgements
of sentence (*1*).

Answer	% Natives	Non-natives
(*a*)	23	9
(*b*)	8	14
(*c*)	46	34
✓ (*d*)	15	44
(*e*)	8	0

them instead of the 'right' answer. This argument cannot legitimately be employed in connection with the next example:

(2) *Whenever it was born I felt ill.*
     (*b*) Each time it was born I felt ill.
     (*c*) When it was born I felt ill.
     (*d*) As soon as it was born I felt ill.

This sentence is grammatical in many Northern Irish dialects, including those used by educated speakers, in sense (*c*). Results in this case should have been biased towards (*c*), since this is the only interpretation that really makes sense: there is no particular reason for selecting (*d*), and, while an interpretation for (*b*) can of course be contextualized, it is much less probable semantically than (*c*). (We do have to concede, however, that, unlike sentence (1), which is ungrammatical in all except the particular northern dialects, sentence (2) is actually gramatically, if not semantically, acceptable in all English dialects. Only in the Northern Irish dialects in question, however, is the sentence both grammatically and semantically acceptable.)

Results show, however, that the grammatical constraints of their own dialects forced a majority of subjects to select the anti-common sense interpretation (*b*). Even with the semantic dice heavily loaded in its favour, interpretation (*c*) did not emerge from most speakers' supposed polylectal grammars as the right answer. The results are given in Table 13.7.

Once again, nearly a quarter of the natives can do no better than to regard this as nonsense—out of context. And only 12 percent (3) of the natives understood this form in the correct Northern Irish sense—and one of them comes from the West of Scotland, where this form is possibly also grammatical. (Interpretations given under (*e*) included: 'whenever I saw a birth . . . ' and 'each time they were born . . . '). The conclusion once again is that, without any context to help them, most native speakers are unable to draw on the rule systems of their own dialect in order to understand a grammatical form new to them—even when the right answer is the semantically obvious one.

(3) *I don't want it but.*
     (*b*) I really don't want it.
     (*c*) but I don't want it.
     (*d*) I don't want it but I'll take it.

Table 13.7 Comprehension judgements
for sentence (*2*).

	%	
Answer	Natives	Non-natives
(*a*)	23	19
(*b*)	58	64
√ (*c*)	12	4
(*d*)	0	14
(*e*)	8	0

This form is grammatical, with 'normal' intonation and primary stress on *want,* in many dialects in Scotland, Northern Ireland, and the northeast of England, where it has the meaning (*c*). We have to recognize that lack of intonation may have caused difficulties here, but the full-stop at the end of the sentence was clearly visible on the paper, and the subjects were explicitly told that there were no misprints of any kind on the test sheet. Results for sentence 3 are given in Table 13.8.

The majority of native speakers, like the non-native speakers, were not able to give it the correct interpretation. Of the 15 per cent (4) subjects who gave the right answer, one was from Scotland and one from the Northeast. The success rate was thus very low indeed, in spite of the fact that some of the subjects must have heard the form, if nowhere else, either from a BBC TV comedy series current at the time and set in the Northeast (in which one of the characters frequently had lines such as *I don't want it though but*), or from a well known Scottish football club manager who appears frequently on TV and radio.

> (4) *Come here till I punch you on the nose.*
>   (b) so that I can punch you
>   (c) while I can punch you
>   (d) until I can punch you

Constructions of this type are usual in many varieties spoken in Scotland, Ireland and Liverpool in the sense of (*b*). The results for this sentence are given in Table 13.9.

Here the native speakers fared better than on the previous sentences— although no better than the non-natives—and of the 50 per cent (13) giving the right answer, five were from Scotland, Ireland or Liverpool. It is also worthy of note that more than a quarter of the native speakers could only interpret this as 'nonsense'. Interpretations written in under (*e*) included '*or* I'll punch you on the nose' and 'keep coming here until I punch you on the nose'.

Finally, for the sake of comparison, a sentence discussed in Labov (1973; see above) was tested in the same way:

> *John's smoking a lot anymore.*

which is grammatical in some American varieties with the meaning 'John's smoking a lot nowadays'. The British subjects did very badly here, 81 per

Table 13.8 Comprehension judgements
for sentence (*3*).

Answer	% Natives	Non-natives
(*a*)	23	19
(*b*)	0	4
√ (*c*)	15	4
(*d*)	62	69
(*e*)	0	4

Table 13.9 Comprehension judgements
for sentence (*4*).

Answer	% Natives	Non-natives
(*a*)	27	34
√ (*b*)	50	49
(*c*)	4	4
(*d*)	12	14
(*e*)	8	0

cent regarding it as nonsense, and none getting the right 'nowadays' answer.

Comprehension in context

Native speakers, then, are not especially successful at comprehending forms from other dialects out of context—an indication of the limitations of passive competence. As noted above, however, comprehension does take place readily in context. There are, nevertheless, limitations even to this ability—limitations which also cast doubt on the extent of passive competence. Firstly, there are a number of examples available in the literature which show that, even given context, failure to comprehend can occur in dialogue between speakers of different dialects.

(*i*) Labov (1973) reports the following exchange between a white American psychologist and a five-year-old black child, Samuel, who had known each other for six months. The psychologist introduces Samuel to Labov, whereupon Samuel turns to the psychologist and says:

Samuel: I been know your name.
Psych.: What?
Samuel: I been know your name.
Psych: You better know my name?
Samuel: I *been* know your name.

'Even after this exchange', Labov writes, 'the white adult did not know that he had failed to understand something'. The problem was that in some forms of American Black Vernacular English, stressed *been* functions as a 'remote perfect' marker. Thus, in this variety, *I been know your name* corresponds to *I've known your name for a long time* in other dialects. The psychologist's ability to comprehend other dialects, even in context, did not extend to the comprehension of this particular form.

(*ii*) Lesley Milroy (forthcoming) reports an exchange in Donegal, Ireland, involving herself and her husband, who are both British, and Sean, a native of the area:

> Sean: How long are youse here?
> J.M.: Till after Easter.
> (*Sean looks puzzled*)
> L.M.: We came on Sunday.
> Sean: Ah, Youse're here a while then.

Here the failure to comprehend is recognized and repaired, but it is real enough while it lasts.

Secondly, lack of comprehension can take place, even given context, at the pragmatic as well as at the grammatical level. Students of the ethnography of speaking have noted that differences in communication norms between language communities can lead to hostile stereotyping and misinterpretation (for example, Scollon and Scollon 1979, on the mutual stereotyping, in interethnic communication in Canada, of English and Athabaskan speakers as 'arrogant'). The same sort of problem may also occur in dialogue between speakers of different varieties of the same language. Again, many examples could be noted. One may suffice.

The following is an interchange between myself and an American shop assistant:

> Asst.: Would you like these things in a bag?
> P.T.: Would you mind?
> Asst.: No, sir, I wouldn't mind at all. We have plenty of bags and it's really no trouble at all, sir.

Here my British use of *would you mind?*, which was intended to function as 'yes, please', was interpreted as a genuine request for information.

Conclusion

Controversy and argument over panlectal and polylectal grammars has continued for several years. One early dispute arose out of Chomsky and Halle's (1968) suggestion that all accents of English could be regarded as having the same underlying phonological forms. It is now clear that, while that might be a possibility for American English, it is not feasible at all for other varieties of the language: on this issue, see Becker (1967); Trudgill (1973); Chambers and Trudgill (1980, Chapter 3).

Next, there was discussion of the problem of the limits of polylectal grammars. Labov's important (1973) paper is the most thorough attempt to investigate this issue. He argues that, while some forms are clearly outside a panlectal grammar, e.g. (*a*) *He smokes a lot anymore* and (*b*) BEV *It ain't no cat can't get in no coop*, there are other forms which should be included, such as negative concord (other than that of the purely BEV type, as in (*b*)), because they are readily comprehended. Then Berdan (1977), in another important data-based study, argues that 'grammars of polylectal comprehension may well exist' but 'documented cases of comprehension across lects fail to provide sufficient evidence for the polylectal grammar'.

Now, in the present chapter, we have noted that it is a rare speaker who acquires or imitates a dialect other than his own vernacular perfectly. We have also seen that native speakers have difficulty comprehending varieties that are phonetically, phonologically or grammatically different from their own if context is unhelpful or absent. And, even given context, grammatical and pragmatic difficulties can cause severe, if often temporary, difficulties. It is the thesis of this chapter that such difficulties indicate that the case for handling the passive competence of a native speaker by means of a grammar is not an especially strong one. The problems that native speakers may from time to time have, at all linguistic levels, with dialects other than their own, and the important role context plays in solving these problems, suggest rather the following.

The more different the productive competence of speaker B is from that of speaker A, the more difficulty speaker A will have in understanding speaker B. At those points where their grammars differ, A will use all the cues he can find, both linguistic and non-linguistic, in helping himself to understand B. He will, given time and practice, get better at understanding B (as Bailey suggests). But there are some forms which he may never come to comprehend fully or analyse correctly. And the fact that even those forms which are understood in context may not be understood out of context suggests that these forms never become part of any internalized, regular, passive polylectal competence.

Where forms from other dialects are comprehended, two factors can be used to explain the phenomenon. The first is *familiarity*. Familiarity with a form, as we have seen, does not inevitably lead to the ability to predict that it is grammatical. Neither does it necessarily lead to an ability to comprehend; but it obviously helps. All native speakers of Standard English have had considerable exposure, for example, to non-standard negative concord (other than the purely BEV type) and it is therefore not surprising if forms containing negative concord are comprehended.

The second and more important factor is *degree of linguistic difference* between the dialects. We do not, as yet, have an accurate measure of this, but there is no reason to suppose that the comprehension of grammatical forms from other dialects proceeds any differently from that of phonetic forms. If A says *face* as [feɪs] and B says [fɛɪs], it is not surprising if they understand one another. If, on the other hand, A says [faɪs] and B says [frəs], it would be equally unsurprising if they had some comprehension difficulties (especially in view of the similarity of B's pronunciation to A's way of saying *fierce*).

The same is surely true of grammatical forms also. If A says *I go* and B says *I goes,* the linguistic difference is so slight that we do not need to postulate a polylectal grammar to explain how they understand one another (anymore than we need to postulate a polylectal grammar to explain why I understand what Dutch speakers mean when they say *Wat is het?* [vat ɪz ət]). On the other hand, the degree of difference between Standard English *There's no cat that can get in a coop* and the BEV equivalent *It ain't no cat can't get in no coop* (combined with the degree of similarity there is between the latter and Standard English *There's no cat that can't get in a coop*), explains the comprehension problem that undoubtedly exists without recourse, again, to the notion of a polylectal grammar.

References

Bailey, C.-J. 1972: The integration of linguistic theory: internal reconstruction and the comparative method in descriptive analysis. In R.P. Stockwell and R.K.S. Macauley (eds.), *Linguistic change and generative theory*. Bloomington: Indiana University Press.

———1973: *Variation and linguistic theory*. Washington, DC: Center for Applied Linguistics.

Bailey, C.-J. and Shuy, R.W. 1973: *New ways of analysing variation in English*. Washington, DC: Georgetown University Press.

Becker, D. 1967: *Generative phonology and dialect study: an investigation of three modern German dialects*. Ann Arbor: University Microfilms.

Berdan, R. 1977: Polylectal comprehension and the polylectal grammar. In R.W. Fasold and R.W. Shuy (eds.), *Studies in language variation*. Washington, DC: Georgetown University Press.

Butters, R. 1973: Acceptability judgements for double modals in Southern dialects. In Bailey and Shuy 1973.

Chambers, J.K. and Trudgill, P. 1980: *Dialectology*. Cambridge: Cambridge University Press.

Chomsky, N. and Halle, M. 1968: *The sound pattern of English*. New York: Harper & Row.

Cochrane, G.R. 1959: The Australian English vowels as a diasystem. *Word* **15**, 69–88.

Knowles, G.O. 1978: The nature of phonological variables in Scouse. In P. Trudgill (ed.), *Sociolinguistic patterns in British English*. London: Edward Arnold.

Labov, W. 1969: Contraction, deletion and inherent variability of the English copula. *Lg.* **45**, 715–62.

———1973: Where do grammars stop? *Georgetown Monograph Series on Languages and Linguistics* **25**. Washington, DC: Georgetown University Press.

Matthews, P.H. 1979: *Generative grammar and linguistic competence*. London: Allen & Unwin.

Milroy, L. (in press): Sociolinguistics and communicative breakdown. In P. Trudgill (ed.), *Applied sociolinguistics*. London: Academic Press.

Newton, B. 1972: *The generative interpretation of dialect*. Cambridge: Cambridge University Press.

Payne, A. (n.d.): The reorganization of linguistic rules: a preliminary report. *Pennsylvania Working Papers on Linguistic Change and Variation* **1(6)**. Philadelphia: US Regional Survey.

Scollon, R. and Scollon, S. 1979: Literacy as interethnic communication: an Athabaskan case. *Working Papers in Sociolinguistics* **59**. Austin, Texas: Southwest Educational Development Laboratory.

Trudgill, P. 1973: Phonological rules and sociolinguistic variation in Norwich English. In Bailey and Shuy 1973.

————1974: *The social differentiation of English in Norwich*. Cambridge: Cambridge University Press.

————1978a: Where does sociolinguistics stop? In W. Dressler and W Meid (eds.), *Proc. 12th Int. Cong. Ling.*, 53–6.

————1978b: Sociolinguistics and sociolinguistics. In P. Trudgill (ed.), *Sociolinguistic patterns in British English*. London: Edward Arnold.

————1980: Acts of conflicting identity: a sociolinguistic look at British pop songs. In M. de Silva (ed.), *Festschrift for R.B. Le Page*. York: University of York.

————1978c: *A sociolinguistic study of linguistic change in urban East Anglia*. Report to the Social Science Research Council.

Wakelin, M. 1972: *English dialects: an introduction*. London: Athlone Press.

Weinreich, U. 1954: Is a structural dialectology possible? *Word* **10**, 388–400.

Wölck, W. 1965: *Phonematische Analyse der Sprache von Buchan*. Heidelberg.

14

Who is really doing dialectology?
K.M. Petyt

Over the history of dialectology, this country appears at some periods among the leaders in the development of the subject—but at others it seems to be behind the times. There are signs in literature going back to the 1300s of a consciousness of regional differences within English, and by the nineteenth century there were a considerable number of publications devoted specifically to dialect. The last 30 years of that century saw a period of intense activity, culminating in the publication in 1905 of the massive *English Dialect Dictionary* and the *English Dialect Grammar*. Skeat (1911) claimed shortly afterwards that: 'The fulness of vocabulary in the Dictionary, and the minuteness of the account of the phonology and the accidence in the Grammar, leave nothing to desire. Certainly no other country can give so good an account of its dialects.' British scholars felt they could rest on their laurels, and wound up the English Dialect Society.

But before long it became obvious that Britain was no longer in the forefront of dialect study, and in a paper published in 1946 Dieth drew attention to the fact that Britain was one of the few blanks on a map of Europe showing which countries had published, or even begun work on, a linguistic atlas. The response was the *Survey of English Dialects* and the *Linguistic Survey of Scotland*—large-scale operations investigating the dialect speech at a network of localities throughout their areas, and leading (after 30 years) to the publication of the splendid *Linguistic Atlas of England* and *Linguistic Atlas of Scotland*.

But dialectology had moved on: several years before these works actually appeared, their whole approach had been challenged—both by linguists and by social scientists. Many scholars felt that the findings of the great dialect surveys, concerned as they were almost exclusively with 'genuine dialect'—to be observed now only among a declining number of elderly rural-dwellers, whose speech showed the development of an earlier system 'uncorrupted' by contact with standard varieties—were hardly relevant to the description of the population at large. A truer picture, it was claimed, would be obtained by examining a representative sample of the population of the towns, seeking the present-day system rather than developments of a Middle English one, and showing the variation between standard and non-standard forms in various sections of the community. American scholars had led the way in this development; Britain was again behind the times. But in the 1970s a number of such socio-urban studies were undertaken.

While dialectologists of this newer school tend to regard the 'traditionalists' as old-fashioned and virtually irrelevant nowadays, the latter continue to work in the way they always have; and tacitly, or even openly at times, they adopt a view shared by many laymen, namely that the more 'modern' studies are not concerned with 'true dialect'.

Which side is right? Who is really doing dialectology? In this chapter I shall look at an area in Yorkshire, probably the county which has received the greatest amount of attention from British dialectologists, and examine studies of both the traditional and the more modern type, in an attempt to see whether either can fairly claim to be the more important.

Probably the greatest figure in the history of British dialectology was Joseph Wright, who was born in a village near Bradford. He was the editor of the *English Dialect Dictionary* (1898–1905) and *Grammar* (1905), but before being appointed to that position he had published a description of his native dialect: *Grammar of the Dialect of Windhill* (1892). Later described (Dieth, 1946) as 'the first really scientific historical grammar of an English dialect', *Windhill* became the model for a considerable number of dialect monographs over the next half-century. It contains a long section on phonology, which traces the development of the sounds from their Old English (or French) origins, a solid treatment of the morphology, a number of illustrative specimens, and a large index which includes many everyday items rather than those found only in this dialect. I shall take Wright's description as the basis for a picture of the 'traditional' dialect of the Bradford area (it may be noted that it does not differ substantially from what may be deduced from 'the monumental work of the late Dr. A.J.Ellis'[1], published three years earlier; it is of course a fuller account, and can generally be assumed to be the more accurate where there appears to be discrepancy).

Obviously I cannot deal here with every aspect of the 'Bradford dialect'; I shall concentrate on part of the phonology. It is a well established fact that dialects differ more in terms of vowels than they do in consonants, so I shall examine the vowel system. Now of course, Wright was working in the days before the concept of the PHONEME was developed, but he was like many dialectologists of the time before phonetics became such a detailed and technical subject, who tended to act like structuralists in that they recorded only phonemic rather than phonetic differences between sounds: they often knew the dialect very well, and so realized, consciously or unconsciously, that only some differences of sound were significant.

---

[1] This was Wright's comment on Ellis (1889) in the Preface to the *English Dialect Grammar*.

Wright sets out the vowels of the Windhill dialect[2], and he is clearly giving something at least very close to the vowel 'phoneme system':

	Short			Long	
i		u	i:		u:
	e ə o			ə:	
	a			a:	

			Diphthongs				Triphthongs	
ei	ui	iu		iə	uə	iuə		ouə
ai	oi	eu	ou	eə	oə		aiə	
				āə				

(Only one aspect of this causes me some doubt: the mid-centering diphthongs /eə/ and /oə/. Ellis shows variation between [e:] and [eə], and between [ɔ:] and [ɔə] in Bradford, and certainly the later evidence shows the existence of [e:] and [ɔ:]. It could be that in Windhill the situation was slightly different from Bradford itself—or, on the other hand, that Wright has gone too far in 'regularizing' and eliminating unimportant differences: he ends up by in effect denying the possibility of a significant difference between words such as *pay* and *pair*.)

As examples of the incidence of the above vowels, I give here for each (*i*) instances where this vowel occurs as in RP, and (*ii*) a number of everyday words where this is not the case:

/i/   (*i*) him, it
      (*ii*) much, such; find, blind; hang (strong vb.); ever, never; week
/e/   (*i*) egg, tell
      (*ii*) have, hang (weak vb.); break; among, wrong; wash
/a/   (*i*) hand, that
      (*ii*) make, take, game, late; father; settle, very
/o/   (*i*) John, ox
      (*ii*) chance, dance; broken, open, over; any, many, yellow; for, always, water
/u/   (*i*) bull, butcher
      (*ii*) butter, husband, some, come, one . . . ; found, ground
/ə/   (*i*) a, of
      (*ii*) berry, bury, worry; Sund*ay* etc; *y*esterd*ay*, yet; sp*i*rit; borro*w*, wind*ow* etc.
/i:/ (*i*) field, see
      (*ii*) bright, night, die, eye, fly, mild; well
/a:/ (*i*) cart, harvest
      (*ii*) doubt, house, now, town . . . ; room; servant; warm; work(N), worst

---

[2] I have not altered Wright's phonetic transcription (apart from indicating length by e.g. [e:] rather than [ē]), and in the material from SED below I have continued to use [i, e, u] instead of their [ɪ, ɛ, ǫ]. I have however adopted [ɔ] both as a pure vowel and in diphthongs, and also [ɛi] and [ɛə]. These transcriptions more accurately reflect the phonetics of these sounds and also the differences between the phonemically distinct pairs /ɔu/ − /o:/ and /ɛi/ − /e:/. Otherwise I have continued to use Wright's symbols except where it is necessary to refer to a sound he does not consider, e.g. [ʌ] or [o:] (which it should be noted does not correspond to Wright's [o:] (now [ɔ:]), but represents a closer long vowel which may contrast with [ɔ:]).

/u:/   (*i*) –
           (*ii*) book, cook; pull, wool; shoulder
/ə:/   (*i*) bird, work (vb.), world (See note 1 below)
/ei/   (*i*) eight, straight
           (*ii*) fight, right; eat, speak, teach
/ai/   (*i*) dry, fine, write
           (*ii*) pick
/ui/   (*i*) ruin
           (*ii*) boot, noon, school . . . ; good, foot; blood
/oi/   (*i*) boil, voice
           (*ii*) close, hole, coal, coat; lose; lane
/iu/   (*i*) new, suit
           (*ii*) blew, grew, through; hook, look, took; enough
/eu/   (*i*) –
           (*ii*) few, strew; shew
/ou/   (*i*) colt, old, roll, soul . . . ; folk, coke; bowl, flow, grow . . .
           (*ii*) bought, daughter, thought
/iə/   (*i*) clear, here
           (*ii*) beat, meal, sea . . . ; bread, deaf, head; again; heard, learn; swear, there
/eə/   (*i*) care, share
           (*ii*) bake, spade, nail, rain, day, way; spoke (vb.), stole; master, rather; weak (See note 2 below)
/oə/   (*i*) –
           (*ii*) order, saw, all, bald; either, neither; calf, half; know, slow, throw (See note 3 below)
/uə/   (*i*) moor, poor
           (*ii*) door, floor, before, more, board, broad, thorn . . . ; go, home, both, nose, loaf . . . ; who
/āə/   (*i*) –
           (*ii*) far, star; dare; sour, tower
/aiə/   (*i*) fire
           (*ii*) –
/iuə/   (*i*) cure, pure
           (*ii*) sure
/ouə/   (*i*) –
           (*ii*) four

Notes:

1) A.J.Ellis and many other sources exclude this vowel from the set for this area, giving /ə/ in all words where Wright has /ə:/. Such forms are readily observable, but Wright would surely have given them had he believed they were the 'genuine dialect' in Windhill.
(2) It was noted above that other evidence suggests the existence of both /e:/ and /eə/. All items listed under (*ii*) here have been observed with the long monophthong.
(3) Similarly, other evidence suggests the existence of /ɔ:/: items under (*ii*) here have been observed with the monophthong.

Sixty years after the publication of *Windhill*, in 1952, fieldwork for the *Survey of English Dialects*[3] was conducted at Wibsey, which is about two miles southwest of the centre of Bradford and thus about 4½ miles from Windhill, which is three miles to the north of the town. Though both

[3]. See Orton 1962, and Orton and Halliday (ed.) 1962. By coincidence, Wibsey was investigated by one Peter Wright!

concern areas of Bradford, there is therefore a difference in both time and locality between these two descriptions, either of which may be responsible for any linguistic differences emerging. In fact these turn out to be few; the most noticeable ones concern the long vowels and the centring diphthongs:

	Windhill				SED			
i:	u:	iə	uə	i:	u:	iə	uə
ə:	eə	oə	e:	ɔ:	ɛə
a:	āə	a:

At first sight there appears to have been an addition of two long vowels /e:/ and /ɔ:/; a loss of /ɔə/ and a very considerable reduction in the load of /ɛə/; /āə/ seems also to have gone, its incidence being taken over partly by /a:/ and partly by a 'new' triphthong /auə/. The following differences of incidence from Wright's list illustrate these 'changes':

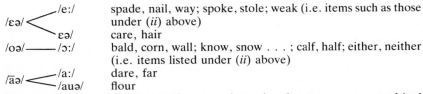

/ɛə/	/e:/	spade, nail, way; spoke, stole; weak (i.e. items such as those under (ii) above)
	ɛə/	care, hair
/oə/——/ɔ:/		bald, corn, wall; know, snow . . . ; calf, half; either, neither (i.e. items listed under (ii) above)
/āə/	/a:/	dare, far
	/auə/	flour

But are these differences due to phonetic change or geographical distance—or are they matters of phonemic interpretation? It was noted above that Ellis recorded both /e:/ and /eə/, and /ɔ:/ and /ɔə/; it seems quite possible that Wright 'standardized' in favour of the diphthong, and that the SED system more accurately shows the phonemic contrasts, including that between /e:/ and /ɛə/ e.g. *way—ware* (as well as that between /e:/ and /ɛi/ e.g. *way—weigh*).

The following points are worth noting also:

(i)   SED agrees with Ellis rather than Wright in recording /ə/ in most cases where the latter has /ə:/.

(ii)   The /eu/ dipthong looks to be very marginal: it is recorded in *show* and *sew*, but *few* is shown to have the RP-like /iu/.

(iii)   Incidence: in *take, make* SED has /e/ as well as /a/ forms;
in *look, took* SED has /u/~/u:/, Wright /iu/. There is no SED evidence of /iu/ in any *-ook* words;
in *shoulder,* SED has /ɔu/, Wright /u:/;
in *water,* SED has /a/, Wright /o/;
in *ground,* SED has /a:/, Wright /u/.

In these last three examples, both forms can be heard in the Bradford area, but probably there was a geographical difference between the two sides of the town, and the Windhill and Wibsey speakers reflect this.

There is then little substantive difference between the accounts of Wright and the SED, and from such descriptions it is possible to extract a detailed and interesting picture of 'The Bradford Dialect'.

But in what sense is this 'The Bradford Dialect'? On the back streets of Bradford do the natives (i.e. those born in Bradford, rather than in

Pakistan or the West Indies) talk like this among themselves? In fact, very few indeed of them do so—one would have to look pretty hard among inhabitants of the town before one found a speaker of this so-called 'Bradford Dialect'. So do most of the native Bradfordians speak Standard English with an RP accent? Far from it; when compared to the above descriptions the speech of the town does appear to have moved closer to the standard language in many ways, but most natives will admit to having been recognized by their speech as coming from Yorkshire, and some have been pinned down more precisely than that.

There is then still 'Bradford Dialect' of some sort, but it is different in many respects from what can be extracted from the works of Ellis, Wright, the SED, and so on. The dialect they describe *can* still be found occasionally, but their descriptions are by no means *representative* of the speech of the general population of the town. Such 'traditional' dialectologists have searched for speakers of 'genuine' dialect, but they have ended up by presenting a picture heavily biased towards a very small minority among the population, and barely relevant to the general situation in Bradford today. One wonders, indeed, whether the term 'genuine' may not be more appropriately applied to the dialect of the majority.

Such would be one of the main criticisms a 'modern' dialectologist would direct against the 'traditionalist'. Moreover, he would claim that this antiquarian preoccupation with 'pure' dialect has led the traditionalist to miss some equally interesting features to be observed in a more representative sample of the population. Two particular types of criticism may be considered in this connection.

Firstly, traditionalists have shown little interest in the present day *systems* of dialects. For example, in phonology they have been more concerned with tracing the regular developments of sounds known to have existed at some earlier period, rather than with establishing the systems of mutually defining significantly different sound-units which stand in opposition to each other in the speech of today. Joseph Wright discussed the developments in Windhill of the various Old English sounds; the SED designed its questionnaire so as to find the reflexes of Middle English sounds; neither was specifically interested in establishing whether at the date of their investigation [reːt] was unambiguously *rate* and [rɛit] was unambiguously *right*, or similarly that [rɛə] was definitely *rare* and [reː] was *ray,* and that there were thus three distinctive sound units in this phonetic area: /eː/, /ɛi/, /ɛə/. In some cases it is possible to deduce this sort of information from traditional works, but often the most appropriate data have just not been recorded, and sometimes we are left with the feeling that there probably was some significant difference, or alternatively that two different transcriptions do not really represent separate phonemes, but we just cannot be sure (e.g. Wright's [eə] above, where /ɛə/ vs. /eː/ seems probable, but one is surprised if Wright really missed this).

Secondly, by concentrating on the most 'pure' data, traditionalists have ignored the variation between this and other common forms. And this variation is particularly interesting, for at least two reasons. On the one hand, it often shows correlations with factors such as social class, sex, age, or formality, and thus tells us something about the social significance of the different variants. On the other hand, this variation is often a sign of linguistic change in progress, and can thus show us how the dialect is developing at the present time.

With these criticisms of traditional dialectology in mind, let us turn now to an example of the more 'modern' approach. The author of this chapter carried out in 1971 a linguistic survey of three industrial towns in West Yorkshire: Bradford, Halifax, and Huddersfield (Petyt 1977, see also 1980: esp. ch. 7). A random sample was drawn from the electoral registers, and just over 100 subjects were interviewed. This number was divided between the three towns in proportion to their sizes with the result that nearly half the informants were in Bradford. A number of people selected in the original sampling could not be contacted or were unwilling to cooperate, so one cannot be sure that the 100 actually interviewed were truly representative of the population at large, but they certainly included a wide variety of speakers: there were roughly equal numbers of males and females, members of all age-groups from 10+ to 80+, and of five social classes (set up for the purposes of this study on the basis of a total 'score' for categories of education, occupation, income, housing, and standard of living). Much of the study was carried out on the lines of Labov's (1966) pioneering work in New York: a structured interview sought to elicit speech of several levels of formality, and a number of particular features were selected for special study. These features or VARIABLES, showed variation between standard and non-standard forms, and the amount of usage of each variant by each different social class, sex, or age-group and in different styles was worked out in an attempt to see whether any interesting patterns emerged. In addition to this examination of variation, the study was also concerned with non-standard features generally, and with the present-day sound systems of the different forms of speech to be heard in the area.

Let us consider first examples of the variation within the town, by concentrating on just three well known 'Northern' features which reveal very different patterns. (Of course, the study investigated a large number of variables, of several different phonological categories as well as some grammatical ones.)

(*i*) First, the vowel in *but, luck, love, mother,* etc. In RP there is a phoneme /ʌ/ which occurs in these words, and which may contrast with /u/ in *put, book, good, wolf* etc. All the traditional dialect descriptions of this area give the impression that this contrast is not possible in Bradford since the /ʌ/ phoneme does not exist in the north of England; /u/ occurs in both the above sets of words. There is historical evidence that this Northern situation was formerly general in England, and that the 'split' into /ʌ/ and /u/ in the Southern half of the country is a relatively recent phenomenon. There is also ample evidence that many Bradfordians do preserve this older pattern, as traditional dialectologists maintain. But a 'quantitative' study such as I carried out (i.e. one which records what occurs every time the variable in question comes up during the interview with an informant, and then works out various 'scores') makes it clear that many speakers have made some attempt to introduce the /ʌ/ vowel into their speech, presumably under the influence of RP. And if the scores of those individuals who share certain social characteristics are averaged, it is apparent that this variation is not haphazard but reveals certain patterns. For example, Fig. 1 is a graph showing the percentage of occasions on which speakers in the different social classes used /u/ in words where RP would have /ʌ/, divided into different levels of formality. It is obvious from this that the use of /ʌ/ relates to social class and style in a way which studies of this sort have shown to be quite common: society is stratified in terms of the proportions of standard and non-standard variants employed by different social classes, with the 'highest' class (I) using the greatest proportion of the more prestigious variants, and other classes following in the order of their social status. Moreover, *all* social classes use higher proportions of the more prestigious variants as the style becomes more formal (the stations along the formality continuum which have been somewhat arbitrarily recognized here are 'casual', 'formal', 'reading passage', 'word list', and 'minimal pairs'). The only unexpected point in this graph concerns the scores for minimal pairs (i.e. where the informant was faced directly with the /ʌ/ − /u/ contrast in pairs such as *putt − put, luck − look,* etc): all classes seem to show a sharp reversal of the trend towards more /ʌ/ in more formal styles. The explanation for this surprising situation is probably as follows: there is no clue in the spelling and no clear pattern of conditioning by the phonological environment to indicate which words have /ʌ/ rather than /u/ in RP; so a Northerner who attempts to acquire /ʌ/ is sometimes unsure which member, if either, of a pair such as *but − put,* etc has /ʌ/. The 'deviant' scores in Fig. 14.1 simply reflect the fact that in this very artificial situation more people 'gave up the attempt' than in other contexts where they were not required to concentrate specifically on this problem.

(*ii*) The lack of /ʌ/ is one of the two Northern features most commonly remarked on by people from other parts of the country. The other is the use of the short /a/ phoneme in a set of a hundred or so words where RP and the Southern half of the country generally has the long /ɑ:/. (This is not, as with /ʌ/, a case of the North and the South differing in the number of phonemes in their *inventory*: both have the short /a/, as in *cat,* and the long /ɑ:, as in *cart*; but the *incidence* of these two phonemes differs, in that in this particular set of words the South has the same vowel as in *cart,* the North that as in *cat*). As with /ʌ/, it is the North which retains the older situation: in the South the vowel has been lengthened in certain phonological environments. But the situation differs from that of /ʌ/, in that whereas the occurrence of /ʌ/ or /u/ is no longer predictable, with the short or long 'A' the pattern of conditioning is still fairly regular. This being the case, it should be easier for the Bradfordian who wishes to modify his speech in the direction of RP to do so without many errors, by formulating some sort of subconscious rule: lengthen /a/ to /ɑ:/ before /f/, e.g. *laugh, raft;* before /θ/, e.g. *bath, path;* before /s/, e.g. *class, past;* before /n/ or /m/ + Consonant, e.g. *dance, branch, grant, command, sample,* and so on.

But whereas the variable involving /ʌ/ presented in Bradford a picture which has been shown to be typical where standard and non-standard

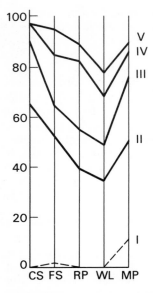

Fig. 14.1 Class and style graph of /ʌ/~/u/ in urban West Yorkshire: percentage scores for nonstandard forms (i.e. use of [u]).

features are in competition—the standard feature being very common among the highest class, and progressively less so lower down the class hierarchy; and all classes using the standard variant more frequently as the style becomes more formal (a pattern which recurred with several other variables in the Bradford study)—the use of the 'long A', though probably easier to acquire, does not reveal such a pattern. In fact, very few informants used the long vowel form at all, and most of those who did so produced only one or two examples during the interview, usually in the more formal situations of the reading passage or the word list; hardly any speakers outside the top social class produced a high enough proportion of long to short vowel forms for this to justify the term 'variable'. This is not the place to speculate about the reasons for this difference among Bradford speakers between these two typically Northern features; it may simply be noted that a traditional type of dialect study would have been unlikely to show it up.

(*iii*) The third example of variation we shall examine presents an unusual graph, and is perhaps the most interesting of the three. It concerns words such as *book, cook, look, took* etc, where RP has /uk/ but in Bradford the /u:k/ pronunciation (see above) can still be heard quite commonly. Fig. 14.2 indicates that the occurence of this nonstandard variant actually *increased* with increasing formality. The very marked increase in the minimal pairs situation might be explained in part by the fact that other evidence shows that in this very artificial situation where attention is focused on possible differences, many informants will try to produce a distinction even if they would rarely do so in natural speech (i.e. the

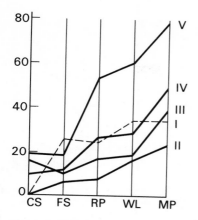

Fig. 14.2 Class and style graph of *-ook* in urban West Yorkshire: percentage scores for nonstandard forms (i.e. use of /u:k/).

performance in respect of /ʌ/ discussed above is untypical). In this case, with the pair *luck—look* many speakers without /ʌ/ will have a homophonous pronunciation as [luk], and so it is not surprising that in the minimal pairs situation they should 'recall' the obsolescent form [lu:k] for the second member. But it was found that even some speakers who pronounced *luck* as [lʌk], and so 'already' had a distinction between the two words, created an extra difference by using the long vowel in *look* (though in conversation they had said [luk]). Moreover, the non-standard variant also increased in the reading passage and the word list, where informants would not be concentrating on finding a difference.

Besides this unusual style pattern, the graph also reveals a disruption of the usual pattern of social class, in that Class I cuts across an otherwise fairly regular array. This class was the smallest in the sample, and certainly was too small to be considered representative (which is why it is indicated by a broken line in these graphs), but with most variables this does not result in irregularities such as we see here. Now many findings of surveys such as this have suggested that unusual patterns of style and/or class differentiation result when a linguistic change is in progress; and two facts lead to the conclusion that such is the case here. Firstly, all the examples of /u:k/ in Class I came from one speaker, who was in his seventies; with the small number of informants in this group this was sufficient to bias the results for the class. Secondly, a graph for the total usage of /u:k/ in all styles by speakers in different age-groups (Fig. 14.3) indicates that below the age of 40 this variant is rare, but then it 'rises' fairly steeply. (The 80+ group is too small and class-biased to be considered representative, but the rise certainly continues.) We may conclude that a change from the regional variant /u:k/ is in progress, and indeed is well advanced, since in everyday speech /uk/ is virtually universal among speakers under 40, and even older speakers show a fairly extensive use of it. But the evidence from the style graph (and also some other types of evidence not discussed here) suggests

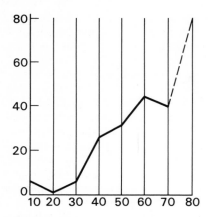

Fig. 14.3 Age-group graph of *-ook*.

that there is as yet no strong feeling of 'inferiority' about the non-standard variant.

This detailed examination of the variation between different forms has shown up facts about the Bradford dialect that a traditionalist, concentrating on hand-picked speakers of 'pure' dialect, would have missed or ignored. The picture of the vowel system which emerges from this study also shows interesting differences from that deduced from the work of Wright and the SED.

The short vowel system shows few differences from the above 'traditional' picture:

$$
\begin{array}{ccc}
\text{i} & & \text{u} \\
 & \text{(ə)} & \\
\text{e} & \text{(ʌ)} & \text{ɔ} \\
 & \text{a} &
\end{array}
$$

Only two are indicated here: (1) /ʌ/ is beginning to appear in certain sections of the population; (2) /ə/ is now for many people of more restricted distribution, being confined to unstressed positions, as in RP; the most persistent stressed environment is before /r/ e.g. *véry, dérelict, térrible, América* etc. But it should be noted that very many changes of incidence have also affected this system, so that the differences from Wright's list exemplified above are now very considerable: in fact, we could say that vowel incidence (with the exception of 'short A', and allowing of course for differences of inventory, such as the absence of /ʌ/), is now very much as in RP.

The long vowel and diphthong systems now appear as:

i:		u:	(ɛi)	(ui)			iə	uə
e:	ə:	o:	ai	ɔi	au	ɔu	ɛə	ɔə
a:		ɔ:						

Among the long vowels, /ə:/ is now quite common, its incidence being much as in RP. Most interesting is the 'new' vowel /o:/, which, though not appearing in traditional descriptions, is quite common. It occurs in words where the traditional dialect had /uə/ e.g. *go, home, road, loaf;* /ɔ/ e.g. *broken, over;* /ɔi/ e.g. *coal, coat;* and /ɔ:/ e.g. *know, throw* (in all of which RP has [əu], to which this [o:] could be considered an approximation). One result of this development is a greater 'symmetry' in the system, since there is now a possible phonemic contrast /o:/—/ɔu/ e.g. *groan—grown* on the back axis, to parallel /e:/—/ɛi/ e.g. *wait—weight* on the front. However, it should be noted that this is not a stable situation, for several reasons: (*a*) the incidence of /ɛi/ is considerably reduced from the traditional situation: it is now common only in words spelled -*ght*, and for many but not all users, in those ending in -*ation*; (*b*) /ɔu/ is also of reduced incidence: it is common only before /l/ e.g. *old, soldier,* and in words spelled -*ow* e.g. *flow, grow* (but not in unstressed position, e.g. *window,* where /ə/ ~ /o:/); (*c*) there is some confusion evident over the incidence of /ɔu/ and /o:/: in many words, especially in those spelled -*ow*, and particularly those which in traditional dialect have /ɔ:/ e.g. *know, throw, blow, crow, mow, own, sow, slow, snow,* etc, variation can be observed between the use of /o:/ and /ɔu/; (*d*) these /e:/—ɛi/ and /o:/—/ɔu/ contrasts do not occur in RP, and there seems to be a tendency among some speakers to lose them, with both /e:/ and /ɛi/ sets and /o:/ and /ɔu/ sets being pronounced [e:] and [o:] respectively (or, higher on the social scale, [ei] and [ou ~ əu]).

Of the diphthongs, /ɛi/ and /ui/ are much reduced in incidence compared to the traditional descriptions; so too are /ɔi/, /iə/, /uə/; /āə/ and /eu/ do not exist for the great majority of people. On the other hand, /ai/ and /au/ are much commoner. These differences are due to the fact that for the majority of the population phoneme incidence is now very close to that of RP.

The system given above appears to be commonest among Bradford speakers today, but there are signs of change in progress. The most interesting concerns the monophthongisation of /ɔə/ e.g. *door, floor, board*[4] to /ɔ:/ (a development well advanced in RP, of course), and also of the parallel phoneme on the front axis, (ɛə/, to /ɛ:/ (also to be observed among younger speakers in some other parts of Britain). The result of this, which was observed among some of the youngest informants, is a system of eight long vowels at four 'heights':

$$
\begin{array}{ccc}
\text{i:} & & \text{u:} \\
\text{e:} \quad \text{ə:} & \text{o:} & \\
\text{ɛ:} \quad \text{ɔ:} & & \\
\text{a:} & &
\end{array}
$$

This can be demonstrated in the /b—/ environment: *bee, bay, bare, bar, bore, bow, boo, burr.*

Some traditionalists have felt that this sort of study is 'not real dialectology'; and indeed a number of informants expressed surprise that I

---

[4] /ɔə/ is a relatively 'new' diphthong, which some people use in an RP-like incidence; in the traditional dialect, as was seen above, all these words would have /uə/.

was bothering with 'all them ordinary words' when they had expected me to be interested in 'real Yorkshire'. Some of them insisted that much of what was heard in Bradford nowadays was just 'sloppy speech' and certainly not 'real Yorkshire'. But the 'modern' dialectologist would maintain that a study such as this, involving detailed examination of every variant which occurs among a representative sample of the population, and with attention both to phonetic detail and to systems of opposing phonemes, produces a picture of the 'Bradford dialect' that is not only truer but also more interesting to a wider range of social scientists, structural linguists, *and* historical linguists (since variation is clearly closely related to linguistic change in progress) than the traditionalist's description of some allegedly 'genuine' dialect.

But sometimes the modern dialectologist too, with his interest in systems and variation, may be guilty of making claims about his view of a particular dialect which are of dubious validity. As one example of this, let us examine some suggestions made by scholars such as Labov and Trudgill about a 'speech community'. Labov (1966, 500), on the basis of evidence from various 'evaluation tests' (a method of investigation also employed in Bradford, but not discussed here), concluded that New York speakers, in spite of differences in performance, were in fact aiming at the same ideal; and that 'New York is a single speech community, united by a common set of evaluative norms'. Trudgill (1974, 133) went somewhat further than this, and claimed that 'speakers of Norwich English belong to a particular speech community which has very many common linguistic features. . . . not shared by any other speech community'; and he went on to set up a common framework, a DIASYSTEM of rules which are supposed to generate all types of Norwich English, and stated his belief that 'members of the Norwich speech community can be said to have internalised this diasystem . . . The diasystem can be said in some sense "to exist" . . . '

Trudgill's evidence appears to be that all Norwich speakers can, for any variety of Norwich English, 'faultlessly imitate it for humorous or other reasons', and 'assign fine sociological meanings to different types of pronunciation'; i.e. his claims are based on (*a*) imitative ability, and (*b*) evaluative norms (as were Labov's). He admits that one could, as 'an intellectual exercise', write a diasystem for *any* two varieties of English, say Yorkshire and Australian, but insists that his Norwich diasystem is essentially different from this: the differences between Yorkshire and Australian are so considerable that a common underlying system would be too abstract to be 'meaningful', and speakers could not perform faultless imitations of each other; but the Norwich system is claimed to have psychological reality, as part of 'the native speaker's linguistic competence'.

Before discussing this viewpoint, let us briefly refer to one or two of its consequences. Trudgill says that because some Norwich speakers distinguish between the vowels of *nose* and *knows,* and because there is a continuum from those who always distinguish them to those who never do so (some Middle-Class speakers), it is unreasonable to set up two separate systems, one with two vowels, the other with only one; rather, the deep-down system has two vowels, but it just happens that some speakers always apply the rules which merge them. He would presumably claim that the latter are able to 'make this distinction . . . *without error, if they wish to for humorous or other purposes'.* A similar case is made out in respect of the vowels of *boat* and *boot:* 'two underlying phonological elements are "kept apart" in the subconscious linguistic knowledge of speakers because a small phonetic distinction is sometimes made between sets of items which they perceive as phonetically "the same", and because the elements are involved in two distinct sets of stylistic alternation: *boat* /u:/~/ʊ/, *boot* /u:/ ~ /ʉ/'. An important difference however is that this time it is the lower classes who apparently perform the feat of applying more rules so that these separate underlying elements are usually realized alike.

How tenable is this notion of a 'speech community'? It seems dubious, on two sets of grounds:

(*i*) THE EVIDENCE ON WHICH IT IS SAID TO BE BASED. This we have seen to be of two main types:

(*a*) *The imitative abilities of members of the community:* Members of the community are said to be capable of faultlessly imitating various subvarieties, which outsiders presumably could not do. But the evidence for this appears to be anecdotal. Trudgill, for instance, does not seem to have tested this ability systematically with all his informants.[5] And anecdotal evidence can be countered by experiences tending to the opposite conclusion: in Bradford, a number of informants said they could not imitate a 'broad Yorkshire' accent, and others who attempted to do so did not do it 'faultlessly'—and surely the finding that the /o:/ and /ɔu/ sets are not clearly distinguished now could be claimed to indicate that it would be artificial to set them up as distinct in some common diasystem. On the other hand, I have come across people from other parts of the English-speaking world who could imitate a broad Yorkshire accent better than some of the more RP-like informants in my sample—which of these would be said to belong to the 'Bradford speech community'?

(*b*) *A common set of value-judgements:* The evaluations by informants of different variants are said to indicate that they are united in their norms. However, none of the evaluation data, whether directly-expressed opinions, self-evaluations, or subjective evaluations of tape-recorded examples, has ever produced 100 per cent agreement on which variants are preferred or aimed at; this is clear in Labov's and Trudgill's work as well as the Bradford survey. Certainly the evidence of the latter does not seem to support the idea of a united speech community: some informants seemed to prefer RP-like forms (e.g.[ʌ]), others seemed to have a regional norm (e.g. [u]). Moreover, there were signs that not all the evaluation tests pointed the same way: it was clear, for example, that the great majority had an [a] standard in words of the *grass, laugh, bath* group (many of them said they disliked the 'long A' variant, and that it was in fact incorrect), but there were clear indications from the subjective evaluations that the [ɑ] form tended to command prestige. What is the evaluative norm in such cases?

(*ii*) THE PROBLEM OF DELIMITING A SPEECH COMMUNITY. This delimitation problem has two aspects, as it were 'horizontal' and 'vertical': in terms of both geographical area and the social scale.

---

[5] See further, Chapter 13 of the present volume. [Ed.]

(a) *Geographical delimitation*. Whereas Norwich, where Trudgill worked, is in a sense an isolated large town, Bradford is part of the West Yorkshire conurbation, which also includes Leeds, Halifax, Huddersfield, Wakefield, and numerous smaller towns. In the past these towns were more physically discrete, and there were probably some noticeable differences of speech between them. But nowadays they merge into one another geographically, and such differences as I found between Bradford, Halifax, and Huddersfield were largely of a 'quantitative' nature: in other words, it is not usually the case that feature *x* occurs in Bradford but not at all in Halifax, or Huddersfield, but rather that it is commoner *on average* in say Bradford than in the others (though *some* Bradford speakers may not have it at all, and some Halifax speakers may have it quite frequently).

In such a situation, what are the 'speech communities'? Hardly Bradford, Leeds, Halifax, etc. Are they smaller than these? Surely not— this would be even more difficult to maintain. Then perhaps industrial West Yorkshire as a whole is a speech community? Certainly it shares many features; but (*i*) there are probably also some well-marked differences between the ends of this geographical continuum; (*ii*) some places on the Western edge of the area may in fact be more similar in many respects to neighbouring Lancashire towns than to Eastern or Southern parts; (*iii*) though there are some markedly different forms in rural areas, there is no sharp urban/rural difference, and it would be difficult to decide just who belonged to the 'industrial speech community'.

(b) *Social delimitation*. We noted that Trudgill set up separate vowels in *nose* and *knows*, claiming that all speakers distinguish these deep down, though some members of the Middle Class never do so in performance. Now to produce a similar diasystem for Bradford it would be necessary to set up /o:/ and /ɔu/, which many speakers distinguish at times—but some RP-speakers in the city never do so, and would probably be *incapable* of doing so. On the other hand, just as Trudgill claimed that all speakers really have distinct vowels in *boot* and *boat* but that the lower classes usually merge them, in Bradford the diasystem would have to contain /ʌ/ and /u/ because even lower-class speakers may occasionally produce [ʌ], and anyway their evaluations show that some of them recognise its significance. However, [ʌ] is a minority phenomenon, and many speakers produce some 'hypercorrect' forms; why should this be, if they really have the distinction in their internalized system? Perhaps it would be more reasonable to have only /u/ in the diasystem, and to have rules for phonemic split which are more likely to be correctly applied higher up the social scale. But this would mean that RP-speakers who consistently and correctly distinguish /ʌ/ and /u/ only do so at a relatively superficial level.

Then perhaps the answer is that the RP-speakers in Bradford are not really part of the local speech community; after all, they are often not as good at faultlessly imitating a broad accent. But is it realistic to exclude them? In many respects they are only the end of a continuum, and they understand the local speech perfectly well; *some* of them may even be able to imitate it.

At the other end of the social scale we have a more serious problem. We noted that Trudgill said it would be difficult to set up a 'meaningful' diasystem for two very different varieties (e.g. Yorkshire and Australian). Consider these two very different varieties:

light fight like find	either	beat feet eat me
A. —— /ai/ ——	/ai/~/i:/	—— /i:/ ——
B. /i:/ /ɛi/ /ai/ /i/	/ɔ:/	/iə/ /i/ /ɛi/ /i:/

With sufficient 'diasystemic incidence rules' such as Trudgill employs for 'phoneme swapping', it would probably be possible to set up a diasystem which will incorporate both the above—but I agree that it would hardly be 'meaningful'; it would indeed be more in the nature of an 'intellectual exercise'. If we take system B as basic, this would mean that the majority of Bradford speakers (who have A) have a deep phonemic incidence that has to undergo considerable changes; but if we take the system of the majority as basic, then the Bradford working-class informant who had system B must have been applying an awful lot of rules to produce his output (and he seemed to do it so easily!).

Perhaps then the answer is that the Bradford speech community does not really include this eccentric individual. But he in fact was the only member of the Bradford sample who spoke the traditional dialect described by Wright and the SED—could we really maintain that he is not a member of 'the Bradford speech community'?! Even a sample of the size usually selected by modern dialectologists could have failed to pick up a single speaker of traditional dialect,[6] but if they then constructed a diasystem for an alleged speech community which excluded such speakers, this would surely be no less a distortion than the description produced by a traditional dialectologist which is based on an unrepresentative selection of 'pure dialect' speakers.

So who is really doing dialectology? The traditionalist gives us a glimpse of a variety which is rapidly becoming obsolete, whereas the modernist is concerned with the systems that may be deduced from the speech of a sample which is more representative of the majority of the inhabitants today. But the modernist frequently makes use of the findings of the traditionalist, and by discussing the notion of a SPEECH COMMUNITY I have tried to suggest some reasons why he cannot afford to ignore them. Apart from the danger of producing a meaningless abstract system, because either too many or too few speakers are included in the 'community', another major problem with this notion is that boundaries (whether linguistic, social, or geographical) are generally imprecise—as the traditionalist has certainly known for a long time, and as the study of variation has brought home clearly to modern dialectologists too; but the notion of the SPEECH COMMUNITY—postulating one community with one set of internalized norms, another with a different set, and so on—makes them precise.

A further reason why modern dialectologists continue to use traditional-

---

[6] See Heath (1980, 8), where he notes that not one 'pure' dialect speaker appeared in the random sample of 80 informants interviewed during his investigation of the speech of the Cannock Urban District.

ists' findings relates to the development (not discussed here) by which many linguists have come to feel that the Saussurian SYNCHRONIC/DIACHRONIC dichotomy is artificial and should be abandoned: synchronic variation in all its aspects, which modern dialectology sees as its proper province, is believed to be intimately related to diachronic change, which has always been a major concern of traditional scholars who trace the development of forms from an earlier stage of the language. The modern dialectologist is often concerned with developments in 'apparent time': speakers of different age-groups are held to provide evidence of linguistic change in progress; the traditionalist has long been concerned with changes in 'real time', and has important material to offer.

It is a fundamental tenet of linguistics that all varieties are equally worthy of study. There is surely a place for both approaches to the study of dialect.

References

Dieth, E. 1946: A new survey of English dialects. *Essays & Studies.*

Ellis, A.J. 1889: *On early English pronunciation,* **V:** *The existing phonology of English dialects.* London: Trübner.

Heath, C.D. 1980: *The pronunciation of English in Cannock, Staffordshire.* Oxford: Philological Society.

Labov, W. 1966: *The social stratification of English in New York City.* Washington, DC: Center for Applied Linguistics.

Orton, H. 1962: *Survey of English Dialects: introduction.* Leeds: E.J. Arnold.

Orton, H. and Halliday, W.J. (eds.) 1962: *Survey of English Dialects: basic material,* **I:** *The six northern counties and the Isle of Man.* Leeds: E.J. Arnold.

Petyt, K.M. 1977: *Dialect and accent in the industrial West Riding.* Ph.D thesis, University of Reading.

———1980: *The study of dialect: an introduction to dialectology.* London: Deutsch.

Skeat, W.W. 1911: *English dialects.* Cambridge: Cambridge University Press.

Trudgill, P. 1974: *The social differentiation of English in Norwich.* Cambridge: Cambridge University Press.

Wright, J. 1892: *A grammar of the dialect of Windhill in the West Riding of Yorkshire.* London: Kegan Paul.

———(ed.) 1898–1905: *English dialect dictionary.* 6 vols. London: Frowde.

———1905: *English dialect grammar.* Published as part of vol. 6 of EDD, also separately.

15

Change and decay in language
Alan R. Thomas

There has generally been resistance within linguistics towards serious appraisal of the notions of death and decay in language. And this despite the considerable concern with the opposite process, with what may be viewed as language 'birth'—the emergence of pidgin and its consequent development into creole. There are, however, a number of questions about languages which are nearing a terminal stage which have no obvious answers. They may focus on the kind of change which they undergo: is it distinctive and of itself diagnostic of impending language death? And is linguistic interference from the dominant language a significant determinant of the nature of such change? Again, as the range of styles available to a speaker of the dying language shrinks, does he simply redistribute his two (or more) languages over functional domains, or does he fill out the deficiencies by code-switching? And, finally, to what extent is language loss to be seen in terms of group or individual behaviour? Little has been done as yet in the way of extensive investigation, though work on Breton (Dressler 1972; Dressler and Wodak-Leodolter 1977) and Scottish Gaelic (Dorian 1973; 1977) is highly suggestive of fruitful lines to follow, certainly in regard to the Celtic languages. An investigation of a dialect of North Welsh is now being prepared, aimed to make a wide-ranging survey of day-to-day use of Welsh in an urban community which will also search out evidence of decay and death. This chapter is in part a review of existing work in the field, and in part a programmatic statement of intention for the coming survey of Welsh.

The scenario for language death as a social phenomenon is a community in the stage of transitional bilingualism, as are all those in which a Celtic language is spoken. Its most salient demographic feature is the rapid decline in the numbers of speakers of the receding language, and in the disparity between the number of speakers amongst older and younger generations. The numbers of Welsh speakers has declined by roughly 5 per cent in every decade since 1901, to its 1971 level of c.19 per cent of the population of Wales. The generational fall-off is shown clearly by the age-group figures in Table 15.1 taken from *Census 1971* (for further discussion see Thomas 1980).

The facts of demographic decline are beyond dispute: the question for the sociolinguist is whether there is evidence of a parallel linguistic decline? Is it the case that a receding language undergoes such drastic restructuring that it becomes depleted as a linguistic system—that it becomes de-structured rather than restructured? There seems to be some suggestion of this in proposals that language death may be seen as a process of pidginization marked by systemic shrinkage (Dressler and Wodak-Leodolter 1977, 37), or by the suggestion that languages have a life-cycle in which cumulative structural expansion is followed by reversion to a simplified form (Hall 1965). Again Dressler (1972, 452), on the basis of evidence of change within the system of consonant mutations in Breton, suggests that one mechanism of language death is the loss by a younger generation of a rule which has become optional for an older one.

Structural change

The kinds of linguistic features which have been associated with dying languages can be illustrated (with considerable simplification) from Dorian's investigations of East Sutherland Gaelic. The most obvious feature is lexical borrowing at an exaggerated rate, regardless of the availability of an indigenous term or not. This leads to massive relexification of the vernacular, and provides the focus for most normative evaluations of popular usage. In Wales, this kind of vernacular usage is frequent enough to have been labelled 'Wenglish', and Dorian (1973, 414) remarks that her informants' evaluative comment on the quality of their own and each other's language similarly focuses on the extent of contemporary borrowings in it. Such borrowing has no direct effect on linguistic structure, though an indirect effect can be the concomitant importation of morphological elements. Denison (1977, 17–19) quotes the introduction of rules for substantival plural formation from Romance into the German of Sauris—resulting, interestingly, in the addition of rules rather than loss of them, since the indigenous German patterns of plural formation are retained alongside the innovations. Thus we have from Friulian an -*s* plural, e.g. [də'kɔda] *tail,* pl. [də'kɔdas], and from Italian an -*i* plural, e.g. [dər prɔfə'soːr(e)] *professor,* pl. [də prɔfɛ'soːri]. Alongside the latter forms, however, there is a Friulian-type -*s* plural [də prɔfɛ'soːrs], though the selection of one form rather than the other has different register implications. The same phenomenon is observed in the treatment of loan-word plurals in Welsh, when the imported -*s* plural is the vernacular norm and an indigenous variant is expected in more 'formal' contexts, e.g. *roced* 'rocket', pl. *rocets/rocedi; bom* 'bomb', pl. *boms/bomiau.*

One important fact about innovations in the lexicon and the morpheme inventory is their salience to the native speaker. However, all Celtic languages have a system of initial consonant mutation of considerable

Table 15.1 Percentage speaking Welsh by age,
1951–1971.

Age	1951	1961	1971
65+	40.7	35.4	32
45+	35.4	31.7	27
25+	27.4	22.7	19
15+	22.8	20.4	17
3+	18.9	15.2	11

complexity, and in all of them the system found in the vernacular seems to be undergoing substantial changes. At least for East Sutherland Gaelic, however, these changes are not salient: since speakers are unaware of them, they are not subject to correction, and they provide potential data in an investigation into language death.

We can exemplify the kind of change which is happening in the Gaelic consonant mutation system from Dorian (1973). The mutation system involves specified phonological alternations in certain word-initial consonants. They are documented as occurring in a wide range of syntactic environments, and for oldest generation speakers are maintained fairly fully: with each succeeding younger generation of speakers, however, the occasional 'omissions' or 'mistakes' made by the oldest become increasingly common, although individuals vary considerably within each decade-group.

All speakers have an inventory of consonant alternations which includes, for instance,

(i) lenition (L), by which an initial obstruent becomes a spirant, e.g. /p/→/f/, /k/→/x/, /b/→/v/;
(ii) nasalization (N), by which a voiceless consonant is voiced, e.g. /p/→/b/, /t/→/d/, /k/→/g/;
(iii) the unmodified radical consonant in each case.

We follow Dorian and use conventional labels for these alternations. The ways in which the consonant mutation system can change are the following,

(i) introduction of a mutation to an environment where previously there was none;
(ii) using both mutations interchangeably in an environment where previously one exclusively occurred, leading perhaps to
(iii) substitution of one mutation for the other in that position;
(iv) loss of mutation in a given environment.

What is happening to the mutation system in East Sutherland Gaelic is well illustrated from the passive construction, which for Gaelic is 'essentially a nominal construction, centred on a possessive pronoun modifying a gerund (traditionally called the verbal noun in Gaelic grammar)' (418–19). In appropriate cases, the possessive pronoun causes mutation of the initial consonant of the gerund, though not all possessive pronouns do, as the list indicates:

	sg.	plu.
1st pers.	mə^L	nə
2nd pers.	də^L	nə
3rd pers. masc.	ə^L	ən^N
fem.	ə	

Since the 3rd singular masculine and the 3rd plural possessive pronouns are usually homophonous as /ə/, we will consider examples which include them: at least in a construction without a subject pronoun, the occurrence of the appropriate mutation after them will be the only marker of person in speech.

The passive in Gaelic can be expressed by either of two constructions, which use different finite verbs and which, in conservative usage, differ also in that one requires a subject pronoun while the other does not:

(*i*)   the *dol* passive:
the verb *dol* ('go') + possessive pronoun + verbal noun,
e.g. $\{$ ^{L}ga   ə^L kumal ə   stɛ $\}$
 /xa   (ə)   xumal ə   stɛ/
lit. 'went his keeping in', 'He was kept in'.
$\{$ ^{L}ga   ən^N kumal ə   stɛ $\}$
 /xa   (ən)   gumal ə   stɛ/
'They were kept in'.

(*ii*)   the *bith* passive:
the verb *bith* ('be') + subject pronoun + preposition + possessive pronoun + verbal noun,
e.g. $\{$ ^{L}ba   aʒ   er   ən^N kumal $\}$
 /va   aʒ   er   ə   gumal/
'They were kept'.

The expected mutation following 3rd singular masculine and 3rd plural possessive pronouns is, of course, the same as with the *dol* passive. However, with the mutation itself redundant in the presence of a subject pronoun, younger speakers tend to generalize lenition throughout the paradigm, even when no mutation is expected. For example,

$\{$ ^{L}ba   aʒ   er   ən^L kumal $\}$
 /va   aʒ   er   ə   xumal/
'They were kept'.
$\{$ ^{L}ba   i   er   ə^L kumal $\}$
 /va   i   er   ə   xumal/
'She was kept'.

Thus younger speakers depart from the conservative norm by introducing a new environment for mutation (3 sg. fem.), substituting lenition for nasalization (3 plu.), and even, in some cases, by loss of mutation with the 3 plu. possessive pronoun.

With the *dol* passive, substantial modification occurs: lenition is generalized throughout the paradigm, thus removing the distinction between 3 sing.masc. and 3 plu. pronouns. The distinction is retrieved, however, by a remodelling of the *dol* passive on analogy with the *bith* passive, in two respects: a pronoun subject is introduced, along with the preposition *er,* e.g.

$$\left\{ \begin{matrix} ^{\llcorner}ga & a\textrm{ʒ} & er & \textrm{ə}n^{\llcorner} & kr\textrm{ɔ}xu \\ /xa & a\textrm{ʒ} & er & \textrm{ə} & xr\textrm{ɔ}xu/ \end{matrix} \right\}$$
'They were hung'.

What we have here are changes of a familiar kind which tend to simplify the grammar, by eliminating redundancies and by breaking down the structural differences between constructions which have similar semantics by analogical levelling.

Language contact

It is therefore unlikely that the process of language death can be diagnosed on the evidence of change in linguistic structure alone. Indeed, in considering change and innovation in contemporary vernacular Welsh, it is often difficult even to separate the strands of linguistic interference from those of indigenous evolution. And then there is still the further question of the point at which linguistic change becomes language decay or death.

Leaving aside the massive relexification referred to earlier, linguistic developments in contemporary vernacular Welsh occur at all structural levels and do not seem to be necessarily dominated (as far as present—admittedly inadequate—knowledge goes) by the fact of language contact. And the fact of language contact is, in some sense, the enabling vehicle for language loss: it seems reasonable to suppose that 'terminal' characteristics of a decaying language would be accompanied by instances of linguistic interference (and, in some cases at least, to be synonymous with them). We might glance at some features of contemporary Welsh in this regard.

There are examples of developments within Welsh which seem to reflect its long-term contact with English. The most obvious is the development of the verbs *gallu* ('be able'), *dylu* ('ought'), *medru* ('to be able') and *cael* ('to have') as modal auxiliaries; for example

Mi *geith* hi ysgrifennu at John. (CAEL)
('She shall write to John.')
Dylai hi fynd. (DYLU)
('She might to go.')
Gallaf wneud hynny yfory. (GALLU)
('I can do that tomorrow.')
Fedri di weld rhywbeth? (MEDRU)
('Can you see anything?')

The auxiliary verbs carry a verbal inflection and are followed by an uninflected main verb: they are formally distinguished from catenative verbs by, for instance, the fact that they can occur as answer-words to *yes-no* interrogatives—thus responses to the question in the last example above might be

Fedraf/Na fedraf.
('Yes / No.')

It can be no coincidence that the semantics of the modal auxiliaries in Welsh—and, in the case of all except *cael*, the selection of lexical verbs to express them—so closely parallels that of English.

It seems plausible, too, that with the modals established in an auxiliary +
main verb syntactic pattern, the breakdown of synthetic tense-marking was
facilitated. There has developed, alongside the inflected main verb, a
construction which has the verb *gwneud* ('to do') functioning as an
auxiliary verb whose function is simply to carry an inflection for tense and
person, followed by a main verb which remains uninflected; for example,

> Tynnodd ef ei gôt.
> ('He took off his coat.')
> Gwnaeth ef dynnu ei gôt.
> (lit. 'He did take off his coat.')

The relationship of the pattern which has an inflected auxiliary verb and an
uninflected main verb to the inflected main verb pattern is not simply
displacive; the analytic pattern seems to be increasingly frequent,
particularly in the vernacular. The choice of one or the other is made on
stylistic grounds, with more intensive use of the conservative inflected
main verb pattern belonging at the 'formal' end of the scale.

Along with this shift in location of the verbal inflection, there has been a
reduction in the number of tense contrasts which occur: effectively, most
vernaculars have only a three-term contrast (leaving aside the verb *bod* 'to
be'), marking prediction, past tense and conditionality (see Jones and
Thomas 1977, Chapter 5 for a discussion of the tense-forms). The
paradigm has been reduced by the formal coalescence of an old perfect and
pluperfect indicative, and the loss of the subjunctive and of an impersonal
passive in all tenses. Reduction of the range of verbal inflections available
can be seen as a process of restructuring which became possible with the
developing of the modal auxiliaries, with redistribution of the semantics of
what had traditionally been labelled subjunctive, etc. into the semantics of
the 'new' auxiliary paradigm. In support of this, observe the development
of an analytic aspectual system to express the traditional functions of
perfect and pluperfect (see Jones and Thomas 1977, Chapter 6) and of a
preposition-based construction to express the passive (see further Jones
and Thomas 1977, 267–79, Awbery 1976).

There also is clear evidence of recent interference from English of a
more superficial kind. The plural morpheme {s} has been borrowed along
with many nouns; its distribution has been extended to encompass
indigenous forms (or borrowings of long standing), alongside their
indigenous plural morphs, for example

pregethwr*s*	alongside	pregeth*wyr*
('preachers')		
ffarmwr*s*	alongside	fferm*wyr*
('farmers')		

For Southern dialects alone (at least for older speakers), the same
process of lexical borrowing has led to a phonological innovation in the
development of a contrast between /s/ and /z/, where previously only /s/
occurred. Thus 'zeal' is borrowed as /ze:l/ by southern speakers, producing
a contrast with /se:l/ ('seal'): for northern dialects, /z/ is regularly assigned
to the closest indigenous phoneme /s/.

Internal change

Except possibly for the developments within the verbal system which were mentioned earlier, there are no instances of syntactic change that I know of which *require* the influence of the structure of English uniquely to explain them. The most obvious ongoing changes are instances of simplification through loss of redundant features; for instance

(*i*)   loss of number and gender marking in adjectives,
tai mawrion → tai mawr
(lit. 'houses big + plu.')
'big houses'
het wen → het gwyn
(lit. 'hat white with vowel alternation y → e to mark fem.')
'white hat'

(*ii*)   reduction of contrasts in person-marking by inflection in finite verb forms, to give an asymmetric pattern; for instance, for the past tense forms of *gweld* ('to see'), for my idiolect:
1st sing. ≠ 3 sing. masc/fem. ≠ all others
wel*es* i ≠ wel*odd* ef/hi ≠ wel*so* ti(2 sing.); ni, chwi, hwy (1,2,3, plu.)
Since the appropriate subject pronoun must accompany the finite verb in all but a few grammatically conditioned contexts in the vernacular, the inflection is redundant;

(*iii*)   a pronominal possessor in Welsh is expressed by a discontinuous morph with the form (taking the 1st sing. as example)
possessive adj. fy . . . pers.pron *i*, with the possessum between them. Thus,
fy het i
'my hat'.
The pattern for nominal possessors, however, is simply to juxtapose possessum + possessor in that order. Thus,
het John   het bachgen
'John's hat'   'a boy's hat'.
On analogy with the nominal possessor construction, that with pronominal possessor occurs frequently—and increasingly in the vernacular of younger speakers—without the preposed possessive adjective, giving *het fi* in place of *fy het i*, also adopting the independent form *fi* of the pronoun in this case. This development is clearly uninfluenced by the corresponding English pattern which requires a pre-possessum possessive adjective—and this in spite of the fact that, in varieties of formal and literary Welsh, the post-possessum personal pronoun is often deleted as a mark of 'good' style, as in *fy het*, leaving the possessive adjective as the only marker of person and possession.

It seems that for most speakers of a receding minority language in a bilingual community (and this would certainly be expected in most Welsh-speaking communities) the evidence of structural change alone may show no evidence of incursion by the dominant language, nor of any loss of expressive power. This latter becomes evident only at the extremity of the 'continuum of oral proficiency' (Dorian 1977, 24) at which grammatical categories may be lost, and where Dorian (1977) finds 'semi-speakers' who provide the ultimate structural evidence of the process of language death. The value of the evidence provided by the reduced structure in the language of semi-speakers, however—where we can be sure that the 'lost' category has not simply been redistributed to another part of the grammar, as with the verbal system in Welsh—is strictly dependent on their place in the continuum of proficiency. Their status as semi-speakers depends on there being other speakers whose language does not have structural loss (otherwise they would be the sole remaining speakers, and the structural integrity of their language could not be assessed, except by comparison with written records). We can consider what factors might prove predictive of imminent language death where the language is not in the terminal stage at which semi-speakers are available in significant numbers, or in the circumstance that one has to make a tentative assessment of its imminence on the basis of fluent speakers' usage alone.

Stylistic range

As Dressler and Wodak-Leodolter show in relation to Breton, the first effect on the usage of a dominated minority language is the restriction of its use to 'private usage in the family and among close neighbours and colleagues (especially among peasants and fishermen), even within the older generations' (1977, 34). Indeed, they go so far as to suggest that ultimately even stylistic variation based on situation and social role can be suppressed, leading to a pidgin-like monostylism: 'There is evidence for the existence of styles dependent on situations and social roles (e.g. fast speech styles). Naturally such styles exist in Breton as well. However, the fact that Breton is restricted to few speech situations leads to the consequence that such a differentiation of styles does not seem to be important any more. The styles merge with one another' (*ibid.* 37). This may be the case with many speakers of Welsh, who have only vernacular style available to them, at least on a systematic basis. (Their situation is compounded by the fact that many speakers, outside the professional classes, do not read and write in Welsh with any regularity: they are effectively (by choice) non-literate, if not actually illiterate.)

Dorian uses instances of change in the consonant mutation system of East Sutherland Gaelic as diagnostic because mutational variants (i.e. 'right' and 'wrong' usage) are not salient stylistic markers, and are not subject to correction. Parallel data in Welsh offers possibilities like the following:

(i)   the preposition *yn* /ən/ ('in'), and the 1 sing. poss. adj. *fy* /ən/ ('my'), both cause nasal mutation of an initial plosive in the following word in more 'formal' styles; thus
/ən + baŋgor/ → /əm maŋgor/   /ən + ka:θ + i/→ /əŋ ŋha:θ i/
'in Bangor'   'my cat'

(ii) the numeral *tri* ('three') causes spirant mutation (frictionalization) of an initial aspirated plosive in a following word; thus
/tri + ka:θ/→ /tri xa:θ/
'three cats'

Vernacular style in the regional dialects has different patterns, however. In northern dialects, at least, nasal mutation in contexts like those given in (*i*) is replaced by soft mutation (de-aspiration of aspirated plosives, and frictionalization of unaspirated plosives). Thus we get

/əm vaŋgor/
/əŋ ga:θ i/ (for those who do not take the further step, described earlier, of deleting the possessive adjective).

For some southern dialects, the spirant mutation in instances like (*ii*) simply does not occur, giving forms like

/tri: ka:θ/

What marks out the speaker whose language has entered the phase of imminent decay is not the fact in itself that these substandard usages abound in his speech (they are, after all, the first-learned, most 'natural' forms, the vernacular of his community), but that his stylistic range is attenuated, so that he makes no significant or consistent adjustment to them where a more conservative, formal style would be expected.

Regularity

Following on this, it might be thought that the process brought about by curtailment of stylistic range would be discontinuation or suppression of monitoring procedures associated with careful speech (cf. Labov 1972, 97–9), so that only the vernacular with the assimilations and elisions of casual speech, would ultimately remain. This would entail, further, substantial regularity over a speaker's usage; with the corrective impetus of self-monitoring removed, one could expect the vernacular norm to be maintained regardless of the presence of contextual constraints to which more sophisticated speakers would respond. However, this is not what typically happens. Attenuation of stylistic range leaves some partial recall so that it does not lead to eradication of all stylistic constraints and their linguistic variants, but to erratic and sporadic application of (at least some of) them; and to uncertainty which may even result in the introduction of new variants. Dressler (1972, 454), for instance, quotes the usage of teenagers in pronouncing [r] in Breton. Originally an apical trill /r/, through French influence a uvular [ʀ] has become acceptable; but, in fact, three varieties—[r], [ʀ] and an innovation [ɹ]—occur in free variation. What we find in the language of speakers who have entered the stage of stylistic shrinkage, then, is partial, sporadic and unsystematic response to stylistic rules. Such a speaker is stylistically dysfunctional without being technically monostylistic—however, a speaker of this kind can be only a marginal participant in situations which demand the formal end of the stylistic range.

Code-switching

There appear to be at least two distinct stages in the process of language decay and death. The first is where the speaker is stylistically dysfunctional, but where his language—in vernacular style—is not significantly different in structure from that of more accomplished speakers. This speaker is likely to be unfavourably evaluated by those who have an extended stylistic repertoire, and to use stigmatized forms when he uses his vernacular in formal contexts (or applies stylistic rules erratically); but, generally, his poor-speaker status is evaluated by his extensive use of borrowed lexical items (a characteristic which is shared to varying extents by more accomplished speakers in *their* vernacular). The second stage is that where, additionally, the speaker's language is structurally dysfunctional with reduced grammatical structure, rendering him inadequate even in vernacular style. However, one strategy which helps to compensate for that inadequacy is code-switching between the dominant and dying languages. One productive area of research will be the role of code-switching in the usage of style-attenuated speakers—the study of code-switching as a developmental phenomenon, at first incidental and possibly phrase and idiom bound, but later necessary to furnish the grammar no longer available in the dying language. Additionally, code-switching has an important function in that it compensates for the reduction of stylistic options in the dying language (and undoubtedly facilitates further loss by displacing stylistic variation).

Group norms and individual performance

Dorian (1973) convincingly displays the reality of generational change in the mutational system of East Sutherland Gaelic. But, as the details of individual performances in her analysis show, age-group norms conceal considerable variation in the usage of individuals. Table 15.2, taken from Dorian (1973, 424), reveals considerable individual variation in the occurrence of appropriate and inappropriate initial consonants in the 40–50 year age-group, in (a) the 3 sing. fem. and (b) 3 pl. of the passive forms discussed before.

It is likely that a potentially fruitful line of further research will be the analysis in detail of individual performances, to investigate the correlation with individual variation of demographic factors (age, social status, sex, educational background) but also in terms of personal commitment to public institutions associated with the minority language, language loyalty (or disregard for it), and the extent to which individuals see the achievement of their ambitions for themselves and their children through a dominant alignment with one culture or the other. Evidence from a community in South Wales (Williams, *et al.* 1978) suggests strongly that educational and language choice can be determined by perceived cultural favouring of career expectations. A tool for such analysis might well be an intensive network analysis (or a number of them) within a community, of the kind described in Milroy (1980), as indeed is projected for a community in North Wales, in the expectation that the data gathered will lead to an analysis which will be sensitive to such personal factors as are mentioned above, as well as to the grosser demographic ones, and also throw light on the role of code-switching in situations of imminent language decay and death.

Table 15.2 Appropriate and inappropriate initial consonants in selected Gaelic verb forms

Informants	(a) 3 sing. fem.		(b) 3 pl.	
	Appropriate initial	Inappropriate initial	Appropriate initial	Inappropriate initial
1	1	1	9	7
2	5	10	1	4
3	—	1	1	11
4	—	2	—	5

References

Awbery, G. M. 1976: *The syntax of Welsh: a transformational study of the passive.* Cambridge: Cambridge University Press.

Census 1971: report on the Welsh language in Wales. Cardiff: HMSO 1973.

Denison, N. 1977: Language death or language suicide? *IJ Soc. Lang.* **12**, 13–22.

Dorian, N. 1973: Grammatical change in a dying dialect *Lg.* **49**, 413–38.

————1977: The problem of the semi-speaker in language death. *IJ Soc. Lang.* **12**, 23–32.

Dressler, W. 1972: On the phonology of language death. *Papers from the 8th Regional Meeting, Chicago Linguistic Society,* 448–57.

Dressler, W., and Wodak-Leodolter, R. 1977: Language preservation and language death in Brittany. *IJ Soc. Lang.* **12**, 33–44.

Hall, R. 1965: *The lifecycle of pidgin languages.* Lignell.

Jones, M. and Thomas, A. R. 1977: *The Welsh language: studies in its syntax and semantics.* Cardiff: University of Wales Press for the Schools Council.

Labov, W. 1972: *Sociolinguistic patterns.* Oxford: Blackwell.

Milroy, L. 1980: *Language and social networks.* Oxford: Blackwell.

Thomas A. R. 1980: Some aspects of the bilingual situation in Wales. *Forum Linguisticum* **27**, 147–63.

Williams, G., Roberts, E. and Issac, R. 1978: Language and aspirations for upward social mobility. In G. Williams (ed.), *Social and cultural change in rural Wales.* London: Routledge & Kegan Paul.

16

Dangerous dichotomies in applied linguistics and language teaching
David Wilkins

In applied linguistics, as in other fields, from time to time we experience a change of focus as a new constellation of ideas comes into prominence. There results an upsurge of research and experimentation motivated by the desire to demonstrate the superiority of the newer ideas over those that had a similar prominence in the preceding period. We may interpret the conflict of newer and older in terms of a binary opposition, and indeed the issues are often explicitly represented as dichotomous contrasts in which the terms stand for the alternative interpretations or perceptions of the phenomena involved. It is anticipated that the research will resolve the conflict that is apparent in the opposition. The present chapter argues that this expectation tends to colour the research itself and sometimes leads to procedures or interpretations which are of doubtful validity. It is further argued that even if such dichotomies have a value in the conduct of research, it would be dangerous to adopt the currently dominant view as a basis for practical decisions in, for example, language teaching, since in a more complex view of human language than we can readily comprehend the terms may well not be mutually exclusive.

Interference v. generalized learning processes

For many years the term APPLIED LINGUISTICS was taken to be virtually synonymous with contrastive analysis. Lado (1957), elaborating on earlier work by Fries (1945) and Weinreich (1953), had shown that at all levels of language it was possible to find an explanation for a large proportion of the errors made by second-language learners by reference to the difference in the relevant characteristics of the mother tongue and the target language. Extensive documentation was provided by Lado himself and subsequently through many contrastive projects for what was then taken to be a more or less self-evident truth, i.e. that the major, perhaps the only, systematic source of difficulties for a learner was the influence of the first language. A psychological account of the process was readily available in the theory of TRANSFER of training. The principal contribution that could be made by (applied) linguists to the teaching of languages was therefore to analyse in depth the differences between the two languages concerned. In this way the nature of the task facing the learner could be fully described.

In recent years the contrastive hypothesis has come under increasing attack and among researchers in applied linguistics has gone somewhat out of fashion. The dominant theme is no longer the effect of the mother tongue upon learning a second language. Instead, researchers examine how far learners, whatever their linguistic background, face common difficulties and undergo common processes in learning a given second language. Following similar research in first-language acquisition, the attempt has been made to discover whether there is a broad developmental sequence in the learning of a second language. Thus, in an early article, Corder, a major contributor to this field, refers to the learner's INTERNAL SYLLABUS (Corder 1973, 268). A considerable stimulus to research was provided by Dulay and Burt (1974), who put forward evidence that learners of different linguistic backgrounds made similar errors in their second-language performance. If it is the case that many errors can be explained in terms of the target language and without reference to the mother tongue, a new hypothesis is needed to account for the processes involved in second-language learning. The hypothesis is that all learners approach the task of learning a second language with similar cognitive abilities, and it is the operation of these abilities upon the language concerned that will determine the particular features of learning the language as a second language.

We can now see how readily the contrast between this and the earlier view can be expressed as a binary opposition. On the one hand the key characteristic of learning is mother tongue interference; on the other hand it is the operation of generalized learning processes. The opposition is not in itself harmful. Unfortunately, however, there is a tendency for the view that is the preoccupation of current research to develop into an orthodoxy, with the result that it is widely and somewhat uncritically accepted in the form in which it is presented. Within research itself there is a tendency to conduct the investigation in such a way as to seek support for one or other of the arguments involved. This in turn affects the quality of the research design and the interpretation of the results produced. It is not the aim of this article to examine and evaluate the evidence on this issue. It is possible, however, to illustrate from this and other issues how viewing things in dichotomous terms, first, can lead to dangerous misconceptions regarding the relations between the opposing hypotheses and, secondly, can engender attitudes towards the evidence available that leave much to be desired.

In the first respect, for example, the opposition is quite misleading in that conceptually there is no necessary contradiction between notions of interference and of generalized processes of learning. It is perfectly possible to include both within a single model of second language learning. There may be aspects of the language learning process that are common to all learners and others that are specific to speakers of a given language. It is therefore not *necessary* that an explanation should be found in one or other of the two views expressed in the dichotomy. However it might be the case that research is best conducted by hypothesizing that one of these views is the correct one. It is then possible to discover how far it accounts for the data observed. It is precisely here that much of the research conducted in this field is open to the second criticism for the degree to which the interpretation of the evidence seems to reflect the predisposition of the researcher. On the one hand there is a tendency to ignore evidence that does not support the preferred view. On the other hand serious consideration is not given to explanations other than the preferred one for data which the researcher has gathered.

Thus, if we take the contrastive hypothesis, we may be surprised that there was not more appreciation in the original work of the fact that it is extremely rare for a learner to transfer inflections (case, tense, number etc.) from the first to the second language, although a theory of interference would seem to predict this. It is not the case either, that every difference between the languages causes difficulty or that the nature of the difficulty can be traced back to interference. Speakers of Slavonic languages will indeed face problems learning the English article system, presumably because there is no article system in most Slavonic languages. However, the absence of articles in the mother tongue means that there will be neither negative nor positive transfer. As a result, the difficulties to be faced are those that are intrinsic to the target language, and it is likely that no reference need actually be made to the mother-tongue in elaborating what these difficulties are. The fact that differences exist and difficulties occur is not sufficient support for the claim that the differences *cause* the difficulties.

Similar flaws can be found in the research of those who favour the notion of generalized processes of second language acquisition. There are some aspects of language where it is very hard to deny the effect of the mother tongue on learning. Pronunciation is a case in point, although it could be argued that motor skills could be expected to be unlike other language skills. As for the interpretation of evidence, there is a world of difference between saying that a set of errors in a given linguistic domain *can* be explained in terms of generalized acquisition processes and that they *are to be* explained in such terms. Thus in an early article (Dulay and Burt 1972), the argument turns on the authors' attempt to find alternative explanations for errors which would normally have been assigned to interference. Once it is shown that such explanations can be found, although objective evidence in support is unavailable and other explanations are at least as plausible, it is argued that the contrastive (interference) hypothesis is unnecessary. It is then further assumed that it is not valid either. Again, there are many instances where it is difficult to conceive how conclusive evidence can be found for either explanation since each seems equally plausible. The omission of auxiliary *do* in the construction of negative sentences in English is a widespread error, but since any equivalent is absent from almost all other languages there is no way of being sure whether it is caused by interference or is the result of general second-language acquisition processes. Indeed it is not clear, even where speakers of different languages make the same error in a second language, that the cause is the same in the two cases. The product is the same, but the process has not necessarily been. It is notoriously difficult to find reliable evidence for reaching a firm conclusion about the causes of errors especially when the errors are gathered in the form of a synchronic corpus. A careful study of longitudinal development may assist but is unlikely to be conclusive. Furthermore, both hypotheses ignore the possible effects of the nature of the exposure (input) which the learner has experienced. It is hard to believe that serious conclusions can be reached about such matters as the order in which categories are mastered, without studies in which the input is carefully controlled and systematically varied.

Behaviourism v. mentalism

The question of the role of the linguistic input brings us to a wider issue which has similarly been presented in dichotomous fashion. Levelt (n.d.) has commented on the seemingly obligatory polarization between BEHAVIOURISM and MENTALISM that characterizes discussion of theories of second-language learning (see, for example, Wilkins (1972, 161–76). We can question whether making binary choices between theories is a desirable procedure, but, in any case, as Levelt observes, it is curious that these particular theories should recur with such frequency. In fact the labels are symbols for the alternative responses to a very general question that is frequently asked in connection with second language learning: is the process of language learning determined by the nature of the language input and contextual variables, or is learning governed by internal, unobservable (innate) processes which require only exposure to meaningful language for their effective operation? The essence of the question is of the greatest importance to the applied linguist and to the language teacher, but asked in this form it is naive. It seems to invite the response that one of the alternatives is true and the other not. Were we to rephrase the question in terms of *how far* each of the embedded propositions is true, we would no longer feel obliged to opt for one or the other.

Having asked ourselves the wrong question in the first place, we have then compounded the error by identifying the former, contextual view with behaviourism and, further, behaviourism itself with a Skinnerian neo-behaviourist model. At this point it would be common to cite Chomsky's review of Skinner's *Verbal Behavior* (Chomsky 1959) as evidence that a behaviourist view of language has been discredited, that contextual factors are of marginal importance in second-language learning, and that language teaching will need to be based on procedures compatible with the view that the key factors in learning are features of the individual and not of the environment in which he or she is learning. Yet, in fact, what Chomsky demonstrated above all was the essential vacuousness of attempting to account for language in Stimulus-Response terms. He did not demonstrate, indeed could not have demonstrated, that no kind of behaviourist theory can account for human language behaviour and certainly not that contextual features are irrelevant to language learning. In our dubious logic, however, we have argued that because behaviourism is concerned with the effect of variables in the input and in conditions pertaining to the learner's own language behaviour, the 'fact' that a behaviourist account has been found wanting has proved that these variables are not a significant factor in language learning. The falseness of the argument is self-evident.

It would be equally naive to suppose that by formulating the original question in 'how far?' terms, we are asking a question to which a precise answer can be given. There may ultimately be no way of establishing to just what extent language learning is a matter of nature or nurture, but at least we are forced thereby to the acceptance that language behaviour and language learning are extremely complex activities. Our current attempts to provide theories to account for them suggest that we are still in a conceptual stone age. With regard to the specific issue under consideration here, the research done on (second) language acquisition in recent years has done a good deal to demonstrate that the individual brings more to the task of learning a language than had hitherto been believed. There remains uncertainty as to how far this applies to learners of second languages studying in an educational institution, but here too fruitful research is beginning to be done (see Krashen 1976, for example). Even so, there is no illogicality in postulating that the operation of internal processes may be accelerated by, for example, the frequency, systematicity or meaningfulness of the language input. These and many other aspects of the linguistic environment which is created for the learner may well have facilitating or retarding effects. It is even conceivable that there are language activities, quite unlike anything currently attempted in the teaching of languages that will prove to promote learning. We should also remind ourselves that success in language learning is dependent on factors of a totally non-linguistic character. Personality and social features, for example, may be crucial in creating an environment favourable to learning. A 'complete' theory of learning would have to include these and relate them to the (psycho-) linguistic variables. If it was argued that such features do not affect the essential nature of the language learning processes, it would be necessary to point out that language teaching is concerned with the *efficient* learning of language, and that it is not a trivial concern to seek the means by which we might discover how to optimize the *rate* at which a language can be learned.

Structure v. function

One of the major areas of decision-making in language teaching involves the question of what language to teach and when. There has to be some basis for deciding what the linguistic content of teaching should be. The conventional approach, reflecting a view of the nature of both learning and language itself, has been to derive the entities to be learned from a description of the structural characteristics of the language in question. At one time, under the influence of post-Bloomfieldian structuralism, this was expressed in terms of 'teaching the structures' of the language. Subsequently with changes in linguistic theory the metalanguage has shifted towards a formulation in terms of rules or even to a relatively pre-theoretical mode such as that adopted above ('structural characteristics').

Whatever the theoretical basis, the essential belief is that the construction of sentences is also the construction of meaning, that is to say, that meaning is consistently created by the lexical items and the relations between them which the structural features of sentences express. In recent years the interest in speech acts has led to this view being challenged. It is suggested that in making utterances we are engaged in socially oriented acts of *doing*. In applied linguistics we have talked of the true objectives of learning as enabling the learner to perform the social (or communicative) *functions* that these acts represent. Thus the 'things' to be taught have been seen as language functions rather than language structures. The fact that there is some frequency of association between certain types of sentence and certain speech acts lends some credibility to this view. Thus, even without taking contextual factors into account, a 'most likely' interpretation can be put upon sentences with performative verbs, sentence types such as INTERROGATIVE and IMPERATIVE and many partially formulaic expressions (e.g. '*Would you mind* pass*ing* the salt?')

However, to suggest that, on the basis of such instances, a choice in language teaching between language functions (illocutionary acts) and language structures can be resolved entirely in favour of the former is to imply something quite misleading about the way in which language generally operates. As is well known, INDIRECT speech acts predominate in normal language use and contextual factors may substantially affect the force of even the apparently conventional acts mentioned above. It follows that language teaching could never be based wholly on familiarizing learners with the conventional expression of speech acts. At the same time there are very few occasions, apart from pathologically deviant cases, where the ordinary linguistic meaning is not operative in the performance of the act. Morgan (1977) has noted that the meaning of a sentence expressing an indirect speech act retains its validity, and an understanding of it is usually necessary for a recognition of the illocutionary force of the utterance even if that force is not wholly derived from the meaning. The only sensible conclusion to reach is that in illocutionary force we have an important new dimension in our perception of the nature of language, but, if, to misquote Austin (1962), our aim is to ensure that language learners know 'how to do things with sentences', this presupposes that they have a command of sentence construction. Language teaching, in other words, is necessarily concerned with both structure and function.

Language v. communication

The role of contextual features enters discussion of another, closely related opposition, that of *language* and *communication*. The extent to which our interpretation of utterances (and not only their illocutionary forces) is affected by non-linguistic factors is well documented. In examining both monologue and dialogue text, it is possible to show that in order to understand fully what is being communicated, the receiver may need to draw on knowledge of the subject-matter, perception of the relevant aspects of the physical situation, familiarity with the producer or with persons referred to, a consciousness of the sets of attitudes, values or prejudices which are either shared by the participants or known to each of them and an awareness of what is socially and culturally expected in certain situations. Further, what could be expressed linguistically within the text may often be omitted altogether. The semantic relation of one sentence to another may be left to be inferred. The general thematic structure of the text may not be marked by any explicit linguistic devices. Steps in an argument may be omitted because they are deemed self-evident, easily deducible or already known to the receiver. The ethnomethodological literature demonstrates how the linguistic may seem to be overshadowed by the non-linguistic in the process of communication so that the role of language as such may be somewhat diminished even in language events (see Turner 1970). It may seem that it is only the receiver who exploits what is pragmatically relevant for interpretation, but in fact the producer himself makes assumptions about what is shared with the hearer or can be recovered by him and it is this that determines what is and what is not made linguistically explicit. What is frequently operating in communication, therefore, is less what can be objectively shown to be 'present' and relevant than what the participants *assume* to be relevant. Rommetveit (1974) refers to these shared assumptions as 'the architecture of inter-subjectivity'.

In the context of the acquisition of a second language we may have little doubt that the ultimate expectation of a learner is to be able to communicate in that language, so that the general aim is indeed communication rather than language for its own sake. Whether that aim should be communication *not* language is another question. The issue manifests itself in two ways. The first relates to just what the responsibilities of the language teacher are. If the language teacher is preparing people to be communicators in the foreign language, should it not be just as much his responsibility to concern himself with the non-linguistic aspects of communication? Indeed might not language, as is suggested below, be left more or less to look after itself? In considering this there are two points that can readily be conceded. First, it might well be the role of the language teacher to draw attention to instances of language use where the failure to recognize the assumptions, values, attitudes that are operating would result in important misinterpretation and where these assumptions etc. are culturally bound and therefore not easily accessible to the learner from another culture. Secondly, in many cases, especially in school systems, the curricular aims of language teaching may not be limited to what would be provided by a purely behavioural analysis of objectives. As a result not all learning activities need be closely associated with features of the language structure. With these reservations, however, it does not seem that the language teacher can be as much concerned with the non-linguistic aspects of communication as with the linguistic. The knowledge that can be drawn upon in acts of communication is encyclopaedic. It would be absurd for the language teacher to attempt to present this knowledge in some systematic way. Such matters are the primary responsibility of other parts of the education system and much must be left to be accumulated randomly in a lifetime of unplanned experience. The language teacher's preoccupation must be the role of language in communication and for reasons that we saw in looking at speech acts, this role should not be belittled.

The second manifestation of the communication v. language issue derives from the psycholinguistic study of certain language activities. It seems to be widely agreed that comprehension, whether of spoken or of written language, is not a literal process of linguistic decoding. In reading we do not first identify letters, then the combination of letters into syllables, of syllables into words and so on up the linguistic hierachy. Much the same can be demonstrated for listening, where whole segments may not be heard and where frequent distortion fails to prevent transmission of the message. In reading, the process is one in which the reader seems to operate on a predicting, sampling, verifying basis which Goodman (1967) has called a 'psycholinguistic guessing game'. The studies carried out reveal a good deal about the skills of an efficient reader and indeed about what skills need to be acquired in order to become efficient. The development of such skills is a learning process. A description of the desired skills is in no way an indication of how those skills are best acquired. However, the evidence on skilled reading has been used (e.g. by Smith 1973) to argue that because linguistic coding skills do not operate in normal reading, it follows that the separate teaching of linguistic sub-skills (letter recognition, syllable recognition etc.) cannot be appropriate or relevant to the learning of reading. A similar form of argument appears in the second-language literature where structural decomposition and recomposition are rejected broadly because the resulting language behaviour does not closely resemble normal communication. Breen and Candlin (1980), for example, reject 'any specification of content in terms of a static inventory of language items' and suggest criteria of selection and organization which do not mention language as such. Techniques and materials which are not 'communicative' are summarily rejected. In both these cases the reasoning seems to be quite false. There is no reason to assume that the learning activity should be an image of the behaviour which it is intended ultimately to produce. To put it another way, it is far from certain (and is indeed improbable) that the most effective way to master a complex skill is by repeatedly attempting to produce the skill in all its complexity. The issue of what constitutes the best learning procedures is one to be resolved empirically, and if at all possible by objective research. The contrast between language and communication is a false antithesis which seems to encourage us to make quite unnecessary choices.

The urge to dichotomize goes far beyond the four sets of oppositions that have been discussed above. The very prevalence of dichotomies suggests that we find them helpful in conceptualizing issues which we seek to clarify. The danger lies in the fact that we also anticipate a *resolution* of the oppositions involved. This expectation rests upon an unjustified optimism with respect to what experimental and controlled research can achieve. As a rule, the more general the hypothesis, the more difficult it is to find conclusive ways of testing it objectively. By contrast, the more specific the hypothesis, the less likely it is to resolve major theoretical differences. If it is true, for example, as is claimed by Krashen (1977), that certain grammatical morphemes in English are acquired in an order which does not reflect the order in which they have been presented in a pedagogically structured exposure, this does not demonstrate that variation in the conditions governing the language input are irrelevant to acquisition. That is indeed one possible explanation, but another is that the input was wrongly structured and that a structure reflecting more accurately what is believed to be the natural sequence of acquisition would facilitate acquisition. A third explanation could be that other features of the manner in which the linguistic input was experienced have affected the intake by the learners. In the language teaching context there are many other methodological variables that operate, and the opportunities for use of the language outside the classroom could also be highly significant. However interesting the possible disparity between what is 'learned' and what is apparently 'acquired', it leaves largely untouched the question of the relative role of input variables and of features intrinsic to the learner.

The general issue is also a familiar one in research into language teaching as such. It is virtually impossible to compare whole methodologies of teaching, however conceptually distinct they may be. It is, however, possible to investigate specific variables. If, thereby, I am able to show that, for example, items of language presented in a combined spoken and written mode are more readily learned and better remembered than the same items presented either solely orally or solely in written form, I have established something useful, but something which can be accommodated within almost any theoretical or methodological framework.

The conclusion to be drawn from our discussion is not that the dichotomies that we have considered are unhelpful. Indeed they are probably essential for the identification of significant topics for research and for the formulation of testable hypotheses. We must however, beware of interpreting research as if it had conclusively resolved the general theoretical issues in one way or the other. We should not be alarmed by this apparent failure. The desire to view all issues in either/or terms is dangerous as a foundation for our pragmatic decision making in that it shows our unwillingness to recognize the true complexity of human language behaviour and of the factors that determine language learning. The fact that communication involves factors other than the linguistic does not mean that the linguistic contribution to communication is insignificant. The fact that complex cognitive processes may be at work in language acquisition does not mean that environmental factors cannot advance or retard learning. If we do not recognize the complexity of language processes, we risk sliding into the narrowly based prescriptivisms that have bedevilled language teaching in the past.

References

Austin, J.L. 1962: *How to do things with words*. Oxford: Clarendon Press.
Breen, M.P. and Candlin, C.N. 1980: The essentials of a communicative curriculum in language teaching. *App. Ling.* **1**, 89–112.
Chomsky, N. 1959: Review of B.F. Skinner, *Verbal behavior*. *Lg.* **35**, 26–58.
Corder, S.P. 1973: *Introducing applied linguistics*. Harmondsworth: Penguin.

Dulay, H. and Burt, M.K. 1972: Goofing: an indication of children's second-language learning strategies. *L Learn.* **22,** 235–52.

——1974: Natural sequences in child second-language acquisition. *L Learn.* **24,** 37–53.

Fries, C.C. 1945: *Teaching and learning English as a foreign language.* Ann Arbor: University of Michigan Press.

Goodman, K.S. 1967: Reading: a psycholinguistic guessing game. *J Read. Spec.* **4,** 126–55.

Krashen, S.D. 1976: Formal and informal linguistic environments in language acquisition and language learning. *TESOL Q* **10,** 157–68.

——1977: Some issues relating to the monitor model. In H.B. Brown, C.A. Yorio and R. Crymes (eds.), *Teaching and learning English as a second language: trends in research and practice.* Washington, DC: TESOL.

Lado, R. 1957: *Linguistics across cultures.* Ann Arbor: University of Michigan Press.

Levelt, W.J.M. (n.d.): Skill theory and language teaching. *Studies in Second Language Acquisition* **1(1).**

Morgan, J.L. 1977: Conversational postulates revisited. *Lg.* **53,** 277–84.

Smith, F. 1973: *Psycholinguistics and reading.* New York: Holt, Rinehart & Winston.

Rommetveit, R. 1974: *On message structure.* New York: Wiley.

Turner, R. 1970: Words, utterances and activities. In J. Douglas (ed.), *Understanding everyday life.* Chicago: Aldine.

Weinreich, U. 1953: *Languages in contact.* New York: Linguistic Circle of New York **1.**

Wilkins, D.A. 1972: *Linguistics in language teaching.* London: Edward Arnold.

17

The structure of language proficiency
Arthur Hughes

A current controversy in foreign-language testing concerns two conflicting views of the nature of language proficiency. On one view, language proficiency is seen as being capable of being broken down into a number of separately testable components; on the other view, it is seen as something 'more like a viscous substance' (Oller 1979), not capable of breakdown into component parts. The first view has been dubbed by Oller (1979) the DIVISIBILITY hypothesis; the second, the INDIVISIBILITY (or UNITARY COMPETENCE) hypothesis.

The divisibility hypothesis can be traced back to Robert Lado, who may be regarded as the father of modern foreign-language testing. In his 1961 book, *Language testing,* he makes a distinction between language skills and what he calls 'the elements of language'. The skills that he has in mind are the familiar ones of speaking, listening, writing and reading (a fifth skill, translation, he regards as less central to the notion of language proficiency). Observing that the mastery of the four skills does not advance evenly (someone may be a much better reader of a foreign language than he is, say, a speaker), Lado insists that for an accurate picture of a person's proficiency each of the skills must be tested separately. This seems entirely unobjectionable. We all know cases of people in whom one skill is highly developed while another is practically non-existent. The man who has learned to read a language in order to obtain information from scientific papers may be quite unable to understand the spoken language, particularly if there is a poor fit between orthography and phonology. It is not possible to predict his listening ability on the basis of a measure of his reading ability. That is why the skills must be tested separately. If we learned that scores on listening tests were accurately predicted by scores on reading tests, or (as we shall see later) that scores on a listening test were predicted better by scores on a reading test than by those on another listening test, we should be suspicious not so much of the notion of separate skills but rather of the quality of the particular tests used, and perhaps of the sample of subjects whose abilities were measured.

As well as the four skills, Lado identifies a number of other variables, which he calls 'elements of language'. The elements are: 'pronunciation, grammatical structure, the lexicon, and cultural meanings. The first of these, pronunciation, is itself made up of three separate elements, namely sound segments, intonation and its borders, and stress and its sequences which constitute the rhythm of language. Within grammatical structure there are two main subdivisions, namely morphology and syntax' (1961, 25). Although, as Lado admits, these elements never occur separately in language, but are always 'integrated in the total skills', they can—and should—be tested separately, particularly if the purpose of a test is diagnostic. A person's pronunciation may be ahead of or behind his knowledge of vocabulary (by comparison with his peers or with native speakers); ability in one cannot be predicted from ability in the other.

Lado's choice and description of 'elements' is clearly influenced by the structural linguistics with which he was familiar. Linguists of other schools might have made different choices, while many would have been reluctant to translate categories of linguistic description into elements of language testing without satisfying themselves that the psychological reality of those categories could be established. Nevertheless, his claim that pronunciation may be ahead of or behind knowledge of vocabulary is perfectly plausible. One thinks of Joseph Conrad, whose English accent, according to Jean-Aubry (1957, 283), was so poor as to prevent him from giving public lectures, but whose English vocabulary was not noticeably deficient. If we should find, as we shall later, that two measures of control of vocabulary correlate less highly with each other than one of those measures does with a measure of accent, then we should be worried not about our distinction between pronunciation and vocabulary but about the accuracy of the measurement.

As was noted above, Lado sees his elements of language being integrated in the skills, but he does not make precise the relationship between elements and skills. He does say, however, that 'in testing the sound segments systematically we have to decide whether to test this element in speaking or listening' (1961, 27) and 'Since the problems will differ somewhat for production and for recognition, different lists are necessary to test the student's pronunciation in speaking and listening' (*ibid*, 45). The implication seems to be that a matrix as in Table 17.1 can be formed in which each cell represents a component capable of separate testing, which will provide information unique to that cell, i.e. additional to that given by all the other cells. This is certainly the way in which Lado's remarks have been interpreted by subsequent writers on language testing. Harris (1968, 11), for example, produces a matrix with 16 cells, admitting that in practice, but for no theoretical reason, 'one can scarcely imagine a test which would attempt to adhere to such a detailed analysis'. Lado establishes the variables and consequent cells essentially on the basis of a mixture of linguistic theory, habit theory and common-sense observation. He does not attempt to justify them in terms of the *processes* involved in language behaviour. There is no mention, for example, of lexical stores,

Table 17.1 Matrix of language elements and skills.

Elements		Skills			
		Speaking	Listening	Writing	Reading
Pronunciation	Sound segments				
	Intonation				
	Stress				
Grammatical structure	Syntax				
	Morphology				
Lexicon					

their possible structure or the means of accessing them. As a behaviourist he is concerned with patterns of behaviour or output, rather than the processes which underly them. Nor does he present any serious empirical evidence for the susceptibility of language proficiency to breakdown into so many separately measurable components. Nevertheless, for the best part of 20 years tests have been produced whose structure betrays a continuing belief in the possibility of such a breakdown. The English Language Battery, for example, a test widely used for the assessment of the proficiency in English of overseas students applying to British universities, has the following sections: sound discrimination, stress, intonation, listening comprehension, grammar, vocabulary, and reading comprehension. It was only with the arrival of a testing heretic, Oller, that the Lado faith was seriously questioned.

As has already been indicated, Oller has called Lado's view of language proficiency the DIVISIBILITY HYPOTHESIS. 'For instance, it might be possible to differentiate knowledge of vocabulary, grammar, and phonology. Further it might be possible to distinguish test variances associated with the traditionally recognized skills of listening, speaking, reading, and writing, or aspects of these skills such as productive versus receptive competencies *vis-à-vis* the hypothesized components (e.g. productive phonology in an oral mode, or receptive vocabulary in a written mode)' (Oller 1979, 424). Opposed to this is the INDIVISIBILITY HYPOTHESIS. 'It may be that language proficiency is relatively more unitary than discrete point testers have contended. Perhaps what has been called "vocabulary" knowledge (as measured by tests that have been called "vocabulary" tests) cannot in fact be distinguished from "grammar" knowledge (as measured by "grammar" tests). This alternative is not apt to be found as appealing as the first mentioned one, but it cannot be excluded by pure logic' (*ibid.*, 424–5). It may not be as appealing, but it is the alternative that Oller favours. It is his contention that all language ability is based on a single internalized grammar or, as he has termed it, EXPECTANCY GRAMMAR (Oller 1975, 1976). Seeming contradictory evidence to this, 'such as the fact that listening comprehension usually exceeds speaking proficiency in either first or second language speakers, would have to be explained on some basis other than the postulation of separate grammars or components of competence. For instance, one might appeal to the load on attention and short-term memory that is exerted by different language-processing tasks. It may require more mental energy to speak than to listen, or to write than to read, and so forth' (Oller and Hinofotis 1980). In support of his preference for the indivisibility hypothesis, Oller (1976) makes reference to the concept of ANALYSIS-BY-SYNTHESIS, the argument that receptive language skills depend on the language user's ability to generate a match for an incoming signal, and the then recent suggestion that productive skills might be similarly related to receptive ones. He also points to the finding of Swain *et al.* (1974) that second language learners tended to make the same errors, whether they were speaking spontaneously, imitating, or translating from their first into the second language. But what he seems to regard as the most convincing evidence are the results of a series of studies that he has carried out with associates, and which are reported in the Appendix of Oller (1979) and in Part 1 of Oller and Perkins (1980).

The procedure followed in these studies has been to require relatively large numbers of subjects to undergo a battery of foreign-language tests, and in most cases to perform some other language-based tasks. Correlations between scores on the various tests (or parts of tests) and tasks are then computed before being submitted to principal component analysis and factor analysis proper.[1] If the divisibility hypothesis is to be supported by such analysis, then tests which purport to measure the same element or skill should be highly correlated, while those which purport to measure different things should be less highly correlated. Factor analysis based on the correlation matrix should result in factors emerging which, when the loadings on them of the various tests are examined, can be associated individually with particular skills or elements. This does not happen. Repeatedly, a large, general factor is obtained; no factor emerges which can be associated with any element; and where there is a factor which appears related to a single skill, its support for the existence of separate skills is questioned by Oller. In his opinion there is 'little hope' for the divisibility hypothesis; the evidence provides much stronger support for the indivisibility hypothesis.

For a number of reasons, we should hesitate before accepting Oller's interpretation of the results of his studies. The first reason concerns the nature of the tests used. As Oller is well aware (see Oller 1979, 174–6), and as hinted at in a quotation above, tests do not always measure what they are supposed to measure. In the study of Scholz, Hendricks, Spurling, Johnson and Vandenburg (1980) into the divisibility hypothesis, two listening comprehension tests correlated with each other at 0.26, but at 0.50 and 0.61 with a test of reading. It seems clear that the two 'listening

---

[1] Oller's choice of statistical methods has been criticized (Palmer and Bachman (1981)). But since Oller's conclusions can be shown to be dubious on other grounds, this is not crucial to the arguments presented here.

comprehension' tests are not measuring the same thing. It is no surprise, then, that there is no factor (to be identified as 'listening comprehension') on which they both show a significant loading. Nor is it surprising, given that tests of 'listening comprehension' typically require the subject to identify the appropriate *written* response (which may be quite complex), that certain 'listening' tests should correlate quite highly with reading tests. This may be a serious criticism of such tests, but the failure of two 'listening' tests to correlate highly with each other is no reason to say that listening comprehension is not a distinct skill. Similarly, the TOEFL test of writing ability used by Oller and Hinofotis (1980) cannot be regarded as an accurate measure of writing ability. The learner writes nothing. He has simply to demonstrate that he can recognize ungrammatical or stylistically inappropriate structures in unconnected sentences. The test is made up of a series of multiple choice items, where the candidate has to indicate which of the italicised words or phrases is 'incorrect'. Thus: '*At first* the old woman seemed unwilling *to accept* anything *that* was offered her by my friend and *I.*' When the test was validated, performance on it correlated at 0.74 with a criterion of 4 short compositions (Harris 1969, 70). While such a correlation may be sufficient to justify using the test as a means of estimating the writing ability of large numbers of students (too many to permit the assessment of substantial pieces of written work), in research of the kind which interests us here, the use of such a test as a measure of the writing skill cannot be defended.

It would not be profitable to examine in this way each test employed in the studies carried out by Oller and his associates. Enough has been said to demonstrate that what they have tested is not the divisibility hypothesis but, if anything, the validity of a number of tests. Even here, though doubt is thrown on a number of tests, it is not clear in the case of the listening comprehension tests whether just one (and which) or both of them are invalid. Oller claims that his studies 'can be viewed as a method of evaluating the theoretical hypotheses and at the same time assessing the construct validity of the various tests that might be included' (1979, 246). Yet, as he observes immediately afterwards, if the tests employed 'had no independent claims to validity, a failure to clarify the choice between the theoretical positions [the two hypotheses] would hardly be conclusive' (1979, 246). But, given that at least some of the tests lack construct validity, apparent support for his position is equally inconclusive.

How, then, should the two hypotheses be tested if the tests which are supposed to measure the elements and skills are of doubtful validity? In discussing the validation of language tests based on the principles he has previously laid down, Lado (1961, 324) says that 'we need to compare the scores on the test with some other criterion whose validity is self-evident, e.g. actual use of the language'. Surely it is the actual use of language, performance in natural language tasks, that should provide the basis for initial research. The productive skills, speaking and writing, since their products allow direct observation, lend themselves most obviously to empirical investigation. The first step would be to obtain comparable samples of both speaking and writing from a number of subjects. These could be then assessed according to any criteria which the researcher might think relevant (grammatical accuracy, success of communication, use of vocabulary, etc.). Reliable and independent judgements of all spoken and written performances would provide the data for statistical analysis which would reveal whether or not there were distinct, identifiable 'elements' and skills.

Oller might argue that at least some of this has already been done inasmuch as the FSI (Foreign Service Institute) interview—with separate rating scales for accent, grammar, vocabulary, fluency, and comprehension—has been used in a number of the studies that he reports. This brings us to a second reason for doubts about Oller's claims. Unfortunately, the assessments of an individual's accent, grammar, etc. in these studies were not made independently. That is, ratings on all five scales were made by the same judges. It would appear from these studies, as well as that of Mullen (1980), that individuals listening to an interview may not be able to distinguish consistently between, say, a speaker's grammar and his vocabulary. Correlations between ratings on the five scales are generally very high (within these, correlations involving *accent* tend to be lower). It could be that the listener forms an overall judgement of 'speaking ability' (and so *perception* of this ability might be thought unitary), but to argue from the high correlations, as Oller and Hinofotis (1980) do, that the five scales are 'equivalent' is mistaken. The high correlations must derive to some degree from the lack of independence of judgements on the five scales. Only when the judgements are independent, when they are made by judges (in sufficient numbers to ensure reliability) who concentrate on only one scale, will it be possible to say whether or not interview ability (or any other 'natural' language ability) can be broken down into separately measurable components.

The third reason for questioning Oller's conclusions concerns the nature of the sample of subjects used in these studies. Too great a range of ability will favour the indivisibility hypothesis. Individual differences (such as the individual's speaking and writing ability) will be obscured. This can be illustrated with an example from soccer. It is generally agreed that kicking and heading are distinct skills. Some players, like Stanley Matthews, have been noted for their control of the ball with their feet; others, like Tommy Lawton, for their heading ability. But if a sample of footballers ranging from international players to the clumsiest beginner were to perform a number of kicking and heading tasks, and their 'scores' were subjected to factor analysis, it is quite possible that only one factor, ABILITY AT SOCCER, would emerge. This is because the large differences of ability *between players* at both kicking and heading, would obscure the more subtle, but equally real, differences between the two skills in individual players. Although no indication of the range of ability of the subjects is generally given, there is a suspicion that something like this is happening in the studies under review. Oller and Hinofotis report that where the bottom half (in terms of ability) of a sample of subjects was eliminated, another factor, LISTENING COMPREHENSION, emerged. They say: 'There is some evidence to suggest that (excluding the oral interview data) if the data represents the whole range of subject variability, the unitary competence [indivisibility] hypothesis may be the best explanation, but if the variability is somewhat less, a moderate version of a separate skills hypothesis would be preferred' (1980, 23). Inasmuch as it is in individual differences that we are interested, we should be concerned to work with samples where 'the variability is somewhat less'. Ideally, the subjects should be of as limited a range of ability within which discrimination can reliably be made. The signs from the Oller and Hinofotis study are that under such conditions more support for the divisibility hypothesis might be found.[2]

It was said earlier that research of the type proposed was 'a first step'. Should separate skills and elements be established, for the practising tester a second step might be the validation of both old and new tests against what would then be dependable criteria. For others, the second step, a very large one, would be an attempt to explain *why* individuals were more or less proficient at particular skills or elements. Research of this nature would have to take account not only of output but also of input (the learner's exposure to the language) and individual differences between learners with regard to aptitude, motivation, and attitude.[3] A full understanding of the structure of language proficiency would presumably involve a detailed account of how utterances are produced and understood. To judge from recent accounts (Butterworth 1980), we are a very long way from being able to do that. Nevertheless, the careful analysis, both qualitative and quantitative, of foreign language output may offer clues as to the nature of the processes by which that output is achieved.

This chapter has been critical of Oller. It would be most unfortunate if it did not also recognize the contribution he has made to the field of foreign-language testing. By opposing the dogma of established theory with a shocking heresy, he woke the testing community, stimulating some to research in order to refute him, others to work in his support. This stage is passing. What is needed now is a period in which researchers work, not to attack or defend extreme hypotheses, but to elucidate the relationships holding between performances of various kinds of language tasks. We know from Kelly (1969) how fashions have come and gone in 2500 years of language teaching. If language teaching (and testing) are not to remain matters of fashion, then they must be the subject of careful, patient, laborious empirical research. After waiting 25 centuries to start, we should be capable of at least a little patience.

References

Alderson, J.C. and Hughes, A. 1981: *Issues in language testing.* London: British Council (ELT documents).

Butterworth, B. (ed.) 1980: *Language production* **1**, *Speech and talk.* London: Academic Press.

---

[2] Yorozuya and Oller (1980) report that in a study of oral proficiency scales they deliberately selected the widest possible range of ability 'to insure optimum variance in scores across interviews'. This suggests that part of the apparent inability of scorers to separate out the elements of a learner's speaking ability may be explained in part by the use as subjects of learners exhibiting a wide range of ability.

[3] For a discussion of the relevance of these factors see Hughes (1981).

Harris, D. P. 1969: *Testing English as a second language.* New York: McGraw-Hill.

Hughes, A. 1981: Reaction to the Palmer and Bachman and Vollmer papers. In Alderson and Hughes 1981.

Jean-Aubry, G. 1957: *The sea dreamer: a definitive biography of Joseph Conrad.* London: Allen & Unwin.

Kelly. L.G. 1969: *Twenty-five centuries of language teaching.* Rowley, Mass.: Newbury House.

Lado, R. 1961: *Language testing.* London: Longmans.

Mullen, K.A. 1980: Rater reliability and oral proficiency evaluations. In Oller and Perkins 1980.

Oller, J.W. 1975: Dictation as a test of grammar-based expectancies. *English Language Teaching* **30,** 25–35.

———1976: Evidence for a general language proficiency factor: an expectancy grammar. *Die Neueren Sprachen* **75,** 165–74.

———1979: *Language tests at school.* London: Longman.

Oller, J.W. and Hinofotis, F.B. 1980: Two mutually exclusive hypotheses about second language ability: indivisible or partially divisible competence. In Oller and Perkins 1980.

Oller, J.W. and Perkins, K. 1980: *Research in language testing.* Rowley, Mass.: Newbury House.

Palmer, A.S. and Bachman, L.F. 1981: Basic concerns in test validation. In Alderson and Hughes 1981.

Scholz, G., Hendricks, D., Spurling, R., Johnson, M. and Vandenburg, L. 1980: Is language ability divisible or unitary? A factor analysis of 22 English language proficiency tests. In Oller and Perkins 1980.

Swain, M., Dumas, G. and Naiman, N. 1974: Alternatives to spontaneous speech: elicited translation and imitation as indicators of second language competence. *Working Papers on Bilingualism* **3,** 68–79.

Yorozuya, R. and Oller, J.W. 1980. Oral proficiency scales: construct validity and the halo effect. *Language Learning* **30 (1),** 135–53.

18

Towards a linguistic typology of aphasic impairment
Renata Whurr

Definitions of aphasia abound. In spite of nearly two hundred years of interest in the subject of aphasia (almost all the clinical forms of aphasia—complete motor aphasia, paraphasia, jargon aphasia, agraphia and alexia—had been described before 1800), there is still no universally agreed classification. Terminological confusion persists, due, in part, to the multidisciplinary interest in the subject (clinical, physiological and behavioural), but also due to the diversity of philosophical and psychological theories on which much of the work has been based. The different disciplines have not as yet managed to avoid the tendency to 'borrow' nomenclature from one another, with the result that a term in one discipline may have a completely different connotation in another. Also, the various disciplinary investigations were carried out largely in isolation, and there was little by way of isomorphism between the different classificatory systems.

The tendency of all three disciplines was to over-classify or to under-classify. Over-classification is illustrated by the proliferation of sub-types of aphasia, which served to bewilder and confuse clinicians, since few patients correspond exactly to the textbook symptomatologies. Conversely, the binary systems expressed in such dichotomies as SENSORY/MOTOR, RECEPTIVE/EXPRESSIVE, FLUENT/NON-FLUENT, and POS-TERIOR/ANTERIOR, although appealing in their simplicity, provided a restricted view and an over-simplification of the problem. Added to these two extreme stands was the constant tendency for the anatomically based localizers and the psychologically based holists to borrow material from both approaches, and thus compound terminological confusion. For example, Broca (1861), while professing the doctrine of regional cerebral localization, distinguished between APHEMIA and VERBAL AMNESIA, whilst Wernicke (1874), another localizationist, drawing on neurophysiological terminology, introduced MOTOR, SENSORY, CONDUCTION and TOTAL aphasia. Then Marie (1906), opposed to the localizationist view, used the terms

BROCA'S and WERNICKE'S aphasia, thus propounding a dynamic theory with localizationist classifications! As early as 1878 Hughlings Jackson had warned 'we must not classify on a mixed method of anatomy, physiology and psychology, any more than we should classify plants on a mixed, natural and empirical basis as exogens, kitchen herbs, graminacae and shrubs'. But mixtures continue to be the norm.

Although it is generally agreed that the term APHASIA at its simplest level means 'an impairment of language function due to focal brain damage', there is little else by way of multidisciplinary agreement. Much of the controversy can be traced to the definition of what aphasia represents, rather than what aphasia is. Most agree that aphasia is an impairment of language function due to brain damage. Few agree as to what is meant by LANGUAGE. 'Language' is a widely used term which has accumulated divergent connotations, many of which are not germane to the discussion of aphasia. As Lesser (1978) has recognized, many of the difficulties of defining aphasia arise from the inherent anomaly of needing to characterize aphasia as a central disorder of language which has repercussions on all modalities of language, while yet having no other framework of analysis by which to describe the underlying disturbance, except in these modalities.

It is surprising that the discipline of linguistics made no systematic, theoretical contribution to the study of aphasia until Jakobson (1954), although both Baudouin De Courtenay and De Saussure had early suggested that the study of the genesis and pathology of language could be rewarding for linguistic theory (see Jakobson 1980). Attempts to provide linguistically based descriptions were produced occasionally, for example by Alajouanine, Ombredane and Durand (1939), Luria (1947), Goldstein (1948), and Brain (1961). The earliest attempt to consider linguistic description as a basis of a classificatory scheme was introduced by the neurologist, Sir Henry Head (1926), who in his study and documentation of the head-injured soldiers of the 1914–18 war recognized four types of aphasia: VERBAL, SYNTACTIC, SEMANTIC and NOMINAL. Each clinical variety represented 'some partial affection of symbolic formulation and expression'. Wepman and Jones (1961), a speech pathologist and a psychologist respectively, identified three types of aphasia: PRAGMATIC, SYNTACTIC and SEMANTIC. The PRAGMATIC aphasic had a disruption in the 'relation of sign to interpreters' (using concepts borrowed from Charles Morris (1938)); the SEMANTIC aphasic had a disruption in the 'relation of signs to objects to which the signs are applicable'; and the SYNTACTIC aphasic had a disruption in the relation of 'signs to other signs'. No cohesive and accurate classificatory system was produced by either of these approaches. Both Head and Wepman and Jones decided to adopt linguistic notions to describe different forms of aphasia. But their terminologies and descriptions are at variance. Head's SEMANTIC category is not equivalent to Wepman and Jones' SEMANTIC category; in fact, it is Head's NOMINAL aphasia that equates with Wepman and Jones' SEMANTIC aphasia. However, there is more agreement regarding the SYNTACTICAL types, and there is some similarity in Head's VERBAL and Wepman and Jones' PRAGMATIC category.

Roman Jakobson (1941, 1954, 1955, 1964a, 1964b, 1971, 1973, 1980) made the first and major contribution as a linguist to the study of aphasia. He claimed that aphasia could not be seen as a unitary deficit which manifested differences ranging along a quantitative dimension. On the contrary, he emphasized the qualitative diversity of aphasic patterns. Linguistic analysis of these patterns, he found, led to distinct and integral syndromes, as well as to a structural typology. He argued (1954; 239):

> if aphasia is a language disturbance, as the term suggests, then description and classification of aphasic syndromes must begin with the question of what aspects of language are impaired in the various species of such a disorder. To study adequately any breakdown in communication we must first understand the nature and mode of communication that has ceased to function. Linguistics is concerned with language in all its aspects, language in operation, language in drift, language in the nascent state and language in dissolution.

Jakobson's first analysis of aphasia was based on the observation that any linguistic sign involves two modes of arrangement—COMBINATION and SELECTION. He distinguished between the MESSAGE, a combination of constituent parts (sentences, words, phonemes etc.), and the CODE, a repository of all possible constituents. The constituents of any message are linked with the code by an INTERNAL relation, and with the message by an EXTERNAL relation. The process of selection is based on the internal relation, and the process of combination on the external relation, of contiguity. He proceeded to outline, on this basis, two opposite patterns of aphasia (based on Goldstein's data). The first type was due to a selection deficiency, where contiguity determined the patient's whole verbal behaviour: this he described as a SIMILARITY disorder. The opposing type, termed a CONTIGUITY disorder, was based on a combination deficiency.

Jakobson stated that every form of aphasic impairment consisted of impairment in either the faculty of selection and substitution, or of combination and conjecture. The former involved a deterioration of metalinguistic operations, while the latter damaged the capacity for maintaining the hierarchy of linguistic units. These were also described as the METAPHORIC and the METONYMIC poles, both processes being continually operative in normal verbal behaviour, and during which competition between both was manifest in any symbolic process. On this basis Jakobson, following in the Saussurian tradition, argued for the bipolarity or dualism of aphasic behaviour, and moreover propounded his dualistic model as a description of the normal language process. However, dichotomous descriptions of aphasia had always proved inadequate, and Jakobson found this was also true of his proposed typology. The language of dissolution could not be compared with language in its normal state. Bipolar linguistic planes and axes did not serve to account for the diversity of language breakdown in aphasia, nor did they lend themselves to producing any sort of correlation with the anatomical substrates of that breakdown. No doubt the inadequacies of Jakobson's typology were due to his limited experience of aphasic patients. He had applied his theories of normal language behaviour to the data described by Goldstein, and inevitably such a vicarious approach was to prove unfruitful. Ten years later, intrigued by the illuminating portrayal of Luria's six types of aphasia,

Jakobson modified his earlier approach, proposing three dichotomies to underlie Luria's six categories. Added to the dichotomy of combination/selection was that of SUCCESSIVITY/SIMULTANEITY (or sequence and concurrence) plus DISINTEGRATION/LIMITATION. Jakobson was still convinced that the opposition of two types of verbal behaviour accounted for all the 'qualitative diversity of aphasic patterns', and could describe distinct and integrative syndromes correlated with structural typology.

But despite these years of interest in the subject, Jakobson actually applied only the most basic of linguistic principles to the study of aphasia. It became evident that the many disturbances could not fit into any dichotomous framework, and that neither the duality concepts of language nor the contrastivity descriptions could satisfactorily account for the complexities involved in aphasic language. Jakobson was very aware of this complexity. In his paper presented at the CIBA Foundation entitled 'Towards a Linguistic Typology of Aphasia' (1964a; 24–5) he stated:

> any linguist who has had the opportunity to observe different specimens of aphasic speech can but confirm and support the views of those neurologists, psychiatrists and psychologists who are getting increasingly clearer insights into the qualitative diversity of the aphasic pattern. A linguistic analysis of these patterns imperceptively leads to the ascertainment of distinct and integral syndromes as well as to their structural typology. The linguistic errors made by the adherents of the unitarian heresy have prevented them discriminating between the various verbal failures of aphasic.

But in spite of this observation, the Jakobson typology failed to take account of linguistic errors in any systematic way. He alluded to the need to apply an autonomous examination to each linguistic level, and to search for correlations between levels. He stated (*ibid.*) that the 'autonomy of levels of grammar, syntax, semantics, can be differentially impaired, and that linguistics provides a greater specification of the linguistic parameters of significance to communication and investigates linguistic behaviour in a far more systematic and insightful way'. While he criticized the unitarists' approach as futile, based on fictitious rubrics which actually ignore phonemic, morphological and syntactic structure in language, Jakobson himself never really developed the structuralist approach in full. Certainly he recognised that there might be an orderly impairment of phonology, prosody, morphology, syntax and semantics in aphasic language; and 'that more account must be taken of the fact that the differences of patterns examined lie not only in the presence and absence of certain properties, but also in the different hierarchies of those patterns' (1980; 107), but he did not suggest how aphasic language actually obeyed a set of rules nor how linguistic analysis could be applied to identify patterns in samples of data. Even recently (1980) Jakobson exhorts that the 'further development in linguistic inquiry into aphasia demands a greater concentration on the description and classification of the purely verbal syndromes, but with constant attention to the whole semiotic framework'.

Jakobson's work inspired a great deal of interest in the linguistic aspects of aphasic behaviour. This interest stimulated a number of research studies which investigated one or other of the linguistic levels, usually in individual patients. However none of the studies heeded Jakobson's suggestion of a systematic account and description of all levels of linguistic organization. As a result, isolated studies had been made on the *phonological* aspect (e.g. Blumstein (1973), Brown (1972), Duchan, *et al.* (1980), Goodglass and Kaplan (1972), Johns and Darley (1970), Johns and Lapointe (1976), Lecours and Caplan (1975), Luria (1970), Whitaker (1971), Miceli *et al.* (1980)) and the *morphological* aspect (e.g. Goodglass and Hunt (1958) and Goodglass and Berko (1960)). Work on the *lexical* level can be illustrated by Kehoe and Whitaker (1973), Marshall, *et al.* (1970), Schnitzer (1972), Lecours and Caplan (1975), Caplan, Kellar and Locke (1972); on the *syntactic* level by Zuriff, *et al.* (1972), Dingwall and Whitaker (1974), Green (1970), Luria (1970), Whitaker (1971) and Zuriff and Caramazza (1976); and on the *semantic* level by Rinnert and Whitaker (1973), Zuriff and Caramazza (1976) and Hier, *et al.* (1980). Sabouraud, *et al.* (1965) proposed a linguistically based classification in terms of two planes, SEMIOLOGICAL and PHONOLOGICAL. He recognised four types of aphasia— SEMIOLOGICAL BROCA'S, PHONOLOGICAL BROCA'S, SEMIOLOGICAL WERNICKE'S and PHONOLOGICAL WERNICKE'S. In this way, Sabouraud, *et al.* proposed yet another bipolar system—albeit at two levels of linguistic function. More recently, Lesser (1978) has emphasized the need to examine the different levels of linguistic processing in language disorders, suggesting that the levels proposed by Jakobson and other linguists represent to some degree psychological processes and perhaps even brain functions, thus having some degree of autonomy, although operating within an interacting whole, and with variable degrees of involvement. Nevertheless, Lesser did not suggest a method of applying the linguistic analysis. It is only very recently that Crystal (1981) has suggested systematic profiling of *all* language levels, in an attempt to find pattern within and across linguistic levels. The methodology is made explicit by Crystal (1981; and see earlier, Crystal *et al.* (1976)). However, he observes that the application of linguistic analysis to aphasic data is in its infancy, and that more data need to be analysed routinely and accurately before a theoretical account can be given.

Is the discussion regarding a linguistic typology in its embryonic stages? An abstract theory has been postulated by Jakobson and others; a methodology of analysis has now been provided by Crystal and colleagues. This suggests that we may be at a turning-point in the history of the subject. However, it will be important, in working towards a truly multidisciplinary typology based on linguistic principles, meaningful to all the disciplines involved in the study of aphasiology, to avoid the pitfalls which have bedevilled the subject in the past. In particular, before suggesting yet another classificatory frame of reference, it is necessary to clarify the objectives in producing a linguistic typology of aphasic impairment. Although Crystal (1981) states there is an urgent need for meticulous analysis of patients' language behaviour, he goes on to say that this should in the first instance adopt a narrower rather than a broader frame of reference. By 'narrower', he means a comprehensive description of the patients' language, initially without reference to neurological or psychological constraints. Yet if a narrow frame of reference is maintained for too long, in one's investigation of the patient, there arises the danger of overrestricting the view, of producing a purely linguistic perspective which lacks clinical relevance. It will need to be remembered that, as Benson (1980; 3–4) argues, 'Aphasia is a clinical problem', and that the 'model building approach is far removed frm the approach of clinical medicine', and again that 'purely clinical descriptions of language are quite different from scholarly theories of language'. Whitaker (1979) goes so far as to argue that 'most linguists have shown remarkably little interest in the brain mechanisms related to language. In fact there is little question that linguistics can proceed to study language independently of neurology'.

Crystal, Benson and Whitaker represent different and unilateral positions. To Crystal, the initial aim is the construction of linguistic analyses uncontaminated by the influences of other disciplines. Benson is concerned with the clinical context of the patient and his symptomatology. Whitaker is concerned with neuro- and psycho-linguistic models of brain and behaviour. No doubt all three would agree with the need for a unified approach with multidisciplinary integration. However, this integrated account will need to observe the neurological correlates *and* the psychological by-products of brain damage, *as well as* a clearly detailed linguistic framework. In this context, linguistic analysis may provide a framework for a future theoretical model of aphasia, but a framework which will require neurological and psychological foundations. Thus, the problem which has yet to be faced is *how* to integrate—how to make operational sense of this notion of 'foundation'. Until such time as proposals concerning the mapping of each theory's constructs onto each other are forthcoming, there seems little point in attempting to produce a classification or definition of aphasia. Rather, what is required is to replace the traditional concern with classification by a more rigorous analysis of medical and behavioural (i.e. psychological and linguistic) variables. Only in this way may there eventually develop a classificatory system which has equal integrity in each discipline. As we have seen, previous attempts at classifying have served to obscure rather than to illuminate. Clinical observations, psychological descriptions and interpretations, plus detailed linguistic analysis of all levels of linguistic operation would seem to provide a more secure foundation for research.

A linguistic typology of aphasic impairment may be premature, but the above descriptive principles can readily be applied to aphasic language in the present state of knowledge, and contrastive patterns demonstrated which at least point in the direction of a typology. For the purpose of illustration, two patients are described below, and their linguistic profiles contrasted. The patients have been chosen to represent the two major (and usually undisputed) types of oral output impairment based simply on the notion of FLUENCY. Fluency ratings are simple measures by which to evaluate output, and the least likely to suffer from misinterpretation. Traditionally, they polarise into NON-FLUENT and FLUENT measures of output. Both categories have some neurological basis, in that the fluent category is more likely to be caused by lesions located in the posterior portion of the brain, whereas non-fluency is correlated with anterior lesions. The patients were victims of cerebrovascular disease with consequent aphasia and right hemiplegia. Both patients were assessed on the Aphasia Screening Test (AST) (Whurr 1974), two months post-onset of their strokes. The AST is a simple diagnostic test which samples all four language modalities. The oral output tasks involve the specific classical tasks of (1) repetition, (2) completing sequences, (3) reading aloud, (4) picture confrontation naming, (5) composite picture description, and (6) discourse. All six test parameters were subjected to detailed analysis at the levels of phonology, prosody, syntax and semantics. For present purposes, only the most general observations, applying to all oral output tasks, will be summarized.

Patient A (non-fluent)

Female; 62 years old; cerebrovascular accident; right hemiplegia; date of onset 24/8/76; date of assessment 7/10/76; occupation housewife. AST results: overall performance 204/205 (i.e. overall mild aphasia); receptive function score 93% (i.e. mild impairment of receptive function); expressive function 81 per cent (i.e. moderate impairment of expressive function). A breakdown of the patient's performance is shown in Fig. 18.1. The patient managed all tests of receptive function except at the complex sentence level, when she failed on the tasks requiring her to carry out complex written and oral commands. In the tests of expressive function, the patient failed to repeat groups of phonemes presented sequentially, and individual words. She had no difficulty in completing sequences, nor in reading aloud at the phonemic and word levels. Her ability to name lexical items in picture confrontation was intact. However, she had difficulty in reading aloud at the sentence level. There were also problems in formulating sentences to describe action pictures and a composite picture. In the writing tasks, copying was intact; writing to dictation was impaired at the word and sentence level, although intact at the phoneme level. Naming in writing, and sentence formulating were severely impaired. The separate tests of calculation demonstrated retained ability in the oral form, but not in writing.

For the purposes of the present chapter, two samples of the patient's speech are presented below—one taken from the picture description task, and one from her free conversation.

Picture description
the little girl is going out/ no/
the little girl is going away/
her daddy has coming with the suitcases/
she's got a ball and a bucket/
and there's the car outside/
there her mummy has got a comb/
and a nailfile/
and lipstick/
envelopes/
and she has—and a case with a scrubbing brush in there/
and a clothes brush/ and some—what's that/
I think/ oh dear/ a powder puff and the safety pins/
she is—she is going to pack the case/

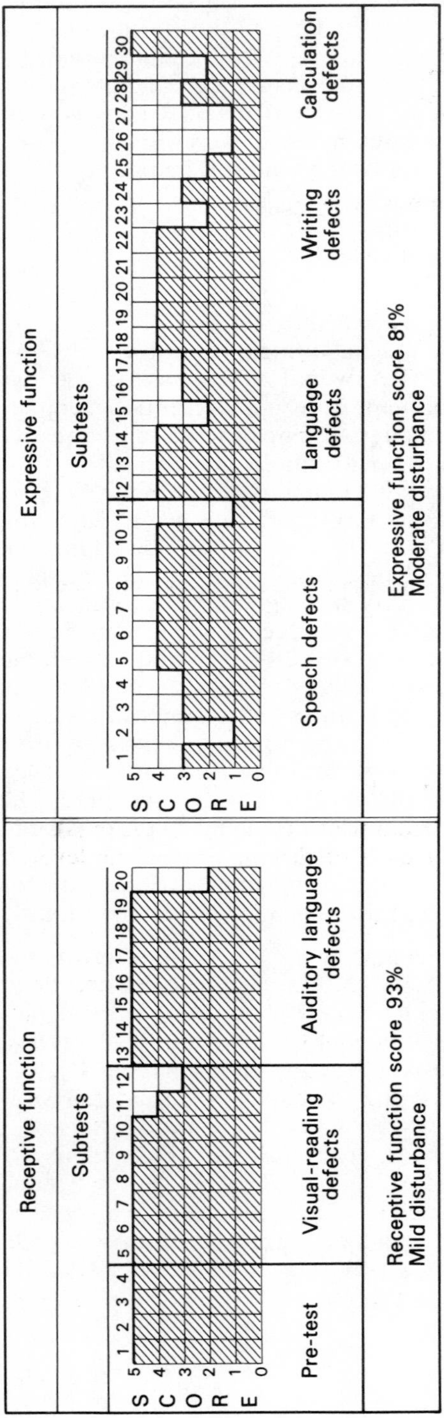

Fig. 18.1 Performance profile of Patient A.

Conversation

T. Did you sleep well last night?
P. Yes.
T. What have you done this morning?
P. Had breakfast and come to the gym.
T. What kind of breakfast did you have?
P. Quaker Oats and marmalade.
T. Toast and marmalade, no?
P. No. Quaker Oats and marmalade.
T. Quaker Oats and marmalade. What was the marmalade on?
P. Bread and butter.
T. Bread and butter. Did you have tea or coffee?
P. Tea.
T. How do you like your tea?
P. Nice and hot and ( ) spoonfuls of sugar.
T. Do you take coffee the same way or differently?
P. No. The same way.
T. 'Cos some people have tea with sugar or in coffee without, or the other way round, don't they?
P. Yes. No, I take the same.
T. Nice and easy to remember.
P. Yes
T. Have you had some this morning yet?
P. No.
T. Oh well, I hope you get back in time for some. Who came and visited you last night?
P. Nobody.
T. It was nice and quiet for once!
P. Yes, yes.
T. Did you watch any television?
P. No.
T. What did you do?
P. I looked ( ) my names, and I got to do.

An analysis of the complete samples, from which these extracts are taken, showed clear patterns of difficulty at each of the main linguistic levels.

Phonology

At this level, the non-fluent patient demonstrated a variety of errors in feature contrasts, systematic processes, cluster and syllable structure processes. For example, feature errors occurred with the fortis/lenis distinction (as in letter *p* [bə], *pen* [ben], *chin* [ʤɪn], letter *z* [sed], *twelve* [tweʊf]), between front and back places of articulation (as in letter *k* [də], *comb* [təʊm], *kicking* /'pɪk-'kɪpʊ-'kɪkɪkɪŋ], *skyscraper* 'skaɪstareɪpəz), between stop and fricative manners of articulation (as in *kippers* ['kefəz], *fence* [pens], *mouth* [paʊd], *teeth* [sɪθ]) and between oral and nasal contrasts (as in *nose* [daʊz], *mouth* [paʊd]). Disturbances of systematic processes were illustrated by a tendency to labialization (e.g. *red* [bʊed], *yellow* [blə-ə'meləʊ]). Vowels tended to centralize. There were several examples of impairment of cluster and syllable structure processes. Cluster simplification occurred in, e.g. *string* [drɪŋ], *green* [gi:n], *Thursday* 'θa:di:, *Friday* 'faɪdi:, and *climbing* ['kaɪmɪŋ].

Prosody

On this level, there was a staccato stress pattern, with equal stress on all items except the nuclear syllable, and little variation in intonation. The placement of stress at word level was appropriate. At sentence level, nuclear tone placement was usually on the last lexical item, e.g. 'a 'man 'is 'walking 'up 'the stàirs/, but there were cases where the tonic syllable occurred in a word which was semantically contrastive, e.g. 'the 'man 'is 'going dòwn 'the 'stairs/. There was a falling nuclear tone in most utterances, except in stereotyped sequences, such as saying the alphabet or counting. There was little other variation in intonation, and overall pitch-range was very restricted.

Syntax

A grammatical profile analysis using the LARSP system (see Crystal, Fletcher and Garman 1976) was made of 44 sentences in the sample (see Fig. 18.2). Of these, 7 were unanalysed, for reasons of unintelligibility (in whole or in part), incompleteness or ambiguity. Of the 37 remaining sentences, there were 21 examples of Minor sentence type, and 16 of Major sentence type. It can be seen from the profile chart that these sentences were primarily at Stages II and III; few sentences contained more than three main clause elements. The occasional example of a more complex sentence type omitted elements of structure (e.g. *had breakfast and came up to the gym*) or resembled stereotyped utterance (e.g. *he said that's alright*). Phrase structure at Stages II to IV is fairly well represented, as is word structure. The profile therefore shows a developing phrase bias, compounded by the patient's use of coordination. This is not a simple developmental profile, though, in view of the occasional examples of more complex sentence constructions (e.g. the passive and emphatic order of *They were taken away, my notes*). It should be noted, also, that despite an apparently well developed verb phrase, only a small selection of verbs was used, e.g. *have, take, say, do, be,* most of these carrying low information. In Sections B and C of the chart, it is notable that the patient was most responsive when the stimulus was a question; non-question stimuli tended to produce only *yes/no* responses. There were occasional pauses and unintelligible utterances, but there were no zero responses: the patient clearly recognized when she had to speak. There was very little redundant language. All responses were statements. Responses to specific questions were generally well structured; when the patient attempted to produce further spontaneous sentences (15 instances), structures tended to become muddled and ambiguous. The patient appeared to need T's guidance as to how to structure responses.

Semantics

There was very low redundancy, compared to normal language, due to the 'telegrammatic' nature of the sentences. On the whole, ideas were organized logically and in sequence, but there was considerable ambiguity and difficulty in comprehension.

Fig. 18.2 LARSP analysis of Patient A (picture description/conversation).

A	**Unanalysed**				**Problematic**	
	1 Unintelligible 0/3	2 Symbolic Noise	3 Deviant		1 Incomplete 2/2	2 Ambiguous

B Responses

Stimulus Type	Totals	Repetitions	Elliptical Major 1	2	3	4	Full Major	Minor	Structural	Ø	Problems
19 Questions	16		4			1	3	7	1		
6 Others	6						1	5			

C Spontaneous 15 | 2 | Others 13

Minor   Social 2/17   Stereotypes 1/1   Problems

Major   Sentence Structure

Stage I (0;9–1;6)

Excl.	Comm.	Quest.	Statement			
	'V'	'Q'	'V'	'N' 1/1	Other 0/1	Problems

Stage II (1;6–2;0)

	Conn.	Clause		Phrase		Word
V X	Q X	SV 2/3	VC/O 0/1	DN 10/6	VV 1/0	-ing 3/0
		S C/O	A X 1/1	Adj N	V part 2/1	pl 2/4
		Neg X	Other	NN	Int X	-ed 0/7
				PrN	Other 1/0	

Stage III (2;0–2;6)

		Clause		Phrase		Word
V X Y	Q X Y 1/0	X + S:NP 2	X + V:VP 2/2	X + C/O:NP	X + A:AP 0/1	-en 2/2
let X Y	VS	SVC/O 2/9	VC/OA	D Adj N 6/1	Cop 2/1	3s 8/2
do X Y		SVA 1/2	VO_dO_i	Adj Adj N	Aux 6/5	gen
		Neg X Y	Other	Pr DN 1/3	Pron 3/17	
				N Adj N	Other 0/2 5/	

Stage IV (2;6–3;0)

		Clause		Phrase		Word
+ S	QVS	X Y + S:NP 1/0	X Y + V:VP 3/1	N Pr NP 1/1	X Y + A:AP 1/1	n't 0/3
	Q X Y Z	SVC/OA 1/1	A A X Y 1/0	Pr D Adj N	Neg V 0/3	'cop 2/1
		SVO_dO_i	Other	cX 3/0	Neg X	'aux 1/1
				XcX 2/4	2 Aux	-est
					Other	-er

Stage V (3;0–3;6)

		Conn.	Clause	Phrase		-ly
how	tag	and 2/3 c	Coord. 1 0/2 1 ·	Postmod. 1 clause	1 +	
		s 0/1	Subord. 1 1 ·			
what		Other 0/1	Clause: S	Postmod. 1 phrase		
			Clause: C/O 0/2			
			Comparative			

Stage VI (3;6–4;6)

(+)				(−)		
NP	**VP**	**Clause**		**NP**	**VP**	**Clause**
Initiator 0/1	Complex 3/1	Passive 0/1	Pron	Adj seq	Modal	Concord
Coord 0/2		Complement	Det	N irreg	Tense 1/1	A position
					V irreg	W order
Other			Other			

Stage VII (4;6+)

Discourse		*Syntactic Comprehension*
A Connectivity	*it*	
Comment Clause	*there* 2/0	Style
Emphatic Order 0/1	Other	

Total No. Sentences Analysed 37	Mean No. Sentences Per Turn 1.5	Mean Sentence Length 5.4

© D. Crystal, P. Fletcher, M. Garman, 1975 University of Reading

Patient B (fluent)

Male; 65 years old; cerebrovascular accident; right hemiparesis (resolved); date of onset 30/8/76; date of assessment 4/10/76; occupation retired civil servant. AST results: overall performance 182/250 (i.e. overall severe aphasia); receptive function score 47 per cent (i.e. moderately-severe impairment of receptive function); expressive function score 32 per cent (i.e. severe impairment of expressive function). A breakdown of the patient's performance is shown in Fig. 18.3. The patient could not repeat sounds, words or sentences, nor could he complete well known sequences such as the days of the week and months of the year. He was unable to name objects or parts of the body, nor could he formulate sentences to describe action pictures or a composite picture. The visual modality provided a more accurate stimulus, since the patient could read aloud a few letters, words and sentences; he also managed to name some colours. In the writing tasks, he could copy, and write the names of a few lexical items, but he was unable to write to dictation or formulate any sentences. The patient's main receptive impairment seemed largely due to gross auditory deficits. There was a severe impairment of expressive function, permeated by the auditory comprehension problem. He was unable to monitor his own utterances, which were fluent, voluble but inappropriate. The only intact skills were visual matching, copying in writing and written calculation. As with Patient A, two speech samples are presented below— one of picture description and one of free conversation.

Picture description
well/ now he's (fertigo)/
here's a wall/ brick/
up against the thing/
now he's got here his wer
then he can get (on)
he's fair all/
he can underneath/
round back/
where the cree
with the tree/ and well er little bird/
little thing/
couple little kiddies/ and that one/
now these two/
now there's little my/ little word/
with a little brick built in/
now here is in the man/ and he's got a bag/
and he's has a little bag/ (   )
now he's also got a bags/
he's umer little code boxal/

Conversation
T. Why did it take you so long to get here this afternoon?
P. How long did it take me?
T. Why did it take you so long to get here this afternoon?
P. Am I about this sort of thing? Oh, I see.
T. Why did it take you so long to get here this afternoon? It took you half an hour to get here.

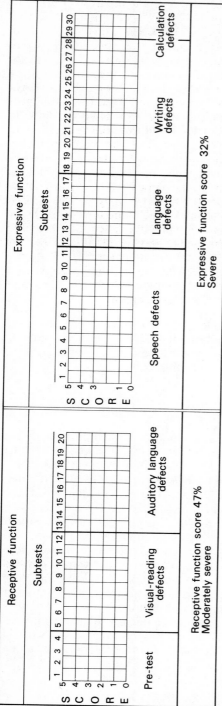

Fig. 18.3 Performance profile of Patient B.

P. So it took me a long while, going somewhere, or or motor the shops, or we go out in the car/ or the clear/ or area/ oh we do all sorts of place/ I could go in/ I could buy some bags/ or packets/ cigarettes/ or anything like that/ or all sorts of thing pretty well/ most things are the thing that I want/

T. How are you managing now at home?

P. Oh, I think practically everything/ for example say well now/ we I hurt my foot/ well I know I hurt it/ hurts me/ there's something about for me/ to comfab it/ that they were to do something to it/ but to be able to hable most things/ have the ability say well it's not my good/ or complete er probability towards always/

An analysis of the samples from which these extracts were taken produced a very different set of error patterns from Patient A.

Phonology

This patient's phonological system was stable, although it was interspersed with jargon (e.g. [fɜː tɪgəʊ]) and neologisms (e.g. [sməik], [bɒksəl]). These were all possible words in English. Almost all phonological contrasts were retained, apart form a few front/back contrasts (e.g. *kicking* [kɪtl̩], *lips* [lɪks], *tree* [kriː]).

Prosody

In this patient there was a wide range of prosodic patterns with varied placement of nuclear tone for emphasis and varied tones expounding nuclear syllables. However, in spite of the range and variety of pattern, prosody appeared not to be used in a meaningful way.

Syntax

This patient produced a wide range of syntactic structures in both the picture description task and the conversation. LARSP analysis of the 63 sentences in the sample is given in Fig. 18.4. Of these sentences, 19— nearly one-third of the data—went unanalysed (for reasons of unintelligibility, incompleteness or deviance). Of the 44 sentences analysed, there were 21 examples of Minor and 23 of Major sentence types. The major types were predominantly SVO and SVOA, but in addition, the patient made important use of Pronouns, Auxiliaries, Complex Noun Phrases, and Connectivity features (though possibly several of these latter were stereotyped). Several syntactic and morphological errors were identified within the analysed sentences, e.g. the omission of Subject or Verb elements of structure, or of prepositions, and the wrong choice of number or tense forms. The superficial impression given by the chart is of a fairly advanced level of grammatical ability, but when one considers the range of unanalysed sentences, and the erratic semantic sequencing and uncertain content of many of the analysed sentences, this impression has to be revised.

Fig. 18.4 LARSP analysis of Patient B (picture description/conversation).

A	**Unanalysed**					**Problematic**		
	1 Unintelligible 7/2	2 Symbolic Noise		3 Deviant 3/2		1 Incomplete 3/2	2 Ambiguous	

B Responses

Stimulus Type		Totals	Repet-itions	Normal Response — Elliptical Major 1	2	3	4	Full Major	Minor	Abnormal Struc-tural	Ø	Prob-lems
6	Questions	6						5		1		
1	Others	1						1				

C	**Spontaneous**	37		1	Others 36	

Minor				Social 9/7		Stereotypes 0/5		Problems	

Stage I (0;9–1;6) — Sentence Type

Major

Excl.	Comm.	Quest.			Statement			
		'Q'	'V'	'N' 2/2	Other 2/1	Problems		

Stage II (1;6–2;0)

Conn. | Clause | Phrase | Word

	VX	QX		SV 1/3	VC/O 0/5	DN 7/11	VV 0/1	-ing 0/3
				S C/O	AX 0/1	Adj N 3/1	V part 2/4	
				Neg X	Other 1/0	NN	Int X 0/1	pl 5/9
						PrN 1/1	Other 5/2	-ed 2/5

Stage III (2;0–2;6)

	VXY	0/1 QXY	X + S:NP	X + V:VP 1/3	X + C/O:NP 0/3	X + A:AP	-en 5/2
	let XY	VS (X)	SVC/O 4/12	VC/OA 1/0	D Adj N 3/2	Cop 4/2	3s 6/1
		0/1	SVA 1/3	VOdOi	Adj Adj N	Aux 5/11	gen
	do XY		Neg XY	Other 1/0	Pr DN 3/3	Pron 14/27	
					N Adj N 1/0	Other 1/4 4/11	

Stage IV (2;6–3;0)

	· S	QVS	XY + S:NP 1/0	XY + V:VP 1/8	XY + C/O:NP	XY + A:AP 2/2	n't
		QXYZ	SVC/OA 3/4	AAXY	N Pr NP 0/4	Neg V	
		0/1	SVOdO,	Other 1/1	Pr D Adj N 2/1	Neg X	'cop 3/1
					cX 4/1	2 Aux	'aux 3/1
					XcX 2/0	Other 3/3	-est

Stage V (3;0–3;6)

	how	tag	and 3/0	Coord. 1 1/0 1·	Postmod. 1 2/1 1· clause	-er
			c 0/8	Subord. 1 0/1 1·		
	what		s 2/2	Clause: S	Postmod. 1· phrase	-ly 0/3
			Other 6/1	Clause: C/O 0/1		
				Comparative		

(+)				(−)			

NP	VP	Clause	NP		VP	Clause

Stage VI (3;6–4;6)

Initiator 1/2	Complex 1/4	Passive	Pron	Adj seq	Modal	Concord
Coord		Complement	Det 2/0	N irreg	Tense 1/1	A position
					V irreg	W order
Other			Other–seq 0/2	−Prep 1/2 −N 0/1 − Pt 0/2 −V 1/4 −S 0/3		

Stage VII (4;6+)

Discourse			Syntactic Comprehension	
A Connectivity	it 0/2			
Comment Clause	there 0/1		Style	
Emphatic Order 1/0	Other			

Total No. Sentences Analysed 44	Mean No. Sentences Per Turn 6·3	Mean Sentence Length 8.1

Semantics

The sample was full of repetitive ideas (e.g. *now there's little my little word with a little brick built in*). These ideas seem to be based on idiosyncratic presuppositions and spurious expectations, e.g. *or we go out in the car* (where *we* had not previously been mentioned). There was an illogical progression of ideas, though despite their lack of logical connection the grammatical form of the sequence was accurate. Collocational relationships were acceptable within phrases, but tended to be lost between phrases. Most of the neologisms replaced nouns, e.g. *the new jinko, the new bib*. There are many examples of perseveration throughout the sample, in particular on the repetition and completing-sequence tasks.

There is therefore considerable evidence from the analysis of these two patients for the existence of contrasting systems operating at all four linguistic levels: phonological, prosodic, syntactic and semantic levels seem to be differentially impaired. There are many points of contrast within each level. For example, a detailed comparison of the two sets of LARSP data would show several significant contrasts, such as:

(*i*) the proportion of unanalysed/problematic sentences to the analysed data (1: 5 in A, nearly 1: 2 in B);
(*ii*) the proportion of spontaneous to response sentences (15: 22 in A, 37: 7 in B);
(*iii*) Social Stage I sentences predominate in A; Stereotyped Stage I in B;
(*iv*) the proportion of clause to phrase structures in Stage II (8: 21 in A, 11: 39 in B);
(*v*) the total number of phrase structures at Stages II, III and IV (82 in A, 140 in B);
(*vi*) the total number of clause structures at Stages III and IV (18 in A, 34 in B);
(*vii*) the total number of expansions between Stages III and IV (14 in A, 29 in B);
(*viii*) the total number of connectives at Stage V (7 in A, 22 in B);
(*ix*) the total number of Stage VI errors (2 in A, 21 in B);
(*x*) the range of structures represented at Stages II, III, IV phrase, V and VI (much greater in B);
(*xi*) the mean number of sentences per turn (1.5 in A, 6.3 in B);
(*xii*) the mean sentence length (5.4 words in A, 8.1 words in B).

These remarks constitute only a partial description of the language patterns which differentiate these patients, but it is already possible to see that the linguistic analysis provides far too many potentially significant variables to permit an easy grouping into binary categories. Not only is the notion of fluency differentially related to the various linguistic levels, taken as wholes (cf. A's phonological, prosodic and syntactic problems, B's grossly impaired semantic system), but further analysis within each level would bring to light further differences. Within the level of grammar, for example, one could envisage a patient with 'fluent' clause structure, but 'non-fluent' phrase or word structure (cf. Crystal *et al.* 1976, Ch.8). Within the level of prosody, one could envisage 'fluent' tone-unit organization, but a 'non-fluent' control of tonicity or tone. And likewise, the various dimensions of segmental phonology and semantics might be used differentially in respect of the notion of fluency. It is impossible to predict, in advance of the detailed description of individual differences between patients, which of the many hundreds of variables are likely to prove most diagnostic, i.e. most capable of being correlated with other clusters of psychological and neurological variables. All that one can do is accumulate detailed and comprehensive profiles of patient behaviour, and begin the task of developing adequate statistical methodologies for handling such variability (a task which has not yet been well discussed).

In the absence of such descriptive statements, the traditional aphasiological foci of attention on matters of definition, diagnosis and classification seem positively misguided. Before these aims can be achieved in a scientifically satisfactory way, there needs to be a correlation of the linguistic findings with those of other disciplines involved. We are still far away from making satisfactory correlations, however, as can be judged not only from the limited descriptive progress made in clinical linguistics, but from the comparably limited behavioural descriptions available in psychology (where the crucial role of task effects on aphasic patients needs to be more fully investigated) and even in neurology (where the descriptive refinements available as a consequence of advances in computerised tomography have yet to be assimilated). Once these correlations can be made, we shall then be in a position to develop comprehensive statistically grounded classifications, based on correlations of clusters of linguistic, psychological and neurological symptoms. Then, and only then, can the issue of definition be satisfactorily addressed.

It is this reversal of the traditional direction of thinking in aphasiology that signals a new phase in the history of the subject. Definition → classification → description has to be replaced by description → classification → definition. Naturally, one will use the classificatory insights of clinical tradition as a heuristic, but there will be no expectation that the conventional binary classification will be retained in due course. Rather, as the data-base of the subject becomes broader, it will be unlikely that these classifications will survive. The controversy then will be how to balance the demands of scientific accuracy in classification, on the one hand, and clinical practicability, on the other: 100 categories of aphasia will presumably be of comparable inutility, at a clinical level, as the current two or three main types are now. It may seem strange to suggest that after two hundred years of study, the science of aphasiology is still in its infancy. But when one looks at the future of the subject in these terms, it is difficult to conclude otherwise.

References

Alajouanine, T., Ombrédane, A. and Durand, M. 1939: *Le syndrome désintégration phonétique dans l'aphasie.* Paris: Masson.

Benson, D.F. 1980: *Aphasia, alexia and agraphia.* New York: Churchill Livingstone.

Blumstein, S.E. 1973: *A phonological investigation of aphasic speech.* The Hague: Mouton.

Brain, R. 1961: *Speech disorders.* London: Butterworth.

Broca, P. 1861: Remarques sur le siège de la faculté articulé; suivies d'une observation d'aphémie. *Bulletin de la Société d'Anatomie de Paris* **36,** 330–57.
Brown, J. 1972: *Aphasia, apraxia and agnosia.* Springfield: Thomas.
Caplan, D., Keller, L. and Locke, S. 1972: Inflection of neologisms in aphasia. *Brain* **95,** 169–72.
Crystal, D. 1981: *Clinical linguistics.* Vienna & New York: Springer.
Crystal, D., Fletcher, P. and Garman, M. 1976: *The grammatical analysis of language disability.* (Studies in Language Disability and Remediation **1.**) London: Edward Arnold.
Dingwall, W.O. and Whitaker, H. 1974: Neurolinguistics. *Ann. Rev. Anthropology* (Palo Alto), 323–56.
Duchan, J.F., Stengel, M.L. and Oliva, J. 1980: A dynamic phonological pattern derived from the intonational analysis of a jargon dysphasic. *B & L* **9,** 289–97.
Goldstein, K. 1948: *Language and language disturbance.* New York: Grune & Stratton.
Goodglass, H. and Berko, J. 1960: Agrammatism and inflectional morphology in English. *JSHR* **3,** 257–67.
Goodglass, H. and Hunt, J. 1958: Grammatical complexity and aphasic speech. *Word* **14,** 197–207.
Goodglass, H. and Kaplan, E. 1972: *The assessment of aphasia and related disorders.* Philadelphia: Lee & Febiger.
Green, E. 1970: On the contribution of studies in aphasia to psycholinguistics. *Cortex* **6,** 216–35.
Head, H. 1926: *Aphasia and kindred disorders of speech.* Cambridge: Cambridge University Press.
Hier, D.B., Mogil, S.I., Rubin, N.P. and Komros, E.R. 1980: Semantic aphasia: a neglected entity. *B & L* **10,** 120–31.
Jackson, H. 1878: Reprint of some of Dr Hughlings Jackson's papers on affections of speech. *Brain* **38** (1915).
Jakobson, R. 1941/68: *Child language, aphasia and phonological universals.* The Hague: Mouton.
–––––– 1954: Two aspects of language and two types of aphasic disturbances. Reprinted in *Selected writings* **2** (The Hague: Mouton, 1971), 239–59.
–––––– 1955: Aphasia as a linguistic topic. *Selected writings* **2,** 229–39.
–––––– 1964a: Toward a linguistic classification of aphasic impairments. *Selected writings* **2,** 289–306.
–––––– 1964b: Linguistic types of aphasia. *Selected writings* **2,** 307–34.
–––––– 1971: *Studies on child language and aphasia.* The Hague: Mouton.
–––––– 1973: *Main trends in the science of language.* London: Allen & Unwin.
–––––– 1980: On aphasic disorders. In *From a linguistic angle: the framework of language.* Ann Arbor: University of Michigan Press.
Johns, D.F. and Darley, F.L. 1970: Phonemic variability in apraxia of speech. *JSHR* **13,** 556–83.
Johns, D.F. and Lapointe, L.L. 1976: Neurogenic disorders of output

processing: apraxia of speech. In H. Whitaker and H.A. Whitaker (eds.), *Studies in neurolinguistics* 1. New York: Academic Press.

Kehoe, W. and Whitaker, H.A. 1973: Lexical structure descriptions in aphasia: a case study. In H. Goodglass, and S. Blumstein (eds.), *Psycholinguistics and aphasia*. Baltimore: Johns Hopkins University Press.

Lecours, A.R. and Caplan, P. 1975: Review of Blumstein 1973. *B & L* 2, 237–54.

Lesser, R. 1978: *Linguistic investigations of aphasia*. Studies in Language Disability and Remediation 4. London: Edward Arnold.

Luria, A.R. 1947: *Traumatiče skaja afazija*. Moscow: House of the Academy of Medical Science.

—— 1970: *Traumatic aphasia*. The Hague: Mouton.

Marie, P. 1906: La troisième circonvolution frontale gauche ne joue aucun role spécial dans le fonction du langage. *La Semaine Médicale* 26, 241–7.

Marshall, M., Newcombe, F. and Marshall, J.C. 1970: The microstructure of word-finding difficulties in a dysphasic subject. In G.B. Flores d'Arcais and W. Levelt (eds.), *Advances in psycholinguistics*. Amsterdam: North Holland.

Miceli, G., Gianotti, G., Catagirone, C. and Masillo, C. 1980: Some aspects of phonological impairment in aphasia. *B & L* 11, 159–69.

Morris, C. 1938: Foundations of the theories of signs. In *International encyclopedia of unified science* 1. Chicago: University of Chicago Press.

Rinnert, C. and Whitaker, H.A. 1973: Semantic confusions of aphasic patients. *Cortex* 9, 56–81.

Sabouraud, O., Gagnepain, J. and Sabouraud, A. 1965: Aphasie et linguistique. *La Revue du Praticien* 15, 2335–45.

Schnitzer, M.L. 1972: *Generative phonology: evidence from aphasia*. University Park: Pennsylvania University Press.

Wepman, J.M. and Jones, L.V. 1961: *Language modalities test for aphasia*. Chicago: Education Industry Service.

Wernicke, C. 1874: *Der aphasische Symptomencomplex*. Breslau: Cohn & Weigart.

Whitaker, H.A. 1971: *On the representation of language in the human brain*. Edmonton: Linguistic Research, Inc.

—— 1976: Disorders of speech production mechanisms. In E.C. Carterette and M.P. Friedman (eds.), *Handbook of perception* 7. New York: Academic Press.

Whitaker, H.A. and Whitaker, H. 1979: Language disorders. In H.D. Brown and R. Wardhaugh (eds.), *A survey of applied linguistics*. Ann Arbor: University of Michigan Press.

Whurr, R. 1974: *An aphasia screening test*. (London: private publication.)

Zurif, E.B. and Caramazza, A. 1976: Psycholinguistic structures in aphasia: studies in syntax and semantics. In H. Whitaker and H.A. Whitaker (eds.), *Studies in neurolinguistics* 1. New York: Academic Press.

Zurif, E.B., Caramazza, A. & Myerson, R. 1972: Grammatical judgements of agrammatic aphasics. *Neuropsychologia* 10, 405–18.